THE COLD WAR AS HISTORY

the text of this book is printed on 100% recycled paper

THE
COLD WAR
AS HISTORY

By

LOUIS J. HALLE

HARPER TORCHBOOKS
Harper & Row, Publishers
New York, Hagerstown, San Francisco, London

First HARPER TORCHBOOK edition published 1975

ISBN: 0 −06 −131890 −6

78 79 80   12 11 10

Practical men may not notice it, but in fact human discourse is intrinsically addressed not to natural existing things but to ideal essences, poetic or logical terms which thought may define and play with. When fortune or necessity diverts our attention from this congenial ideal sport to crude facts and pressing issues, we turn our frail poetic ideas into symbols for those terrible irruptive things. In that paper money of our own stamping, the legal tender of the mind, we are obliged to reckon all the movements and values of the world.

GEORGE SANTAYANA

Contents

CONTENTS

CONTENTS

Preface

THE title of this book represents the common distinction between current events and history. In the close-up view of human society the role of accident seems to predominate. An airplane carrying the future ruler of Algeria falls into the hands of the French, who are trying to subdue the revolt of which he is a leader; or the Prime Minister of Great Britain has to undergo a prostatectomy at a moment critical for the British Government; or the Secretary General of the United Nations is killed in an airplane crash. When we read about such accidents in the newspapers, hours after they have occurred, they seem decisive. As we are able to detach ourselves and broaden our perspective, however, they come to seem inconsequential. Finally, when we achieve the large historical view we see Algeria, for example, emerging with a logical inevitability from its colonial history, and the capture of Ben Bella by the French, if not forgotten, is seen to be an accident of no ultimate significance for the secular movement that is its context.

In the larger view a pattern, an order of some sort, becomes apparent. Roman history from day to day must have seemed a succession of accidents to the men on the spot. We ourselves, however, can see how Rome was rising, over a period of centuries, to dominate the Mediterranean world and half Europe; we can see how, by this very process, it was becoming overextended and in various ways corrupt; and we can see how at last it crumbled away. There is something more here than a meaningless succession of events. There is a movement, a progression, a development. The events fall into patterns that are logical.

The same element of logic appears in the great militant ideological movements of history. A Jesus or a Mohammed or a Karl Marx inspires a vast movement associated with doctrinal belief—which initially possesses its votaries with ideological zeal; which leads to crusades and wars of conquest; and which at last settles down to a peaceful coexistence with the rival ideologies that, in the hour of its zeal, it had committed itself to overcome and eliminate.

With this logic in mind, I have undertaken to treat the Cold War as a phenomenon not without precedent in the long history of international conflict; as a phenomenon that, experience has taught us, has its own dynamics; as a phenomenon that, typically, goes through a certain cycle with a beginning, a middle, and an end.

It is true that, as yet, we are too close to the Cold War to see it in such a perspective as that in which the Punic Wars, for example, may be seen. Consequently, the title of this book represents aspiration only. It represents the aspiration to do for the Cold War, which belongs to our present, what Thucydides did for the Peloponnesian War, which belonged to his own present and in which he took part. If the aspiration is too ambitious, still, even the most limited success in its realization might be held to justify it.

At the same time that I have tried to see the Cold War in this distant perspective, I have been concerned with the human actors in terms that are sometimes intimate. I have shown, close up, individuals struggling like Laocoön with the enveloping problems of the day. This human detail does not, however, seem to me inconsistent with the large perspective. The essence of history, in a certain view, is the contrast between the immensity of its movement and the limitations of the individuals who, often with the greatest gallantry, put themselves at grips with it.

*   *   *

It may be thought that, as an American, I can hardly write with such detachment as I profess about a contest in which the involvement of my own country involves me, personally, in partisanship. The truth is that, granted my partisanship, I still feel a powerful sympathy for the Russian nation, for the Russian people, as well as for my own country and people. No one, it seems to me, can review the thousand years of Russian history without feeling emotional about the Russians—as Sir Bernard Pares did when he wrote his *History of Russia*.

In trying to understand a great conflict like the Cold War one should, in any case, rise above the dust of the battlefield to take a compassionate view of the exceedingly human beings on both sides. Professor Herbert Butterfield of Cambridge has written:

Behind the great conflicts of mankind is a terrible human predicament. . . . Contemporaries fail to see the predicament or refuse to recognize its genuineness, so that our knowledge of it comes from later analysis—it is only with the progress of historical science on a particular subject that men come really to recognize that there was a terrible knot beyond the ingenuity of man to untie. . . . In historical perspective we learn to be a little more sorry for both parties than they know how to be for one another. . . . As regards the real world of international relations I should put forward the thesis . . . that this condition of absolute predicament or irreducible dilemma lies in the very geometry of human conflict. It is at the basis of the structure of any given episode in that conflict.

The pages that follow will illustrate Professor Butterfield's theme. If you put a scorpion and a tarantula together in a bottle the objective of their own self-preservation will impell them to fight each other to the death. For the moment, at least, no understanding between them is possible. If either stopped fighting he would immediately be killed. From the point of view of each, the basic situation is that the other is trying to kill him. There is 'a terrible knot almost beyond the ingenuity of [the actors] to untie.' There is a condition of 'absolute predicament,' of 'irreducible dilemma.' The situation is tragic. The proper attitude for the observer, therefore, is one of sympathy for both parties.

In the Cold War various historical circumstances (which I shall describe) put Russia in the role of challenger—superficially, at least, in the role of aggressor. But the historical circumstances, themselves, had an ineluctable quality that left the Russians little choice but to move as they did. Moving as they did, they compelled the United States and its allies to move in response. And so the Cold War was joined.

This is not fundamentally a case of the wicked against the virtuous. Fundamentally, it is like the case of the scorpion and the tarantula in the bottle, and we may properly feel sorry for both parties, caught, as they are, in a situation of irreducible dilemma.

* * *

Citations of publications in the footnotes refer to the list of publications at the end of the book, just before the Index.

This history was written under the auspices of the Graduate Institute of International Studies in Geneva as part of its program. I acknowledge with warm appreciation the important assistance it gave me.

I am most grateful to the following persons who gave me help that ranged from the supply of items of information to suggestions based on a critical reading of chapters in draft: Peter Calvocoressi, Reginald Kazanjian, the Hon. George F. Kennan, Albert Legault, Charles Burton Marshall, Philip E. Mosely, Sir John Slessor, the Hon. Clare H. Timberlake, and Arnold Wolfers. I am also grateful to Miss Ulrike Wuttig, who spent many days typing and checking and picking up after me in a most intelligent fashion. On top of that, she took upon herself the sole authorship of the Index, a great labor carried through with skill.

L. J. H.

Geneva, 1966

CHAPTER I

The enlargement of Moscow's empire at the end of World War II

THE circumstances out of which the Cold War arose are simple enough in outline. The traditional boundary of the Russian Empire (and of its Soviet successor) had been roughly along a line extending from the eastern Baltic to the Black Sea. West of that line there had, in recent times, been an unhappy group of buffer states: Finland, Estonia, Latvia, Lithuania, Poland, and the Balkans. West of the buffer states, in turn, had been Germany, Austria, Italy, France. Traditionally, the gigantic power of Russia had been contained or balanced, to the West, by one or another of the western European great powers, or by a combination of them.

In the twentieth century the principal European power that served to contain the power of Russia had been Germany. Thus the elements of an equilibrium, of a balance of power, had existed in Europe before World War II, however precariously. Those elements no longer existed in 1945, when the War ended. When the War ended, the military forces of the Soviet Union were in occupation of most of the buffer area, and even of areas well beyond it. They were in occupation of all Poland, and of Germany to a line a hundred miles west of Berlin. They were in occupation of Hungary, and of the eastern part of Austria. They were in occupation of Rumania and Bulgaria. They were in Yugoslavia, if not actually in occupation of it. In other words, the Soviet Union had suddenly, as if by sleight of hand, effected the military conquest of the eastern half of Europe. It had simply swallowed up half of Europe—or was in the process of swallowing it up. Moscow's army had reached a line that ran through the middle of Europe from north to south.

What was there on the other side of this line to balance and contain this suddenly expanded Russian power?

The uncaptured half of Europe, on the other side of the line, lay prostrate. And Russia, at this time, was still advancing, still ex-

1

panding. With the rapid withdrawal and disintegration of the American Army, there was no military obstacle to the Red Army if it chose to continue to the English Channel.

What the situation of Europe represented, in the years from 1945 to 1947, was a crisis in the balance of power. It was the fourth such crisis that Europe had experienced in a hundred and fifty years, since the end of the eighteenth century.

Napoleon's France had temporarily upset the balance of power at the beginning of the nineteenth century, overrunning Europe as far as Moscow. To restore the balance on that occasion a great coalition of states, putting themselves on a war-footing, and many years of desperate fighting, had been necessary.

In the early twentieth century Kaiser William II's Germany had similarly challenged the European balance of power. Again a coalition of states, fighting desperately for four years, had been necessary to defeat this second challenge.

The third occasion arose toward the end of the 1930's, when Hitler overthrew the European balance of power, as Napoleon had done, and overran Europe from the Channel to the gates of Moscow. Again a great coalition had fought an exhausting war to put him down and to restore the European equilibrium.

The European equilibrium was not restored, however, upon the achievement of victory over Hitler. On this third occasion, as we have seen, Russia was left in possession of half Europe, while the other half lay prostrate before it. The western allies, having put down the terrifying specter of Hitler, were now confronted with the no-less-terrifying specter of Stalin. For them this was a bitter conclusion indeed of a war that had required so much courage and sacrifice on their part.

It is essentially true, then, to say that since the end of the eighteenth century four great wars have been fought to maintain or restore the European balance of power. The fourth was the Cold War, which began almost immediately after World War II.

*   *   *

The picture I have sketched above seems to me essentially true. But it leaves out much; and it is enormously simplified. I shall have to begin complicating it from this point on.

For one thing, I have, in this preliminary fashion, sketched the circumstances that brought about the Cold War without any reference to ideological issues. Yet most persons regard the Cold

War as essentially an ideological war; and I would, myself, be far from denying the ideological element. (I shall deal with the question this raises in the next chapter.)

For another thing, I have referred only to Europe, and to the European balance of power. This is a rank oversimplification. The Cold War has been worldwide; both its immediate predecessors were properly called world wars; and even the Napoleonic Wars had spread to America (in the War of 1812) and to India. Let me begin the process of complicating my picture, then, by taking account of the world beyond the frontiers of Europe.

In crude terms of power—of power politics and the balance of power—Europe in the nineteenth century was co-extensive with the wide world. Nowhere else in the world was there any power to match that of the European powers, to stand against it. In the nineteenth century, therefore, Europe came to dominate the whole world. It came to dominate the Far East and the Pacific. It came to dominate south Asia—the East Indies, Indochina, Burma and India, Persia and the Middle East. It came to dominate Africa, from the Cape to Cairo. North America was essentially a colonial extension, and in part a colonial possession, of Europe, sheltering behind British sea-power. The same was true of South America.

In the course of the nineteenth century, then, European power had been projected all around the world. Under these circumstances, the European balance of power had become essentially a world balance of power. The stage for the political maneuvers involved in the European balance had become nothing less than the whole world. When Britain came into conflict with Russia in Tibet, or along the northwest frontier of India, that conflict was essentially a European power-conflict. It was essentially a conflict over the European balance of power. When France and Britain and Russia, extending their power in east Asia, began to come into conflict with one another in the interior of China, what was at stake was the European balance of power.

This situation changed materially at the end of the nineteenth century, with the rise to world power of two states outside the European continent. One was the United States of America, the other Japan. After the 1890's it really does become an anachronism, therefore, to speak of the 'European' balance of power. For the European balance of power is no longer self-contained. It has, rather, become part of a larger balance that involves independently existing powers outside Europe.

When Napoleon upset the balance of power in Europe the European powers were able, by themselves, to put him down and to re-establish it. They did not have to look for succour to powers outside Europe—and, in any case, such powers did not exist. This was not the situation, however, in either of the World Wars, and it has clearly not been the situation in the Cold War.

In both World Wars, and again in the Cold War, the European states that were trying to maintain the *status quo* against the challenger had to look to the United States for succour, since they, themselves, lacked the required strength. In World War I Kaiser William, having defeated Russia, would surely have made himself supreme over Europe if, at the last hour, the weight of the United States had not been thrown into the balance against him. In World War II, again, Hitler would surely have defeated England and Russia, as well as France, and would have made himself supreme over Europe and the Mediterranean, if, again, the weight of the United States had not been thrown into the balance against him. Finally, it seems unlikely that western Europe would have recovered and maintained its independence, during the score of years after 1945, if the weight of the United States had not again been thrown into the balance—this time against the Soviet Union.

What has happened in the twentieth century is that the world-wide balance of European powers has come to involve military powers all around the world—China, Japan, and the United States—as well as the powers on the European continent. Still, however, as in the past, the fulcrum of the balance, the center of gravity, remains in Europe.

We must bear in mind, here, that Russia is a European, not an Asian power. This might not be clear to anyone who knew only the map of Russia in the twentieth century, and who noted how that map embraces more Asian than European territory. But it is quite clear to anyone who knows Russian history. The basic Russian stock is Slavic, and there are no purer Europeans than the Slavs. They were in Europe as long ago as we have any knowledge, as long ago as neolithic times. Their center was north and west of the Black Sea—far to the west of the Ural Mountains, which we identify as dividing Europe from Asia. They are a purely European people, not Asian in any feature.

The beginnings of Russian history, moreover, are in the area between the Baltic and the Black Sea, inside Europe. For a thousand years this is Russia, the home of the white European people we call Russians. It was not until the modern age and the period of general European expansion that the Russians moved into Asia, settling the great empty spaces of Siberia until they had given Russia Asian territory more than equal to her home territory in Europe. It is true that the Russian people were repeatedly subjected to Mongolian influences, and that their empire came to include a variety of Asian nations, but this hardly makes Russia an Asian nation any more than England's involvement in India made England an Asian nation.

Nevertheless, it is clear that Russia always has been, and remains today, a frontier nation, a nation on the outer edges of Europe, away from its center.

How about the United States?

Since the United States is basically a nation of European stock it is in that sense a European nation. Its language, moreover, is a European language, its culture a culture of exclusively European descent.

The fact is that, in modern times and at an accelerating rate, Europe expanded eastward across Siberia to the Pacific on one side, and westward across the Atlantic and North America to the Pacific on the other side. What we have today is an expanded Europe that stretches all around the world, to the Bering Straits in Siberia, and to the Bering Straits in Alaska.

Both Russia and the United States, then, may be regarded as European nations on the outer edge of Europe. If we think of this expanded Europe, stretching all around the northern hemisphere, we can see what has happened. What has happened is that the preponderant power has shifted away from the center of Europe, on the old European continent, to the outer edge in both directions.

But the center of the balance is still the old European continent. It is in the heart of Europe that the confrontation of Russian power and American power is staged. Russia and the United States have a common boundary in Bering Straits, while on the European side they are four thousand miles apart. Yet it is not in Bering Straits that the two colossi confront each other. In Bering Straits, where they touch each other, they have their backs to each other, and it is, rather, across the heart of Europe that they confront each other face to face.

While the preponderant power of European civilization has, then, moved out of the ancient European continent, westward into America and eastward into Russia, the old continent is still the center of the power-struggle. It is still the center of the world balance of power that has developed out of the European balance of power.

* * *

I have hesitated to use the term 'balance of power' because, in itself and in what it is often taken to represent, it arouses such widespread disapproval. Social scientists criticize it because it is misleading if taken literally. At the same time, volumes have been written about the various balance-of-power 'systems' that have existed in history. I use the term here neither literally, as a balance that can be expressed in pounds avoirdupois, nor with reference to any particular system. I use it to mean, simply, such a distribution of power among a number of centers as prevents the acquisition by any one of enough power to make itself master of the rest.

Such a distribution is essential to the stability of any society. In the United States it is represented, not only by the constitutional system of checks and balances but also by the distribution of political power among the several groupings of business-men, of working men, of farmers, etc. At the turn of the century, when big business threatened to upset this balance, the other centers of power combined to put it down by means of the 'trust-busting' legislation. After World War II, when labor threatened to upset it, the other centers combined to put it down by such legislation as the Taft–Hartley Act.

It is a paradox that even a dictatorship depends on a balance of power, which it maintains by manipulation, among the elements of the society over which it presides. The dictator divides to rule. Stalin, to hold his position, had to balance the Army, the secret police, the Party, and the bureaucracy off against one another. If ever there is a world government, its power to survive and to govern will also depend on a balance of power among those over whom it presides. It will not, in other words, exist as an alternative to the international balance of power.

We may decry the international balance of power, but when it is upset by a Hitler or a Stalin we all become alarmed and combine to correct the situation. We all combine to restore the previous balance of power, although sometimes without admitting that that is what we are doing.

It would have been better, in the two World Wars, if the restoration of a balance of power had been the victors' conscious and proclaimed objective. They would then, one supposes, have seen that it was essential to avoid the complete destruction of the defeated enemy's power, since that power would be needed in the postwar balance.

In the conclusion of the Napoleonic Wars, France, under a successor regime, had been restored to the family of nations, in which she immediately re-assumed a role that was indispensable to the balance.

World War I ended less happily. Germany, under a successor regime, was not immediately restored to the family of nations. A stable international system was not re-established, and no enduring peace ensued. Just as there could not be a stable international system after 1815 in which a healthy France did not play its part, so there could not be a stable international system after 1918 in which a healthy Germany did not play its part. In 1919, however, the victorious powers undertook simply to eliminate, for an indefinite future, the power of Germany. It happens that the elimination of German power, in the close of World War I, was matched by the elimination of Russian power, which had already occurred. Otherwise we might have seen in 1918 the kind of situation that confronted us in 1945.

Among the consequences of World War I were the rise of a new Russia and the rise of a new Germany, both profoundly antagonistic to the *status quo* represented by the traditional Western powers that had won the War, as well as to each other. And so peace was never truly established after the War. A peace of sorts, a truce, survived for a few years, not by virtue of a stable equilibrium of power but of an unstable equilibrium of weakness. In the immediate aftermath of the War, neither Russia nor Germany was in a position to seek the establishment of its own hegemony.

Then Hitler mobilized German power for a new attempt. Again, in overcoming Hitler's Germany, the victorious allies of World War II undertook to erase German power from the map of Europe for an indefinite future. But this time Russian power remained in being, and the Western allies could not keep it from pouring into the vacuum left by the elimination of German power. It poured

into eastern Europe, and how much farther it would spread no
one at the time could tell.

This new challenge to the balance of power, and the reaction of
the Atlantic world under American leadership, represents the
genesis of the Cold War.

The Cold War, then, belongs essentially to the same class of
international conflict as the Napoleonic Wars and the two World
Wars. There is the same challenge of a military colossus threatening to overwhelm and subjugate its neighbors, threatening to
extend its sway indefinitely. There is the same belated organization of a defensive coalition against that colossus. There is the same
build-up of military power on both sides, and a mutual confrontation. And in this case as in the others, it all ends with the frustration
of the challenge, with its containment or defeat in one way or
another.

The reader undoubtedly has in mind already the one most
conspicuous difference between the Cold War and the three
earlier wars. The three earlier wars were wars of military combat,
wars in which armed forces faced each other, and pummeled each
other, and drenched the landscape in blood. But the Cold War has
not been a war in this sense. It has not been a war in which fighting
and bloodshed have had anything except an incidental or an
accidental role. The contestants have confronted each other, they
have shouted threats and abuse at each other, they have flexed
their military muscles to intimidate each other—but they have not
struck at each other. One side or the other has sometimes advanced
or backed off a few inches. By and large, however, since this cold
combat was joined the two sides have between them kept to the
territorial *status quo*. If it is right to regard the Cold War as World
War III, we must at least admit that it has been conducted quite
differently from World Wars I and II.

The reason for the difference, I think, is that the revolutionary
new weapons of the nuclear age are so deadly that their use cannot
be seriously risked. The contestants on both sides know that they
may all be killed if they strike. Consequently, however they may
threaten, they draw back rather than strike when that appears to
be the choice before them. It follows that, so far at least, we have
much to thank nuclear weapons for. Whatever the future may
hold, their advent upon the scene has so far spared us much. It
has kept the Cold War cold.

Nevertheless, like its predecessors, the Cold War has been a worldwide power contest in which one expanding power has threatened to make itself predominant, and in which other powers have banded together in a defensive coalition to frustrate it—as was the case before 1815, as was the case in 1914–1918, as was the case from 1939–1945.

CHAPTER II

The behavior of Moscow as a reflection of Russia's historic experience

Writing in the 1830's, Alexis de Tocqueville made the following remarkable prophecy:

There are on earth today two great people, who, from different points of departure, seem to be advancing toward the same end. They are the Russians and the Anglo-Americans.

Both have grown great in obscurity; and while the attention of mankind was occupied elsewhere they have suddenly taken their places in the first rank among the nations, and the world has learned, almost at the same time, both of their birth and of their greatness.

All the other peoples appear to have attained approximately their natural limits, and to have nothing left but to conserve their positions; but these two are growing: all the others have stopped or continue only by endless effort; they alone advance easily and rapidly in a career of which the limit cannot yet be seen.

The American struggles against the obstacles that nature places before him; the Russian is at grips with humanity. The one combats wilderness and savagery, the other combats civilization decked in all its armament: moreover, the conquests of the American are won by the plowshare, those of the Russian by the sword.

To attain his end, the first depends on the interest of the individual person, and allows the force and intelligence of individuals to act freely, without directing them. The second in some way concentrates all the power of society in one man.

The one has liberty as the chief way of doing things; the other servitude.

Their points of departure are different, their paths are divergent; nevertheless, each seems summoned by a secret design of providence to hold in his hands, some day, the destinies of half the world.[1]

One may draw two conclusions from the fact that de Tocqueville was able to make this prediction so long ago.

One is that what is predictable must (always barring a cataclysm) be inevitable. Nothing is surely predictable except as it is

[1] Translated from *De la Démocratie en Amérique*, concluding passage of the first half—i.e., of Vol. I.

bound to happen. If it may or may not happen, then one cannot predict its happening with authority; one can only guess and gamble that it will happen. But de Tocqueville was not guessing and gambling. He saw the future development of America and Russia as implicit in their contemporary circumstances. He saw their future in their present as one sees the leaf in the bud. Therefore we may conclude that the polarization of the world between two superpowers was not the accidental product of accidental circumstances.

Walter Lippmann once wrote that prophecy 'is seeing the necessary amidst confusion and insignificance. . . .' The development that de Tocqueville prophesied so long ago belonged to the realm of the necessary.

The other conclusion that I draw from his prophecy is that the role of Communism in the polarization of the world is secondary, that it does not belong to the realm of the necessary. For de Tocqueville, when he wrote his prophecy, knew nothing of a young university student in Germany called Karl Marx, or of an unborn revolutionary called Lenin. He did not foresee the coming of Communism to Russia. He did not anticipate the substitution of a Communist regime for the czarist regime. He foresaw that what in fact came to pass would come to pass regardless of the ideological label attached to the authoritarian regime that governed Russia.

The implications of this seem to me essential to an understanding of the Cold War. The behaviour of Russia under the Communists has been Russian behaviour rather than Communist behaviour. Under the Communists Russia has continued to behave essentially as it behaved under the czars. There has been the same centralization and authoritarianism. There has been the same conspiratorial approach to international relations. There has been the same profound mistrust of the outside world. There has been the same obsession with secrecy and with espionage. There has been the same cautiousness, the same capacity for retreat. There has been the same effort to achieve security by expanding the Russian space, by constantly pushing back the menacing presence of the foreigners across the Russian borders.

What the Revolution of 1917 did was simply to reinvigorate the traditional principle of authoritarianism in Russia. It replaced a decadent and enfeebled authoritarian dynasty with a new, vigorous, and ruthlessly determined authoritarian dynasty. All this is implicit in the fact that de Tocqueville was able to predict both the polarization of the world and the ideological contest between the two superpowers without foreseeing Marxism–Leninism.

The Cold War, then, represents an historical necessity to which the Communist movement is incidental rather than essential.

*   *   *

By contrast with America, Russia has always been a closed society. It has been a secret society under the czars as under the Communists—and, at an earlier stage, under the princes of Muscovy as under the czars. It has been a society in which all the functions of a Government that was constitutionally all-powerful have traditionally been carried on in the dark, out of a fear that has been repeatedly justified in the awful history of the Russian people. Consequently Russia, neither Asian nor seeming quite European, speaking a language not understood outside its confines, has had about it an air of darkness and mystery that is the antithesis of the aura that surrounds the American society.

Of other societies that have been hostile and aggressive it has been evident that they were driven by ambition. Athens, Rome, Hitler's Germany, and pre-war Japan were driven by ambition. These societies were intoxicated by their dreams of power. It would be wrong to assign a like cause to the long history of Russia's expansion and hostility. And today as well, I think, we are misled by an essentially nominal situation when we say that Moscow's expansion and hostility represent an ambition to spread its so-called 'Communist system' throughout the world. Such an ambition is, at best, secondary.

From the beginning in the ninth century, and even today, the prime driving force in Russia has been fear. Fear, rather than ambition, is the principal reason for the organization and expansion of the Russian society. Fear, rather than ambition in itself, has been the great driving force. The Russians as we know them today have experienced ten centuries of constant, mortal fear. This has not been a disarming experience. It has not been an experience calculated to produce a simple, open, innocent, and guileless society.

If all my ancestors for ten centuries back had died violent deaths at the hands of their neighbors, it is quite likely that I would have been brought up from childhood to be suspicious and hostile toward my neighbors. It is likely that I would have been brought up to be dangerous to my neighbors, that I would have been brought up to the practice of an astute course of deception designed to outwit and to foil them. And while I might on occasion feel myself profoundly attracted to them, as one is always attracted to a powerful enemy, no smiles of friendship on their part would ever persuade me to relax my guard in their company. Like Foreign Minister Molotov visiting his wartime ally, Prime Minister Churchill, I would keep a loaded revolver by my bedside.

Throughout Russian history real circumstances have justified the fear by which the Russians have been governed. For ten centuries they have survived the greatest trials experienced by any people in the world today only because they have been so governed. They have survived those trials only because they learned at an early stage to trust no one, to be suspiciously alert, to keep their own counsel, and to substitute guile for superior strength where superior strength was lacking.

The basic factor in producing this national sense of insecurity has been geographical. Throughout its history Russia has been without natural frontiers to serve for its defense.

Physically, as we all know, Europe is a peninsula on the vast Eurasian continent. As such, it is confined and rugged; it is tightly bounded by the sea on almost every side; and it is criss-crossed by mountain-barriers. As far eastward as the Carpathians and the Black Sea, it is compartmentalized by natural frontiers. On the east, however, between the Carpathians and the Baltic, Europe opens out into a great plain that is continuous with the immense plain of central and northern Asia. There is no proportion here. One could fit the whole European peninsula into the middle of this Asian plain and perhaps have as much space left over in it.

For century after century, this Asiatic hinterland was an unknown realm, a mysterious realm of darkness and danger. Europe, and Russia itself, simply faded out on the edge of this plain, which then receded into the endless Asiatic distances. Beyond the eastern horizon was cultural obscurity, barbarism, or fabulous empires like the Empire of Prester John.

The Europeans on the eastern marches of Europe, which means the Russians, were naked to any enemies that might, at any time, come pouring out of this darkness to attack them. On the map there are mountain-ranges running north and south, the Urals, which form the watershed between the European and Siberian parts of the plain; but they are, for the most part, hardly more than gentle swellings in the landscape. They provide no defensive barrier.

In the first centuries of the Christian era a sort of 'population explosion' among the nomadic peoples of Mongolia caused an outpouring, in all directions, of whole nations on horseback. The peaceful Slavs of eastern Europe lay defenseless in their way. Successive hordes, pouring out of the eastern darkness, swept over them, burning and slaughtering as they passed.

In the second half of the fourth century one of the greatest Mongolian invasions, that of the Huns, swept over the Slavs and did not spend itself until it had reached what is now France. The Huns disappeared in due course, only to be replaced, generation after generation, by fresh waves of invaders. There were the Bulgars, the Avars, the Khazars, the Magyars, the Pechenegs, and so on—up through the Tartars, the so-called 'Golden Horde,' which did not disappear from Europe until the end of the fifteenth century. The original Russians were the victims of these successive invasions. Lying defenseless on the plain, they were slaughtered and subjugated and humiliated by the invaders time and again. (This is something to remember when we read about the elaborate defenses that the Russians have erected along their common boundary with China.)

The original Russians, small bands of Slavs along the Volkov and Dnieper rivers, were not only defenseless to the east. They were defenseless on all sides. They were without frontiers, exposed to attacks by teutonic peoples in the north and west, and by Lithuanians and Poles in the west, as well as by Mongols in the east.

One is reminded of Matthew Arnold's 'Dover Beach':

> And we are here as on a darkling plain
> Swept with confused alarms of struggle and flight,
> Where ignorant armies clash by night.

That has been the whole history of Russia for ten centuries. Americans found themselves in a great continent that was almost uninhabited (estimated aboriginal population north of the Rio Grande: $1\frac{1}{2}$ million), in which their chief struggle was against the natural wilderness. But the chief struggle of the Russians was against the armed hordes of hostile nations.

*   *   *

Somehow the Slavs on Europe's outer fringe survived, until we hear of the formation in the ninth century of the first Russian state. The ninth century, one recalls, is the great century of the Viking invasions. It is the century when these primitive Scandinavians pour out of Scandinavia as the Mongols had been pouring out of Mongolia. They invade all the rivers of western Europe, burning and pillaging. They invade the Mediterranean, spreading over Sicily and the southern part of the Italian peninsula. They are the Danes who invade the British Isles and exact the Danegeld. They are the Norsemen who settle Normandy. They discover Greenland and North America. They also flow south over the river-roads of eastern Europe, to the Black Sea and Constantinople. They come down from the Gulf of Finland, ascending the Volkov River to its headwaters, then crossing over to the headwaters of the Dnieper and descending that river to the Black Sea.

In 862, the Slavs who lived at Novgorod, on the northern reaches of the river-road, asked a company of Viking warriors to come and protect them from the Pechenegs, who were among the most savage of the Mongol invaders. Twenty years later, the defensive organization of Slavs under Viking leadership established its capital at Kiev, on the Dnieper. This is the first Russian state, the so-called Kievan State. It struggles for three and a half terrible centuries to survive, but at last goes under.

In the thirteenth century came the greatest Mongolian invasion of all, that of the Golden Horde under Genghis Khan. These Tartars were irresistible, if only by their endless numbers. Everywhere they killed part of the people, enslaved others, burned, pillaged, looted, destroyed. In 1240, after the best resistance it could make, Kiev fell. Two years later a visitor found that the city had only two hundred houses left, and that the surrounding countryside was littered with skulls and bones. It is not possible to imagine the sum of horror that was experienced here. 'The heathen from all sides,' says an ancient chronicle, 'came victorious into the land of Russia.'

Sir Bernard Pares has written:

Kiev was a great and generous attempt to do the impossible:—along a single thin road running almost on the frontier of Europe, with a nascent civilization, a scattered population and a hopeless political organization which had little in it but the fine spirit that prompted it to keep at bay the unceasing and successive waves of population which

were driven by economic necessity out of Asia's storehouse of peoples.
. . . It is this that is the charm of the history of Kiev,—that against such
hopeless odds the chivalrous fight was kept up so long. Klyuchevsky
has said that a people becomes a nation by passing through some great
common danger, which remains afterwards as a great national memory.
Russian patriotism glows in the period of Kiev. We find more of it here
than at any later time except at such tense moments as the invasion of
Napoleon in 1812.[2]

For two centuries after the fall of Kiev, such Russians as survived will be under the suzerainty of the Tartars. Nevertheless, a
new Russian state now begins to form and develop farther north
and east, no longer on the uncovered plain but in the northern
forest. The phoenix is born again at Moscow. This new state of
Muscovy is able to survive and to grow only by the most guileful
dealings with the Tartar overlords. The task of the princes of
Muscovy is to save the new realm from the fate of Kiev by acting
as intermediaries for it with the Tartar khans; fawning upon them,
placating, appeasing, paying tribute; knowing when to advance
and, above all, when to retreat. (The retreat of a successor to the
princes of Muscovy in the Cuban crisis of October 1962 represents
a traditional Russian maneuver, based on a cautiousness and
patience learned during the long centuries when the Russians
demonstrated their powers of survival under the rule of their
Mongol conquerors.)

The Russians played for time, and with time the Tartar Empire
at last rotted away. When the liberation came, under Ivan the
Great in the late fifteenth century, it came by the typically Russian
combination of advance and retreat. In 1480 Ivan challenged the
suzerainty of the Tartars. When they responded by moving on
Moscow he fled and sued for peace. Twice he made his army retreat. Then, suddenly, the Tartar regime collapsed; the Tartar
Khan was killed in his sleep; his sons were overthrown. 'It is just
in such a slow and inconspicuous way,' writes Pares, 'that other
great decisions in Russian history have often come of themselves.'[3]

Russia's experience for the first six centuries was not such as
makes for an open, friendly, and guileless society. It was not such
as makes for a liberal and pacifistic society. On the contrary, all
the circumstances of Russian history have, from the beginning,
imposed the necessity of complete discipline under autocratic

[2] Pares, p. 41.   [3] Pares, p. 88.

authority—this as the price of survival. The United States, expanding over a rich and empty continent, could afford the luxury of democratic self-rule, of individualism, of free enterprise. The whole Russian society, by contrast, had to be organized for continuous military defense. Its Government had to be in a position of total control, so that it could maneuver freely, and so that it could command the forces necessary for the vital defense of the besieged and embattled society.

The reign of Ivan the Great marks the establishment of the autocratic czarist system, as well as the liberation from Tartar rule. It was Ivan who first took the title of 'Sovereign of all Russia,' and who first referred to himself as 'Caesar'—'Czar' in the Russian.

The knowledgeable reader will recall that Constantinople, having lasted a thousand years as the capital of the Eastern Roman Empire, finally fell before the Turks in 1453. The niece of the last Eastern Caesar, before the fall of Constantinople, had become the wife of Ivan the Great. It was this association with Constantinople that moved him to take for himself the imperial title, in succession to the fallen line of Eastern Caesars. So the autocracy dictated by circumstances was reinforced by the adoption of the tradition of the Byzantine Empire. By devious ways, the mantle that originally belonged to Augustus ended upon the shoulders of Ivan and his successors.

*   *   *

From the days of Ivan the Great until our own time, a period of five centuries, the history of Moscow is one of steady, continuing expansion. Yet this expansion, in a way peculiar to Russia, is not an aggressive expansion. Right up to our own day it is a defensive expansion, an expansion prompted by the lack of natural defensive frontiers in a world of mortal danger on all sides. Where mountain-ramparts or impassable waters are lacking, sheer space must do in their stead. The huddled defensive community—in Kiev, in Novgorod, in Smolensk, or in Moscow—is impelled, by whatever means, to drive the encircling danger back. And the process of driving the danger back becomes, to the eye of the outsider, the process of imperial expansion.

Throughout this expansion, and until our own day, Russia continues to be embattled and besieged. It is true that Moscow threw off the Tartar yoke in 1480. In 1571, however, the Tartars of the Crimea captured and burned Moscow. According to the reports, they killed 800,000 Russians and carried away 130,000 prisoners. This was the kind of incident that would be repeated time and again throughout the long history of Russia's defensive expansion—down to Hitler's invasion and slaughter of the Russians in our own day.

After the sixteenth century, however, the threats to Russia's survival all came from the west. In 1606 Russia was invaded, and Moscow was captured, by a Polish army. For six years, then, Muscovy was largely under Polish occupation, while Moscow was either occupied or withstanding siege. In 1611 Moscow was burned down again, all except for the Kremlin and the inner town. That same year, Swedish troops captured Novgorod.

In 1613, with the liberation of Moscow from the Poles, the coronation of Michael Romanov inaugurated a new dynasty. There followed a long series of wars with Swedes, Poles, Turks. And all the time Russia was expanding steadily. To the east, it expanded at last across Siberia. To the south, it expanded along the shores of the Black Sea. To the west, under Peter the Great, it emerged on the Baltic. In 1812 it was the French who invaded Russia. The Russian earth was scorched. Again Moscow fell into the hands of the invader.

The repeated blows continued in the twentieth century as for a thousand years before. In 1917 the Russian state collapsed completely, if temporarily, under the assault of Kaiser William's army. The invaders advanced deep into Russia. Virtually all the territory gained since the days of Peter the Great was lost. And with the loss of Finland the Russian frontier was forced back to within artillery-range of the new capital, St. Petersburg, that Peter had established on the Baltic. The loss of the whole Ukraine meant the economic ruin of Russia.

However, under the hammer-blows, first of the German assault, then of assault by the expeditionary forces of the Western allies, including the United States, the Russian state was reconstituted, a new dictatorship was forged by Lenin and then Stalin, and again the innate strength of the Russian land and people was gathered up, at terrible sacrifice, to withstand the next attack.

The next attack was to come under the directing will of Adolf Hitler. Again all the best Russian earth would be scorched. Again, when the assault was over, the land would be littered with the dead bodies of Russians, of which between seven and eight million were left dead when the Nazi tide had at last receded. And again the end of it all would be a further expansion of the territory under Moscow's sway, this time to embrace most of Europe to a line a hundred miles west of Berlin.

So, in the face of continual assault and defeat, Russia would emerge to fulfill de Tocqueville's prophecy, a giant power under the sway of one man, holding in its hands the destinies of half the world.

CHAPTER III

American behavior as a reflection of experience opposite to that of the Russians

The Russians have always been aware of their weakness and their danger; the Americans have, since an early date, been aware of their strength and their safety. The Russians have achieved success by way of repeated failure; the Americans believe that they have never lost a war. The Russians have regarded the outside world with awe, and have felt their own points of inferiority; the Americans have regarded the outside world without respect, and have gloried in their superior way of life.

Neither the Russians nor the Americans have found it easy to establish rewarding relationships with the world outside their borders. The Russians have repeatedly tried to Westernize themselves and have repeatedly recoiled from the West; while in the East they have encountered races and cultures that were altogether alien. (Dostoyevski is said to have remarked that Russians should turn to Asia, because it is only in Asia that they are accepted as Europeans.) The Americans, on the other hand, have traditionally been concerned to avoid involvement in what they regarded as the nefarious political combinations of a sinister Old World.

We have to recall that the American nation had its beginnings, in the seventeenth century, as a nation of refugees from the tyrannies, the persecutions, and the power-politics of the Old World. Americans have traditionally thought of themselves as the fortunate few who escaped from the Old World and, escaping from it, turned their backs on it for ever. And they have thought of their new-found continent as vastly superior to the other continents inhabited by a less fortunate mankind.

It was not only the Pilgrim Fathers in the early seventeenth century, crossing the Atlantic in the *Mayflower* to found the new society, who embodied this escape. Every generation since, right on into the twentieth century, has seen the inpouring of refugees from the Old World who, upon their arrival, shake the dust of the

Old World from their feet forever. My own grandfather came to America as part of the emigration from the European continent after the failure of the revolutions of 1848, and he never had any desire to go back. Again in the 1930's there was an influx of refugees from Hitler's spreading empire.

In our American mythology, the refugees and their children had established in their God-given land a new and entirely different kind of society, a society in which there were no lords and commoners, a society in which all men were free and equal, in which all men were brothers, in which the wicked devices of the Old World (the princely 'balances of power' and 'spheres of influence') were happily unknown. Even in my generation, which went to school after World War I, all of us Americans were brought up on this distinction between the Old World and the New. We learned to congratulate ourselves on our escape from the Old World, and we became conscious of our mission to preserve the heritage of that escape. George Washington had warned us, in words that had since acquired a semi-sacred character, against succumbing to the wiles of the nations in the Old World who would try to involve us in their constant quarrels. He had said: 'The great rule of conduct for us, in regard to foreign Nations, is, in extending our commercial relations, to have with them as little Political connection as possible.'

A generation later President Monroe, in the enunciation of the 'Doctrine' that bears his name, had said: 'The political system of the European powers is essentially different...from that of America.' The system he was referring to was the system identified with the term 'balance of power.' 'Balance of power' was un-American.

Not only had God given us a virgin continent, replete with all goods, on which to establish our society, he had given us the great oceans to protect it. Part of our American mythology, then, was that we were beyond the reach of the wicked. In an address of January 27, 1837, the young Abraham Lincoln had said:

All the armies of Europe, Asia, and Africa combined, with all the treasure of the earth (our own excepted) in their military chest, with a Bonaparte for a commander, could not by force take a drink from the Ohio or make a track on the Blue Ridge in a trial of a thousand years.

Moreover, even as late as the 1920's Americans were, for the most part, genuinely isolated. One can hardly imagine, today, how remote a farmer in Kansas—or a druggist in Oklahoma, or a doctor in Montana, or an engineer in Ohio—was from the political problems of Europe. He thought of Europe in terms of the old continent from which his forebears had escaped.

I recall in the 1930's, along an unexplored river in Central America, coming upon an old Englishman who had been there since the beginning of the century. The first question he asked me about the outside world was how the Boers were behaving. The Boer War belonged to his present as later events did not. In the same way, I have no doubt that to most Americans in the 1920's King George III was more real than King George V. References to the British still evoked the image of the wicked 'Red Coats' whom we had chased out of our continent.

Beginning about the turn of the century, the American people found themselves faced with an apparent choice between either taking an active part in world affairs or continuing to enjoy their traditional detachment. The United States, in the course of a war for the liberation of Cuba from Spain, unexpectedly found itself responsible for the defense of colonial territory in the midst of the Far Eastern theater where Britain, France, Germany, Russia, and Japan were contending for power and empire. The unintended acquisition of the Philippines imposed on the United States an overseas commitment that was incompatible with a continuing policy of abstinence from world affairs. It could not remain within its New World and still provide for the defense of these Asian islands against a power like Germany, which was trying to get them for itself, or a power like Japan, which had embarked on an imperial expansion that would encompass the area in which they lay.

Quite aside from this, the foundations of the long-standing world order on which American detachment depended were crumbling at the turn of the century. Until then the European balance of power, which had become a world balance of power, had been maintained by Great Britain, which had by itself played the role of balancer. This is to say that Britain, keeping itself free of permanent involvement in rival systems of alliance among the powers, had been able to shift its weight from one side to the other as necessary to keep the balance. It had been able to do this because of the security afforded by the moat that the English Channel represented as long as it was under English naval control. And as the European balance became a world balance Britain was able to do it by that naval supremacy over the seven seas in consequence of which it was able to hold off any potential enemy from the approaches to its island kingdom while bringing its own power to bear wherever it might be needed along the shores of the five continents. This was the strategic basis of the *Pax Britannica* that prevailed in the world from the final overthrow of Napoleon in 1815 to the end of the century.

At the end of the century, however, this strategic basis was being undermined by the rise of German, Japanese, and American sea-power, which were rapidly putting an end to British naval supremacy. The British, seeing that they could no longer 'go it alone,' tried for an alliance with the United States that would combine the two navies in a partnership, failed, and concluded an alliance with Japan instead.

One is left to contemplate the defaulted possibility that the United States, at the turn of the century, might have associated itself with Britain to maintain the world order that Britain could no longer maintain by itself—the possibility, in fact, that the United States might have taken over Britain's long-standing role as balancer when the rise of air-power reduced the security of the British Isles. Such contemplation is not altogether idle because it provides a basis for appreciating the failures of the first half of the twentieth century—failures that to us, in the second half of the century, must appear particularly notable and tragic.

In the twentieth century the United States, standing behind the Atlantic Ocean as Britain had stood behind the Channel in the nineteenth, dominating that ocean as Britain had dominated the Channel, might for a couple of generations more, at least, have kept the peace that was in fact lost. If the United States, in association with Great Britain or alone, had actively and clearly committed itself to the maintenance of the balance of power, and had developed its Navy accordingly, Kaiser William would have had to limit his ambitions. The failure of any German challenge would have been a foregone conclusion, for Germany would have been within reach of the United States while the United States would not have been within reach of Germany; and therefore the challenge would not have been offered.

I said above that, at the turn of the century, the American people confronted an apparent choice between either taking an active part in world affairs or continuing to enjoy their traditional detachment. The choice was only apparent, however, since their traditional detachment depended on the *Pax Britannica* that was coming to an end. There was no course of action or inaction by which the United States could have continued its isolation in a New World that was no longer strategically detached from the Old.

With the opening of the twentieth century, the responsibility fell to the United States of taking England's place as the balancer, or associating itself with England in that role, by actively using its weight for the deterrence and the frustration of any challenger to the world order who was trying to make himself predominant. Surely Anglo-American power—used shrewdly, knowledgeably, skilfully—could for an indefinite period have continued to maintain the condition of relative peace and order that had prevailed since 1815. All depended on the United States. All depended on its recognition of the new responsibility, and on its knowledge of how to meet it.

Here, however, we face a foregone conclusion. What men and nations are by their nature and upbringing cannot be excluded from the given factors that determine the course of history. Nothing in the experience of the American people, after the War of 1812, had equipped them even to recognize that an international responsibility had fallen to them with the passing of the nineteenth century. What stood for wisdom among them was still, of necessity, the ancient wisdom of the Founding Fathers, which had been handed down from generation to generation and was still taught in the schools.

Had the counsels of the Founding Fathers, adopted by the American nation, involved it in disaster, then they might have stood discredited. On the contrary, however, at the turn of the century we Americans could look back on a history of success that supported an unqualified self-confidence, and that confirmed us in our traditional policy.

If the Russians have been shaped by a record of failure, the Americans have been shaped by a record of success. The quick American victory in the Spanish–American War of 1898, including a dramatic and unanticipated naval triumph off the distant shores of Asia, impressed the American people as it did the rest of the world. The first time the United States had occasion to strike, on its own initiative, at a kingdom of the Old World, it saw that kingdom go down under the first blow. This was surprising, at the time, and rather intoxicating. Suddenly Americans were conscious of being, not only a world power, but the greatest of all nations. And this, they could hardly help feeling, was the reward of their virtue. They were 'the Chosen People,' as William Allen White put it. God had provided them with a virgin continent, unmatched on the face of the earth, so that they could erect an entirely new society that, by its example, would serve for the regeneration of mankind. Less than a score of years after the Spanish–American War, when the United States again had occasion to strike at an Old World tyrant, he too succumbed to the irresistible power and virtue of the democratic armies from the New World.

No wonder that the American people, in the twentieth century, have tended to succumb to what Sir Denis Brogan has called 'the illusion of American omnipotence'! It is this illusion that has made so many simple Americans feel that the failures and frustrations of American policy in the period after 1945 could be explained only as the consequence of treason or gross incompetence in Washington. Americans have not, in recent times, appreciated the limitations of American power as Russians have always appreciated the limitations of Russian power; and just as failure has been the making of the Russians, so success has threatened to be the undoing of the Americans.

Whatever the considerations that may appear vivid to us today, it was unthinkable at the turn of the century that the American people should involve themselves in England's wicked power-politics. It was unthinkable that they should come to the side of the British monarchy, which had tyrannized over them and exploited them under George III, and which still practised its diabolical colonialism over a worldwide empire.

Not wickedness or stupidity or a more-than-human selfishness prevented the American people from adapting themselves to the new circumstances of the world at the beginning of the twentieth century—by betraying their own history, by rebelling against the teachings of their Founding Fathers, by abandoning their essential tradition. Unprepared to recognize the facts of international power-politics, let alone to manipulate and to master them, they persuaded themselves, at first, that the Kaiser's bid for European hegemony had no bearing on their own well-being and security, which were inviolable; that his triumph or defeat was properly a matter of indifference to them. And they maintained this attitude until the Kaiser's submarines were, at last, hunting their prey in the waters off New York Harbor.

When Americans began to lose their lives by hostile action in waters that lapped their own coasts—and that in spite of the security that the Atlantic Ocean was thought to provide in and of itself—then the nation responded with bewilderment, alarm, and excitement. This, for the American people, was their first lesson in the facts of twentieth-century life. Unfortunately, it was a lesson that they failed to learn.

The American people, shaped by their long tradition, could not accept considerations of power-politics as reasons for going to war. If those considerations nevertheless drove them to war, then they would have to persuade themselves that their motives were, in fact, of a higher order. Defending the sea-approaches to their own land against the German submarine, they told themselves that what they were really defending was a moral principle called 'Freedom of the Seas.' It was 'Freedom of the Seas' that was at issue. Ostensibly, the United States intervened in World War I on behalf of 'Freedom of the Seas.' It would not, however, have felt the same obligation to intervene on behalf of this freedom if the German submarines had not been operating off its own shores.

So, in 1917–1918, the United States, morally and psychologically unequipped to do so, came into the War at the eleventh hour to restore the balance of power, while pretending that it was doing something altogether different and nobler.

The result was that the lesson was not learned the first time, that it had to be repeated in 1941, and that it would be finally learned only in 1947, when at last the United States, now grim and realistic, would abandon its isolationist policy and all its outworn traditions in order to meet the challenge of Stalin's Russia—which was the successor, in this respect, of Hitler's Germany.

In 1917, however, even 'Freedom of the Seas' was not enough to placate the national conscience in the face of such an abandonment of the national tradition as the entry into the War represented. The abandonment could be justified only if it brought an end, once and for all, to the wicked power-politics of the Old World, followed by a reconstitution of that World on the lines that had been tried and proved in the New World. So the War became a 'war to make the world safe for democracy.' It became a 'war to end wars.' The American people persuaded themselves that, without selfish interests of their own, they had entered the War for the salvation of mankind—to put an end to power-politics, and to put an end to all the sordid conceptions that went with power-politics, like 'spheres of influence.' They persuaded themselves that they had entered the War, not to restore the balance of power, but to put an end to the whole system of which it was a part.

The persistence of the national attitude that this represented was such that as late as 1945, a whole generation later, the President of the United States, returning from the Crimea Conference at Yalta, said to the Congress: 'The Crimea Conference . . . ought to spell the end of the system of unilateral action, the exclusive alliances, the spheres of influence, the balances of power, and all the other expedients that have been tried for centuries—and have always failed.'

There is a sort of fatality about these matters. If the American people had been told the truth in 1917, if they had been fed on the reality instead of on dreams, then they would not have fought, and the War would have been lost, and anarchy would have triumphed and would have prevailed over the world. So the American people were told the opposite of the truth, and they fought for it, and the War was won.

The price in postwar disillusionment, however, was immense. The American people, already in a state of revulsion at the un-expected horrors of trench-warfare, found that, after all their sacrifices, and after finally achieving victory—after rescuing the Old World—the shining new world that they thought they had fought for was not forthcoming. It was still the unregenerate Old World of before the War, the world of secret treaties, spheres of influence, balances of power. The result was that a major portion of the American nation concluded, with passionate embitterment, that a disastrous mistake had been made in abandoning the sacred precept of the Founding Fathers to stay out of foreign quarrels; and they determined that the mistake should never be repeated.

While this revulsion was essentially naïve and pitiful, it was fed by real failures on the part of the victorious French and British. President Woodrow Wilson had proposed a settlement of the War that, in its essential features, would have constituted a genuine and enduring peace. This was what his famous 'fourteen points' meant. This was what his projected 'peace without victory' meant. There could be no peace in which the victors undertook to keep the vanquished prostrate in perpetuity, preventing them from regaining their feet. That, however, was precisely the kind of settlement that the French and British leaders, driven by the hatred and the thirst for revenge that the War had aroused in the peoples they represented, forced through at Paris. It was a 'peace settlement' in name only, for it did not restore Germany, under its anti-imperial successor Government, to the family of nations, or even allow it the means to earn its living. It did not, to use the phrase applied by Abraham Lincoln to a similar situation, 'bind up the wounds of war.' 'Only a peace between equals can last,' Wilson had said; but the very essence of the Versailles Treaty was the establishment of inequality.

John Maynard Keynes, quitting the Paris Peace Conference in disgust, had written in 1919: 'If the . . . War is to end with France and Italy abusing their momentary victorious power to destroy Germany and Austria-Hungary now prostrate, they invite their own destruction also, being so deeply and inextricably intertwined with their victims by hidden psychic and economic bonds.'[1] In spite of Wilson, the European victors did abuse 'their momentary victorious powers.' And so there was no real peace; and what Keynes had predicted came to pass; and it all eventuated in a renewal of the War, this time under the rubric of 'World War II.'

It may be said, then, that part of the revulsion of the American people, which projected them back into their traditional isolationism, was produced by the Versailles Treaty. They had been betrayed in what they had had some right to expect, as well as in what they had been pitifully naïve to expect.

There is a fatality about these matters. The way World War I was fought, and the way it was concluded, made a second world war virtually inevitable. The way the American people became involved in World War I made it virtually inevitable that they would not learn the lesson of that war. This lesson was that, whether they liked it or not, the chief responsibility for policing the balance of power, and thus maintaining the foundations of international stability, had passed to them.

If the American people had learned the lesson of World War I, and if the other Atlantic victors had learned to act with a lofty wisdom; then all the subsequent disasters might have been averted. The economic collapse of the 1930's might have been averted; the

[1]Keynes, p. 5.

failure of Germany's Weimar Republic might have been averted; the rise of Hitler might have been averted. But everything conspired against this. Above all, our common human nature conspired against it. And so we had to go through the horror again. We had to pay the price of taking the lesson all over again.

Even then, however, we did not learn it. Even then, the American people did not immediately achieve an understanding of the realities, and of their role in dealing with them.

So World War II was followed by the Cold War.

CHAPTER IV

The creation, in 1945, of the power vacuums on either side of Russia into which it tended to expand

Arjuna stayed his chariot between the two armies. He saw in either relatives, benefactors, and friends. He saw kindred civilizations opposed, and destruction certain for one of them and perhaps for both. His limbs trembled, his purpose weakened, and instead of proclaiming battle, he spoke thus to the god Krishna, who was his charioteer: 'I desire not victory nor kingdom nor pleasures. . . . Those for whose sake we desire such things—they stand opposite to us in the battle now. . . . Slaying these poor sinners, we shall fall ourselves into sin. They, blinded by greed, see no guilt in the destruction of kindred, no crime in hostility to friends, but we, we who have seen, why should we not refrain? When kindred are destroyed, the immemorial traditions perish; when traditions perish, anarchy falls on us all. Were it not better for me to go unarmed, unresisting, into the battle and be slain by them instead?'

THIS is how the Hindu classic, the *Bhagavad-Gita*, opens—with Arjuna in his chariot, at the outset of a great battle, paralyzed by the prospect of killing those who are his kindred, his fellow men, because in their greed and their blindness they have turned against him. It opens with Arjuna's question to his charioteer, who is the god Krishna: whether it would not be better to let himself be slain than to destroy his lapsed kindred, and by destroying them to destroy, as well, the foundations of civilization and order.

Krishna then answers Arjuna that it is his duty to slaughter his opponents, even though in doing so he destroys his kindred, his friends, and the common civilization. What he should renounce is not destruction but the fruits of destruction and the hope of dominion after destruction.

In a brief essay entitled 'Hymn before Action,' E. M. Forster cites this episode, and reports its conclusion in the following words: 'Arjuna drives into the battle rejoicing, and wins a great victory. But it is necessarily and rightly followed by disillusionment and remorse. The fall of his enemies leads to his own, for the fortunes

30

of men are all bound up together, and it is impossible to inflict damage without receiving it.'

The essay in which E. M. Forster cited this episode appeared in 1912. I call attention to this date. Two World Wars since 1912 have not robbed the essay of its point.

Before both Wars the Atlantic nations were paralyzed with horror, and hesitated long before the prospect of destroying an enemy made up of those who were their own kinsmen, their fellow men. They hesitated long before undertaking the destruction of an enemy whose fall would entail their own fall as well. In both cases, they drove into battle, at last, and won a great victory. But in both cases the great victory was followed by disillusionment and remorse. The fall of their enemies led to their own—'for the fortunes of men are all bound together, and it is impossible to inflict damage without receiving it.'

After World War I the point made by a Hindu mystic so many centuries ago, the point repeated by an English novelist in 1912, was made again by the English economist from whom I have already quoted the sentence: 'If the European Civil War is to end with France and Italy abusing their momentary victorious power to destroy Germany and Austria-Hungary now prostrate, they invite their own destruction also, being so deeply and inextricably intertwined with their victims by hidden psychic and economic bonds.'

Neither the wisdom of the author of the *Bhagavad-Gita*, nor the insight of E. M. Forster in 1912, nor the knowledge of John Maynard Keynes in 1919 influenced those who, upon the occasion of World War II, once more drove into battle and won a great victory. And again the great victory was followed by disillusionment and remorse.

The traditional wisdom of the *Bhagavad-Gita* was too recondite and sophisticated for the nations that Roosevelt and Churchill (not to mention Stalin) led into battle. They were governed by a simpler conception: that war and anarchy were caused by the existence of 'aggressor nations,' and that peace and order would reign undisturbed if the nations called 'peace-loving' destroyed the power of the nations called 'aggressor.' So the policy associated with 'unconditional surrender' was pursued, and the objective of making Germany helpless for an indefinite future was adopted.

*   *   *

The basis for the Cold War was laid when the two Western allies, the United States and Great Britain, looking forward to their victory, adopted the objective of utterly destroying German power and preventing its reconstitution for an indefinite future. This objective was adopted without any thought that American power or British power, alone or together, would fill the vacuum thus created. Indeed, President Roosevelt made it clear, as we shall see, that American power would be rather promptly withdrawn from Europe after the victory had been gained.

The adoption of this objective is properly associated in our minds with the decision that the Atlantic allies took, in January 1943, to require the unconditional surrender of Germany, Italy, and Japan. The unconditional-surrender decision was the decision to make no compromise peace with the German, Italian, or Japanese nations, even though they should overthrow and replace the gangster regimes that, having captured power over them, had led them into war. It was the decision to go on to a total victory, a victory that would make it possible, then, to erase the power of Germany, Italy, and Japan from the map of the world.

It is clear to most of us today, and there were those to whom it was clear at the time, that this was an unwise decision, a decision based on a judgment distorted by the passions and the mythological conceptions of wartime.

We may suppose that such a decision, for which the United States bore the prime responsibility, would not have been made if we Americans had ever allowed ourselves to regard World War II as a struggle to re-establish a balance of power—which is what it was. For the American and the British people, even more on this second occasion than on the first, the War was simply a struggle between the forces of good and the forces of evil. To put the matter in the terminology of the day, it was a struggle between the 'peace-loving nations' and the 'aggressor nations.' This terminology was particularly unfortunate because it pertained to the 'nations' apart from the regimes that governed them. What it meant was that Germany, Italy, and Japan would be 'aggressor nations' even under responsible democratic regimes. They were what they were as a matter of national character—just as the United States, Great Britain, China, and the Soviet Union were 'peace-loving nations' as a matter of national character.[1]

---

[1] For the documentation of this see Halle, 1959, pp. 284–6; and 1962, pp. 58–62 and 171.

In this mythology of a world divided between 'peace-loving' and 'aggressor' nations it was, by definition, the nature of 'peace-loving' nations always to love peace and of 'aggressor' nations always to aggress. Therefore the way to achieve a permanent peace was for the 'peace-loving' nations to disarm the 'aggressor' nations, and to keep them disarmed in perpetuity.

Popular sophistication, even among the most advanced nations, had not yet reached the point where political leadership could dispense with the uses of such mythological conceptions as this. Woodrow Wilson had had to offer the American people a myth for which they would fight, and Franklin D. Roosevelt had to do the same.

This is not to say that Roosevelt, any more than Wilson, was a cynical politician who knowingly misled the people. He corresponded to Walter Bagehot's definition of a politician as a man of common mind and uncommon abilities. A product of the Wilsonian era, he had been brought up to the ideal model of a world in which international organization was the noble alternative to the ignoble power-politics that had been traditional in the Old World. German power, in this conception, could be erased, and the consequent vacuum need not be filled by any other national power, or combination of national powers, because an international organization to maintain peace and order would do away with the role that national power had hitherto played in international relations. 'Peace-loving' nations, among which the Soviet Union was included, would no longer engage in the sordid game of power-politics but would, rather, submit themselves to the wise decrees of an international community organized for the expression of a collective will.

The American experience for a century before 1914 had not been such as to nurture the wisdom that rests on a knowledge of reality. It had, rather, been such as gives scope to our human propensity for self-delusion. The premise of American thinking in the period of World War I had been that a complete alternative must be found to power-politics, and Wilson had persuaded himself that he had found such an alternative in his proposed League of Nations. A generation later, Roosevelt, who had not moved beyond this conception, allowed himself to believe that his proposed United Nations Organization would serve as the complete alternative to power-politics, rather than as a device for taming them, for keeping them within the bounds of some order.

In this view of international organization and power-politics as mutually exclusive alternatives, Wilson and Roosevelt alike reflected the naïveté of the American mind in the first half of this century.

On the overt record, however, Wilson was less naïve than his successor, for he had taken the position that the establishment of peace required that Germany, under a respectable successor regime, resume its role as an equal in the community of nations. He had been careful to make a distinction between the governing regime, which was transitory, and the nation, which was permanent and ineradicable, attributing the war-guilt only to the former. This provided a basis for making peace with the German nation after it had replaced the Kaiser's regime by one that was responsible and legitimate. Roosevelt, on the other hand, attributed the war-guilt to the nation itself. It followed from this attribution that the replacement of the Nazi regime by a respectable successor would not entitle the German nation to any greater consideration by those who were undertaking to overcome it. It would not save the nation from punishment and the destruction of its power, or even mitigate these consequences of its defeat.

Wilson had been a stubborn thinker in his own right. Roosevelt was not. The better politician of the two, Roosevelt was more disposed simply to represent the common mind and give it expression. This is not to say that he was without political courage. In the years preceding the Japanese attack on Pearl Harbor, when the American nation had been deeply divided over foreign policy, when there had been no common mind, he had seen the need for a timely intervention to put down Hitler, and he had steered the country in that direction without an excessive regard for the political risk to himself. He was never a craven politician, however prudent and circumspect.

With the cataclysmic attack on Pearl Harbor, the nation that had only the day before been paralyzed by division found itself united in a determination to strike down the aggressors and crush them into the ground. In this mood, it was not disposed to distinguish between 'peace-loving' Japanese and 'aggressor' Japanese, between 'peace-loving' Germans and 'aggressor' Germans, between 'peace-loving' Italians and 'aggressor' Italians. As always in wartime, the great abstractions now took possession of the national mind. In place of Japanese, German, or Italian men, women, and children, there arose an apparition called 'The

Enemy,' a beast whose inborn nature fulfilled itself only in aggression. Wilson had deliberately taken the Kaiser to be the ruthless master of the German people, whose overthrow would free them to rejoin the community of nations. But Roosevelt, sharing the common mind rather than shaping it, took Hitler to be merely the servant of the German people, representing a ruthlessness that had its origin and native abode in them. Hitler was simply their agent. It followed that the replacement of the governing regime in Germany would be merely the replacement of one agent by another who was bound to represent the same thing. Such a replacement would offer no basis for the reacceptance of Germany in the community of nations. The German nation would continue, still, to be 'The Enemy,' with whom one could make no peace. It would still be one of the 'aggressor' nations, upon the permanent suppression of which the peace of the world depended.

This was the conception on which the Atlantic powers based their unconditional-surrender decision. By that decision, the opposition inside Germany was put on notice that the overthrow of the Nazis and their replacement would avail Germany nothing. Germany under any kind of regime—under the regime of an Ebert or an Adenauer as under that of a Hitler—would still be 'The Enemy.'

The non-Communist opposition in Germany was composed of men whom George Kennan has described as 'very brave and very lonely.' These men were our true kinsmen. They were representatives of our own civilization who had dedicated themselves to its restoration in Germany. When, at great personal risk, they made contact with the Atlantic leadership, informing it of their intention to rid Germany of Hitler, they were refused support simply because they were Germans. Alone and without encouragement, then, they nevertheless mounted their attempt of July 20, 1944, against Hitler, which did not come far short of succeeding. At least one of the survivors has testified to the difficulty created by the allied refusal of cooperation with the German resistance.[2]

If we had been worldly-wise we would have known that the real world is not divided between peoples that are all 'peace-loving' and peoples that are all 'aggressor.' We would have known that there are forces of good and forces of evil that contend for

[2] Kennan, p. 367. See also the report of an address by Eugen Gerstenmaier in the *New York Herald-Tribune*, Paris edition, July 21, 1964, p. 2.

power within every nation, within Germany and the United States alike. In that case our aim would have been to see the Nazis replaced in the seats of power by the 'peace-loving' forces in Germany, and then to make a genuine peace of reconciliation with a Germany under the government of those forces.

The decision to eliminate German power from Europe, rather than make such a peace, is what laid the foundations of the Cold War.

In the day of our victory, on May 7, 1945, the elimination of German power was total, as it had not been on November 11, 1918. We had not only eliminated the military and industrial plant of Germany, but had allowed the entire structure of the German state to collapse and disappear. The vacuum of military and economic power was completed by a political vacuum. No German Government, no German political authority, remained in the land.

It is evident that such a vacuum can hardly persist, even for a week. It is bound to be filled by something. What would fill it in the moment of victory was the victorious armies: the American, British, and French Armies under General Eisenhower; and the Red Army that served Stalin's dictatorship. For the moment the victorious forces, jointly or severally, would administer the German area of Europe as conquered territory.

But what then?

At the Yalta Conference in February 1945 Roosevelt told Churchill and Stalin that he did not believe he could obtain the consent of Congress to keeping American troops in Europe 'much more than two years.'[3] In fact, under irresistible popular pressure, the United States proceeded, immediately after the War, to demobilize and to dismantle its wartime military structure. It followed the total elimination of German military power with the drastic reduction of its own. From 1945 to 1947 it reduced its armed forces from twelve million men to 1·4 million.[4] Clearly, the United States could have had no intention of filling the vacuum, or of filling it for long.

---

[3] Feis, 1957, pp. 531–2.

[4] Noel-Baker, pp. 46–7. There are those who suppose that the American monopoly of atomic power, at this time, made the United States potentially supreme over the earth, and consequently in a position to impose its will on the Soviet Union to any extent that it pleased. For a discussion of this view, which I regard as mistaken, see Chapter XVII below.

Britain, as we shall see, was an exhausted country, without the resources to fill the vacuum.

France was itself a vacuum.

That left only Russia, which did not demobilize after the War and did not dismantle its wartime military establishment. Instead, it kept in its armed forces five to six million men, fifty thousand tanks, and twenty thousand aircraft. And it began the construction of a navy that, in the number of its submarines, was to exceed the combined navies of the world. Only Russia, then, would be in a position to fill the vacuum.

At this point it is proper to note that the Atlantic allies did not, in fact, carry out the postwar policy they had projected for Germany. They did, on the contrary, in 1949 and 1950, make a genuine peace of reconciliation with a dismembered Germany under the government of an anti-Nazi successor regime that represented the forces of moderation and decency in Germany. And they supported the restoration of German power to fill the vacuum. But by then it was too late. By then all eastern Europe, including an important part of Germany itself, had fallen under the power of Stalin. By then the Cold War had got started and had reached a peak of intensity.

*   *   *

The question arises whether the allied leaders were blind to what seems so clear to us today, when it is set forth in the terms that I have used above. Part of the answer is that in America, at least, the terms that I have used above were not current before the post-war period. The term 'power vacuum,' for example (with its dramatic implications for those who know that 'nature abhors a vacuum'), had not yet come into the language. And in our public speech, at least, we rejected all the conceptions of power-politics as inapplicable to the projected postwar world. In our public speech, we had not effectively moved beyond Wilson.

This is part of the answer. Another part is that, in fact, neither Washington nor Whitehall was blind to the danger of an over-bearing Soviet Union that would get out of bounds after the War. This danger could hardly have had a large role in the thinking of the Atlantic allies during the first half of the War, when the danger from the Axis powers was still so immediate, and when the Soviet Union was still on the defensive before the invading armies of Nazi Germany. This, be it recalled, was the period when they committed themselves to the thesis that the German people were congenital aggressors who would have to be rendered permanently powerless, after they had been brought to unconditional surrender. I can testify, however, that there was no time when the danger from the Soviet Union was not a topic of anxious conversation among officers of the State Department; and by the winter of 1944–1945, as the day of victory approached, it became the predominant theme in Washington.

One who remembers this vividly is repeatedly surprised by expressions of the view, which has been widely accepted since the War, that the men in Washington were blind to the Soviet danger, or regarded it with indifference because of ideological affinity for what Moscow represented. We can understand how this view has gained acceptance if we take account of the distinction between public and private thinking. In the period with which we are dealing, the enemy was the Axis, and the Soviet Union was an ally. The overriding objective was to win the War against the Axis, and to do this it was necessary to rally opinion against the Axis and in support of solidarity among the allies. To have expressed hostile suspicions of the Soviet ally publicly, under the circumstances, would have been to commit what was then regarded as a political crime, that of undermining the war-effort.[5]

On the public level, then, the Soviet Union was our loyal ally, one of the 'peace-loving' states. On the public level, the possibility of a tolerable postwar world depended on the replacement of power-politics by an international organization based on unanimity among the 'peace-loving' great powers, including the Soviet Union. And on the public level this was regarded as possible. On the private level, however, there was widespread anticipation of the struggle to contain the Soviet Union that would follow the total destruction of German power. Since the record contains only what was said on the public level, historians and

[5] At the end of August 1943, when the newspaper-columnist, Drew Pearson, charged that Secretary of State Hull and high officials of the State Department were opposed to the Soviet Government, Mr. Hull replied by denouncing the accusations as 'monstrous and diabolical falsehoods.' President Roosevelt publicly stated that they were detrimental to American foreign relations and to the unity of the United Nations.

When Hitler attacked Russia, in June 1941, and Churchill prepared to announce British support for Moscow, his private secretary asked him whether this was not a case of bowing down in the House of Rimmon (a reference to 2 Kings 5:18). 'Not at all,' he replied. 'I have only one purpose, the destruction of Hitler, and my life is much simplified thereby. If Hitler invaded Hell I would make at least a favorable reference to the Devil in the House of Commons.' (Churchill, 1950, p. 370).

other commentators have at least superficial grounds for believing that Washington was blind to the Soviet danger.

It is true that the anxious anticipation of the Cold War, while widespread, was not universal. Most persons, in government or out, take for their own the views that represent public respectability at any given time—which is to say that the public view was not without influence on private views. In government or out, there were those for whom belief in salvation by international organization had acquired something like a religious quality. And there were well meaning persons, not a few, who believed that Stalin's Soviet Union represented a social experiment on which the hopes of mankind depended. Nevertheless, my recollection remains that the predominant worry in Washington, as the War approached its end, was over the deadly struggle to contain the Soviet Union that could already be foreseen.

If, nevertheless, nothing was done to prepare for this struggle, that is simply because, by this stage of the War, the government of circumstances had replaced the government of men. The Atlantic allies were already inescapably committed to policies that had been conceived in the days when the only objective was to overcome the Axis aggressors. It was too late to persuade the public that a 'soft' peace might well be made with a Germany in which 'peace-loving' forces had gained control. It was too late to persuade the public that a balance of power, in which Germany had its part, must be restored. It was too late to tell the public that, in the absence of such a balance, it must not expect peace at the end of the War, and must therefore resign itself to keeping the armed forces up to something approaching wartime strength. It was too late to abandon the whole conceptual structure, however false, on which the War was being fought. It was too late for statesmanship. Everyone now felt himself borne along, irresistibly, by the swelling stream of circumstances. I have no doubt that this was true, as well, at the highest level.

Any practicing politician, especially in critical times, finds that his hands are always quite full with the immediate problems of the day. He moves from day to day, and when he does look ahead at problems to come he can only hope that he will find some way of solving them when he gets to them. Franklin D. Roosevelt, too, was being swept along by the stream of circumstances, with constantly fewer options as the war progressed. He was aware of the fact that the Soviet Union was looming as the great problem that would confront the Atlantic allies at the end of the War. Always a gallant optimist, however, he apparently convinced himself that he could somehow, when the time came, cajole Stalin into being a good fellow. In any case, a man who is fighting desperately to save his house from a fire that is raging in it may find it hard to worry about how he is going to pay an installment on the mortgage that will come due at some future date. He may even find it hard to worry about the damage that the water from the fire-hoses will leave. (It is those who come afterwards who may profess themselves scandalized by such a reckless use of water.)

I doubt that anyone who has not lived through a great war can appreciate the degree to which the simple objective of winning it comes to exclude every other objective. It is hard to believe that, if once the war is won, any new problem that arises could be truly serious.

In any case, by the last year of the War in Europe intractable circumstances were dictating the decisions of the leadership in America and Britain. In both countries, that leadership was worn out. Roosevelt had been President since 1933, living in a constant state of crisis for almost twelve years without respite, confronted every day by fearful dilemmas, by decisions almost beyond mortal capacity to make. He was like a soldier who has been in battle continuously for months without relief. At last he had reached the point where he simply trusted to a sort of native virtuosity to get him through from day to day, from hour to hour.

Those who saw President Roosevelt in the last year knew that he was near death. He could no longer comprehend the vast scene of action over which he presided. He could no longer read the papers that were put before him. The last time he addressed Congress he was no longer able to stand on his feet for the occasion but addressed it sitting down. All the flesh had gone out of his face, and he looked so ghastly that the press-photographers had to be kept at a distance. Then a blood-vessel burst in his brain, and he was dead.

These are circumstances that should be borne in mind by those who are scandalized at President Roosevelt's failure to deal adequately with all the problems that the closing days of the War presented to him.

Prime Minister Churchill, too, was a man in need of restoration as the War drew toward its end. He had borne the responsibility for decision and leadership through the black days of 1940 when Britain was being smashed in its own home-islands by the superior Nazi air-power. He had continued to bear it through the days when British sea-power went down, and sank to the floor of the ocean, before the advancing Japanese in the Far East. After that, he had found that his role must, of necessity, be increasingly subordinate to Roosevelt's as the military resources committed by the United States became increasingly greater than the British resources. He could argue against American policy, but in the end he had to go along with it. He, too, was reduced to the point where he put his name to documents that he had read without understanding, and that he did not believe in.[6] He could not fight over everything, and as time went on he fought over less and less. Finally he, too, was letting himself be carried away by the stream of circumstances.

Prime Minister Churchill, it is evident, saw the danger of Russian hegemony in Europe as clearly as anyone. But what could he do? He fought hard in the decisive days of the War for what may or may not have been the right strategy, that of invading the European continent from the southeast so as to limit the westward advance of the Russians. But he was overborne in this by an American insistence that military operations aimed at unconditional surrender only should not be subordinated to ulterior political considerations regarded as Machiavellian.

By the closing days of the War, then, at least as far as the Atlantic allies were concerned, statesmanship was exhausted, men were worn out, and circumstances had risen, at last, to full command.

It is hard to doubt that, if statesmanship could still have averted the Cold War in 1942, after that it was too late.

[6] For example, both Roosevelt and Churchill, at the Quebec Conference of September 1944, approved the so-called 'Morgenthau Plan' for the postwar dismemberment of Germany and its conversion 'into a country primarily agricultural and pastoral in its character.' When Roosevelt returned to Washington, Secretary of War Stimson read out loud to him some of the sentences in the document that he and the Prime Minister had initialed. The President, Stimson later wrote in his diary, 'was frankly staggered by this and said he had no idea how he could have initialed this. . . .' (Stimson and Bundy, p. 581.) Churchill, too, found himself embarrassed to explain his action in retrospect. (See Churchill, 1953, pp. 156–7.)

CHAPTER V

Russia's conquest of the Baltic states and East Poland in 1939–1940, and what Stalin's postwar intentions in eastern Europe may have been

In the course of its expansion over the centuries the Russian Empire, by the end of the eighteenth century, had come to include Finland, Estonia, Latvia, Lithuania, and Poland. None of these had ever existed as an independent nation-state in the modern sense of the term, and one can hardly say that the first three had ever enjoyed independent statehood of any sort. Nevertheless, they represented distinct ethnic entities, and in the course of the nineteenth century, with the spread of nationalism, national self-consciousness awakened and grew in each of them. In the latter part of the nineteenth century the czars attempted to suppress their respective national distinctions by a process of forced Russification that, in its failure, provoked their bitter hostility.

Russia's defeat in World War I brought independence to these countries and enabled them to set themselves up as sovereign members of the family of nations. The Soviet Union under the administration of the Bolsheviks, while recognizing the right to national independence in principle, opposed it in practice within the area of the former czarist empire, to which it was heir. Where it could prevent the constituent nations of the empire from becoming independent—as in the case of the Ukraine, Byelorussia, Georgia, Armenia, and Azerbaijan—it did so. It consented to the independence of Finland, the three smaller Baltic states, and Poland only after they had won it by force.

Strategic considerations bearing on the defense of Russia had prompted the Russians to engulf the Baltic nations and Poland in the first place. These strategic considerations were not altered by the succession of the Bolsheviks to the power and the responsibility that had been borne by the czars. This was vividly impressed on the minds of Lenin and his colleagues, including Stalin, during the period from 1917 to 1920, when they saw their country invaded from all sides. They had seized power in the expectation

42

that the revolutionary movement they represented would immediately be successful throughout Europe, and thereafter throughout the rest of the world. This would mean the disappearance of the system of national states that Marxist orthodoxy identified with the rule of the capitalist bourgeoisie. There would no longer be a Russia, a Poland, a Germany; there would no longer be international relations; there would no longer be problems of national defense. Trotsky later reported that, when the Bolsheviks met to organize their Government and the question of foreign relations was raised, Lenin exclaimed: 'What, are we going to have foreign relations?' And when he was himself appointed Foreign Commissar of the new regime Trotsky said: 'I shall issue a few revolutionary proclamations and then close up shop.'[1] Addressing the Seventh Congress of the Russian Communist Party in March 1918, Lenin said: 'There is no doubting the truth that if our revolution remained the only one, if no revolution erupted in other countries, our position would be hopeless.'[2] He urged the Congress to ratify the Treaty of Brest-Litovsk, by the terms of which the most important part of the Russian Empire would be lost, on the ground that a true friend 'will come to our aid: the world revolution.'[3]

With the failure of revolution outside Russia, however, the Bolsheviks were confronted by a problem that they had never expected to have to face at all, that of defending the encircled Russian state as the czars and their predecessors had had to defend it for a thousand years past. The old strategic imperatives now bore upon them as upon the czars before them, and they saw the need of territory beyond the Russian land proper if the Russian land proper was to be made secure. Inheriting the responsibility of the czars, they found themselves with no realistic alternative to taking up the policy, together with the diplomatic and military instruments, by which the czars had discharged that responsibility. The ideological principles that had been dreamed up by men far from the seats of power turned out to be inapplicable when the seats of power had been attained. This is the history of every revolutionary ideology that has ever come to power.

The loss of Russia's western territories implied the catastrophic loss of such military security as the Russian state had won

---

[1] Trotsky, p. 341. Cited by Aspaturian and Keep, p. 248.
[2] Cited by Fischer, p. 220.   [3] Cited by Fischer, p. 221.

for itself since the beginning of the eighteenth century. Its insecurity was now to become an obsession with Stalin, who came to power in the 1920's, as it had been with his pre-Bolshevik predecessors, and he would move to remedy it as soon as he could. The opportunity came, at last, in 1939 and 1940.

By the terms of a secret protocol in the treaty that Stalin's Russia concluded with Hitler's Germany in August 1939 (and by the terms of a supplementary provision added a month later), Finland, Estonia, Latvia, Lithuania, and eastern Poland were assigned to the Soviet orbit. Consequently, in the summer of 1940 the Red Army occupied Estonia, Latvia, and Lithuania, and incorporated them in the Soviet Union. Already in September 1939, it had occupied eastern Poland. It had been less successful in the forcible recapture of Finland, which it attempted in 1939. The unexpectedly determined resistance of the Finns had induced Moscow to settle for a cession of Finnish territory that reduced the strategic vulnerability of Leningrad.

These moves in 1939 and 1940 represent the beginning of the westward expansion under Stalin that was to eventuate in the Cold War. Hitler's invasion of Russia interrupted the expansion from 1941 to 1944; but it was then resumed, on the recoil, with all the momentum of hot pursuit. The Red Army, pursuing Hitler's retreating forces, was to carry to a line a hundred miles west of Berlin. Behind that line the agents of Stalin were to engage in activities so purposeful and ominous as to arouse alarm, at last, throughout the Atlantic world.

We may be sure that, from an early stage, Stalin was determined on the reincorporation in the Russian empire of the three small Baltic states, of eastern Poland, and of Bessarabia.[4] He had demanded the agreement of the British and French to that reincorporation in 1939, and had been refused. He had then, in effect, made Hitler's agreement to it a condition of the Nazi–Soviet Pact. Visiting Moscow in December 1941, British Foreign Minister Eden had been taken aback by the rough insistence with which Stalin had demanded that the British agree to its postwar realization as a condition of the wartime alliance. Clearly, the lands to be reincorporated represented the 'glacis' that Stalin

---

[4] Bessarabia, like the small Baltic states, had broken away from the empire in the period from 1918–1920 and been recaptured in the summer of 1940. The justification for absorbing eastern Poland was that it contained more Ukrainians and Byelorussians than it did Poles. This appears to have been the fact. See Feis, 1957, p. 30, fn. 32.

deemed essential to Russian security. On the other side of the western frontier to be formed by it he was determined to have 'friendly' governments in power; but he had not, one supposes, made up his mind that they should be puppet governments, or even that they should be Communist.

When the Bolsheviks had seized power in Russia in 1917 they had counted on the support of the masses in neighboring countries. Marxist doctrine had misled them into believing that wherever they went they would be welcomed by the masses as liberators. Their first disillusionment on this score had come in 1920 when Lenin had ordered the Red Army to invade Poland. He had known that the military strength for such an undertaking was inadequate, but he had thought of the invasion as simply a means of detonating the expected uprising of proletarians and peasants in Poland. With this in mind, he had appointed three Polish Communists as a 'Polish Provisional Revolutionary Government' to accompany the invading Army and set up their administration in Warsaw. The Polish workers and peasants failed, however, to welcome the invaders of their country; revolution was not detonated; and the end was military disaster. This was a shock to Lenin, who for a moment fell into depression. 'The disillusionment,' he told a group of Communists in Moscow, 'is too great.'[5]

Stalin, who had been involved in this disillusioning experience, sustained a repetition of it in 1939 when he ordered the Red Army to march into Finland. At the same time, following the pattern of 1920, he set up a 'people's government of Finland,' composed of Finnish Communists who had been living in Russia. Again the expectation was that the Finnish masses would welcome the Soviet soldiers as liberators, that a limited military force would therefore suffice to detonate the revolution that Marx had predicted. Again, nothing of the sort happened; large Russian military reinforcements had to be summoned to the scene; and at last prudence dictated to a disillusioned Stalin the acceptance of a compromise whereby the independence of Finland was retained.

There is a world of difference between the task of military liberation and that of military subjugation. The former is self-liquidating: when it is done the troops can march home. The latter involves a commitment of forces to which no end and no limit can be foreseen. Once a nationalistically aroused population has been antagonized by conquest and occupation, to set it free again becomes too dangerous. No task, however, is more unwelcome to a military commander or more demoralizing to his troops than the indefinitely continued suppression of a hostile population. Presumably Stalin, after his experience in 1939, preferred a self-governing Finland to the burden and danger of controling a rebellious population of helots. Otherwise, one supposes, he would have occupied and subjugated Finland as a defeated enemy in 1944 and 1945—for Finland had been Hitler's ally in the War.

Finland, when the War was over, gained Moscow's acquiescence in its rejection of Communism and in the establishment of its status as a self-governing democracy of the western type. Part of the price it paid was to renounce for the indefinite future any military cooperation with the opponents of Russia, or any foreign relations inimical to Russian security.

I daresay that Stalin would not have rejected out of hand the possibility of a similar arrangement with Poland. This might hold for Czechoslovakia, for Hungary, for Rumania, and for Bulgaria as well. Stalin was not a crusading ideologist. He was, rather, an illegitimate czar in Russia whose preoccupation had to be that of securing himself in his position. Securing himself in his position meant, in the realm of foreign affairs, securing the geographical base on which that position rested. This objective required all his resources of skill and cunning, leaving nothing over for any independent additional objective such as the realization of the Marxist prophecy for its own sake.

I have already noted how the experience of Poland in 1920 and Finland in 1939 had taught Stalin that Communism could not, in spite of Marxist dogma, count on popular support. Lacking popular support, its expansion would require a commitment of force that, being unlimited, might well have given him pause. There was another reason as well why the prospect of expanding Communism might have given him pause. He had already had occasion to learn that a Communist party outside the orbit of his power might not be amenable to his will—that it might, in fact, be defiant and, by its defiance, offer world Communism an alternative leadership. The occasion for learning this lesson was the rebellion against Moscow's authority, in 1927, of the Chinese Communists under Mao Tse-tung.[6]

[6] See [pp. 195–6] below.

That Stalin learned this lesson is suggested by his failure to support the Chinese Communists against the Chinese Nationalists, at the end of the War, until it appeared that they were going to win anyway, when he found himself having to make the best of an accomplished fact.[7] It is also suggested by his attitude toward the Communist movement in Yugoslavia during the War.

Just as the Japanese invaders of China had been opposed by two rival groups—a conservative group under Chiang Kai-shek and a Communist group under Mao—so the Nazi invaders of Yugoslavia had been opposed by two rival groups, a conservative group under General Mihailovich and a Communist group under Tito. Just as the Chinese Communists under Mao were more wholehearted in resisting the Japanese invaders than the Nationalists under Chiang, so the Yugoslav Communists under Tito were more wholehearted in resisting the Nazi invaders than the Cetniks under Mihailovich. Moscow, faced with these alternative Yugoslav regimes, long remained on friendly terms with Mihailovich and his Cetniks, withholding from Tito and his Communists any official recognition, any public countenance at all, and any assistance. The British swung over to the Communists, abandoning the Cetniks, well before Moscow could bring itself to do likewise. It is evident that Tito, a Yugoslav nationalist who had, from the beginning, opposed Moscow's domination of the Yugoslav Communist Party, did not have the subservience that Stalin looked for in foreign Communist leaders.[8] After the War, likewise, Stalin did not favor the efforts of the Greek Communists, supported by Tito's Communist regime in Yugoslavia, to achieve power in Greece.[9]

Stalin had repeatedly indicated to Roosevelt and Churchill that he was by no means bent on spreading Communism by revolution when the War ended. 'We have not found it easy,' he said, 'to set up a Communist system.'[10] While Stalin never felt any burdensome obligation to be truthful, it is possible that he sometimes meant what he said. Presumably he knew that a rival Communist regime would be more threatening to his position than

[7] See [p. 200] below.

[8] Anyone who doubts this has only to read Tito's own account of his difficult relations with Moscow, and that of his close collaborator, Vladimir Dedijer, in Dedijer.

[9] See [pp. 85–6] below.

[10] Feis, 1957, pp. 203–4.

a rival anti-Communist regime, and a Communist regime with a power-base of its own was sure to become a rival.[11]

Even the strongest statesman is the creature of circumstances that do not represent his will. We make a mistake when we suppose that what happens in the world happens in accordance with plans that had been made in advance by those who preside over its happening. The fact that this is virtually never the case, or that it is only marginally so in particular instances, is disguised for observers, and for the historians who come after, by a verbal falsification that is universally practiced and accepted. Lenin, for example, was taken by surprise at virtually every turning in the events that occurred in Russia in 1917. He improvised to meet them, and finding himself unexpectedly in the seat of supreme power he continued to improvise to deal with circumstances that he had not foreseen. The verbal falsification consisted in his nominal identification of what happened in Russia with his plans and predictions, however different it actually was. He called his Bolshevik *coup d'état* the uprising of the proletariat that Marx and Engels had prophesied, and he called his subsequent Government the dictatorship of the proletariat. Since the nominal is always more real to us than the real, we have supposed ever since that the Communist regime in Russia represents the realization of the plans made by Marx and elaborated by Lenin. But it is not so in reality. In reality, Lenin, too, was the creature of circumstances that did not represent his will.

There is no reason to take it for granted, then, that what happened in Europe in the three years after the War was, in its main features, the realization of plans with which Stalin had anticipated the opportunities that victory would bring. We may more reasonably suppose that his main intentions were to establish the most defensible frontiers possible about an area limited by what he would be able to control from Moscow; to promote in the countries on the other side of those frontiers a degree of dependence on Moscow that would prevent them from participating

---

[11] 'Because Moscow had always refrained at the crucial moment from supporting the Chinese, Spanish, and in many ways even the Yugoslav revolutions, the view prevailed, not without reason, that Stalin was generally against revolutions. This is, however, not entirely correct. His opposition was only conditional, and arose only when the revolution went beyond the interests of the Soviet state. He felt instinctively that the creation of revolutionary centres outside Moscow could endanger its supremacy in world Communism, and of course that is what actually happened.' Djilas, pp. 119–120.

in the conspiracies of a world that he, along with all Russians, assumed to be hostile; and to promote weakness in the countries beyond them. How he realized these intentions would in large part be a matter of improvisation as the situation developed. Statesmanship is always nine-tenths improvisation anyway.

I see no reason to believe that what actually happened after the War was, in any considerable degree, what Stalin would have wished to happen. I see no reason to believe that he would have welcomed the prospect of having to hold half of non-Russian Europe in forced subjection, or the prospect of a situation that caused American power to remain in Europe and be regenerated. The dynamics of the situation, rather than his will, determined what happened. The vacuum of power in central Europe, at the end of the War, drew the Soviet Union, with a certain irresistibility, into positions of commitment from which it would then find it almost impossible to disengage. When the successor Government to Stalin's tried to effect a limited disengagement—in Austria, in Hungary, and in Poland—it thereby produced, in the uprisings of 1956, a political earthquake that shook the very seat of its power in Moscow.

These, I think, are the terms in which we must look at what happened in Poland, in Czechoslovakia, and elsewhere in the area that, whether by intention or force of circumstances, fell under the domination of Moscow at the end of the War.

CHAPTER VI

*The divergence between Russian and Western views of the
world that made postwar planning difficult*

B Y the closing days of the War, the government of circumstances had taken over from the government of men. At this
time a series of joint decisions on the postwar settlement were
made by the three leaders of the coalition against Hitler. These
decisions were to prove effective to the extent that they reflected
the strategic circumstances at the end of the War. Where more
than one interpretation of their terms was possible, the interpretation that reflected the strategic realities was almost certain to be
the one that would prevail.

If we may suppose that the traditional Russian view of the
world was the basis of Stalin's thinking, his horizon hardly extended beyond the Eurasian continent within which Russia had
always been confined. His vision was of a society occupying the
interior of that continent and encircled by sinister forces that
purposed its destruction. These forces were implacable and so
powerful that the greatest guile was necessary in dealing with
them. Stalin's long-term objective would be not only to strengthen
Russia against its encircling enemies by measures of forced industrial and military development, but to weaken those enemies
by every kind of conspiratorial device. For this latter purpose the
Communist movement, with its fifth columns and the appeal of
its nominal Marxism, was indispensable. Stalin must have
assumed that there had always been a Cold War, which would
continue after the defeat of Hitler as before. It would continue
until Russia had made itself so strong, and its encircling enemies
had declined into such weakness, that its mortal danger would at
last be at an end.

The Anglo-American view of the world, by contrast, was
global. Englishmen and Americans had spread around the world,
navigating the one great ocean that embraces the planet. The
world for them was a globe rather than a flat plain encircled by
enemies. Consequently, they thought of their own security in

terms of the organization of this aquaterrestrial globe as a whole. In World War I the objective of making the world 'safe for democracy' implied an organized society of nations that would establish a universal order for the maintenance of peace. The same conception prevailed in World War II and was the basis for the postwar planning that the Atlantic powers initiated as their victory came into sight.

We Americans had failed to learn the main lessons of World War I. We had thought of the League of Nations as an alternative to national power everywhere, making power-politics and the balance of power unnecessary. Now we planned the creation of a successor organization on the same premise. The failure of the League to maintain peace and security had been generally attributed to two causes. The first and chief of these was that the United States had remained outside it. The second was that it had not had military forces at its disposal for the enforcement of peace and security. The avoidance of these two mistakes, it was thought, would enable its successor to be effective where it had failed.

Nothing was spared, therefore, to insure American participation this time. The planners were more concerned with the acceptability of their plan to the United States Senate than with its acceptability to the Russians or to any other prospective members. American soil was chosen for the site of the new organization's headquarters so as to make it awkward for the United States not to participate.

The concept of providing military forces to police the new world order was subject to a major limitation that, as everyone recognized, had to be accepted. There was no way of providing the organization with military power sufficient for enforcement actions against any of the so-called great powers. In fact, in the world as it was and would continue to be, the real power to maintain international order would still remain with them. And since theirs was the power, theirs must be the responsibility. It must therefore be the great powers, acting in concert, who directed the means of enforcement placed at the disposal of the international organization. For this purpose they would have to constitute themselves a committee (the Security Council). Such a committee, however, could direct enforcement actions only on the basis of unanimity. At this point the planners were dealing not with a theory but a fact. The United States Senate would not agree to American membership if the vote of the United States with respect to enforcement actions could be overridden, and one might take it for granted that Moscow would not agree to Russian membership if the Russian vote could be overridden. The keystone of the arch, then, would be the unanimity of the great powers.

This conclusion had a happy relevance to the nominal circumstances in which the postwar planning was being done. In those circumstances, the United States, Great Britain, the Soviet Union, and China (with France temporarily absent) were comrades-in-arms together, joined in the brotherhood of their Grand Alliance against Hitler, Mussolini, and the Japanese warlords. What was foreseen as the basis of the postwar organization was the perpetuation of this Grand Alliance, to which President Roosevelt had given the name 'United Nations.' The projected successor to the League of Nations, then, would be the United Nations. It was already in being, requiring only remodeling and expansion for permanence.

This conception is not to be held in contempt by us who have seen the failure to realize it. It may have been the best that could be improvised at the time. The fault, I think, and it was a major fault, was to expect too much of it. The fault was to count on it as a means alternative to the international balance of power for the maintenance of international stability. Since there is every reason not to regard international organization and the balance of power as mutually exclusive alternatives, between which an either–or choice has to be made, we must look to traditional thinking for the American disposition to do so.

One of the prime American objectives in World War I had been to do away with power-politics and the balance of power, regarded as evil in themselves, to eliminate them permanently from the conduct of human affairs. Because we had failed to learn the lessons of that War, this was an objective again in World War II. The American people and the Senate would be the less likely, now, to accept the proposed new international organization if it merely supplemented the balance of power. They would be less likely to accept it if it failed to do away with power-politics and everything associated with them. I have already reported how, upon his return from the conference with Churchill and Stalin at Yalta, in the Crimea, Roosevelt told a joint session of Congress:

The Crimea Conference . . . ought to spell the end of the system of unilateral action, the exclusive alliances, the spheres of influence, the balances of power, and all the other expedients that have been tried for centuries—and have always failed. We propose to substitute for all these, a universal organization in which all peace-loving nations will finally have a chance to join.

It is in terms of the belief that international organization would make the traditional means of security unnecessary that we must view the catastrophic dismantling of American military power at the end of the War.

Churchill knew better, but his freedom to follow his own leading was limited. He could undertake a few deals on his own, such as the deal with Stalin whereby Britain recognized Rumania and Bulgaria as a Russian sphere of influence, in return for Russia's agreement to a dominant role for Britain in Greece. Such exceptions apart, however, he has to follow Roosevelt.

It is hard to imagine what Stalin made of all this. The projected United Nations Organization was not a conception for which the Russian understanding was shaped. The Russians may well have had some difficulty in judging the motives and the thinking of the Americans who expounded it to them with such intensity of belief. It may be that its chief importance for them was as a possible trap.

On the other hand, Stalin's private reaction may not have been altogether negative. There may have been some enticement in the prospect of playing a leading role, along with the traditional leaders of Western civilization, in a worldwide organization representative of that civilization. I cannot entirely dismiss from my mind a notion that Stalin, representing the traditional Russian outlook, was somehow attracted to the strange world and the strange ways of the civilization that Roosevelt and Churchill represented. The other side of Russian hostility has always been attraction. There has always been a consciousness of the contrast between Russian backwardness and the sophistication of the more advanced societies to the west—the contrast between a certain Russian awkwardness and the graces that Roosevelt, especially, represented so well—and this consciousness has made for love as well as hate. Stalin was a Georgian peasant with a gangster background, while Roosevelt and Churchill were patricians of the gentlest lineage. When I see the photographs of Stalin sitting stiffly alongside Roosevelt and Churchill at Teheran or at Yalta

—wearing his clothes like a little boy dressed up for visitors, while the other two sit at ease in theirs—I find it plausible that, with a part of his mind, Stalin was impressed at finding himself in such company, a member of such an exclusive club. Roosevelt counted too heavily on his power to charm Stalin, but his optimism may not have been without a basis, however small.

Such speculation aside, the United Nations was an Anglo-American conception that must have had relatively little positive importance for the Russians, their minds dominated by the security problems that were immediate rather than global.

One thing is clear. The fact that the unanimity of the great powers was an indispensable condition for the realization of Washington's postwar plans weakened its power to resist the demands the Russians made in connection with more particular issues. It impelled the American Government to back down, time and again, from any final confrontation with them, since all would be lost if they should be provoked into withdrawing from the great wartime coalition that was now to be perpetuated in the postwar world. From Washington's point of view no other problem was more important than that of the postwar international organization, the success of which would pave the way for the solution of all other problems. The realization of the plans for the United Nations Organization must therefore take precedence over such particular issues as that of the future of Poland.

When, in April 1945, the San Francisco Conference was about to meet to conclude and sign the Charter of the United Nations, the White House and the State Department were thrown into consternation by word from Stalin that Soviet Foreign Minister Molotov would not be able to attend. Urgent appeals were made to Stalin. The emotion surrounding Roosevelt's death, which had just occurred, was invoked to sway him. At last, to Washington's immense relief, he consented to send Molotov after all, as a magnanimous gesture in these exceptional circumstances.

The cause of the original notification that Molotov would not attend the San Francisco Conference was the developing dispute between Moscow and the Atlantic allies over the question of Poland's future. For Stalin, one surmises, the Polish question was more important than that of international organization.

CHAPTER VII

The tragedy of Poland, 1939–1945

Such sporadic or occasional independence as the nations on Russia's western frontier had been able to enjoy over the generations had depended on a balance of power, however precarious, among the great powers that encircled them: Russia, Germany, Austria, Turkey. This balance had enabled the little buffer nations to play their big neighbors off against one another.

Under the circumstances in which World War II was ending, however, this possibility was virtually excluded. The policy associated with unconditional surrender, together with the projected withdrawal of American power, meant that there would be no power in the west to balance the overwhelming power of Russia to the east. This left the East European buffer states, from Finland to Bulgaria, with no wide range of choice. They had to come to whatever terms they could with Moscow, depending on such good will toward them as they might find it possible to evoke. They were not altogether without bargaining power, since Moscow might be expected to make some concessions in order to avoid getting itself into a position in which it had to hold down rebellious peoples by sheer force.

This was demonstrated by Finland. The Finns, combining concession and resistance to the most constructive end open to them, finally achieved a *modus vivendi* with the Russians that enabled them to maintain their own political system—although this involved heavy sacrifices and a degree of moral sordidness imposed by Moscow. All one can say is that any possible alternative would have been worse at the time, and that by the end of the 1950's conditions in Finland had justified its policy.

The situation of the Poles was particularly difficult and painful, and their national temperament virtually disqualified them from coping with it. Poland had been, and continued to be, the Don Quixote among nations—by contrast with the Finnish Sancho Panza. Romantically proud and patriotic, the Poles were in the habit of thinking of their country as a great power, by right if not in fact. Unlike the Finns, they conducted themselves, repeatedly, with little appreciation of the limits of what was possible for them. They were excessively preoccupied with questions of honor, but their patriotic devotion to their own national glory tended to blind them to the feelings and interests of the non-Polish peoples in their vicinity. The desire for an expanded national territory, which had been the fatal disease of so many European nations in the late nineteenth and early twentieth century, had led them into acts of folly. When this much has been said, however, one must acknowledge the attractiveness of so spirited a nation, as well as the sympathy that it deserves for the cataclysmic tragedy of its wartime and postwar experience.

It was Poland's misfortune that the Atlantic powers and Russia had waited too long to contain that expansion on which Hitler embarked in 1936, when he reoccupied the Rhineland. By the spring of 1939 he had already conquered Austria and Czechoslovakia with the acquiescence of an intimidated France and an intimidated England. The abandonment of Czechoslovakia by England and France (the latter of which had been bound to it by a formal alliance) destroyed confidence in the readiness of the French and the British to stop Hitler at any point. The consequence was that the East Europeans who had not already been captured by Hitler moved to save themselves, or to get whatever they could for themselves, in circumstances that represented what seemed to be the final breakdown of the established order. The Poles seized four hundred square miles of Czech territory; Hungary took almost five thousand square miles; and Stalin's Russia entered into an agreement with Hitler's Germany for the partition, in effect, of the East European buffer states from the Baltic to the Black Sea. The joint partition of Poland by its two powerful neighbors was part of that agreement.

It would have been understandable and even proper if, confronted as they now were by irresistible power on both sides, the Poles had laid down their arms and accepted their subjugation, living thereafter in hope of a day when, by passive resistance and the evolution of circumstances, they might again achieve their independence. This was what the Czechs had done, and it was what the Danes would do a few months later. At this point, however, the British and French gave the Poles those guarantees of their protection which, while encouraging their resistance, could no longer save them.

England and France went to war on September 3, 1939, two days after Hitler's invasion of Poland, in order to stop his further expansion. The topical reason, however, was to honor the obligation they had assumed to defend Poland. Having assumed too late an obligation that they could no longer discharge effectively, they now made the honorable gesture of attempting to discharge it. This obligation, together with their inability to discharge it in the face of Russian as well as German opposition, would involve them in the greatest embarrassment as World War II approached its end, and would contribute notably to that worsening of relations between the Atlantic powers and the Soviet Union which was to eventuate in the Cold War. There is a sense in which the Cold War, like World War II, began with a Western attempt to rescue a Poland that was beyond its reach.

Hitler's Army invaded Poland on September 1. Britain and France declared war on the 3rd but remained militarily quiescent. Stalin's Red Army invaded Poland on the 17th, and on the 19th the Nazi invading Army from the west met the Communist invading Army from the east. The Polish Government escaped to France and, upon the fall of France, took final refuge in London. It was this Government in exile that had now to address itself to the almost insuperable problem of restoring Poland to independence in the aftermath of the War.

Poland had gained its independence after World War I because both of the great powers between which it lay had been defeated and prostrated. In this Second World War, such hope of independence as might be based on the prospect of Germany's defeat would, in default of a coinciding Russian defeat, depend on Russian acquiescence. Under the circumstances, the Polish Government in exile had, at all costs, to keep on good terms with Moscow. This would make demands on the capacity for restraint and self-discipline of a people that was habitually swayed by romantic notions.

The one issue above all others that would test the capacity of the Poles was that of the territory to the east of the so-called 'Curzon line,' territory that had been in dispute between Russia and Poland since the latter's restoration as a sovereign state at the end of World War I. Poland had won it from the Bolsheviks by force of arms in 1921, but its claim to regard it as Polish national territory was weakened by the fact that the Poles who inhabited it were outnumbered by its Ukrainian and Byelorussian population. This was the territory that the Red Army occupied in 1939 by agreement between Stalin and Hitler. If anything was clear, it was that Stalin was determined to keep it after the War. The possibility that the Polish Government in exile could remain on good terms with the Russians depended entirely on its being willing to let it go—as the Finns had let some of their eastern territory go. On an issue like this, where Moscow was adamant, the Poles really had no choice.

The Polish Government, exiled in London, was in an extraordinarily difficult position. The authority of any government that is excluded from the country it claims to govern is bound to be in doubt, especially as the days, the months, and the years of its absence from the home-scene accumulate. Its first great problem, then, is to maintain, in a form that is manifest, the allegiance of the people for whom it pretends to speak, since it is on this allegiance that its authority depends. These people, however, may be scattered, remote, or inaccessible. The vast majority of the people for whom the exiled Polish Government pretended to speak were, of course, captives of Nazi Germany in occupied Poland. The contact that the London Government had with them was through an underground organization in Poland. This organization was increasingly faced with rival underground organizations, so that there was a problem of maintaining its own authority. There was also a problem of maintaining *rapport* between it and the London Government. Finally, there were whole Polish armies, at various stages of the War, in France, in Italy, in the Middle East, and in Russia. The London Government had to have a care for its authority over them, and had to maintain the position of being able to speak for them as well as for the Poles in captive Poland. These requirements severely limited its freedom of action, especially when it came to anything so drastic as giving up Polish territory. At no time did it feel itself in a strong enough position for this.

The circumstances, moreover, were not such as were conducive to agreement on what constituted realism. The London Government was in a position to have a realistic appreciation of the international scene, with the various forces that conflicted upon it; but it was remote from the domestic scene in Poland. The Underground knew the domestic scene at first hand but was remote from international realities. The commanders of the Polish armed forces abroad were apt to view the political problems of Poland's future in romantic terms.

The reality was that, unless both Germany and Russia were defeated, Poland at the end of the War would be in no position to enforce large claims upon the international community. This, however, was not a reality to appeal to the Don Quixote in the Polish character. The realists in the London Government had to face the fact that a substantial part of its scattered constituency was looking forward to the creation, at the end of the War, of a great and aristocratic Poland that, while balancing off Germany and Russia against each other, would organize eastern Europe into a grand federation under its leadership. Such dreams were not conducive to the acceptance of a policy on the Finnish model, involving national self-abnegation, self-sacrifice, and a determination to fight only for the minimum requirements of independent survival.

The agony of the circumstances in which the London Poles had to make their terrible decisions are beyond description. They had to abide the continuing violation and massacre, in the homeland from which they were exiled, of their kindred, for whom they were unable to provide any relief. The Nazis, during their four-year occupation of Poland, killed over six million Poles. This is an unimaginable figure. It may help us appreciate it, however, if we note that the slaughter of the entire population of Switzerland—every man, woman, and child in Geneva, Lausanne, Berne, Zurich, Basel, Lugano, as well as in every village, farm, and mountain-valley—would not amount to so much. The Poles in exile could not know who or what would be left when they recovered their own country, if they ever did.

The Russians, it appears, during their occupation of eastern Poland before the Nazis drove them out, and after their re-entry in 1944, were not notably more considerate of Polish humanity. Poland's rescue from the Nazi wolf, at last, was by another wolf, and this was what the exiles were being asked to accept. It was in almost unbearable agony of spirit, then, that they had to make decisions that would have tested the *sang froid* of a Talleyrand.

One incident, finally, was too much for them. Thrown off their balance by it for a brief moment, they were never able to recover.

When the Russians invaded eastern Poland in 1939, among the prisoners whom they took were 14,300 Polish officers whom they segregated in three prison-camps. On July 30, 1941, shortly after Hitler's surprise attack on them, the Russians concluded an agreement with the Poles in London ending the state of war between them, and thereupon arrangements were made for the Polish General Anders to organize a Polish army in the Soviet Union out of the released Polish prisoners and refugees in Russia.

But where were the 14,300 officers who should have been available to command them?

The Russian authorities kept putting the question aside, or giving abrupt and unconvincing answers to it. One does not, however, simply mislay so many human beings. The disappearance of these officers, which posed a practical as well as a humane problem, became a sort of nightmare that haunted the Poles in London over the months that lengthened into years; but all their efforts of investigation and inquiry were frustrated by Russian brusqueness and indifference. Then, on April 13, 1943, Radio Berlin announced the discovery in eastern Poland, in a forest called Katyn, of mass graves containing the bodies of over ten thousand Polish officers, each one of whom had been shot in the back of the head. The massacre, according to Radio Berlin, had been committed by the Russians while they were still in occupation of eastern Poland.

Two days later, Moscow countered by accusing the Germans of the massacre.

Even today we still do not know conclusively whether it was Stalin's Russians or Hitler's Nazis who did the deed. Certainly the Nazis, who killed some three and a half million Polish Jews, leaving only a hundred thousand alive, were capable of it. At the time, because Nazi Germany was the enemy and Soviet Russia the ally, British and American opinion was predisposed to attribute the guilt to the Nazis. There is evidence, however, that the officers had been killed long before the Germans replaced the Russians in eastern Poland, and this evidence is made more plausible by the earlier behavior of Moscow, when the Poles had tried to find out what had happened to them, and by the self-contradictory explanations that it offered later. In fact, the behavior of Moscow from start to finish makes it hard not to conclude that the guilt belongs there.

The revelation of the Katyn massacre was, in any case, the occasion of the fatal mis-step by the Polish Government in London. Two days after Moscow had denied the German accusation the London Government, with good reason to suspect that the accusation was true, announced that it had asked the International Red Cross to send a delegation to Katyn so that the German charges might be 'verified' by a competent international body. The Polish request to the Red Cross followed an hour after a similar German request, thereby giving the impression of a co-ordinated action. Then, having made this imprudent move, the London Government officially demanded of Moscow, on April 20, an explanation of what had happened to the missing officers.

Moscow's response was simple and brutal. It broke off relations with the Polish Government in London, accusing it of having 'sunk so low as to enter the path of accord with the Hitlerite Government.'

No one can suppose that it was the Polish Government's response to the Nazi accusation that alone brought Stalin to break with it. There had been difficulties all along, the chief of which arose from the Polish refusal to consider giving up eastern Poland in the postwar settlement. Stalin was determined to have a 'friendly' although not necessarily a Communist government in Warsaw after the War, and he must already have been doubtful that the Government in London met this requirement. Its clear disposition to accept the Nazi charges would have stung him if they were false, but must have stung him even more painfully if, as one must suppose, they were true. For in the latter case the Polish reaction would have evoked both the memory of his collaboration with Hitler in the rape of Poland and the memory of his gullibility in letting Hitler, in his betrayal of their agreement, take him by surprise.

The London Poles, under heavy pressure from Whitehall and Washington, found a formula for retracting their request to the International Red Cross, and avowed their continued desire for friendly relations with Moscow 'on the basis of the integrity and full sovereignty of the Republic of Poland.' But the break was not to be mended, or it was not to be mended without concessions that the London Poles would not make; and for the Poles, whatever the justice of their position, this was bound to be fatal. Sometimes the right, to survive, has no choice but to pay its respects to might.

Eight days after the break Stalin told a newspaper-correspondent that he wanted a strong and independent Poland with which, after the War, to establish 'good-neighborly relations' of 'mutual respect.' This may well have been what he really did want. For the government of such a Poland, however, he wanted a regime that would accept the absorption of eastern Poland into the Soviet Union, and that would deal with him in terms that took realistic account of the distribution of power.

At the Teheran Conference, in the winter of 1943–1944, Stalin told Churchill that what was needed was a Polish Paasikivi. Juho Paasikivi was the remarkable Finnish statesman who had played a leading role in the 1940 peace negotiations with Russia. He was to play such a role again in the spring of 1944. Finally, as Prime Minister and then as President of Finland from November 1944 on, he was to demonstrate an appreciation of the realities of power that was far better calculated than ideological affinity to evoke Stalin's respect. In the Finnish nation, however, Paasikivi had a Sancho Panza behind him.

*   *   *

The situation produced by the break between the Polish Government and Moscow was more important than any other topical factor in leading to the break between Russia and the Atlantic powers at the end of the War. It also epitomized that break; for the dilemma that faced the Poles from the beginning was that they could save their country from one wolf only by delivering it to another. This same dilemma, albeit in a less absolute form, faced the Atlantic allies.

England had gone to war for the independence of Poland. When Poland fell, and then France, it had taken the Polish Government under its protection as a refugee. It could not now cast that Government out simply because, by its faithful representation of Polish nationalism, it had antagonized the Russian wolf. The Government in Washington, like the Government in Whitehall, had accorded the exiled Polish Government the status of legitimacy and now found itself essentially in the position of the British Government. The interests represented by the Polish Government in London were under Anglo-American protection. Churchill might, in exasperation, tell the London Poles that Britain had not gone to war to defend Poland's eastern frontier, that in fact it identified itself with the 'Curzon line' favored by Moscow—and he did tell them this. Roosevelt might tell them, as he did, that concessions were unavoidable, since the United States and Britain would not go to war with Russia over Poland. The reply of the London Poles was that they had no authority to cede

Polish territory, and there is a sense in which this was undoubtedly true.

As late as February 1944, when the advancing Red Army was already at the frontier of prewar Poland, the Polish Underground passed a resolution, which they sent to their Government in London, stating that they were prepared to accept an enlargement of Polish territory on the west that had been proposed as compensation for the proposed reduction on the east; that they rejected, however, the proposed reduction on the east; and that they were 'determined to fight the new Soviet aggression.' They said they would never submit to force, and this was a noble but a foolish saying, for in the end they would no more be able to resist Stalin's force than they had been able to resist Hitler's force in the beginning. Whitehall and Washington were bound to the exiled Polish Government, which in turn was bound to a nation of Don Quixotes.[1] So the Polish dilemma became their own.

Just as the Polish campaigns of World War II began with collaboration between Hitler and Stalin, so they ended with something like local and tacit collaboration between them. This was the natural consequence of the Polish determination to fight them both.

In the end, the Polish Underground decided to fight the Germans first and to oppose the Russians only afterwards. The advancing Red Army accepted the help that was consequently tendered by the local units of the Underground—after which, however, it disarmed them and imprisoned their leaders rather than leave them intact in its rear. When the Red Army reached the gates of Warsaw the Warsaw Underground, in response to a call to do so broadcast over Radio Moscow, rose up against the occupying Nazis, moved by a natural desire to make the liberation of the capital a Polish accomplishment in the greatest degree possible. What they had not expected, however, was that the Red Army would choose this moment, when it stood within sight of the city, to halt its advance and encamp.

Moscow maintained that there were sound military reasons for this halt, as there may well have been; but it is clear that there were also political reasons. By not moving to rescue the Warsaw Poles, who had risen only in the expectation of imminent rescue,

---

[1] General Anders, commanding the Polish Army in Italy, also expressed his determination to fight the Russians.

the Russian leaders could be assured that the Nazis would have
the time and means necessary to do a thorough job of annihilating
an Underground that, once rescued, was prepared to turn on its
rescuers.

For two months and one day the embattled Poles, using the
sewers of Warsaw for shelter and communication, fought a hopeless battle against the Nazis, whose victory was in a sense guaran-
teed by the Red Army which stood by.

The consternation, at this point, not only of the London Poles,
but of the British and American Governments as well, was complete. Churchill and Roosevelt pleaded with Stalin, if he would
not come to the rescue himself, at least to facilitate the dropping
of supplies into Warsaw from airplanes based in Italy by allowing
damaged aircraft with wounded aboard to land behind the Russian lines. Stalin was candid in the reason he gave for his refusal.
He had, he said, come to the conclusion that the Warsaw uprising
had been inspired by persons antagonistic to the Soviet Union.[2]

In their two months and one day the Nazis were granted the
time to destroy Warsaw, razing its buildings and slaughtering its
population. That done, they marched out to the west while the
Red Army, assured that all effective opposition had been quelled,
marched in from the east. What the Red Army found when it
entered Warsaw was 'little but shattered streets and the unburied
dead.'[3]

Statesmen generally make their decisions at a level of abstraction above that at which flesh-and-blood suffers. This is inevitable. So, in its measure, is the suffering. Within our human limitations there is no possibility of ultimately understanding why this
should be so. Because statesmen in the capitals of the Atlantic
nations hesitated before the prospect of suffering and destruction
that might be entailed in an undertaking to stop Hitler, the Polish
people and the people of half the world were racked and decimated.

[2] The Commander of the Royal Air Force in Italy at the time, Marshal Sir John
Slessor, has reported that the Russians 'even refused to allot me one airfield where
damaged aircraft with wounded men on board could land, instead of having to fly
all the way back to Italy.' In six weeks 'R.A.F., Polish and South African aircraft under
my command flew 181 sorties into Warsaw, of which 31 heavy aircraft failed to return,
a loss rate of over 17 per cent.' (From a letter in *The Observer*, London, August 16,
1964.) Again the Western allies were trying to save Poles who, again, lay beyond reach
of their salvation—thereby encouraging a resistance that could not succeed.

[3] Churchill, 1953, p. 145.

There is a sense in which the Cold War, like World War II, began with flesh-and-blood in Poland.

* * *

One has the impression that Stalin was genuinely reluctant to create a satellite regime for the postwar government of Poland. Neither the Polish satellite regime that had been prepared by Moscow in 1920 nor the Finnish regime prepared in 1939 had ever had a chance to govern, and the lesson of these failures may not have been lost on him. In any case, he may have been less than eager to create a situation that the British and Americans were inescapably committed to oppose. Taking their basic hostility for granted, he may not have wished to provoke them unnecessarily. Even though he could make his will supreme in Poland, he had the traditional Russian consciousness of weakness in terms of the whole wide scene.

Until the last moment, then, he seems to have hoped that he could bring the London Poles to some such agreement as he was soon to enter into with the Finns. It was not until late July 1944, when the Red Army was crossing the 'Curzon line' and entering into what Moscow, itself, recognized as Polish territory, that a provisional Polish executive, the Committee of National Liberation, was set up by Moscow for the administration of the liberated Polish territory. In August this executive moved to Lublin, which it declared to be the temporary capital of Poland, and by the beginning of the new year a succession of carefully managed formalities had transformed it into the 'Provisional Government' of Poland, recognized as such by Moscow.

Beginning with the inauspicious new year, then, there were two Governments of Poland, one recognized by Whitehall and Washington, the other recognized by Moscow. It made a difference in practice, if not in principle, that the first was in England while the other was in Poland. Here we have the first major disagreement among the wartime allies foreshadowing the Cold War.

At the Yalta Conference in February 1945, and afterwards, both Churchill and Roosevelt fought, as they were morally obliged to do, for the re-establishment of Poland under an independent and legitimate regime. However, although they could propose it was only Stalin who had the power to dispose. A formula was agreed upon under which the Polish people were nominally given the right to self-determination by free elections. Moscow interpreted this formula to suit itself and, from now on, ruthlessly imposed its own solution without regard to Western protests.

So the territory under the control of Moscow was extended westward to include the whole of Poland, while resentment and alarm grew in the West.

CHAPTER VIII

The fall of Rumania, Hungary, Bulgaria, and Czechoslovakia

IN the Armistice and subsequent Peace Treaty with Finland Russia obtained territorial concessions that left the Finns militarily defenseless and therefore at its mercy. This assured Moscow of their 'friendliness' even under a liberal democratic regime of their own choosing. It made unnecessary the dangerous and expensive task of military occupation.

In Poland, on the other hand, military occupation was an automatic consequence of the campaign against the German forces, and the hostility of the legitimate political elements in the country made it appear that the only 'friendly' government the Russians could expect would be a puppet government of their own imposing.

The campaign against the German forces also had the military occupation of Rumania and Hungary as an automatic consequence. It would have required a remarkable self-restraint on the part of the Russians if, in the course of such occupation, they had refrained from strengthening the domestic position of the local Communists, who were prepared to cooperate with them as others were not. Such interference in domestic affairs, however, was bound to arouse popular hostility that would, in turn, increase the need for such interference if Moscow was to be assured of 'friendly' regimes in the two countries. So a little tyranny requires more tyranny until all compunctions against its practice are at last abandoned.

In any case, the extraordinary self-discipline of the Finnish people in exercising the freedom that was left to them could hardly be expected elsewhere. It was a foregone conclusion, for example, that a free Rumania would be an anti-Russian Rumania.

Faced with this situation, the two Atlantic allies involved themselves in a contradiction that was to be a fruitful source of misunderstanding in Moscow. In trying to follow, simultaneously, the paths of realism and idealism they found themselves in the position of a man who makes promises that are mutually irreconcilable. Thus, as a matter of *Realpolitik*, they agreed, on repeated

67

occasions, with Moscow's contention that the governments of the countries on Russia's western frontier must be 'friendly' to it.[1] On other occasions, however, and as a matter of ideological principle, they prevailed on Stalin to recognize the right of those same countries to exercise self-determination through free elections. Except in the case of the realistic Finns and perhaps the Czechoslovaks, these two positions were in conflict; for freely elected governments would probably not be 'friendly' to Moscow. This conflict did not constitute a serious embarrassment for Stalin, who allowed himself to consider that freedom, as applied to elections, might be abridged in any degree (e.g., by withholding it from non-Marxist elements in the population) without thereby ceasing to be freedom. This, however, was not the view of the American and British statesmen. Their interpretation of the word 'free' was universalistic, and they appear to have been less concerned than Stalin with the import of 'friendly.'

The British tradition, which Churchill represented, was more realistic than the American tradition, which Roosevelt represented. There is reason to believe that Churchill and Stalin, left to themselves, might have come to a good understanding on postwar arrangements in eastern Europe—with the possible but by no means certain exception of Poland. On the one occasion when they were, in fact, left to themselves (chiefly because Roosevelt was facing an election in the United States) they did come to such an understanding. Visiting Stalin in Moscow on the night of October 9, 1944, Churchill proposed to him in effect that, since the Red Army was already in Rumania and Bulgaria, these two countries be considered as belonging to a Russian sphere of influence, while Greece be considered as belonging to a British.[2] Stalin immediately agreed. This was language that he understood. It was the language, one supposes, of a Paasikivi. He subsequently

[1] In operational terms, a 'friendly' government would presumably mean, as a minimum, a government committed to enter into no alliances with potential enemies of Russia and to resist, within its jurisdiction, any military moves by them that menaced Russia. Moreover, it would have to refrain from thwarting Russian foreign policy in any way. What might be called ideological friendliness was not directly involved. Stalin was a power-politician before he was an ideologist.

[2] Churchill, 1953, p. 227. Churchill comments: 'Of course we . . . were only dealing with immediate war-time arrangements. All larger questions were reserved on both sides for what we then hoped would be a peace table when the war was won.' If we take this without a grain of salt we cannot say that the agreement aimed at spheres of influence in the classic sense of the term. A grain of salt, however, would not be out of place.

showed his good faith, when it came to this kind of agreement, by living up to it.

This kind of agreement, however, was abhorrent to American thinking and unlikely to be popular with the British electorate, among whom idealism was not closely circumscribed by an appreciation of the realities of power. The American vision, which was congenial to the British as well, was of a worldwide international community, democratically organized under a sort of parliament of nations, in which all the members enjoyed self-determination by free elections on the Western model. In this vision there were no spheres of influence, and power-politics had become obsolete. With this in mind, the United States, at the Yalta Conference in February 1945, presented the project of a 'Declaration on Liberated Europe' according to which the American, British, and Russian Governments undertook jointly to assist 'the people in any European liberated state or former Axis satellite . . . to form interim governmental authorities broadly representative of all the democratic elements in the population and pledged to the earliest possible establishment through free elections of governments responsive to the will of the people; and to facilitate where necessary the holding of such elections.'

This was not the kind of undertaking to which a man like Stalin, who had not withheld his signature even from the Atlantic Charter of 1941, would have found it hard to subscribe. It was a Declaration, couched in the most general language, to be published to the peoples of the world at the close of the Yalta Conference; so that it could be regarded as having a rhetorical and propagandistic significance. It represented the kind of thing one said on hortatory occasions in public as opposed to the kind of hard agreement that was kept private—like the agreement with Churchill on Rumania, Bulgaria, and Greece. Furthermore, the language could well be taken by a Marxist to have a meaning quite different from that which it had for a Jeffersonian democrat. In the pure Marxian tradition 'the people' does not include the bourgeoisie, for example; and 'the will of the people' is Rousseau's 'general will,' which has nothing to do with the will of a majority, and which is represented only by a mandarin élite—in this case, the Communist leadership.[3] Finally, ever since the failure to

---

[3] For a discussion of these concepts see Halle, 1962, pp. 38–51 and 136–141.

produce, in 1917, the revolution prophesied by Marx, the new masters of the Russian state had accustomed themselves to the device of nominalism, the device of calling what actually happens by the nominal terms that identify it with what was supposed to happen—as when the dictatorship of Stalin was called 'the dictatorship of the proletariat.' Therefore, a commitment to free elections and to governments responsive to the will of the people presented no insurmountable problem to Stalin, who proceeded to accept it.

The reality of power-politics was what counted for Stalin. The Western leaders accepted this priority to the extent of acknowledging the requirement of 'friendly' governments on the frontier of his empire. Churchill went further in accepting it by according first place to Stalin's will in providing for the disposition of Rumania and Bulgaria at the end of the War. What counted for Roosevelt, however, and here Churchill followed him, was the idealism of freedom which might conflict with the reality of power-politics. Under the circumstances, it is not surprising that, in what actually happened at the end of the War, the ideal did not prevail over the reality of Stalin's unbalanced power in eastern Europe; that the Russian requirement of 'friendly' governments was not sacrificed to the Western ideal of free elections.

Having subscribed to the 'Declaration on Liberated Europe,' but having his triumphant military forces in Poland, Rumania, Bulgaria, and Hungary, Stalin proceeded with the necessary degree of ruthlessness, as occasion required, to eliminate from the public life of these countries the elements that were not 'friendly' to his Russia—even though, where that was the case, they represented a majority of the population. As often as Churchill remonstrated, Stalin or his spokesmen reminded him by clear hints of the good faith that they, for their part, were showing in leaving the British free to deal as they pleased with Greece. So the entire column of states along Russia's prewar border, from the Gulf of Finland to the Black Sea, plus Bulgaria, fell captive to the expanding empire whose sway was now enlarged toward the west by so much. The absorption of eastern Poland and of Ruthenia resulted in a common frontier between the Russian state and Czechoslovakia, which would now, in its turn, have to meet the requirement of producing a government 'friendly' to Moscow.

*   *   *

In terms of its internal circumstances, none of the other eastern European states, not even Finland, was in as good a position as Czechoslovakia to reconcile the requirements of self-determination by the procedures of Western democracy with the requirement of a governing regime 'friendly' to the Soviet Union. The Finns and Poles alike had been antagonized by generations of Russian tyranny; but the peoples of Czechoslovakia had suffered, rather, under the yoke of the Viennese Hapsburgs, and they were moved by panslavism to associate themselves in their own minds with the Russian peoples. In Czechoslovakia, therefore, it was not a foregone conclusion that free elections would produce a regime 'unfriendly' to Moscow. Moreover, the legitimate Government of the country, which like the Polish Government had taken refuge in London, represented the high order of statesmanship for which Czechoslovakia had been noted ever since its founding after World War I. And this statesmanship did undertake, as World War II approached its end, to achieve the kind of accommodation with Moscow that the Finns were later to achieve for themselves. It even appeared to have succeeded, until the development of the Cold War imposed an extra strain on a situation that may, in any case, have been too fragile to survive.

Thomas G. Masaryk, the founding father and first President of Czechoslovakia, had exemplified the Platonic ideal of the philosopher statesman. Eduard Benes, the second President, who presided over the Government in its English exile, was Masaryk's disciple as well as his successor. Both men earned worldwide reputations for the high character of their statesmanship—which was not, however, to be rewarded in the end by a final realization of the cause to which they devoted it.

Czechoslovakia, challenged and then assaulted by Hitler's Germany in the 1930's, was first betrayed by the French and the British, and in the end by the Russians. The French and British betrayal propelled Moscow into the Nazi–Soviet Pact and, in sacrificing the military means by which Czechoslovakia might have opposed and contained Hitler, allowed him to start World War II with a strategic advantage that almost enabled him to take Britain and Russia captive, as well as France.[4]

In 1938 Hitler had embarked on a policy of threatening war

[4] One could make a plausible case for it that this was averted only by the British invention of radar, which enabled Britain to survive the Nazi aerial assault of 1940. So dangerously do we live.

unless Czechoslovakia accepted partition at his hands. Czechoslovakia was armed to resist, and had a defensive alliance with France. In those days, however, both France and Britain, in a condition of moral slump, haunted by the fear of poison-gas and aerial bombardment, were ready to pay virtually any price to avoid war with Hitler. They were ready to pay even the price of delivering up to him their Czechoslovakian comrade and ally. At Munich in 1938 they paid this price—but without ultimately avoiding the war from which it was supposed to save them. This was the historic appeasement of Hitler that failed to appease him.

At Munich the British and French—in the absence of their Czech colleague and without consulting the Russians, whose military security was at stake—agreed to the Nazi seizure of Czech territory in return for Hitler's assurance of what the British Prime Minister called 'peace in our time.' Benes had been President of Czechoslovakia when this had happened, but in the subsequent events he rose above all bitterness. A year later, when 'peace in our time' came to an end, when the War broke out over Poland, he had formed a Government in exile in London. Here he had cooperated loyally with the British.

The postwar prospects of Czechoslovakia were essentially the same as those of Poland. In the case of a Russian victory over Hitler, Moscow would be left free to impose its will on the country. Benes, in his London exile, understood this. Experience had taught him not to depend on support or rescue from the Western powers. Therefore, he and his exiled Government determined from the start to make the best terms possible with Moscow. Unlike the unhappy Poles, he and his colleagues managed to avoid any defiance or any provocation of Moscow throughout the course of the War. They did not overestimate the possibilities that were open to them. From London they took the initiative to negotiate with Moscow a treaty that should govern postwar relations between the two countries. When Benes approached Stalin for this purpose he found him friendly, well disposed, and even rather generous in his attitude.

Early in 1943 Moscow assured Benes that it was prepared to see Czechoslovakia restored, after the War, as an independent country, and that it would not interfere in the domestic affairs of the restored country. These assurances were repeated on more than one occasion. In 1945, at a dinner that he gave for Benes,

Stalin offered a toast in which he said that Benes had once been right to suspect the Soviet Union of wishing to Bolshevize Europe, but that Soviet policy had since been reoriented. After the War, he said, the various Communist parties would become nationalist parties, giving the national interests of their respective countries priority.[5]

What are we to make of these assurances? Were they honest or calculated to deceive?

We need not altogether dismiss the possibility that both honesty and deception entered into Stalin's motives. One can imagine that he was genuinely averse to undertaking the forced Bolshevization of a Czechoslovakia that, in addition to being oriented toward the Western conception of democracy, was the strongest, the richest, and the most advanced of the eastern European countries. He may have felt that he could maintain, with a non-Communist government under Benes, the kind of relations that he was later to maintain with the Finnish Government under Paasikivi; and this would be preferable to the burden of holding the country in subjection. At the same time, he might also have been moved by a desire to allay Benes's suspicions of the Moscow-trained Czech Communists who were to be given key places in the Czech government after the War, men whom he denigrated in talking to Benes.

Whatever the measure of Stalin's honesty, and even if he was being wholly dishonest, Benes had virtually no choice but to accept such terms as he could draw from him. He was, moreover, in no position to keep the Communists out of his postwar Government since they were the strongest single party in Czechoslovakia at the end of the War. In the genuinely free elections, with secret ballot, of May 26, 1946, the Communists polled more than twice as many votes as the next strongest party (Benes's own), obtaining more than 35% of the total votes cast. In this one instance, then, elections did mean a government 'friendly' to Moscow.

Czechoslovakia, although bound by strong ties to the West before Munich, was the most pro-Russian, or the least anti-Russian, of the countries along Russia's western border. It had, at this time, experienced oppression by the Germans and betrayal by the French and British, but it had been neither oppressed nor betrayed, as yet, by the Russians. Under all these circumstances,

Benes could not have excluded the Communists from his postwar Government.

In March 1945 President Benes met in Moscow with the Czech Communist leaders who had been living there. With them he organized a provisional Government, including a substantial Communist element, to govern his country as it became accessible in the wake of the liberating Red Army. Out of the twenty-five cabinet posts seven went to the Communists. These seven included the posts of Prime Minister and of Minister of the Interior, with jurisdiction over the police.

It is often accepted as axiomatic that, where the Communists gain control of the Ministry of the Interior, they gain control of the government and of the country. That this is not a foregone conclusion, however, is shown by the Finnish experience; for in 1948 the Finns, upon evidence that their Communist Minister of the Interior was on more confidential terms with the Russian Government than with his own, removed him from his post; and Moscow, presumably impressed by the toughness of the Finns, held its hand.

In the spring of 1945 Benes's provisional Government, following on the heels of the Red Army, set up its administration at Kosice, inside the eastern border of Czechoslovakia. There it issued the 'Kosice Program,' setting forth the policies of the new regime, which would base its foreign policy on 'the alliance of the State with the Soviet Union. . . .' This new Government now accepted Russian annexation of Ruthenia, which had constituted the eastern tip of Czechoslovakia, as the Poles refused to accept Russian annexation of eastern Poland. After the elections of May 1946, a permanent non-Communist Government, under a Communist Prime Minister and with substantial Communist representation, was established in Prague. It appeared that, as in Finland, a *via media* had been found between the demands of 'friendship' with Moscow and the appeal of freedom on the Western model.

This hope, although not clearly unfounded, was to be disappointed. In June 1947 the offer of assistance in the rehabilitation of Europe made by Secretary of State Marshall, later to be known as the Marshall Plan, exerted on the Czechoslovak Government, as on the other governments along Russia's European frontier, a tug that aroused Moscow's anxiety if not its alarm. In the winter of 1947–1948 there were signs that the strong position of the Communists in Czechoslovakia was weakening. Throughout Europe and the West as a whole, a reaction was manifesting itself to the ruthless expansionist policy of Stalin's empire since 1944. The Cold War had begun.

In February 1948 the Communist Minister of the Interior, supported by the Communist Prime Minister, defied the Czechoslovakian Cabinet, which was attempting to exercise over him the discipline that the Finnish Cabinet, that same spring, was to exercise over its own Communist Minister of the Interior. Six days later, a Deputy Foreign Minister of the Soviet Union arrived in Prague. The police, obeying the orders of the Communist Minister of the Interior, then went into action. There was some blood shed. The forces of freedom were suppressed. Parliamentary democracy was abolished. And so Czechoslovakia was forcibly transformed into a police-state under a puppet Government subservient to Moscow.

*   *   *

I pause at this point to note that so far in these chapters I have examined the westward expansion of the Russian empire at the end of the War, first in abstract general terms, then in terms of specific events. At the level of abstraction adopted in Chapter I, I described how Russian power inevitably poured into the vacuum left by the destruction of power on its western frontier. The metaphoric image, here, was seductive in its implication that politics obeys laws as simple and absolute as those of classical physics. When we see what actually happens in operational terms, however, in terms of armies marching, statesmen negotiating, and people voting, the whole situation appears to offer a range of possibilities incompatible with the rigidity of physical laws. Accidents seem to play their part. The mistakes of individual statesmen are seen to be significant. The respiratory ailment that impaired Roosevelt's strength in the winter of 1944–1945 has its effect. Unusual human weakness or unusual human virtue appears to alter what might otherwise have been the course of events. One hesitates to deny that Finland might have gone the way that Czechoslovakia finally went. One hesitates to affirm that Czechoslovakia never had the possibility of retaining such freedom as Finland managed to retain.

We must beware of the absoluteness of the great abstractions represented by the metaphor of the power vacuum. We must assume a range of choice in the actual play of events. But the range may be small at any one time (although cumulatively large over the generations), and so the metaphor may not be altogether misleading.

If one puts food before a sufficiently hungry child, warning it that indigestion may be the consequence of eating it, our knowledge of human nature makes it predictable that the child will end, after whatever hesitation, by eating it nevertheless. Moscow, one supposes, was not unmindful of future trouble in the prospect of swallowing the more-or-less indigestible nations that lay before it in Europe as the War ended. Therefore it maintained a considerable degree of self-restraint in its confrontation with Finland, of which it had already had some experience, and it showed some hesitation in confronting other possible victims. There was an initial reluctance over Poland, and an abstemiousness of some duration with respect to Czechoslovakia. In each particular instance, however, in which one has the power to dispose of a frightening enemy at the gate, and to replace him with a trusted servitor, a failure to exercise it must seem to be a folly by which one invites one's own destruction.

It is really not conceivable that the rulers in Moscow, with a thousand years of desperate struggle for survival behind them, would have abjured power-politics after the War and cooperated in the organization of a postwar world that represented the ideals of Anglo-Saxon political philosophy. This would have been for them to commit a kind of suicide, for it would have implied the dissolution of the secret and tyrannical regime on which they depended, inside Russia, for their own survival.

The range of choice, then, was small, the element of predetermination large. In the end Poland or Czechoslovakia might have retained a bit more freedom, Finland might have retained less. But this would not have represented a basically different situation. When the whole structure of power that had balanced and contained Russia on the west was shattered, then it was practically if not theoretically inevitable that the Russian power would expand. And so it did.

History is like a Shakespearian tragedy. Hamlet need not have suffered the fate that befell him—but only if he had not been Hamlet.

CHAPTER IX

What happened in Yugoslavia, Albania, Germany, Greece, Italy, and France at the end of the War

WHERE the retaining walls that surround a great power go down the result may be disaster, not only for its neighbors but also for the great power itself. Napoleon, one supposes, might have consolidated the conquest of half Europe if only he could have stopped halfway. But he could not stop halfway; the whole of Europe was more than he could digest; and the result was Waterloo. One may plausibly believe that Hitler lost Austria, in the end, and everything else as well, including Germany, simply because he could not stop with Austria. From an early stage the rulers of the Roman Empire were seriously embarrassed by the overextension that had taken place under Hadrian's predecessors.

The same danger was implicit in Russia's postwar expansion. The outermost conquests proved impossible or too costly to hold. Albania and Yugoslavia broke away, and the rebelliousness of the East German population required desperate measures for its suppression. To the extent that China could at any time have been considered part of the empire directed from Moscow it was a liability, weakening Russian security rather than enhancing it.

One may conclude that it was the misfortune of Russia, as well as of the West, that the area which fell under its domination in the course of the War or in its aftermath was not limited to a relatively narrow strip along its former western border. One may also conclude that it was Russia's good fortune that Italy and France, which for a moment appeared on the verge of also falling under its sway, did not do so. In the end the expansion was limited. Khrushchev had occasion to appreciate, if Stalin did not, that matters would have been better all around if it had been even more limited. In 1955 and 1956 he and his associates would move, on the precedent of the Emperor Hadrian, to accomplish the retrenchment that the uprisings of the latter year in Poland and Hungary brought to a halt.

* * *

Moscow under Stalin forcibly imposed Communist regimes on Poland, Hungary, Rumania, and Bulgaria, and was to do the same in Czechoslovakia. Such a procedure was not needed, however, in Yugoslavia and Albania, where local Communists would find it possible to do the job by themselves.[1] If Stalin had been an ideologist, intent on the spread of Communism to embrace the world, he should have rejoiced at this as representing the fulfillment of Marx's prophecy and Lenin's—the delayed fulfillment of the predictions in the realization of which Lenin had been so deeply disappointed when, after his seizure of power in Russia in 1917, the Communist revolution failed to take place elsewhere. As a practitioner of *Realpolitik*, however, it appears to have troubled Stalin; for the implications of self-liberation, as opposed to liberation by Moscow, were independence. When the Red Army liberated a country from the Axis it simultaneously brought that country under Russian control. There was no assurance that native liberators would do the same. Add to this that Yugoslavia and Albania were separated from Russia by the width of Hungary and Rumania, so that they were not so vulnerable to the pressure of the Red Army.

We have already seen how reluctant Stalin appears to have been to transfer his support from the anti-Communist resistance-group commanded by General Mihailovich to the rival Communist resistance-group commanded by Marshal Tito.[2] After the War he seems to have given some thought to how he could bring both Yugoslavia and Albania under his firm control. The result was that in February 1948 he ordered Yugoslavia and Bulgaria to join themselves together in a federal union and, when they had done so, to bring Albania into that union with them. What he had in mind, one surmises, was that, through his control of Bulgaria, he would be able to hold the rest of the projected Bulgar–Yugo–Albanian state, on whose frontiers the Red Army would stand, under his control. But the Yugoslavs were already too independent to obey him in this, and before the year was out they would break with him completely.

One may well ask how much or how little it means that, in 1944–1945, Yugoslavia and Albania nominally underwent the

---

[1] This is not to say that they could do it without the use of force and fraud against their own populations. The way the Yugoslav election of November 11, 1945, and the Albanian election of December 2, 1945, were organized is sufficient evidence of this.

[2] See p. 47 above.

Communist Revolution predicted by Marx and became, nominally, Communist states under Dictatorships of the Proletariat.

As was the case with the Russian Revolution of 1917, it is hard to find any points of resemblance between what happened in the two Balkan countries and what had been predicted in *The Communist Manifesto* a century earlier. In the *Manifesto* Marx and Engels had predicted that the revolution would take place when and where the proletariat (meaning industrial workers) had become an 'immense majority' of the population. The revolution itself would then be the uprising of this proletarian majority against the capitalist exploiters who had held it in bondage; it would be the 'self-conscious, independent movement of the immense majority in the interest of the immense majority.' The ensuing Dictatorship of the Proletariat would likewise be the dictatorship 'of the immense majority in the interest of the immense majority.' And, in the Marxian prophecy, the disappearance of nationalism and the nation-state would accompany the revolution, since 'the workers have no country.'[3]

Yugoslavia, only less than Albania, was predominantly a country of peasants and mountaineers. The nominally Communist movement that liberated it from within and gained control of it at the end of the War, the movement that Tito and the other professional revolutionaries of his entourage led, was a movement of peasants and mountaineers inspired by patriotic rather than proletarian zeal. This, except nominally, was not at all the revolution that Marx had predicted; and Tito's subsequent rule was not at all the predicted Dictatorship of the Proletariat, except nominally.[4]

The fact that nationalism was the motive which brought Communist regimes to power in Yugoslavia and Albania was a guarantee that they would not for long make themselves subservient to the national interests of Soviet Russia. For the moment,

[3] For a discussion of the Russian Revolution in these terms, see Halle, 1965, Chapter VII.

[4] The abolition of private enterprise and the expropriation by the state of the means of production, in the Communist countries, has been taken by some as the hallmark of true Marxism; but this was merely the institution of state capitalism, which Lenin himself, in May 1918, could defend only as a temporary necessity associated with the 'painful transitional period from capitalism to socialism.' (Cited by Fischer, p. 236.) Socialism, which is, in turn, a transitional period in the final progress to a Communist society, was nominally achieved in the Soviet Union by 1955, according to Foreign Minister Molotov's letter in the October 8, 1955 issue of *Communist*, an official organ of the Soviet Communist Party. But state capitalism nevertheless persisted in Russia. How the world has been beguiled for half a century by this nominal nonsense!

however, ideological indoctrination had its effect. Tito's movement in Yugoslavia and Enver Hoxha's in Albania, although they
were both more obliged for their success to the British than to the
Russians, turned with ideological passion against the capitalist
West and made their obeisance to what they still regarded as the
shrine of Marxism–Leninism in Moscow. They began, at least, by
faithfully submitting themselves to the leadership in the Kremlin.[5]

So it was that, in the immediate aftermath of the War, Moscow
appeared in the West to have extended its dominion to the shores
of the Adriatic. In 1946 and 1947 it was easy to believe that
Greece and then Italy would be the next to fall. And after that,
perhaps, France.

*　　*　　*

The policy that governed the victorious allies in fighting World
War II made it certain that, in the moment of victory, there
would be a vacuum of indigenous power from Russia to the
Atlantic. That vacuum could be filled only by Russian power
coming in from the east or by other power coming in from the
west. The basic question to be resolved was that of the line at
which the respective powers of East and West should meet. This
would be determined in part by the will of statesmen and in part
by circumstances independent of their will.

It is not clear that Stalin wanted to extend the area of his
dominion as far west as possible, since he was cautious of provoking an Anglo-American reaction and since he knew that the
area over which he could maintain effective control was limited.
There can be no doubt, however, that Britain and the United
States, for their part, were averse to committing their power too
far east. We quite mistake the situation, then, if we think that
there was a simple competition, during the last year of the War,
in which Moscow was trying to draw the line between the two
sides as far west as possible while Britain and America were trying
to draw it as far east as possible.

The British Foreign Minister, Anthony Eden, on a visit to
Washington in March 1943, told Roosevelt (as reported by
Roosevelt's *alter ego*, Harry Hopkins) that:

he believed one of the reasons Stalin wanted a second front in Europe
was political; that if Germany collapsed, he had no desire, in Germany,

---

[5] The disillusionment that followed is poignantly described in Djilas.

to take full responsibility for what would happen in Germany and the rest of Europe, and he believed it was a fixed matter of Russian foreign policy to have both British and U.S. troops heavily in Europe when the collapse comes.[6]

In January 1944, at the first meeting of the European Advisory Commission, an inter-allied council that had been set up to make recommendations on such matters, the British member submitted a proposal, approved by the War Cabinet, whereby the Russian zone of occupation in Germany should extend to a line 110 miles west of Berlin. Dr. Philip E. Mosely, who was intimately involved in these negotiations, reports that the subsequent Russian acceptance, without bargaining, of this zone of occupation 'appeared a sign of a moderate and conciliatory approach to the problem of how to deal with postwar Germany.' At that time the representatives of the War Department in Washington, who were concerned with planning the postwar occupation of Germany, 'implied that they expected all of Germany up to the Rhine to be in Soviet control upon Germany's defeat. . . .' On the other hand, Prime Minister Churchill, in his war memoirs, comments that 'in those days a common opinion about Russia was that she would not continue the war once she had regained her frontiers, and that when the time came the Western Allies might well have to try to persuade her not to relax her efforts.' These statements suddenly evoke for us, in our own time, the almost forgotten outlook of that distant day when the men in government carried on as best they could in spite of the blindness that afflicts us all until hindsight comes, too late, to relieve it.[7] When the British proposal was put forward the forces of the Axis were still deep in Russia; the only forces that the Atlantic allies had on the Continent were still pent up in southern Italy; Hitler's power was still supreme in the rest of Europe. At the time Stalin was complaining bitterly about the failure of the Atlantic allies to open a 'second front' in western Europe, leaving the Russians to meet, by themselves alone, almost the entire burden of battling the Axis forces.

As for the United States, Roosevelt based his policy on the expectation that, as soon as it could manage to do so after the end

[6] Cited by Feis, 1957, p. 122. This reading of Stalin's mind has since seemed wildly implausible, but it is not a foregone conclusion that he would, without misgivings, have embraced an opportunity to occupy all Germany.

[7] Mosely, 1950; and Churchill, 1953, p. 508. Mosely should be read in the light of the later and more comprehensive account in Franklin, 1963.

of hostilities, it would insist on withdrawing completely from Europe—as it had at the end of World War I. Therefore he could not assume for the United States commitments that would involve a long-continuing military presence on the far side of the Atlantic after the War. Anticipating American withdrawal, he tried not to become deeply involved in projected European territorial settlements. Let the British, he said, have the principal share in worrying about them.[8] At Yalta in February 1945, he told Stalin and Churchill that 'he felt that he could obtain support in Congress and throughout the country for any reasonable measures designed to safeguard the future peace, but he did not believe that this would extend to the maintenance of an appreciable American force in Europe.' He 'did not believe that American troops would stay in Europe much more than two years.'

I cannot see into Stalin's mind, but I doubt that this statement aroused misgivings in it. As for Churchill, he reports in his memoirs that it caused 'formidable questions' to rise in his own mind. 'If the Americans left Europe Britain would have to occupy single-handed the entire western portion of Germany. Such a task would be far beyond our strength.'[9]

One gathers that Churchill was more concerned with the south of Europe than with the north, that his principal anxiety was to keep Russia away from that main artery of the British Empire, the Mediterranean. His persistence in arguing for an invasion of Europe from the south rather than the west, his zeal for an aggressive strategy in Greece, Albania, and Yugoslavia, his project for landing troops at the head of the Adriatic and striking north through the Julian Alps—all this was presumably calculated to

[8] In a memorandum of February 21, 1944, to Acting Secretary of State Stettinius, Roosevelt said: 'I do not want the United States to have the postwar burden of reconstituting France, Italy and the Balkans. . . . It is definitely a British task in which the British are far more vitally interested than we are.' (Cited in Feis, 1957, p. 340.)

[9] Churchill, 1953, p. 353. Churchill could not have been altogether unprepared for the President's statement, since the President had frequently indicated, when postwar settlements in eastern Europe were under discussion, that the United States must be in a position to withdraw from Europe after the War. It should be added that at a later session of the Yalta Conference the President, perhaps troubled by the implications of his statement for his own bargaining position, modified it by saying that the American people might change their minds about maintaining forces in Europe if an effective international organization was created (see Feis, 1957, p. 532). One wonders whether he thought that this would· influence Stalin's attitude toward the proposed organization favourably or unfavourably. By this time, however, it is plausible that the dying Roosevelt was hardly thinking at all, that he was simply improvising his positions on the issues as they arose.

exclude Russia from the Balkan Peninsula and the Adriatic, and it might have had the effect of saving Austria and Czechoslovakia as well. It would hardly, however, have interposed a barrier to a Russian advance across Poland and northern Germany in the direction of the North Sea and the Channel. The relative lack of British sensitivity to the prospect of such an advance is exemplified by the gratuitous proposal of the War Cabinet, in the winter of 1943–1944, that the Russian zone of occupation in Germany extend to a line 110 miles west of Berlin.[10]

We must recall that it hardly occurred to anyone, in the days of the wartime alliance, that those who were defining the zone to be occupied by the Red Army in the moment of Germany's unconditional surrender were defining what would, for at least a generation after the War, be the Democratic Republic of Germany, a Russian puppet state; or that the Western zones of occupation would become the Federal Republic of Germany, a sovereign state with irredentist claims on the territory of the Democratic Republic. On the contrary, Germany was to be occupied only for as long a period after its surrender as would be necessary for the creation of a new German governmental structure and the ideological reorientation of the German people. While this was being done the country would be administered as a political and economic whole by a Control Council comprising representatives of the three occupying powers. After that, the Americans, the British, and the Russians would withdraw from Germany. No division of the country in two, even for one day, was ever contemplated.

Since the prospect of occupation was not looked upon (even by the Russians, one surmises) as an opportunity for permanent national aggrandizement, and since in certain contexts it appeared as a burden, there may have seemed the less reason, in the Western capitals, for not assigning a large share to the Russians.

The intention had been to establish a joint allied administration over the country as an undivided whole. The Control Council,

[10] Churchill appears to have been embarrassed when it came to explaining this in his memoirs, as he had been embarrassed when it came to explaining his endorsement of the 'Morgenthau Plan' for the partition and 'pastoralization' of Germany at the Second Quebec Conference (see Churchill, 1953, p. 508). The historian must not, I think, try to make good sense of everything that harrassed statesmen do or fail to do when they are under severe pressure and have for long been stretched to the limits of endurance. Nevertheless, it is hard to imagine the War Cabinet proposing to Moscow that the Red Army occupy the Balkan Peninsula.

composed of one representative of each occupying power, would make the decisions that the powers would then carry out in their respective zones. The decisions of the Council, however, could be made only on the basis of unanimity, so that any member could prevent any decision from being adopted. In the absence of a decision, each occupying power was free to act independently within its own zone. Here we see the application to a specific situation of that principle of unanimity among the great powers on the basis of which the organization of the whole world had been planned.

In default of unanimity, which was no more attainable in the Control Council than in the Security Council of the United Nations, Russia exercised a largely independent control of its own zone, which in 1949 became the German Democratic Republic; while the Western allies, in agreement with one another, pursued their own course in what became the Federal Republic of Germany. So Germany was divided after all. And so the western boundary of the rapidly expanding Russian empire was now advanced to a line four-fifths of the way from Russia's prewar boundaries to the boundaries of Holland, Belgium, and France. The Atlantic nations were already in the shadow of the Russian empire.

How much farther would its expansion carry?

*   *   *

Today we know that the line from Lübeck, just south of Denmark, to the head of the Adriatic represented the farthest westward advance of the Russian empire in its postwar expansion. We also know that its extension to so distant a line was a source of weakness rather than of strength. But we did not know this in the period from 1944 to 1948. We assumed, rather, a firm Russian grip on the whole area that appeared to have fallen under the Russian power; and we could not know, at the time, that an expansion which had already covered so much of the distance to the Atlantic seaboard and the western Mediterranean would stop before reaching them. Ahead still lay only the power vacuum—the weakness of nations broken and prostrated by war.

The formal situation in Greece at the end of the War was like that in the other small eastern European countries. During the War there had been a Greek Government in exile and, in Greece itself, organizations of resistance fighters—of which the chief was

the National Liberation Front, the E.A.M. By the time of liberation a marriage of these hitherto separated entities had been
effected, taking the form of a Government of National Unity in
which the E.A.M. had five Cabinet posts. The E.A.M., however,
had means of power in Greece that made it independent of the
Government in which it was formally participating, and inside
the E.A.M. the leading element was the Communist. The
Government that had been in exile was hardly able to re-assert
its authority upon returning. The reins of power appeared to be
in the hands, rather, of the Communist-dominated E.A.M. In this
kind of situation elsewhere in eastern Europe, Communist take-
overs would occur; and it seemed plausible that Greece, too, was
on the way to becoming a 'People's Republic.'

In this single case, however, the overshadowing military force
was not the Red Army but the British Army. The Government of
National Unity had been brought into Greece in the train of the
liberating British forces and was essentially a British puppet. The
British Ambassador in Athens assumed a proconsular role, and in
one instance a British Minister of State, Mr. Hector McNeil,
visited Greece to install a new Greek Government of British
choosing.

The forcible British intervention in Greece, which prevented a
Communist take-over, had to cope with more opposition from the
United States, which was outraged by the sacrifice of principle to
expediency, than from Russia. The evidence indicates that in
1945 and 1946 the Greek Communists, whatever their own in-
clinations, were directed by Moscow to cooperate with whatever
Greek regime the British supported. Aside from the fact that this
accorded with the agreement of October 9, 1944, between
Churchill and Stalin, Stalin presumably had two not unrelated
motives for it. One, which could hardly have been admitted even
to fellow Communists outside the Kremlin, was that a Communist
Greece, because beyond the reach of his control, would have a disruptive influence on his empire. The other was that the Communization of Greece might be expected to provoke severe reactions from the British and the Americans, with dangerous
consequences.[11]

So the Greek Communists were beaten out of Athens, one way
or another, and most of them took refuge in the north, where they

[11] See pp. 68–9 above.

could find sanctuary and perhaps succour in Communist Albania, Yugoslavia, and Bulgaria. In fact, by the spring of 1946 they were finding, in these countries, active support for spreading guerrilla operations that came to take on the dimensions of civil war in Greece. This, so far from representing Stalin's will, represented the degree to which the area over which he could make his will effective was limited. In a meeting of February 1948 he scolded Vice-President Edvard Kardelj of Yugoslavia, demanding that the Communist insurrection in Greece, which Yugoslavia was supporting, be brought to an end. Milovan Djilas, who accompanied Kardelj, reports Stalin as saying: 'What, do you think that Great Britain and the United States—the United States, the most powerful state in the world—will permit you to break their line of communication in the Mediterranean? Nonsense. And we have no navy. The uprising in Greece must be stopped, and as quickly as possible.' [12]

Ever since 1944 the Russian empire had been extending itself westward with spectacular rapidity. On the southern front Bulgaria had fallen, Yugoslavia had fallen, Albania had fallen. No one in the West could know that Greece would not fall in its turn, and then Italy. By 1948 the general view in the West was that, in accordance with Communist ideology, Stalin had the domination of the entire world as his goal. In fact, as we now know, the forces under his leadership were going beyond where he wanted them to go. They were being drawn into the power vacuum to a greater extent than he wanted. He was not altogether in control of the situation. No statesman ever is.

*   *   *

The eastern part of Austria, including Vienna, fell to the Russian empire at the end of the War by a sequence of events similar to that which resulted in the Russian capture of the eastern part of Germany. No one could know, in the following months and years, that the rest of Austria would not be drawn into the empire as well. And it seemed not unlikely, by the winter of 1947–1948, that the Communists would capture power in Italy and France. This could well have happened even without Stalin wishing it—although in that day the possibility of his not wishing it was hardly conceivable.

[12] Djilas, p. 164.

In Italy and France alike, the Communists had been out-
standingly effective in the wartime resistance movements. Consequently, at the end of the War their credit was high and their
political strength massive.

In Italy they emerged as one of the three strongest political
parties, the Christian Democrats and the Socialists being the other
two. From Moscow's point of view this ostensible strength may
have seemed less than reliable. In 1945, for example, one of the
intellectual leaders of the Italian Communist Party publicly
expressed his contempt for the basic Marxist doctrine of dialectical
materialism, and it appears to have been common for Italians
who voted Communist to attend mass like everyone else, and to
submit themselves to the authority of the parish priest. From
the point of view of the West, however, the Communist strength in
Italy appeared as Russian strength, and the threat of a Communist
electoral victory appeared as the threat of Stalin's rule in Rome.
Consequently, there was increasing alarm as the Communist
membership rose.[13]

As everywhere in eastern Europe at this time, the Italian Communists were entirely ready to enter into coalitions and into coalition governments. In Italy they found an ally in the Socialists,
one of the other two parties. Although some of the Socialists split
off from their Party rather than stomach the association, this
partnership still promised to bring the Communists into supreme
power. They already had prominent places in the coalition
governments of the day. In the first Government of the new
Italian Republic, which took office in July 1946, they held four
Cabinet posts: Justice, Finance, Transport, and Postwar Relief.
The Socialists who had entered into partnership with them
obtained the Ministry of Foreign Affairs in addition to three other
posts. Under the circumstances, it did not appear implausible to
alarmed observers in the West that what was happening in
Rumania, in Bulgaria, in Hungary, in Yugoslavia, and in
Albania, and what was yet to happen in Czechoslovakia, would
happen in Italy as well.

The situation in France was not essentially different. 'The
rumours persistently circulating for months after the liberation
about an impending Communist coup,' Viscount Chilston has
written, 'might have become a reality had it not better suited the

[13] It was 1,762,056 in December 1945. Six months later it was 2,125,000. This made
the Italian Communist Party the largest in the world outside Russia.

Communist book to temporize.'[14] The membership of the French Communist Party rose from 385,000 in 1944 to one million a year later, and in the elections of October 1945 it came out first among the French political parties. It was now the strongest party in France. In the first Cabinet under the Fourth Republic, which took office in January 1947, the Communists, in addition to holding a Vice-Premiership, held the Ministry of National Defense and three other posts. This was alarming.

Meanwhile, in France and Italy economic and social breakdown appeared as an increasingly imminent possibility. In the terrible winter of 1946–1947 all western Europe, including the British Isles, was balanced on the brink of collapse. Anarchy impended, and no one could doubt that it would result in a Communist take-over.

It was this imminent and frightening prospect, in the context of Russian expansion, that finally drew the United States back across the gulf of the Atlantic to the European continent. It was this that drew it back into the vacuum from which it had expected to withdraw completely. By returning, however, it would finally collide with the Russian empire, which was being drawn ever farther into that same vacuum. So the Cold War would be joined.

[14] Toynbee, 1955, p. 486.

CHAPTER X

The defeat of Japan and the expansion of Russia in the Far East

THE collapse of Hitler's Nazi state, with what remained of its military apparatus, finally occurred in the first week of May 1945. So the War in Europe came to an end amid the far-flung ruins of a society so recently mighty.

By this time Japan's defeat was also assured. The only questions remaining were those of what military action was necessary to seal it, and how it should then be registered in a Japanese act of submission. The postwar world was coming upon the victors before they were ready for it.

By the spring and summer of 1945 the Japanese, who had so recently spread their power far over the Pacific and far over eastern Asia, had been beaten back and were increasingly in disarray. In their home islands they were now dissevered from their remaining forces overseas. The overseas communications on which they depended for their food supplies had been cut, and no food was coming in. They were at the point of helplessness, unable to feed themselves, unable to defend themselves against the attacking Anglo-American forces that now surrounded and bore in upon their home islands. Their industrial production had virtually stopped, their industrial areas having been smashed. Harbors and channels had been closed by mines. Anti-aircraft defenses were no more. The fire-control services, required to put out fires after incendiary air-raids, had virtually stopped operating. Over eight million Japanese were homeless, and the number was increasing every day. Manifestly, this was the end. It remained but to go through the forms of surrender.

During July 1945, according to the official report of the American Chief of Staff, 'Fighters from Iwo Jima swept the air over the Japanese islands, strafed Japanese dromes and communications and gave the superbombers freedom of operation. The Third Fleet augmented by British units hammered Japan with its planes and guns, sailing boldly into Japanese coastal waters. The warships repeatedly and effectively shelled industries along the coasts. These mighty attacks met little opposition.'[1]

By the summer of 1945, then, the Japanese had virtually stopped defending themselves because they no longer had the means to defend themselves. In the face of a demand by their opponents for an unconditional surrender that, to their minds, implied unthinkable consequences, they were nevertheless trying to put themselves in a position to sue for peace and for mercy. This required the replacement of Prime Minister Hideki Tojo's warmaking regime, which had been responsible for the attack on Pearl Harbor, by a regime with which the Western powers would feel they could treat.

Accordingly, as early as June 1944, General Tojo was replaced by General Kuniaki Koiso, whose new Government, abandoning all hope of victory, proceeded to address itself to the objective of a negotiated peace that would save whatever was still salvageable. Koiso's lack of success and the catastrophic deterioration of the military position led to his replacement by the aged Baron Suzuki, a moderate man acceptable to the party that favored concluding peace. His new Cabinet was composed, in large measure, of what had been the moderate opposition to the extremist war policy.

So, even by the fall of 1944, the militaristic fire-eaters who had brought Japan to such a pass were being discredited. They were being replaced by the moderates who had hitherto had to stand aside.

Although the defeat of Japan could no longer be in question, the war continued still because those in the positions of command could not find the levers by which to bring it to a halt. A confused and exhausted statesmanship did not know how to arrest the self-continuing destruction and take a new course. The Anglo-American powers kept up their assaults because the order had been given long before and the commitment not to negotiate a peace with any Japanese regime at all seemed to leave them without an alternative. They had committed themselves to the doctrine that Japan, like Germany and Italy, was an 'aggressor nation' by nature, irrespective of the regime that governed it at any particular time, and that its power had therefore to be totally eliminated for an indefinite future as a pre-condition of peace in

---

[1] Marshall, p. 243.

the world. No compromise might be considered, no terms might be negotiated. All the indications in the winter of 1944-1945 that the Japanese were prepared to negotiate a peace, and the approaches they attempted to the Anglo-American powers, were disregarded. The Anglo-American powers remained on the course they had taken at an earlier stage, a course directed at the objective of smashing Japan rather than make a peace. Their objective was the power vacuum, to the east as to the west of the Soviet Union (which in the official mythology of the day was a 'peace-loving nation' like the United States and Britain). By now, no less in the East than in the West, the government of circumstances had long ago taken over from the government of men.

There were in the West men of great standing who, as individuals, had not been altogether misled by the official rhetoric and mythology of wartime. One was the American Secretary of the Navy, James Forrestal; another was the Secretary of War, Henry Stimson; another Joseph Grew, former American Ambassador to Tokyo and now Undersecretary of State. They raised their voices in the final stages of the War, when the atomic bomb and the Russian forces alike had already been loosed against the Japanese, but not earlier. For the whole conception represented by the doctrine of unconditional surrender had, itself, never been at issue. It had never been open to debate or discussion. The President had proclaimed it and his subordinates had had no occasion, even if they had had the inclination, to challenge it. After 1942 it was simply too late to question the mythic doctrine on the basis of which the grand strategy of the war was being conducted.

Only at last, when all else was ruin, did these few statesmen raise their voices in favor of the one concession that enabled the Japanese to make their act of submission without implicating themselves in what would, in their eyes, have been a sacrilege: the offering up of their Emperor to the mercy or the vengeance of the victors. The American moderates, among whom General Douglas MacArthur must be honorably listed for the occasion, were moved by practical considerations as well as by the scruples of civilized men. They were not unmindful of the fact that the authority of the Emperor would be indispensable to them in the occupation and pacification of Japan. They raised their voices now, when all else that might have been saved had already been lost, and so in the final days they saved from the wreckage of Japan the central principle of authority on the basis of which its reconstitution could be undertaken. The Japanese were permitted to make their unconditional surrender conditional on the safety of their Emperor.

In terms of reason there is no accounting for the fact that the Western allies, even as late as the spring and summer of 1945, anticipated that the defeat of Japan, which in fact remained only to be formalized, would still cost a long effort and sacrifices of a magnitude hard to contemplate. 'General Marshall told me,' President Truman later reported, 'that it might cost one half million lives to force the enemy's surrender on his home ground.' According to Secretary Stimson, the information given him was that American forces alone might suffer a million casualties.[2]

It is against this background that we must see the anxiety of the Anglo-American allies, in 1944 and 1945, to bring the Russians into the war against Japan. Just as there had been fear that the Russians would stop their pursuit of Hitler's forces when they had driven them from Russian territory, leaving the Western allies to carry the whole burden of fighting them from that point on, so there was fear that the Russians, even after the defeat of Germany, would leave the Western allies to carry the whole burden of defeating the Japanese in Manchuria, in China, and in Korea, as well as in the Pacific islands.

From an early stage, then, the United States pressed Stalin for a commitment to come into the War against Japan (with which Russia had concluded a treaty of neutrality in April 1941). Because his armed forces were already too fully occupied in Europe, he had long resisted this pressure. At last, however, in October 1943, he caused rejoicing in Washington by telling Secretary of State Hull that, 'when the Allies succeeded in defeating Germany, the Soviet Union would then join in defeating

---

[2] Truman, p. 417, and Feis, 1961, p. 12. What was foreseen was an invasion of the Japanese home islands followed by combat for every square mile of Japanese soil. The fanaticism of the 'aggressor' people, it was held, precluded their unconditional surrender otherwise. The fact that even the most extreme fanatics have to eat appears not to have been considered. Perhaps a proposal of simple blockade (including internal blockade by the bombing of internal communications) would have been regarded, in the atmosphere of the day, as the manifestation of an insufficiently offensive spirit. Moreover, because the patience of the allied peoples had already been so tried by the years of wartime sacrifice, there was an atmosphere of urgency, a universal assumption that victory must be achieved in the shortest possible time. The starvation of the Japanese, even if these mythical creatures were capable of starvation, might have seemed too long a process.

Japan.'[3] The fact that he made no conditions for this commitment seemed, in the circumstances of the day, magnanimous.

The matter was discussed further between Roosevelt, Churchill, and Stalin at Teheran the following month, and there appears to have been informal agreement on the concession to Russia, after the War, of the Kurile Islands, half of Sakhalin, and privileges in the port of Dairen. It is evident from the entire record, to the extent that it is available, that Stalin at this time was not notably intent on territorial aggrandizement in the Far East and that neither Roosevelt nor Churchill were worried by such a prospect. Here, and at this stage, all was amicable. For almost a year after, however, there was anxiety in the Western capitals at Stalin's unwillingness to concert military plans for the defeat of Japan when the time came for the Russians to take part in it. At last, in October 1944, discussions of a common strategy were begun and an understanding was reached that the Russian forces would be ready to fight Japan some three months after the defeat of Germany. To the gratification of Washington, it now transpired that the Russians were willing to undertake even wider operations in the Far East than had been hoped. When they indicated, now for the first time, that they would expect some reward for such undertakings, in the postwar settlements for the Far East, there was no alarm.

Nations generally fight only one war at a time. In October 1944 the United States was still fighting the War that had not yet ended. It was not yet fighting the War that had not yet begun. 'Sufficient unto the day is the evil thereof.' A fierce and exclusive concentration on the evil of the day was especially characteristic of the United States in the Far East, where its anxiety over the imagined magnitude of the military task reflected an almost neurotic exaggeration of the unhuman Japanese capacity to keep on fighting when there was nothing left to fight with. One who lived through those days in Washington recalls how everyone in the intragovernmental competition for place and influence was concerned to show that he, at least, was not so weak-minded as to underestimate the satanic enemy or to be 'soft' on him. In this atmosphere, anyone who took seriously rumours or reports that the enemy was ready to quit, however much he might pretend that he was, discredited himself. Anyone who suggested charity

[3] Hull, p. 1309, cited by Feis, 1957, p. 234.

toward the Japanese nation, now that it could no longer ward off the overwhelming blows that were being rained upon it, showed himself lacking in the toughness that the conduct of war requires. And if anyone anticipated that the Japanese might shortly be the allies of the United States, their strength an asset rather than a liability, he kept his thoughts in the secret compartment of the mind to which all embarrassing thoughts must be relegated for the sake of outward respectability.

So the whole situation was misconceived, and errors of judgment were committed that would, in retrospect, seem inexplicable. President Truman, who replaced President Roosevelt only in the middle of April 1945, had his misgivings; but he had not yet acquired the mastery of his job that might have enabled him to override the advice of the seasoned counselors whom he had inherited and who surrounded him. In any case, it was too late for him to salvage anything from the situation except the symbol of the Emperor.

I make one possible exception to this. It is conceivable that in mid-April it was not too late, yet, to spare the men, women, and children of Hiroshima and Nagasaki.

The atomic bomb had not figured as an element in the planning of those who contemplated what would be required to bring the Japanese to unconditional surrender. This was simply because it had not been invented. The successful test of a prototype, which marked the date of its invention, did not come until July 16.

In the minds of those who directed the vast enterprise by which the atomic bomb was invented it had been thought of chiefly for use against Germany. Produced in time, it would have served as an alternative to the allied landings in Normandy, and to the great ensuing campaign of so many millions of men, from West and East alike, until they met in the heart of Germany. Coming too late for that purpose, it was welcomed instead as an alternative to the invasion of the Japanese home islands at a cost in American and British lives that haunted the allied planners.

In a sense it came too late for use against Japan too, since Japan was already beaten. This was not, however, as the men of the time saw it, and so the announcement of the successful explosion in New Mexico came to them as a cause of relief and rejoicing. It would be used, now, to save the lives and the human suffering that otherwise would be entailed in an agonizing prolongation of the War.

It is evident today that in these last months of the War the whole basis of allied strategic thinking, the fundamental assumptions on which it rested, had shifted away from reality. Everyone was too engrossed with the mythological specters that come to dominate the mind in wartime, too battered by pressures endured too long, too exhausted from the interminable ordeal, for a fresh view of the situation. Statesmanship, now, had at last been drawn down to the point of disappearance. So it was, as Churchill later reported in his memoirs, 'that the decision whether or not to use the atomic bomb to compel the surrender of Japan was never even an issue. There was unanimous, automatic, unquestioned agreeement around our table; nor did I ever hear the slightest suggestion that we should do otherwise.'[4]

Moved by a good intention, the statesmen gathered at Potsdam issued, on July 26, what was meant to be a warning to the Japanese, in the interests of humanitarianism, of what was in store for them if they delayed their unconditional surrender. But it was couched in the conventional rhetoric of wartime oratory, so that today one must wonder how anyone could have expected the Japanese to read it as anything except another item of daily bombast.[5]

Nevertheless, the Japanese were trying to have the War brought to an end, and they were trying to communicate with the allies for that purpose. Communication, however, has often been peculiarly difficult for the Japanese, whether as a matter of linguistic

[4] Churchill, 1953, p. 639. 'Up to this moment,' Churchill reported (p. 638), 'we had shaped our ideas towards an assault upon the homeland of Japan . . . by the invasion of very large armies. We had contemplated the desperate resistance of the Japanese fighting to the death with Samurai devotion, not only in pitched battles, but in every cave and dugout. . . . To quell the Japanese resistance man by man and conquer the country yard by yard might well require the loss of a million American lives and half that number of British. . . . Now all this nightmare picture had vanished. In its place was the vision—fair and bright it seemed—of the end of the whole war in one or two violent shocks.' If the Japanese ability to communicate had been greater the allied leaders would have known that 'this nightmare picture' was false. There were those in the councils of the great at this time who later reported that they had opposed the use of the atomic weapon against Japan, but they must have done so *sotto voce*. Because governments operate by consensus, it takes great arrogance as well as a reckless courage for anyone involved in the process of government to go against a consensus that has already formed.

[5] The alternative to unconditional surrender, said the *Potsdam Declaration*, 'is prompt and utter destruction.' By these few words, it was thought, the Japanese had been given a warning of the atomic bomb that made the decision to use it on their cities a choice made by them in rejecting the alternative!

formation or of a psychological inhibition that manifests itself in national reticence. They, too, were distraught in these days, and now they simply missed their footing in the delicate diplomacy that the situation required.[6]

The Governments of the Western alliance, having given the warning that was no warning, and having received from the Japanese Government a rejection that had not been intended as a rejection, the former now gave orders to the military commanders that set in motion a sort of automatic process, not closely guided or managed. This process did not end until the entire stockpile of two bombs, then available, had been expended in blowing apart, not one city only, but two cities. The second bomb fell and the second city was destroyed simply because, the process having begun, continued, and the machinery of the Japanese Government did not move fast enough in proclaiming the unconditional surrender that had become unavoidable.

I have given this much account of the circumstances that led to the actual employment of the atomic bomb in action because, in ways that defy definition, this terminal resort to its use created the psychological atmosphere of the postwar world upon which the nations now looked out as the smoke cleared away from the ruins. This was a somber victory.

In the world that now emerged, two facts dominated. One was the expansion of the Russian empire, which spread around the globe from the Elbe River to the Sea of Japan. The other was the atomic bomb. It is hard to believe that the fearful brooding presence of the bomb over this postwar scene would have been the same if its possibilities had not been so catastrophically demonstrated in bringing World War II to its belated conclusion. One despairs, today, of evoking, for a generation that did not experience it, the hopelessness with which this instrument of abrupt annihilation seemed to invest the future of the world, in that hour of what might otherwise have been celebrated as a glorious victory.

*   *   *

On August 6, 1945, the first of the two atomic bombs obliterated Hiroshima. On August 8 Moscow, apparently acting in haste and

[6] See, for example, Feis, 1961, pp. 97–8. This book gives a fuller account of these matters than would be appropriate here.

ahead of its planned schedule, declared war on Japan, and the Red Army advanced into Manchuria. On August 9 the second bomb fell on Nagasaki. On August 10 Japan announced its readiness to surrender. On August 14 the terms of surrender were agreed upon and the War was over.

At the Yalta Conference in February Stalin had confronted Roosevelt with certain 'Political Conditions for Russia's Entry into the War against Japan.' These included new conditions beyond those included in the informal understandings reached at Teheran a year earlier, exemplifying in this the Russian device of trying at every stage of negotiation to go beyond what had already been agreed upon, and they showed scant respect for the Chinese sovereignty of which the United States for half a century had made itself the protector. But Roosevelt, who by now was nearer his death than anyone dared allow himself to believe, was not disposed to resist; and a Churchill who was acting more and more like a sleep-walker signed what Roosevelt, his unquestioned leader in the Far Eastern enterprise, had seen fit to accept. One war at a time was enough for the exhausted vitality of these two severely pressed men; neither had strength left to address himself to the future Cold War while the present hot war remained, as each thought, so far from finished.

Add to this that, as it then seemed, Stalin could get even more than what he claimed without the need of any agreement by Roosevelt or Churchill. With respect to China he asked, in effect, for control of the Manchurian Railway and of two Manchurian ports on the Yellow Sea: Dairen and Port Arthur. Since, however, there was civil war in China between the ruling Nationalists and the challenging Communists, all Stalin had to do, it was thought, was to support the Communists in order to gain far more than what he was claiming.

Those who have been concerned to explain the weakness of the Western statesmen at Yalta, in these matters, have pointed out that Russia would surely have entered the war against Japan even without Western encouragement, and that in the absence of the Yalta agreement it would not have felt more inhibited in the claims it made for postwar compensation out of such Japanese and Chinese territory as lay under its hand. One may accept this as true, regretting only the subscription of the United States and Britain to an unnecessary intervention followed by unjustifiable rewards. But we are wise after the event; and it remains true, in any case, that the weakness of Western statesmanship at this time is essentially irrelevant to the fact of Soviet expansion.[7]

Addressing the House of Commons after the Yalta Conference, Churchill declared: 'It is a mistake to look too far ahead. Only one link in the chain of destiny can be handled at a time.'

Near the beginning of his wartime leadership, in a tribute to his fallen predecessor, Neville Chamberlain, delivered in the House of Commons on November 12, 1940, three days after Chamberlain's death, he had also said:

It is not given to human beings, happily for them, for otherwise life would be intolerable, to foresee or to predict to any large extent the unfolding course of events. In one phase men seem to have been right, in another they seem to have been wrong. Then again, a few years later, when the perspective of time has lengthened, all stands in a different setting. There is a new proportion. There is another scale of values. History with its flickering lamp stumbles along the trail of the past, trying to reconstruct its scenes, to revive its echoes, and kindle with pale gleams the passion of former days. What is the worth of all this? The only guide to a man is his conscience; the only shield to his memory is the rectitude and sincerity of his actions. It is very imprudent to walk through life without this shield, because we are so often mocked by the failure of our hopes and the upsetting of our calculations; but with this shield, however the fates may play, we march always in the ranks of honour.

When the War came to its final end the Red Army had spilled out beyond the borders of the existing Russian empire to occupy Manchuria, and also Korea from the Manchurian border to the 38th parallel, which would soon become a front in the Cold War. The Kurile Islands and the southern half of Sakhalin Island, taken from Japan, had been added to that empire, which was now separated from the Japanese home island only by the twenty-five-mile breadth of the Soya Strait.

The War had stopped at last. Over the world that was left towered the new Russian empire and the atomic bomb.

[7] I suspect that, at this time, Stalin too was improvising his moves without studied forethought to a greater extent than we commonly think. Although his view may have reached further into the future than Roosevelt's or Churchill's, he too was, for the most part, fighting one war at a time. This, to take an example, is the impression given by the tenor of his conversation with Roosevelt of February 8, for which see Feis, 1957, p. 518.

CHAPTER XI

The United States in search of a workable foreign policy

THE process of Russian expansion did not come to an end with the termination of hostilities against Germany and Japan. As we have seen, it continued through what remained of 1945, through 1946 and 1947, and into 1948. The immediate threat that it appeared to pose was not limited to the as-yet-unconquered part of Europe, to the Mediterranean highway, or to the Far East. In Iran a particularly wanton course of political and military aggression appeared to threaten the entire Middle East and India.

By the terms of an Anglo-Russian-Iranian Treaty of 1942, Russian military forces had been stationed in northern Iran for the duration of the War, to be withdrawn within six months of the conclusion of hostilities. In the fall of 1945, after hostilities were over and as the date for withdrawal approached, these forces proceeded to foment and support a separatist movement in northern Iran that was patently aimed at bringing the area into the Soviet structure. At the same time they blocked the way of Iranian Army units dispatched by the Government in Teheran to quell the movement. This was as if the American forces in Britain had organized and armed a Scottish separatist movement, and had then barred the way to troops dispatched by the London Government for the purpose of putting it down.

One suspects that, as in Poland in 1920, as in Finland in 1939, the high priests of the Communist movement in Moscow had been led by their own scriptures to take an excessively optimistic view of the ease with which the Marxist revolution could be set off in foreign countries. As had been the case with the Poles and the Finns, however, the Iranians resisted. The Treaty deadline of March 2, 1946, for the withdrawal of the Russian troops approached, and as yet the separatist movement had not succeeded. On March 1, then, Moscow announced that it would continue to keep troops in Iran beyond the deadline, 'pending clarification of the situation.' The Iranian Government appealed to the Security Council of the United Nations. The Russians, confronted by failure and extreme public embarrassment, at last accepted defeat and withdrew their forces from Iran.

Although the attempted aggression had failed, the nakedness of the display alarmed those who were committed to a postwar organization of international relations that depended on acceptance by the Soviet Union of the 'peace-loving' role in which it had been cast for the purpose of defeating the 'aggressor nations' of the Axis.

The importance of what happens in history is judged by its ultimate success or failure, which is known to hindsight. For those who live at the time, however, it is not known, and therefore another order of importance prevails. The aggression against Iran had an importance in early 1946 that, because of its ultimate failure, would fade from the historical record. To recapture the atmosphere of the time, however, with all its anxiety, we must recall the profound fear for Iran, for the Middle East, for the Mediterranean, and for western Europe that was felt by those who had for so long looked forward to the establishment of a peaceful world order when the 'aggressor nations' should at last have been overcome and disarmed by the 'peace-loving nations.'

* * *

Today, seeing so clearly the relationship of the postwar power vacuums to Russian expansion, we can see that the United States should have postponed the demobilization of its armed forces until the international arrangements of the postwar world had been completed. President Truman and the Administration over which he presided saw it hardly less clearly at the time.[1] In their public statements and Congressional testimony they were explicit about it, although confining themselves to general terms and avoiding such references to Russia as would have made the negotiations of the day more difficult.

The Administration was quite without choice, however, in the matter of demobilization. From the moment the fighting ended, Washington was overwhelmed by the virtually unanimous and impassioned demand of the American people that the

[1] E.g., reporting the anxiety of the State Department in a dispatch to *The New York Times*, September 23, 1945, Samuel A. Tower wrote: 'The effectiveness of the Department of State, now engaged in developing negotiations and policies in Europe and the Pacific, hinges on the might this country is prepared to throw behind it, hence its concern over an ill-considered dissipation of our power.'

soldiers be returned to their homes and their normal civilian lives immediately. If the Administration did not accede completely to this demand, the Congress was prepared to take matters into its own hands. There really was no choice. The question was not one of whether but of how—how to provide the administrative procedures and transportation to discharge some twelve million men and restore them to their homes forthwith. President Truman and General Marshall, the Chief of Staff, found themselves compelled to promise that 'the men are coming back home, and coming as fast as the services can get them out.' Both were constrained to give the strange assurance, in response to excited criticism, that 'there has been no relationship whatsoever between the rate of demobilization and any future plans of the Army.'

The Administration knew the danger of demobilization before a peace-settlement, and was not silent about it, but the practical problem with which it was now faced was that of how to provide even enough troops for the occupation of Japan and of the American zones in Germany and Austria. The answer was, in principle, simple. If all the wartime forces were to be discharged, then new forces would have to be provided chiefly out of the generation that had just reached the age for military service.

In his Message to Congress of January 6, 1947, the President said that by July the Army would be reduced to 1,070,000 men (he did not here forecast the fact that by 1948 the active Army would consist of only 554,030 men). At these reduced levels, he observed, serious difficulties were being experienced in maintaining the American occupation forces. Under the circumstances there are wistful connotations to his statement, in the same Message, that 'we live in a world in which strength on the part of peace-loving nations is still the greatest deterrent to aggression.'

The Russian Government, presiding over a population upon which it enforced obedience, did not reduce its armed forces, in the postwar period, below a figure of between five and six million men. We may suppose that these were for the most part battle-hardened troops. The American postwar forces, by contrast, were largely composed of newly inducted, inexperienced boys who would need more training and hardening, before they were ready for combat, than they were likely to get in the limited period for which they were required to serve.

All these facts become understandable when we recall that the United States, from 1945 to 1947, was not yet out from under the sway of its long isolationist tradition. Just as its intervention of 1917 to 1919 in the power politics of the Old World had appeared as only a temporary departure from that tradition, so the renewed involvement that began with the attack on Pearl Harbor was widely regarded as temporary. President Roosevelt was making a sound judgment, in terms of the situation as it then existed, when he foretold at Yalta in February 1945 that the American people would not agree to keep American troops in Europe for much more than two years after the end of hostilities. With the conclusion of the War, the American people simply assumed that the time had at last come to return to what it considered normal.

It was soon to learn that what has been normal in the past is never quite applicable to the present and may be altogether inapplicable to the future.

From the summer of 1945 to the spring of 1947 was a period of uncertainty for the American people and its Government. It began with the official assumption that the new international organization, based on unanimity among the five great 'peace-loving' powers, would henceforth maintain a peaceful world order from which power-politics—including such devices as the balance of power and spheres of influence—had been banished. The vision, which went back a long way in American history, was of a Jeffersonian organization of all mankind.

Even by the end of the War, however, when this period began, it had already become evident to Americans that the realization of this vision would not be immediate. At least for the time being, then, the official foreign policy that had been projected for the postwar world could not be made to work. What this meant was that, for the moment, the United States was without a workable foreign policy. It was, to be specific, without a workable foreign policy until the spring of 1947.

What was required in the first instance, for the replacement of the projected foreign policy by a policy applicable to the developing circumstances, was a conscious recognition of the realities to which it would have to be applicable. The American Government and the American people would have to dismiss from their minds and banish from the logic of their language the concept that nations were divided between an 'aggressor' and a 'peace-loving' species, of which the former was represented by Germany and Japan (if not also by Italy), while the latter was represented by Russia. They would then have to accept the need to re-establish a balance of power by filling the remaining power vacuums and thereby limiting the further expansion of the Russian empire. Such a conceptual change as this, while it might take place more rapidly in the subconscious mind, could hardly be explicitly formulated and adopted as such until after an interval of intellectual confusion and inner conflict, during which some persons would continue to adhere with a sort of blind desperation to the outdated concepts and their attendant language, while others would recognize the increasingly manifest realities without being able to find a coherent intellectual pattern or forms of words into which to fit them.[2]

*   *   *

One who was there may permit himself to recall some items in the eventful process by which a new intellectual pattern and a new form of words were brought forward and implanted in the American mind.

On March 5, 1946, four days after Moscow had announced its intention of keeping its troops in Iran, whatever agreements it had made to the contrary, the most famous public figure of the day, having traveled from England to Fulton, Missouri, there delivered a formal address in the presence and under the auspices of the President of the United States, although his retirement from public office by the British electorate a year earlier meant that he spoke in a private capacity. It is significant of the atmosphere which still prevailed at this date that Mr. Winston Churchill caused widespread shock in the United States by uttering, in the presence of the President—who must have had advance knowledge of what he would say and who was therefore implicated—what everyone had had in his mind but had hitherto hesitated to proclaim in public. These were the words that then seemed so indiscreet, however true:

A shadow has fallen upon the scenes so lately lighted by the Allied victory. Nobody knows what Soviet Russia and its Communist international organization intends to do in the immediate future, or what are the limits, if any, to their expansive and proselytising tendencies. . . . From Stettin in the Baltic to Trieste in the Adriatic, an iron curtain

---

[2] The tragedy of those who adhered to the obsolete concepts is most notably exemplified by Mr. Henry Wallace, the former Vice-President under Roosevelt, whose long and distinguished career now ended in a sort of public disgrace. The need for forms of words is central, exemplified up to 1945 by such terms as 'peace-loving' and 'aggressor', later by 'containment.'

has descended across the Continent. Behind that line lie all the capitals of the ancient states of Central and Eastern Europe. Warsaw, Berlin, Prague, Vienna, Budapest, Belgrade, Bucharest and Sofia, all these famous cities and the populations around them lie in what I must call the Soviet sphere, and all are subject in one form or another, not only to Soviet influence but to a very high and, in many cases, increasing measure of control from Moscow. . . . Whatever conclusions may be drawn from these facts—and facts they are—this is certainly not the Liberated Europe we fought to build up. Nor is it one which contains the essentials of permanent peace.

Mr. Churchill went on to say: 'From what I have seen of our Russian friends and Allies during the war, I am convinced that there is nothing they admire so much as strength, and there is nothing for which they have less respect than for weakness, especially military weakness.'

This speech shocked the public in part because of its direct reference, in such blunt terms, to Russia by name. The one item that appeared to produce the greatest shock of disapproval, however, was the use, here for the first time, of the term 'iron curtain.' In a matter of months this term would be an accepted part of everyone's vocabulary, for the American mind was now changing fast. Those who responded with initial disapproval would shortly be using it themselves.

*　　*　　*

The lack of a conceptual scheme for appreciating the postwar situation, and of a formulated policy for dealing with it, was most seriously felt in the State Department, which had the responsibility of advising the President on the situation and of dealing with it under his direction.

To put ourselves back in these times we must recall that in 1945 and 1946, by contrast with what was to come, there had as yet been almost no development of Russian studies in the United States. The sophistication of a later day was, as yet, lacking. The institutes of Russian studies that were to proliferate on American campuses in the late nineteen-forties had not yet been founded. Experts in the Russian language, in Russian history, in Russian society, or in Russian doctrine were not readily to be found within the borders of the United States.

The deficiency that this represented was in part the consequence of the fact that until 1933 we had not recognized nor entered into official relations with the Soviet Union. In the late 1920's, however, certain Foreign Service Officers in the State Department had the foresight to bethink themselves of the need that would arise if the day came when the United States did find itself involved in relations with Russia.[3] Consequently, certain younger officers were selected for two years of intensive training in the Russian language and in the general background of Russian affairs. Two were assigned to receive this training in each of four successive years, after which budgetary reductions put an end to the program. Of the eight young officers put through this training, two would later serve as American Ambassador in Moscow. They were Messrs. George F. Kennan and Charles E. Bohlen.

In February 1946, when Mr. Kennan was deputy chief of mission at the American Embassy in Moscow, he sent the State Department a paper, sixteen pages long, in which he undertook to analyze and explain Moscow's international behavior, to suggest the behavior that was to be expected of it in the future, and to draw certain conclusions for the consequent formulation of American foreign policy.

Able analyses of international situations by officers in the field had been received in the State Department before this, and have been since. For the most part they are lost in the floods of paper that deluge the Department and submerge its staff every day. The timing of Mr. Kennan's communication, however, was strategic. It came at a moment when the Department, having been separated by circumstances from the wartime policy toward Russia, was floundering about, looking for new intellectual moorings. Now, in this communication, it was offered a new and realistic conception to which it might attach itself. The reaction was immediate and positive. There was a universal feeling that 'this was it,' this was the appreciation of the situation that had been needed. Mr. Kennan's communication was reproduced for distribution to all the officers of the Department (so that even one who was exclusively concerned with Latin American affairs at the time received his copy). We may not doubt that it made its effect on the President. It was communicated to the War and Navy Departments as well.

[3] The two officers who appear to have taken the principal initiative were G. Howland Shaw and Robert F. Kelley. I am indebted for the information on it that I give here to Mr. Kelley and to Mr. Reginald Kazanjian, who as a Foreign Service Officer was close to these matters at the time.

This document presented the picture of a Soviet governing regime, with absolute mastery over the Russian society, swayed by an unreasonable but neurotically powerful hostility to the world beyond the area of its control. Marxism is merely the 'fig leaf of . . . moral and intellectual respectability' that covers the nakedness of a policy that is brutally cruel, disingenuous, and unlimited by any scruples. This regime, by its own attitude and devices, is virtually insulated against knowledge of the outside world that does not support its mythical preconceptions. It works to undermine and destroy the world that it regards as representing 'capitalist encirclement,' and does so on two planes: the official plane of overt governmental activity and the 'subterranean plane of actions undertaken by agencies for which the Soviet government does not admit responsibility.'

The governing power of the Soviet Union is not, however, schematic or adventuristic. Impervious to the logic of reason, it is highly sensitive to the logic of force. Its success as a form of internal power 'is not yet finally proven.' The supreme test will be its power to survive such crises as were caused by Lenin's death and will be caused, again, by Stalin's passing. In the absence of a genuinely popular allegiance to the doctrines in which it clothes itself, its internal system is bound to be strained by 'recent territorial expansions.'

The American response, said Mr. Kennan, must be in the first instance to achieve an understanding of Russian realities and to communicate that understanding to the American public. Then our American society must look to its own inner soundness and the presentation to other nations of 'a much more positive and constructive picture of the sort of world we would like to see than we have put forward in the past.'

In urging that an understanding of the realities be communicated to the American public, Mr. Kennan wrote: 'I am convinced that there would be far less hysterical anti-Sovietism in our country today if the realities . . . were better understood by our people.' The paper ends with a warning: 'the greatest danger that can befall us in coping with this problem of Soviet Communism is that we shall allow ourselves to become like those with whom we are coping.'

From this notable document, composed at the same time as Churchill's Fulton Address, dates the formulation of a new American and Western policy to meet the brand new threat and challenge that finally stood revealed when the smoke of war had cleared away. Mr. Kennan was brought back to Washington where, in the following year, he would organize and head the Policy Planning Staff in the Office of the Secretary of State.

One more document deserves special mention in this chronicle. Mr. Kennan was to have the leading role, under the authority of the Government he served, in carrying out his own recommendation that an understanding of the realities by which American policy was challenged be communicated to the American public. The principal device by which this was accomplished was an article in the quarterly, *Foreign Affairs*, which appeared in its issue of July 1947. Its title was 'The Sources of Soviet Conduct' and it bore, in place of an author's name, the letter 'X'. Since this article represented the newly formulated position of the United States Government, it would have been self-defeating to put it forward simply as the thought of one man, even if the discipline of the career service had not limited the public expression of personal views by its members.

The impact of the article on the American public, and even in larger spheres, was a counterpart of the impact that the communication from Moscow had had in the State Department. It met, among the members of the public, the same need that the earlier document had met among the members of the Government. From the beginning its authoritative character was known, and there was no point to trying to keep secret the name of its author, which now for the first time sprang into public prominence. It represented, in the broadest terms, the formulated policy of the United States for the postwar world, thereby bringing to an end the period of transition and uncertainty that had begun with the winter of 1944–1945.

The principal addition that this document made to the earlier communication from Moscow was a word and a concept. The word was 'containment.' 'It is clear,' the text read, 'that the main element of any United States policy toward the Soviet Union must be that of a long-term, patient but firm and vigilant containment of Russian expansive tendencies. . . . Soviet pressure against the free institutions of the Western world is something that can be contained by the adroit and vigilant application of counter-force at a series of constantly shifting geographical and political points. . . .' This was followed by the prediction that, if containment were effectively applied 'over a period of ten or fifteen

years' (i.e. until 1957–1962), the result might be a radical modification of the Russian threat as it then existed.

The peroration is worth quoting in conclusion:

> Surely, there was never a fairer test of national quality than this.
> In the light of these circumstances, the thoughtful observer of Russian–
> American relations will find no cause for complaint in the Kremlin's
> challenge to American society. He will rather experience a certain
> gratitude to a Providence which, by providing the American people
> with this implacable challenge, has made their entire security as a
> nation dependent on their pulling themselves together and accepting
> the responsibilities of moral and political leadership that history plainly
> intended them to bear.

It is not amiss to note that the new conception by which American and Western policy was henceforth to be guided represented a
notably higher level of the mind than had the preceding conception of a world divided between 'aggressor' and 'peace-loving'
nations. The American society was rising to the occasion. The only
question was whether it would hold to such a high level. There
were moments in the years to come when no one could be sure.

CHAPTER XII

The Greek–Turkish crisis of 1947 and the proclamation of the Truman Doctrine

FOR a generation or more—if not, indeed, since 1898—the American people had been in the process of reluctantly abandoning the isolationist policy of a profoundly cherished tradition. By the winter of 1946–1947 that long, painful, and embittering process had, at last, been virtually completed. What was needed, now, was a new and definitive formulation of America's place and policy in the world. Such a formulation, when it came, was bound to be entangled in the formulation of the operational requirements imposed by the immediate danger that would occasion it. The immediate danger had received explicit public recognition in Churchill's Fulton Address of March 5, 1946. At the same time Mr. Kennan, in his private communication to the State Department, had provided a clear and sophisticated definition of it that, in itself, supplied the grounds for a new formulation of American policy. Kennan had also set forth, in his communication, the necessity of informing the American people of the challenge posed for their country by the power and behavior of Stalin's Russia. His article in *Foreign Affairs*, however, which was to serve this purpose so notably, would not appear until the summer of 1947.

It will be helpful now, as we recall the unfolding of these matters, to keep in our own minds the distinction, not clearly perceived at the time, between immediate policy to meet the immediate challenge and, what was so long overdue, the permanent new orientation of the country towards its external environment.

Secretary of State George C. Marshall had been in office only a month when he undertook to deal with the basic orientation of the United States in an address at Princeton on Saturday, February 22, 1947.

Twenty-five years ago [he said], the people of this country . . . had the opportunity to make vital decisions regarding their future welfare. I think we must agree that the negative course of action followed by the

United States after the first World War did not achieve order or security, and that it had a direct bearing upon the recent war and its endless tragedies. . . . I am therefore greatly concerned that the young men and women of this country . . . shall acquire a genuine understanding of lessons of history. . . . You should fully understand the special position that the United States now occupies in the world, geographically, financially, militarily, and scientifically, and the implications involved. The development of a sense of responsibility for world order and security, the development of a sense of overwhelming importance of this country's acts and failures to act, in relation to world order and security—these, in my opinion, are great 'musts' for your generation.[1]

Secretary Marshall left his office in the State Department early on the afternoon of Friday, February 21, to go to Princeton, where he would give his address next day. It was after he had already left that the British Ambassador telephoned the Department to request an immediate appointment with him, saying that he had two notes from his Government to lay before him without delay.

Rather than ask the Secretary to come back to Washington, Undersecretary Dean Acheson, who was Acting Secretary in his absence, suggested that the Ambassador send a representative with copies of the notes to discuss them with the officers of the Department chiefly responsible for the matters with which they dealt. Then whatever staff-work was needed could be got under way immediately, in anticipation of the Secretary's return Monday morning. First Secretary Sichel of the British Embassy, dispatch-case in hand, thereupon went to the Department, where he called upon Mr. Loy Henderson, Director of the Division of Near Eastern Affairs. He pulled the two notes from his dispatch-case and handed them to Henderson to read.

The first referred to the deteriorating situation in Greece, where the Government was at the brink of economic and military perdition, where it appeared that the Communist rebels might be about

---

[1] The language of this statement is so awkward as to cry out for comment. Our traditional American contempt of what is regarded as merely literary cultivation is a heavy handicap to American statesmanship. What the Secretary of State said in this, his first major public utterance since taking office, was denied any possibility of moral or intellectual authority by the crippled English in which he said it. No one would note it as Churchill's Fulton Address was noted; no one would remember it as Lincoln's Gettysburg Address (which was no richer in content) was remembered. If the same failure did not attend Kennan's utterances, that was simply because, by the distinction of his mind, he was exempt from the painful incapacity of his colleagues.

to capture the country for Stalin's rapidly expanding empire—which would thereby emerge, at last, upon the shores of the Mediterranean. Until now Britain, pursuing the policy set by Churchill in 1944, had been providing the economic and military assistance that the Greek Government needed to stave off this disaster. Now, because of Britain's own economic crisis (the note said), it could give no further financial assistance after March 31. His Majesty's Government hoped that the United States would be able to take over the burden. The Greek requirements for 1947 were estimated at between $240 million and $280 million.

The second note that Henderson read, as Sichel sat by, had a similar message about Turkey, where Britain had also been giving economic and military assistance needed by Turkey if it was to hold its own against the active pressure that Moscow was putting upon it.

My office, in those days, was around the corner from Henderson's. I remember him as one of our most energetic and dedicated Foreign Service Officers, a man who burned with an inward flame that showed in his eyes. He was not the relaxed British type of diplomat that I surmise Sichel to have been. The only account we have of this occasion reports how Henderson immediately grasped the catastrophic import of the two notes and wondered at Sichel's calmness in delivering them. The legendry that is history must always have men rising to occasions like this without hesitation or uncertainty, simply because that is the way the men remember it afterwards. Whatever is unworthy of the occasion disappears immediately from memory. I would myself expect that the first thought of virtually any man in Henderson's position would be: 'There goes my week-end!'—while at the same time, in a confused way, the larger meaning would be assembling itself in his mind. Nevertheless, in Henderson's case I find it plausible to believe that the flame immediately rose high, that Sichel had occasion to be impressed by the way his eyes flashed with it.[2]

What the two notes reported was the final end of the *Pax Britannica*. Now, after two World Wars, Britain had exhausted the last of the means with which, for almost a century and a half, it had maintained its power and discharged its responsibilities over

[2] The account to which I refer in this paragraph is in Jones, pp. 3–8. This neglected book is almost unique in the vivid picture it gives of the human beings involved in the crisis of these weeks. To Jones, who was associated with them, it was not an abstraction called the State Department or the Government of the United States that acted.

the wide world. Consequently, it was not only withdrawing from Burma and India, it was also withdrawing from the eastern Mediterranean, where it appeared certain that it would be replaced by Stalin's new empire, already moving into the area— unless the giant American nation, acting quickly and against its ancient tradition, could bring itself to go in first. The British notes informed the American Government that it had thirty-eight days.

*   *   *

It was not only Greece that, in the winter of 1946–1947, balanced upon the brink of perdition. So did Britain and all of western Europe. We, who know of the last-minute salvation to come, can hardly recapture, today, the alarm inspired by the picture that confronted the makers of American policy as they looked out across the ocean at a world that was collapsing.

The degree to which Britain and western Europe had been exhausted by the War did not become evident until now, two years after its termination. In 1945 Britain still had some reserves of gold and foreign exchange left, and that year the United States and Canada opened credits of $5,000 million for it to draw on. The expectation was that these resources would tide the British over until they had reconstructed the industrial productive power that would enable them to re-establish the export trade by which they might earn for themselves what was needed to pay for necessary imports of food and raw materials.

This, however, was not happening. Britain's productive power was not becoming re-established. Its limited reserves and the $5,000 million credit were being expended for currently needed food and fuel, rather than for capital investment. Soon, when they were used up, and in the absence of rescue from outside, the British people would starve, and in the winter they would freeze for lack of fuel. Britain was like a soldier wounded in war who, now that the fighting was over, was bleeding to death.

The plight of Britain—which was no different from the plight of other free countries in Europe—was made vivid, now, by what lawyers call an 'Act of God.' The winter of 1946–1947 was one of extraordinary severity. Beginning on January 25, a succession of blizzards without precedent struck the British Isles. At this time Britain was already in the midst of a crisis caused by the shortage of coal. This shortage had already forced a number of factories that produced for export to shut down temporarily. Twelve days before the blizzards struck, the Government had reduced coal allocations to all industries by fifty per cent—simply because that was all the coal available. There had already been some temporary cut-offs of electricity because of the coal shortage. And food was being severely rationed.

The blizzards that now began simply froze transport in Britain, as well as killing the winter wheat. Everywhere, the factories that were still open began to close. By February 7, two weeks before the British informed the State Department that they would have to withdraw from Greece and Turkey, more than half of British industry had come to a halt. On that date the Government announced in the House of Commons that for several days all electricity would be cut off from industrial consumers in most of England, including the Midlands, and that electricity for domestic use would be cut off for five hours of each day. Immediately, five million workers were thrown out of work and were left with little or no heat in their homes.

The approaching crisis in Greece and Turkey was, then, merely the symptom of a far wider crisis in Britain and throughout Europe. Britain could no longer continue its rescue operation in Greece and Turkey because it stood in need of rescue itself. Britain was collapsing as Greece was collapsing; and so were France and Italy, in both of which the Communists seemed about to take over as they already had in the eastern European countries. This was once more the eleventh hour—as in 1917, as in 1941. If the United States did not intervene now, all would be lost.

Again, however, now for the third time, the United States would intervene.

Secretary of State Marshall had assumed his office four days before the blizzards hit England. Many who knew him or had followed his career were impressed by certain points of similarity between him and our national hero, George Washington. Like Washington, Marshall was a dignified figure who did not unbend easily. He had Washington's severity and self-discipline. He made the most of limited endowments. He did not possess intellectual brilliance or the gift of eloquence. But he could distinguish what was more important from what was less important. As with Washington, it was sheer moral character that gave him his innate dignity and an element of greatness. He was a great man without being a particularly good Secretary of State—for it was in the military life, rather than in political life, that he found himself at home.[3] He accepted the political and diplomatic posts for which President Truman chose him out of his sense of duty only.

Whatever the deficiencies of General Marshall's preparation for such an office as that of Secretary of State, he was fortunate in having as his deputy in that post a man who shared none of them. Undersecretary Dean Acheson was the perfect foil for General Marshall. Also a man of strong character, and of a moral courage that sometimes amounted to recklessness, Acheson's intellectual powers were impressive. To those who had the opportunity to observe his mind in action those powers were, on occasion, stunning. The parallel of Alexander Hamilton's relationship to George Washington springs to mind.

Acheson had the kind of wide-angle vision that could comprehend the entire world situation at a glance, and in his exposition of it to those who were his peers he had a logical persuasiveness that even his opponents could not resist.[4] A brilliant conversationalist more than an orator, he was at his best in analyzing a difficult international situation before a small group, such as a Congressional committee or an interdepartmental meeting. With his fertile intellect and the eloquence of his logic, he was to have the most creative role among those who now addressed themselves to the great emergency.

The man who presided at this crisis found himself President of the United States without having ever been a candidate for the office and without having ever considered himself qualified for it. Mr. Truman was a man of simple background, with limitations of education that, unlike Abraham Lincoln, he was never quite able to overcome by his own endeavor. A Missouri machine-politician, he was always dazzled by the great world of Washington, which he entered by way of election to the Senate. In 1944, a maneuver by President Roosevelt and his associates to drop Vice-President Wallace had brought Truman into the Vice-Presidency by what

[3] Even as American Chief-of-Staff during the War he had not appreciated political considerations at their full value. Representing the American disposition to divorce military activities from their political context, he opposed himself firmly to the British disposition to formulate military strategy with political ends in view. He had been brought up, like all American Army officers of his generation, to believe that the only purpose of military operations was to crush the enemy, to destroy him or make him helpless, and that any politically motivated modification of that purpose, or any political limitation on the means for its attainment, was morally repellant.

[4] Because I have deliberately adopted an historical perspective, I allow myself to refer in the past tense to men who are still alive and active. May they forgive me if I seem to write their obituaries prematurely!

was hardly more than an accident of politics; and it was an unprepared, a bewildered, even a frightened man who suddenly felt on his own shoulders the burden under which Roosevelt had just broken. His own conception of his inadequacy, at that moment, seemed plausible to all who knew him, so that he was without the support of an opinion that would have given him strength.

In most respects Mr. Truman was never to appear well fitted to be President of the United States in a day when the future of the world depended on extraordinary and commanding statesmanship by the American Government. Yet the American Government under his administration rose to the demands of that day. Future historians will surely find that the record of his Administration was not inferior to that of his better qualified predecessor.

Mr. Truman's personal humbleness was offset by a profound respect for the office he now occupied, and by a sense of his responsibility to that office. The Missouri politician who had always been at home with the petty deals and combinations of machine-politics at the local level now showed himself able to rise to the level of an exalted office—at least on the great occasions of his testing. At the height of a crisis, and for the moment that it lasted, the little man became big. There were several occasions when he faced the choice between what appeared to be his own political future and what he conceived to be the obligation of his office. Before such a choice he never hesitated. One such occasion was on the night when he decided to take upon himself alone all the responsibility for American intervention in Korea, rather than incur, for the nation, the risk and delay attendant upon seeking a prior Congressional resolution in support of it. Another occurred on the night of April 10, 1951, when he dismissed the American general who, as the popular hero of World War II and now as commander of the forces in Korea, was the idol of the American people. On this occasion he preferred to pay the expected price of political disaster and humiliation to himself rather than leave the authority of his office impaired by a craven failure to exercise it.

At the great turning-point of 1947 this was the man who presided in Washington. As his Secretary of State he had a soldier of the highest prestige. As second in command of the State Department he had a man of commanding intellect and fierce personal integrity who, like himself, would at critical moments be willing to sacrifice his own political life rather than abstain from doing what he conceived to be right. And in George Kennan, whose role was principally in the background of events, he had in his Government a man of Shakespearian insight and vision who saw the international scene as a stage on which those who represented the historic achievements of human civility were challenged by powerful forces of evil. One of Mr. Truman's qualities was his ability to appreciate these men and to support them as they supported him.

I have, in these paragraphs, named four utterly diverse men. Two of them, President Truman and Secretary Marshall, I saw at close quarters only once or twice, and I never had any communication with them. The other two, however, came to be cherished personal friends. I know very well that, where the great occasion was lacking, none of them was larger than life-size. They were not made of bronze but of flesh, each with his human limitations and weaknesses—as had been the case with Washington, Hamilton, and the other distinguished figures of their generation. They lived only occasionally at a level of exalted purpose, and all their speech did not consist of words of wisdom. Nevertheless, in these years of which I am writing these contrasting personalities represented among them the highest endowments of humankind.

There were other men too—James Forrestal, Robert Patterson, Averell Harriman, William Clayton—who contributed notably to the realistic reshaping of American policy in these days, and who represented that quality of character which is not conspicuous in every Administration. Beyond them were hundreds of others, perhaps thousands, in Washington or at American missions abroad, who did not spare themselves. It is a false legend that the men of government are all self-serving politicians or time-serving bureaucrats. So they may be in the mass, just as the mass of scholars and teachers, of intellectuals, of journalists, may be petty in the pursuit of their careers; but the honor of mankind is repeatedly saved (as it would be once more in the years after 1945) by those who can, when the occasion requires, rise above their ordinary selves. Of such men government is not, in my experience, more devoid than the other spheres in which responsibility makes its claims.

I should not omit, here, the mention of one more man who also met the trial of these days and played an indispensable role. Senator Arthur Vandenberg, like President Truman, was undistinguished in most of his career. He had been a provincial isolationist politician until late in World War II, and he did not achieve his full stature until the same call for greatness was sounded in Congress as in the halls of the Executive Branch. Dean Acheson has, in some of his memoirs, left a moving picture of the tacit partnership between himself and Vandenberg, at opposite ends of Pennsylvania Avenue, that now enabled the two Branches of the Government to march forward together.[5]

I am not one who thinks that great men make history. Still, I would rather not do without them.

* * *

The situation that the men in Washington faced on February 21, 1947, was uncompromising in its demands. The British were not suggesting that the United States might see its way clear to easing their burden in Greece and Turkey by giving them some additional help with it: they were saying that they had no choice but to drop it forthwith. Again, their domestic situation was not a matter of statistics that had disturbing implications for the future; their economic activity was slowing to a halt, men, women, and children in increasing numbers were experiencing cold and hunger. The hour had struck in England as in Greece.

Mr. Sichel's call on Mr. Henderson was followed by nineteen days of intense and fruitful activity in Washington. At the end of that time, on March 12, President Truman went before a Special Joint Session of Congress to deliver a Message that, in its historic importance, ranks at least with the Message of April 2, 1917, in which President Wilson asked Congress to recognize the existence of a state of war with the Imperial German Government.

President Truman was not a Woodrow Wilson. He commanded no such eloquence as deserves to be remembered in itself. The higher vision was never his. Wilson had written his classic Message by himself the night before its delivery. Truman had to depend entirely on the governmental bureaucracy, operating by negotiation and compromise among its members, to provide him with a text. The process by which this was done is described in almost hour-by-hour detail by Joseph M. Jones, who participated prominently in it.[6] Mr. Jones, as a professional practitioner, takes this procedure for producing presidential addresses for granted and manifests his loyalty to it. However, the detached reader of

---

[5] See Acheson, pp. 139–140. [6] Jones, Part IV, Chapter 2.

his account may allow himself to view it with an appropriate horror.

In judging the President's Message to Congress we should bear in mind the opposition between the perspective of current events, in terms of which men act, and the perspective of history, in terms of which their actions are recalled and judged. In the perspective of history, the conquest of Constantinople by Mohammed II in 1453 is important, *inter alia*, because it inaugurated the revolution in warfare produced by the introduction of artillery. For Mohammed, however, what was important was not the inauguration of a revolution in warfare but the capture of a city. For the Truman Administration, what was important was to obtain Congressional authorization and appropriations for aid to Greece and Turkey. The proclamation of abstract doctrine, although it would loom larger for the historian, had to come second. The host of bureaucrats working directly under Mr. Acheson were operators rather than political philosophers. This is what Mr. Truman was too. Woodrow Wilson was the last American President to be both an operator and a philosopher, but it is not a foregone conclusion that in this situation he would have done better than Truman.

The President's historic Message was badly composed. Read today, it seems consistently to put last things first and first things last. It lacks coherence. Like all the products of multiple bureaucratic drafting in committees and subcommittees and supercommittees, each sentence or each group of two or three sentences is a separate paragraph in itself. This is the natural consequence of a drafting process in which isolated declarations are shifted around freely, withdrawn here, inserted there, and repeatedly juggled. If the specialist on peanuts in one of the committees insists on the inclusion of a sentence about peanuts it can be placed virtually anywhere in a text that comes to a full break at the end of every two or three lines. It might be impossible, however, to insert it in a text that developed with unbroken coherence from a beginning through a middle to an end, and such a text, consequently, could not survive the process of drafting and revision.

Although an attempt was made to achieve smoothness, coherence, and fine language by adding public-relations specialists to the other specialists engaged in the drafting process, these worthy persons could not possibly supply what was needed. Their business was not statesmanship but salesmanship, and salesmanship for them generally meant the short, hard-hitting phrases of the advertising business. Mr. Jones reports drafting sessions in which participants offered observations beginning: 'The only way we can sell the public on our new policy is. . . .' The task for statesmanship, however, was not to sell a program to the public by advertising devices; it was, rather, to expose the world situation to the public in all its massive reality, so that its implications for action became clear. This Woodrow Wilson would have known how to do.

I think it appropriate to mention these matters here because the inarticulateness of the Truman Administration would, at last, prove to be its Achilles' heel. From 1948 to 1952 it would lose the support of a public to which it could not, in words of authority, explain the policy it was pursuing. By its inarticulateness it would leave the field open to opposing demagogues. At last, because it could not say effectively why the Korean War had to be fought as it was being fought, the public became alienated and rebellious. Nations do not go on making sacrifices of blood and treasure without the inspiration of the word. Nothing is more pitiful than to find successive American Administrations since 1945 hiring the services of uneducated public-relations experts to provide themselves with a synthetic eloquence that is foredoomed to failure.

In his Message to Congress the President, after an initial account of economic and social conditions in Greece (which referred to the dearth of poultry), went on to say that the Greek Government was unable to cope with 'the terrorist activities of several thousand armed men, led by Communists, who defy the Government's authority at a number of points. . . .' 'Greece,' he said, 'must have assistance if she is to become a self-supporting and self-respecting democracy. The United States must supply that assistance. . . . There is no other country to which democratic Greece can turn.' The Greek Government, he continued, was not perfect. Nevertheless, 692 American observers considered the recent election for the Greek Parliament 'to be a fair expression of the views of the Greek people.'

The President then turned to Turkey—which 'also deserves our attention.' Omitting any certification of democratic virtue in this case, he merely said that, 'as in the case of Greece, if Turkey is to have the assistance it needs, the United States must supply it.'

Up to this point the President had dealt with the world crisis as if it were a question of repaving a highway in Missouri. At this point, however, it was possible to insert almost verbatim a series of paragraphs on American foreign policy and its objectives that had been drafted by the Subcommittee on Foreign Policy Information of the State–War–Navy Coordinating Committee. These paragraphs began as follows:

One of the primary objectives of the foreign policy of the United States is the creation of conditions in which we and other nations will be able to work out a way of life free from coercion. This was a fundamental issue in the war with Germany and Japan. Our victory was won over countries which sought to impose their will, and their way of life, upon other nations.

To ensure the peaceful development of nations, free from coercion, the United States has taken a leading part in establishing the United Nations. The United Nations is designed to make possible lasting freedom and independence for all its members. We shall not realize our objectives, however, unless we are willing to help free people to maintain their free institutions and their national integrity against aggressive movements that seek to impose upon them totalitarian regimes. This is no more than a frank recognition that totalitarian regimes imposed on free peoples, by direct or indirect aggression, undermine the foundations of international peace and hence the security of the United States.

The peoples of a number of countries of the world have recently had totalitarian regimes forced upon them against their will. The Government of the United States has made frequent protests against coercion and intimidation, in violation of the Yalta Agreement, in Poland, Rumania and Bulgaria. I must also state that in a number of other countries there have been similar developments.

At the present moment in world history nearly every nation must choose between alternative ways of life. The choice is too often not a free one.

One way of life is based upon the will of the majority, and is distinguished by free institutions, representative government, free elections, guarantees of individual liberty, freedom of speech and religion, and freedom from political oppression.

The second way of life is based upon the will of a minority forcibly imposed upon the majority. It relies upon terror and oppression, a controlled press and radio, fixed elections, and the suppression of personal freedoms.

It may be noted in passing that the simple ideological conception set forth in these lines, as a basis for the policy of containment, would plague the United States for years to come when it found that, to contain the Russian empire, it had to support regimes that could not meet the ideological test. (Apparently there was already some doubt that the Turkish regime could meet it.) As in 1917, as in 1941, it was still not possible to tell the American people what the real issue was, that the real issue was the balance of power.

At this point in the passage taken from the Subcommittee, not standing out from it in any way, came the single sentence that set forth what would afterwards be known as the 'Truman Doctrine.' It read: 'I believe that it must be the policy of the United States to support free peoples who are resisting attempted subjugation by armed minorities or by outside pressures.'

After this the Message gradually worked its way back to the principal subject, from which it had digressed for the sake of these generalities. The President asked Congress 'to provide authority for assistance to Greece and Turkey in the amount of $400 million for the period ending June 30, 1948.' He also asked for authority to assign personnel to work in Greece and Turkey. That done, he ended with a few stock phrases: 'Great responsibilities have been placed upon us. . . . I am confident that the Congress will face these responsibilities squarely.'

What was important at the time was the institution of certain programs in Greece and Turkey. What would be important in historical perspective was the commitment of the United States to active responsibility for freedom and justice throughout the world, the commitment implicit in the policy of containment set forth in the sentence that presented what everyone afterwards discovered to be a 'Truman Doctrine.' I suspect that the significance of this sentence, thrown in by public-relations specialists, was not fully appreciated at the time. Otherwise, why did nobody see how inappropriate and weak it was for the President of the United States, who is alone charged by the Constitution with making its foreign policy, to begin it with the words, 'I believe it must be'—as if he were a private citizen putting forward a proposal for the consideration of the authorities? Perhaps the statement, as it appeared in the original Subcommittee document, began with 'We believe it must be.'[7]

---

[7] Those who are incredulous at the suspicion that no one before March 12 appreciated the full significance of the sentence might read the account of the formulation of the 'Point Four' policy in Chapter I of Halle, 1965.

However that may be, the sentence announcing that the United States, finally abandoning its traditional isolationism, would now undertake, in succession to Great Britain, to establish a *Pax Americana* all around the globe—this sentence was so negligently placed in the text, and so negligently composed, that it could go quite unnoticed. The London *Times* was not unrepresentative of press-comment on the Message when it observed that 'Mr. Truman's speech does no more than extend the prospect of American support to a new area, the Eastern Mediterranean and the Middle East.'

As always, the topical situation was what dominated men's minds. Later, those who had been responsible would be surprised and delighted to find out how they had made history.

CHAPTER XIII

The Marshall Plan and Moscow's reaction to it

IN February and March 1947 the United States, acting in haste
to meet an emergency, decided to replace by its own means
and devices the support for Greece and Turkey that Britain was
no longer able to continue. The commitment to do so, however,
made sense only as part of a larger commitment, which was
therefore implicit in it. There is no such thing as filling only one
corner of a power vacuum. It follows that the Truman Doctrine
was implicit in aid to Greece and Turkey, rather than being
merely the independent consequence of a statement in President
Truman's Message of March 12. Nothing essential would have
been altered by leaving the statement out.

It became widely apparent, immediately after March 12, that
the United States could not stop with the rescue of Greece and
Turkey. A commitment had been assumed of which the limits
were, for the moment, unknown. This was evident to Acheson in
the State Department, who immediately ordered the initiation of
staff studies to determine how many countries were going to need
how much American aid of what kind. It was also apparent to the
most perceptive of journalistic commentators, Walter Lippmann,
who in his column of March 13 wrote that the decisions represented by the President's Message 'call for an estimate of how
the total military and financial resources, that can be made
available, may most effectively be applied to meet demands which
arise from every quarter of the globe.'

An event acquires historical importance only by its consequences. The consequences of Mr. Truman's Message of March
12 did not stop with aid to Greece and Turkey. They continued
with the European Recovery Program and the policy of actively
containing the Russian empire from the Elbe to Korea. They
continued with the measures of opposition to further Russian
expansion which finally inaugurated the Cold War. All this was
implicit in the President's Message of March 12, which thereby
represents a turning-point in history.

The emergency that the Government in Washington faced had two aspects. The collapse of Europe from Britain to Greece was alarming in itself, since it implied a proliferation of chaos to which, for a variety of reasons, the United States could not have been indifferent even in the absence of the Russian menace. The other and complimentary aspect was the Russian menace. The United States was now committed to meeting the emergency, but it had some choice of how much emphasis to place on the one aspect or the other in the formulation of the course it followed and the rationale by which it justified that course. Throughout all the developments after March 12—indeed, after February 21— the tension between the emphasis on rescue and the emphasis on containment is manifest.

In this critical spring of 1947 the overt and all-out political conflict between Russia and the West, which would come to be called the Cold War, presented itself as an imminent danger but not as a foregone conclusion. Under the circumstances, the men in Washington were mindful of the need to avoid any conduct that would put the responsibility for starting the Cold War, if it should start at all, on the West rather than on Russia. (Another way of saying this was that, if Europe should at last be divided into two opposed camps, the United States should not be the one that divided it.) The general view, inside the American Government as well as in the more sophisticated American press, was that it had been a mistake, in the Message of March 12, to have sounded the trumpet-call for ideological battle against Russia, and to have put the programs of aid to Greece and Turkey in that context.

The European reaction to the ideological emphasis of the President's Message tended to confirm this view. Much of western Europe felt itself almost in the grip of the Communist power, which had been rising from within at the same time that it loomed ever more menacingly from without. The western Europeans were, for the moment, too much at the mercy of Moscow to join the United States in a policy provocative of it. If the United States was going to challenge Moscow to ideological and political combat (which might eventuate in military combat) they would, in their weakness, have to make it clear that they were not associating themselves with that challenge. It was questionable whether they would feel free to accept an undertaking to rescue them that might well provoke counteraction by Moscow. The situation was one of extraordinary delicacy. As we now know, when the offer of rescue came at last, in the form of the Marshall Plan, it undoubtedly did contribute to the final fall of Czechoslovakia and its incorporation in the Russian empire.[1]

Moreover, as long as Europe was not yet irreparably divided between East and West, it was of practical importance to avoid any conduct that would in itself produce such a division. The recovery of a western Europe that was economically severed from eastern Europe would thereby be made far more difficult, expensive, and uncertain. There was every reason, then, to shape developments so that the Russians would be tempted to participate in a general program of reconstruction for all Europe. This was the last chance, really, to arrest the accelerating trend toward complete political division and conflict. If such a division was to be realized anyway, the responsibility had better rest with Moscow than with Washington.

Finally, there was an exceptionally sensitive appreciation in Washington of the reasons why the initiative for formulating a European recovery program, and its formulation, should be European rather than American. I say 'exceptionally' because it has been a fault of the American style in international relations to be too dynamic and unreserved in these matters. Most Americans believe that, in diplomacy as in military operations, it is always an advantage to have the initiative. This is, I think, quite wrong with respect to programs of international cooperation, since the passive party whose cooperation is solicited is always in a stronger position than the party who actively solicits.

In addition, as an excessively self-confident nation we have been disposed to assume that a plan made by Americans is bound to be a better plan than any plan made by foreigners on their own. And we have sometimes been insensitive to what makes for self-respect in others no less than in ourselves. Europeans have had occasion, more than once since 1947, to resent the apparent assumption on our part that we know better than they what is best for them.

It is therefore worth noting that the shaping of policy in April and May was the work of a few mature and worldly individuals of unusual psychological sensitivity. I refer particularly, at this point, to Messrs. William L. Clayton and George Kennan in the

[1] See pp. 74–5 above.

State Department. The former was Undersecretary for Economic Affairs, the latter had just founded the Policy Planning Staff, which had as its first task the formulation of a policy to meet the European emergency. These two men, with their assistants, operated under the direction of Undersecretary Acheson as Secretary Marshall's chief-of-staff. It is remarkable that, as was not the case in February, there was no obstructive proliferation of committees, of public-relations staffs, and of bureaucratic machinery generally. The handful of men involved were able, consequently, to give effect to their personal sensitivities and insights in a way that almost never happens in a large and naturally insensitive bureaucracy.[2]

To the names I have just mentioned I should properly add that of an individual who played an appreciable role while remaining outside the ranks of government. Walter Lippmann, for a generation before as since, brought to his profession as journalist a sense of history that enabled him to see through current events to the secular movements underlying them. He also had the delicacy of perception, the psychological sensitivity, that distinguished Kennan and Clayton. He, as we shall see, was apparently the first to present, in a column of May 1, the basic concept on which the European Recovery Program was to be based.

*　　*　　*

In his newspaper column of April 5 Lippmann made a report, sensational at the time, in which he said what, as he put it, the responsible men inside the Government would be saying if they were not under constraint to keep up appearances and morale: that Europe was on the brink of economic collapse. To prevent the crisis which would otherwise 'spread chaos throughout the world,' he said, 'political and economic measures on a scale which no responsible statesman has yet ventured to hint at will be needed in the next year or so.' On May 8 Acheson was, on behalf of the Government, to make a more detailed presentation of the same catastrophic situation in his Address before the Delta Council in Mississippi.

---

[2] The Policy Planning Staff, when it carried out this first assignment, consisted first of two and then of three men beside Kennan. They served as individuals, not as representatives of other departments. There was no organization of all the limbs, branches, and twigs of government for a massive combined effort to imitate the uses of the mind.

For seven weeks, from March 10 to April 24, Secretary Marshall had been in Moscow at the meeting of Foreign Ministers who were trying, without success, to agree on a common policy toward Germany and Austria. The course of action pursued by Russian Foreign Minister Molotov at that meeting suggested to the other participants that Stalin's Government was not averse to collapse and chaos in the West. Upon his return to Washington, Secretary Marshall delivered, on April 29, a radio-address to the American people in which he reported the apparent Russian disposition to obstruct or delay the settlement of matters essential to the recovery of western Europe. He concluded by observing that the United States could not ignore the factor of time. 'The recovery of Europe,' he said, 'has been far slower than had been expected. Disintegrating forces are becoming evident. The patient is sinking while the doctors deliberate. I believe that action cannot await compromise through exhaustion. New issues arise daily. Whatever action is possible . . . must be taken without delay.'

In his column of May 1, commenting on the report by Marshall, Lippmann wrote that it would not do for the United States to allocate to each European government separately its contributions to European recovery.

So after we have discussed the separate needs of Britain, France, Italy, and the rest, we should suggest to them that they meet together, agree on a general European program of production and exchange, of imports and exports to the outer world, and that they arrive at an estimate of the consolidated deficit for as much of Europe as can agree to a common plan. Such a consolidated deficit will be smaller than the sum of the separate national deficits.

One sees how the basic concepts were assembling, during these fruitful weeks, in men's minds. There was the acceptance of a responsibility for urgent and massive action in Washington. There was the objective of European recovery for its own sake, rather than merely as a means of containing Russia. There was the agreement that the whole undertaking must be essentially European, however dependent on the American contribution. Finally, there was the concept of a united Europe in which the component nations had traded out their respective deficits among themselves to produce a consolidated deficit, less than the sum of its parts, which would then be met by the United States as its contribution to the community of European nations as a whole.

The carrying out of the whole conception proceeded, now, in a quiet and relaxed fashion that provides a contrast, not only with the developments leading to the Message of March 12, but with the manner in which we Americans generally address ourselves to crises. Intelligence, on this occasion, appears to have been dominant over enthusiasm. No bugles were blown. There was no preparatory staging of a great event. In fact, the occasion on which Secretary Marshall would announce what was thenceforth to be known as the 'Marshall Plan' appears not to have been regarded as of any particular importance until its immediate and far-reaching consequences became manifest.

It was not until May 28 that Secretary Marshall decided to accept Harvard's invitation to speak at its commencement exercises on June 5, and then he did not have in mind any particular subject for his remarks. When the suggestion was made that he use the occasion to set forth the ideas on European recovery that had been developing he accepted it in spite of Acheson's objection that a commencement address was unlikely to get the attention in the press that one would want for these ideas. The Secretary's Special Assistant, Charles E. Bohlen, drafted it, and the Secretary revised his draft in the airplane on his way to Harvard. It is evident that no one in Washington, with the possible exception of Acheson, had attached first importance to it.

Here, then, is another example of how we fail to see the historic significance in current events until it becomes manifest in their consequences. The historic significance is not there to be seen as yet. On the same day as Secretary Marshall was casually announcing the 'Marshall Plan' at Harvard President Truman, in Washington, was denouncing as an 'outrage' the Communist coup that had just taken place in Hungary—and it was President Truman's statement that made the bigger headlines next morning.[3]

Acheson, afraid that what Marshall said would pass unnoticed or unappreciated in Europe, took quiet action on his own to avert this. On June 4 he invited to lunch three British correspondents assigned to Washington and, after impressing them with the importance of the Secretary's Address next day, urged them to telephone the text to London as soon as it was released, and to see to

---

[3] *The New York Times* headlines on June 6 were:

> TRUMAN CALLS HUNGARY COUP OUTRAGE;
> DEMANDS RUSSIANS AGREE TO INQUIRY;
> MARSHALL PLEADS FOR EUROPEAN UNITY.

it that a copy was delivered to Foreign Minister Ernest Bevin immediately, whatever the time of day or night.

In his Address Marshall described the economic and social plight of Europe and indicated that assistance to meet it would accord with American policy. However, he said:

before the United States Government can proceed much further in its efforts to alleviate the situation and help start the European world on its way to recovery, there must be some agreement among the countries of Europe as to the requirements of the situation and the part those countries themselves will take in order to give proper effect to whatever action might be undertaken by this Government. It would be neither fitting nor efficacious for this Government to undertake to draw up unilaterally a program designed to place Europe on its feet economically. This is the business of the Europeans. The initiative, I think, must come from Europe. . . . The program should be a joint one, agreed to by a number, if not all, European nations.

He said that at the proper stage the role of the United States would be to support such a program 'so far as it may be practical for us to do so.'

I don't suppose that any of those who, sitting on their folding chairs in Harvard Yard, listened to the Secretary of State, appreciated the fact that they were present at an historic occasion. The Secretary did not appreciate it himself.

*   *   *

The threat of an imminent collapse in western Europe had drawn the United States across the Atlantic in 1917 and again in 1940–1941. It was, I think, a foregone conclusion that the same threat would draw it again in 1947. Circumstances dictated this, and the statesmen merely gave expression to it. Much depended, however, on the shrewdness, the intelligence, the very style of the expression. Statesmanship might have faltered and fumbled. Confusion might not have been avoided—and, in fact, it was not altogether avoided in the initial move to assist Greece and Turkey. The fact that this was not now the case is attributable to the statesmanship of a few men, with whatever reservation one may wish to make in favor of luck or providence.

Foreign Ministers Bevin in London and Bidault in Paris eagerly embraced the Marshall proposal on its own terms, which they could not have wished to alter. Here was occasion for a degree of international accord that is rare even among the best of allies. The Marshall proposal posed no such dilemma for the West Europeans as it would have if it had been cast in the form of a challenge to Moscow, or if, taking advantage of the weakness of their position, it had suggested any kind of imposition by Washington. In these months of April, May, and June, then, and for more than one reason, the statesmanship of a few outstanding individuals had a scope and influence that the muddle of bureaucracy, domestic politics, and international relations usually forbids.

When the text of Marshall's Address was delivered to Bevin at his home there began, immediately, a period of intense and momentous diplomatic activity in the European capitals. That activity, based on the vision of a united Europe with its own consolidated program of recovery, supported by the United States, culminated at the end of June in a series of meetings at which the Foreign Ministers of Britain, France, and Russia were to organize the initial planning.

For the West the element of suspense, when the first of these meetings began in Paris on June 27, was provided by the question whether the Russians would come in or stay out. The final realization of the developing Cold War depended on the resolution of this question. If the Russians stayed out, requiring their satellites to stay out too, then Europe would be finally cloven and the Cold War would be finally under way. On the other hand, an implicit if not explicit condition of eastern European participation was the renunciation by Moscow of the policy that was now opening up the Cold War. In his Harvard Address Secretary Marshall had said:

Our policy is directed not against any country or doctrine but against hunger, poverty, desperation, and chaos. . . . Any government that is willing to assist in the task of recovery will find full cooperation, I am sure, on the part of the United States Government. Any government which maneuvers to block the recovery of other countries cannot expect help from us. Furthermore, governments, political parties, or groups which seek to perpetuate human misery in order to profit therefrom politically or otherwise will encounter the opposition of the United States.

The Marshall proposal, and its eager acceptance in London and Paris, confronted Moscow with the final decision whether to join the West or fight it.

Events since late in the War had been marching consistently in the direction of the all-out political conflict on the brink of which the world stood, in these critical months, as the United States reversed its withdrawal from Europe and came back, once more, to help man the ramparts of the West. In June 1947 one might still cherish the hope, however, that the Soviet Union, rather than confront the aroused and mobilized resistance of the West, would come to terms. The door was being held open for it. This would have entailed a change in the course it had been following, but such a change might well appeal to the counsels of prudence in Moscow.

We can have no knowledge of the deliberations that took place in the conference rooms of the Kremlin after June 19, when the British and French Governments proposed to the Russian Government a prompt meeting of the three Foreign Ministers to prepare a program of European recovery along the lines of the Marshall proposal. By that time the East–West conflict had, at least by implication, been drawing American military power, such as it was at this time, back across the Atlantic. As early as the spring and summer of 1946, as Russian pressures on the Middle East and the eastern Mediterranean had begun to arouse alarm, the United States, well in advance of the policy decision proclaimed on the following March 12, had thought it best to make a quiet demonstration of strength and will by sending the battleship *Missouri* and the aircraft-carrier *Franklin D. Roosevelt* to cruise in Mediterranean waters. This action could not have gone unpondered in a mind like Stalin's. The Greek–Turkish program, set afoot after the British note of February 21, 1947, had involved American reinforcement of the Greek and Turkish military defenses. Finally, an American commitment to the economic recovery of the western European countries, directed at their independent survival, inevitably implied a moral commitment and a course of policy that could not easily stop short of military support if circumstances called for it. The United States was, at this time, the only power with an atomic armament; presumably Moscow and Leningrad were as vulnerable to it, in case of a fight, as Hiroshima and Nagasaki. The top priority that Moscow gave, in these days, to the development of an atomic armament of its own is proof that it was not disdainful of the atomic power that the United States held in its hand. Traditional Russian caution and capacity for retreat had ample occasion, then, to manifest themselves in June 1947.

On the other hand, the stiffening attitude of the United States was bound to feed the fear and hostility that had always dominated Moscow's attitude toward the foreign world that surrounded and enclosed it. This was the encircling danger that it had always sought to push back by the enlargement of its empire. The historic impulse to push this danger back had been re-enforced since 1917 by the influence of that Marxist indoctrination whereby it came to be held as dogma that the so-called capitalist-imperialist nations were under the government of sinister and deeply conspiratorial ruling groups, groups that were fanatically moved, by irresistible historical forces, to attempt the destruction of the new Russian state and everything it represented. There could be no appeasement of these ruling groups or anything except a pretended accommodation with them. The stiffening attitude of the United States, then, was bound to promote the traditional Russian fear that would impell Moscow almost convulsively to tighten its grip on the territories beyond its western frontier which it already did or could control.

Moscow must have been moved, then, by contrary impulses: the impulse to appease a superior strength, if only as a matter of duplicity, and the impulse to strengthen its defense by taking advantage of every opportunity to weaken the encircling power and achieve the geographical expansion of its own. The latter opportunities must have been particularly tempting at this time.

I suspect that Moscow now made an imprudent miscalculation. Seeing the West apparently about to fall into chaos, it underestimated its basic strength. (So Hitler, seeing the superficial signs of decadence in France, Britain, and America, had thought them more decadent than they were.) Stalin and his advisers may have been too impressed by the American demobilization of 1945–1946, and by the social as well as economic disarray of Italy, France, and Britain—as well as Germany.

Here, again, Marxist doctrine may have been misleading. The so-called 'business-cycle' had always impressed the Marxists— quite rightly, I daresay—as a fundamental weakness of societies governed by the principle of free enterprise. The 'business-cycle' meant periodic economic depressions, amounting to far-reaching crises, that might be expected to increase progressively in severity until the death of free enterprise ensued. A consequence of World War I had been the catastrophic depression that began in the United States at the end of 1929, spread to the rest of the capitalist world, and led to that revolutionary rise of the Axis regimes which betokened a breakdown in the traditional order. Now the Marxist oracles were predicting, on the basis of *a priori* theory, that World War II would be followed by another economic depression and consequent breakdown of the Western social order. When, in 1946 or 1947, the Russian economist Varga published his opinion that such a breakdown was not imminent, he was censured, disgraced, and eventually brought to recant. I suspect, then, that Stalin gambled on the expectation that a recovery from the crisis of 1946–1947 would not take place. He thought that Russia was surrounded by a degree of weakness that, with whatever precaution, it could safely exploit. I surmise that now in 1947, as again in 1950 and in the events leading up to the Cuban crisis of October 1962, Moscow underestimated the West. The picture of confusion and indiscipline that liberal democracies normally present to the outside world tends to mislead those who represent authoritarianism. This was surely the case in 1917 and in 1941. I think it was again the case in 1947.

Finally, I cannot help thinking that, in the circumstances of 1947, the element of aggressive crudeness in Stalin, of which Lenin had complained in his last years, was dominant. One would expect such a disposition to become more marked as old age and the extended experience of supreme power exercised their corrupting influence. At a certain point he had a way of rudely smashing his way to his objective, careless of the incidental damage. While there were surely elements of uncertainty and restraint in his approach to postwar problems from 1943 to 1947, circumstances may now have seemed to him to have moved to the point of an East–West confrontation such as he may, at an earlier stage, have hoped to avoid. In these circumstances he responded to the impulse of ruthless aggressiveness that he had manifested repeatedly in his career, the impulse to act in the fashion of the barbarian chieftain who uses his boots on the bodies of his opponents.

As his trusted agent and counselor Stalin had, at this juncture, Foreign Minister Molotov, one of the only old Bolsheviks who had survived Stalin's purges in the 1930's, a man whose distrustful hostility to the outside world may have amounted to an obsession. In 1942, when as Russian Foreign Minister he had been the official guest of Prime Minister Churchill at the latter's country home in England, at a time when Russia and England were allies, he had slept with a loaded revolver by his bedside, and his bed-clothes had been arranged so as to enable him to jump out of bed, in case of need, without delay.[4] In negotiation he customarily showed all the flexibility of a stone wall. Representing Russia in the United Nations, he made the word *nyet* famous throughout the world.

Stalin had already embarked, in any case, on a policy of refusing any accommodation to the West, any cooperation with it. This had become evident to Marshall at the Moscow Conference and had been a prime factor in the decision he took, upon his return, to move forward immediately—with Russia, without Russia, or if necessary against Russia—to rescue and restore Europe. At Moscow, Stalin and his Government had showed a disposition to prevent the development of a free and independent Germany, to drain Germany of its resources for the enrichment of the Russian economy, and to let Russia's erstwhile allies struggle with the consequent problems as best they might. It seemed clear that the greatest possible weakness, in the area beyond his control, was his objective. He did not, one supposes, anticipate the effective *riposte* that the Marshall Plan would prove to be.

In this speculative vein, I see reason to believe that Moscow was taken by surprise when the Marshall Plan was presented for its acceptance or rejection—just as it was again taken by surprise in 1950, when the West under American leadership reacted so resolutely to the Communist aggression in Korea.

When Moscow received the invitation of June 19 to participate with France and Britain in planning along the lines of the American proposal, it might conceivably have decided that the postwar expansion of its power could not prudently be continued, that in accordance with the dialectical rhythm of history the time had now come for a pause and a concurrent appeasement of the opposition. It might have decided that the time had come to concentrate on problems of consolidation and internal development, including the development of an atomic armament. But the old tyrant of the Kremlin, supported by Molotov, may be presumed to have seen only the evidence of what looked like irrevocable weakness in the camp of the 'capitalist imperialists.'

When, at the end of June, the French and British Foreign Ministers met in Paris with Molotov, the doubt about what Russia's response would be was soon resolved.

[4] See Churchill, 1950, p. 337.

CHAPTER XIV

*The success of the European Recovery Program
in spite of Moscow's opposition*

M R. MOLOTOV, meeting with Messrs. Bevin and Bidault in
Paris, refused Russian cooperation in any combined program of European recovery, on the grounds that such a program
would be in violation of national sovereignty.

Two days after the Paris meetings that produced this result, on
July 4, 1947, the French and British Governments invited all the
European countries except Russia and Spain to a conference to
be held in Paris a week later for the purpose of formulating a program such as Secretary Marshall had suggested. Important elements in the small Communist countries of eastern Europe must
have been desperately eager to accept, and Moscow's interdiction
of such acceptance was bound to arouse resentment among them,
however stifled in its expression. The nationalism that Moscow
had invoked as its reason for rejecting the Marshall proposal
would not be unmoved, in these countries, by such a demonstration of their servitude. Even as early as this, one may suppose,
there would be stirrings of what would later become known as
'Titoism.'

Moscow did, in fact, forbid acceptance of the Anglo-French invitation by the states under its hand. The communication of its decision to that effect was subject to a momentary slip-up in Prague,
where the Czech Government accepted by unanimous decision of
the Cabinet, only to withdraw its acceptance (by unanimous
decision of the Cabinet) after receiving a telephone-call from
Moscow. The declinations of the other eastern European states
were first made known by Radio Moscow, at a time when some
of the declining governments did not yet know that they had
declined.

And so Europe was finally divided. From this point on we can
talk of East Europe and West Europe—rather than of eastern and
western Europe. The central condition on which the Cold War
was to be based, the mutual opposition of two Europes, one led by

Russia and the other by the United States, had at last been established.

It is convenient to have nominal opening and closing dates for great conflicts like the Cold War. Such dates are generally provided by formal declarations of war, by formal surrenders and peace-treaties. However, since the conflict which began to be called 'the Cold War' in 1947 was never formalized, such formal instruments to mark its beginning and its end are lacking.[1]

In any case, the Cold War was not an altogether new conflict. The French and British statesmen who, in the second half of the nineteenth century, strove to contain Russia in the Balkans, in the Middle East, in India, and even in China, would not have found it novel. Russia, from its own point of view, had been engaged in a continuous competitive struggle with the outside world throughout all the centuries of its history and, especially since 1917, Moscow took such a struggle for granted. Lenin and Stalin always considered that they were engaged in a life-and-death combat with the West. In that combat there were truces; there were parleys, diplomatic maneuvers, and feints of various sorts; there were intervals of relative relaxation while both sides recovered their breath; there were temporary accords of a tactical nature—but there was no real peace. Even the alliance with Britain and the United States against Hitler had been tenuous and for the occasion only. Stalin and his henchmen may not have consciously rejected possibilities of permanent accommodation with the West, but their minds were controled by an atavism that lay far below the conscious surface. Something like a cold war between Russia and the Atlantic powers was going on all through the period of the alliance: it was marked by Moscow's constant reproaches and recriminations against Washington and London; the representatives of the United States and Britain found themselves treated in Moscow almost as if they had been the agents of enemy powers. The basic relationship was symbolized by the loaded revolver that Molotov considered it advisable to keep by his bedside when a guest of the British Prime Minister at Chequers.

In the context of the continuing struggle between Russia and the West, however, it was not at first clear whether the postwar

[1] The term 'Cold War,' as the name of the struggle between the two camps, gained currency when Mr. Walter Lippmann used it as the title of a book published in late 1947. It had been loosely used in the 1930's to describe the activities of 'fifth columns,' etc.

phase would be one of relative accommodation and restraint or one of outspoken mutual opposition. In the West, at least, accommodation could still be regarded as a possibility up to the end of June 1947. That, however, was the point-of-no-return.

In the conclusion of World War II Russia, almost by force of circumstances, had begun a rapid and already far-reaching expansion over Europe toward its Atlantic rim. The United States, which had intended to withdraw from Europe, had been alarmed by this expansion and had come back into Europe to stop it from going any farther. This return of the United States constituted a challenge to Russia, which it had the option of accepting or not. By the end of June it became clear that it had accepted it.

*　　*　　*

A week after the failure of the Paris meetings at which Russia had refused to join in a common program of European reconstruction, on July 12, the sixteen European nations (except Spain) that were not under Moscow's domination met at Paris in a conference of which one commentator observed that it marked the beginning of a new period in world diplomacy, following upon the period that had begun with the Moscow Conference of Foreign Ministers in October 1943, and had ended with the Moscow Conference of Foreign Ministers in March 1947. 'It was,' he said, 'the first conference held, not only without Russia, but in defiance of Russia, and under a barrage of hostile Russian propaganda. It was the first conference reuniting friend, foe, and neutral of the late war. . . . And it was the first completely successful postwar conference.' [2]

The Paris Conference of sixteen, in only four days of meeting created a Committee of European Economic Cooperation to lay the basis for a common program. On September 22 the Committee presented a report setting forth the anticipated combined deficit for the next four years that the United States would be asked to meet. Acting on that report, the Congress of the United States passed, and on April 3, 1948, the President signed, the Economic Cooperation Act, which authorized the allocation of $5,300 million to meet that deficit in the first year (interim assistance having

[2] Sebastian Haffner in *The Observer* (London), July 17, 1947; quoted in Calvocoressi, 1952, p. 105. Germany's interests were represented at the Conference by the Western European occupying powers, Britain and France. Spain, regarded as a Fascist state, was excluded on ideological grounds.

already been made available, since the emergency was not waiting on these processes). On April 16 the sixteen European nations created the Organization for European Economic Cooperation, which had for its aim 'the achievement of a sound European economy through the economic cooperation of its members,' and for its immediate task that of insuring 'the success of the European Recovery Program.'

Nothing in the European Recovery Program could have been interpreted as antagonistic to Moscow except the fact that it was undertaken in spite of Moscow's objections. The West European countries were seeking simply their own salvation and recovery from the effects of the War. In doing so they were, however, associating themselves with the United States, which had taken a stand against any further Russian expansion. The choice that had been put before them at the beginning of July 1947 had been that of resigning themselves to helplessness and the descent into chaos, or facing the active opposition of Moscow by undertaking to save themselves with American help. Their decision in favor of the latter course now identified them as members of the camp opposed to Moscow, and therefore as proper objects of its hostility.

In the general view then current, of which Churchill made himself a spokesman, it was only the American monopoly of atomic power, available for the protection of the West, that made this disregard of Moscow's opposition possible. Even so, in the months that followed the first meeting of the sixteen nations, Europeans and Americans alike had to steel their nerves to live and carry on in the expectation of a new World War that might begin at any moment with the occupation of a defenseless West Europe by the Red Army.[3]

[3] From the beginning of the 1930's to almost the end of 1962 the populations of the West lived continuously in a terrible fear. The general economic breakdown of 1929–1930, which foreboded the breakdown of the social order everywhere, was followed by the rise of Hitler and the Japanese war-lords, to the point where it no longer seemed possible to stop them. The terrors of World War II were followed by those associated with the prospect of an imminent general breakdown of civilization and the obliteration of all that made life worth living, or even possible, under the Muscovite tyranny that was spreading from the East. The emotion of fear is not easily recaptured, and now a new generation is growing up that, one hopes, will be spared the experience. However, for those of the new generation who want to know, and for those of their elders who want to recapture the brooding terror that lasted for some thirty years, I recommend J. R. R. Tolkien's trilogy, *The Lord of the Rings*, Boston, 1954–1956, which enshrines the mood and the emotion of those long years in which we, in the West, saw almost no possibility of saving ourselves from the intolerable darkness that was overspreading the world from the East.

The problem of resisting the hostile Russian power was complicated in varying degrees for the West European nations by the Communist parties that operated from within their borders under the discipline of Moscow and in support of its foreign policy. As we have seen, their resistance to the Nazis in the occupied countries had given the Communists prestige and had greatly strengthened their position when the Nazis were finally overcome and swept away. They had promptly become one of the three strongest parties in Italy, so that they had to be given four Cabinet posts in the first Government of the new Italian Republic. In France, after October 1945 the Communist Party had been the largest and strongest of the political parties, having polled a higher percentage of votes than had ever been polled by one party in the history of France. Consequently, it had held a Vice-Premiership and four other Cabinet posts (including the Ministry of Defense) in the first Government under the Fourth Republic. Here appeared to be a menace of Muscovite conquest from within as grave as the menace of Muscovite conquest from without. The two menaces in conjuntion were cause for alarm or despair among realistic and reasonable men. Moreover, continuous suffering from cold and hunger, as West Europe failed to recover after 1945, seemed likely to produce increasing numbers of recruits for the Communist parties, regarded as the parties of protest.

If one has been slipping at an accelerating rate toward the abyss of disaster, which one has almost reached, one can hardly hope that one's slide will be halted, at last, just on the brink. The aggressive intransigence that Moscow now manifested, as the West approached the brink, was surely based on the expectation that it would not be able to save itself from going over. It represented the deep-seated psychology that impells one to turn upon those who appear stricken and helpless.[4] At this time Moscow was openly proclaiming the imminence of economic collapse in the United States as well as Europe, and there can be little doubt that this is what it confidently expected.

The expectation was not to be realized.

Although it could not yet be seen at the time, by the summer of 1947 the tide was already beginning to turn. The forces of resis-

---

[4] The psychology is not limited to human nature. A flock of crows, for example, will sometimes swarm in fury upon one of its members who has been disabled. Defenselessness in others invites the assertion of one's own relative power, arousing the instinct of the bully in man and beast, in nations and in crows alike.

tance to further Communist expansion were rallying, not only in Washington but at all sorts of obscure points, and were growing in strength. The support and protection of the United States, with its atomic armament, now encouraged and emboldened those forces. As has been the case more than once in our time, the cohorts of freedom overcame their normal demoralization and disarray at the eleventh hour.

As early as May 4, 1947, with the Communists still the strongest party in France, Premier Paul Ramadier asked four of the five Communist members of his Cabinet to resign and, when they refused, dismissed them. The fifth followed them out. For a moment it appeared that the Ramadier Government might fall in consequence, and Ramadier, himself, said with a certain plausibility that if he was forced to submit his resignation he would feel that he was 'signing the abdication of the Republic.' He did not resign, however, the Republic did not abdicate.

The fatal if as-yet-hidden weakness of the Communists was that they were serving the interests of a foreign government rather than those of France, and this could hardly be disguised for long. In the long run they were bound to awaken the opposition of the forces of nationalism, which, in the long run, in France as elsewhere, were bound to prevail over them.

This was demonstrated again in November, when the Communists, who dominated the French labor movement, tried to arrest France's economic recovery and bring about a general breakdown by widespread strikes. At the same time they called strikes in Italy, and it was evident that a violent movement against the developing European Recovery Program was under way. In a statement supporting insurrectionary disturbances that accompanied the strikes in Marseilles, where the red flag was hoisted over the *Palais de Justice*, the political committee of the French Communist Party declared its support for the 'working and democratic population of Marseilles in its struggle against the American Party.' On this occasion the Ramadier Government finally did fall. For a few days France had no government. Some two million workers were idle. Vitally needed coal was no longer being mined, food supplies were cut off, and starvation impended. The Communist-dominated Confédération Générale du Travail adopted a resolution disapproving American aid to France. By the end of November the Communists in the National Assembly had almost brought its proceedings to a halt by obstruction and

disorderly behavior. At one point they took over the tribune and
held it overnight. The new Government of Mr. Robert Schuman,
however, stood firm, and in December the strikers began to weary
of what their Communist leadership was imposing on them.
When the Communists called a strike of the workers in the Paris
Métro on December 8 it had to be abandoned because of the lack
of response. Finally, on December 9, the strikes collapsed completely. The next day business as usual was everywhere resumed.

The result of this Communist attempt, and its failure, was a
general loss of Communist strength in France. The Communist-
dominated confederation of labor-unions probably lost almost a
quarter of its membership. A strengthened Government now closed
down the principal Communist newspapers and took other measures
to bring the Party under control. This was the turning-point for
the French Communist Party, which now began to decline in
membership and political strength. It had shot its bolt and missed.

At the same time as it moved to meet the November strikes,
the French Government found the hardiness to take a firmer line
with Moscow. It raided a Russian repatriation camp near Paris
and expelled twenty Russian nationals for interference in internal
affairs, thereby provoking Moscow to reprisals that it justified, in a
note of December 9, on grounds of 'the hostile position adopted
by France toward the Soviet Union.' The French Government
declared the Russian note unacceptable.

It was not a coincidence that the Italian Communists, through
their control of the Italian labor-movement, fomented widespread strikes and public disorders in Italy at the same time that
their fellow conspirators across the border were doing the same
thing in France. The Italian disorders and strikes continued
sporadically for a few months without achieving any decisive success. Here, too, the Marshall Plan was a target. Addressing a congress of the Italian Communist Party in January, its leader, Palmiro Togliatti, described the principal task of the Party and its
allies as that of combatting 'the policy of financial groups and the
Marshall Plan.' In Italy too, however, the Communist Party,
which included a bizarre mixture of persons who could hardly
have been regarded as Communists in Moscow, had reached the
peak of its strength, from which it would, in the years to come,
gradually decline.

We can see now how natural it was that, by the winter of 1947–
1948, the resistance to Communism should have been building up

in Europe and throughout the West, that the prestige and good-will gained by the Communists in defeating Hitler should have been declining.

For one thing, the nature of the police-administration that had descended on eastern Europe, that had made of it virtually a complex of concentration camps—this was becoming known in the West, and it was damaging the image of the Russians as liberators. Here, I think, the Russians were in some measure the victims of their own national backwardness. Throughout eastern Europe, from Poland to Bulgaria, the ruled were, for the most part, more advanced, less primitive, than their new rulers from the East. In Poland, in Hungary, and elsewhere, the Russians brought with them the crude administrative methods that they were accustomed to use on their own childlike and submissive population. Commenting on the Russian administration of Poland over a century earlier, under the czars, Bernard Pares noted how difficult it was for them to 'grant to Poland . . . rights which were not yet given in Russia,' and observed that 'it was as if Russia could only hold Poland by uncivilizing it.'[5] 'This,' George Kennan has remarked, 'was far more the case in 1945, for the methods and concepts of the N.K.V.D. were then as backward and archaic as those of the *oprichniki* of Ivan the Terrible, whereas the Poles had progressed considerably in political maturity since the post-Napoleonic period.'[6] A crudeness and brutality that had been native to the ancient Russian empire was thus identified with the Communist movement to its discredit.

In addition, the outspoken allegiance of the national Communist parties in the West to Soviet Russia, rather than to their own national societies, was repellant to all those who were moved by a normal patriotism. This made itself felt especially after June 1947 when the possibility of war with Russia began to present itself. On February 22, 1949, Mr. Maurice Thorez, Secretary General of the French Communist Party, did its cause no good with the French people by stating, in effect, that if the Red Army entered France the French Communists would side with it against their own Government and Army. Four days later, Togliatti said that if the Red Army invaded Italy 'the Italian people would have the evident duty of helping the Soviet Army in the most effective manner possible.'

---

[5] Pares, p. 325.   [6] Letter to the author.

Here we see the Communists affronting nationalist feeling, to their own loss, in the West. We can imagine that in East Europe, too, although it was not yet apparent, they were beginning to lose popular good-will by the winter of 1947–1948; again, both because of the traditional brutality with which they imposed their control and because of the priority they gave to Russia's national interests over those of the countries on which they so rudely imposed it.

I have already noted that the Communists were beginning to lose, by the winter of 1947–1948, the very great strength they had had in Czechoslovakia at the end of the War. Now, with the battle-lines drawn, Moscow ordered the February coup in Prague, whereby such freedom as Benes had managed to preserve for Czechoslovakia was lost under a dictatorship of the Communist Party. This coup, appearing in the West as an example of continuing Russian aggression and expansion, outraged opinion and contributed substantially to the passage of the Economic Cooperation Act through the American Congress. Three months later, as we have seen, the Finnish Government, moved by considerations of nationalism, succeeded in ridding itself of its Communist Minister of the Interior because he had shown himself more obedient to the policy of Moscow than to that of Helsinki.

It was not only in the popular appeal of Communism that the winter of 1947–1948 was a turning-point. In the same winter there began an economic recovery in West Europe that quite exceeded the expectations of those who had launched the European Recovery Program. In a little over two years, of what had been intended as a four-year program, Britain's dollar-deficit had vanished, with the consequence that American assistance under the Marshall Plan could be terminated at the end of 1951. Eire, Sweden, and Portugal had already been able to dispense with any further assistance of the sort by the middle of the year, at which time the American administrator of the assistance, Mr. William C. Foster, said: 'The progress of recovery in Western Europe is now such that we could limit dollar assistance to a few special cases' if it were not for the need to support the West European countries, who were now rebuilding their military strength, against what he referred to, in language that had by now become commonplace, as 'the Soviet design to subvert and subjugate' them. By the middle 1950's the West European countries, in contrast to those of East Europe, were beginning to enjoy such a prosperity as they had never known before.

The dark and sordid chapters in history far exceed those that show the grace of which men, at their best, are capable. The latter are what save the honor of mankind. The conception and the realization of the European Recovery Program belong to the latter. On both sides of the Atlantic, intelligence and thoughtfulness combined with high purpose. The British Government, in announcing the Program's completion in Britain, expressed its gratitude to the Government and people of the United States for giving to Britain, at a critical moment in its history, 'the means to regain her economic independence and power.' Speaking to the House of Commons, Mr. Hugh Gaitskell, Chancellor of the Exchequer, said: 'We are not an emotional people, and we are not always very articulate. But these characteristics should not be allowed to hide the very real and profound sense of gratitude which we feel toward the American people, not only for the material help they have given us but also for the spirit of understanding and friendship in which it has been given.'

Because such moments never last is no reason why they should be forgotten.

CHAPTER XV

The creation of the Cominform; the return to conscription in the United States; and the conclusion of the Brussels Pact

THE continuing expansion of Russia at the end of World War II alarmed the Western nations, impelling them to draw together for a common resistance. So the retirement of the United States into its own hemisphere, which had just begun, was halted and reversed. This, in turn, alarmed Moscow.

We can understand the Russian reaction to the Western reaction only as we bear in mind the belief of the Russian leaders that the encircling 'capitalist' world was bent on the destruction of the Soviet state. The Marxist–Leninist scriptures could be read to show that, at a certain stage of history, the 'capitalist-imperialist ruling circles' abroad would, out of fear and hatred, unleash against the Soviet Union a war more terrible than any known before. This belief represented a collective version of the persecution-mania that psychiatrists are familiar with among individuals, a mania that makes such individuals dangerous to their neighbors. Like many conceptions of the obsessed mind, however, it was based on partial truths. All sorts of real circumstances could be marshaled and interpreted to make it convincing. From 1918 to 1922 Russia had been invaded from every side by the Germans, the Austrians, the French, the British, the Americans, the Poles, and the Japanese. At Munich in 1938 the French and British had reached an agreement with Hitler that could be interpreted as a device for getting him to turn his armies against the Soviet state. The slowness of the Western allies to open a 'second front' on the Continent in World War II could be interpreted as a strategy for allowing the Nazis to bleed Soviet Russia white. (This would be especially plausible to those who were capable of discontinuing the pursuit of their Nazi quarry until that quarry had completed the destruction of Warsaw.) For thirty years, and at terrible cost, the Soviet state had survived all these machinations of the 'capitalist imperialists' against it. Now the Truman Doctrine and the Marshall Plan showed that a new assault was in preparation. So what passes for the whole truth is fabricated out of half-truths, quarter-truths, and the mere semblances of what is feared in the recesses of the obsessed mind. It was this conception of the Soviet leaders that, after the spring and summer of 1947, made any mutual understanding and accommodation between East and West impossible.

If, since 1944, the scorpion had showed itself ostensibly aggressive toward the tarantula, that was only out of the defensiveness induced by its knowledge that the tarantula was secretly bent on killing it. The tarantula's natural reaction simply confirmed this knowledge.

Alongside this basic Soviet attitude there had undoubtedly been some expectation in Moscow, during the war years, of being able to live at peace with the West after the War was over. It is normal for the human mind to hold, at certain levels, beliefs that stand in contradiction to other beliefs held at other levels. Stalin may well have thought that, if only he could now acquire, along his western frontier, the strategic 'glacis' of 'friendly' states that had always been his objective, he would have a bulwark behind which he could, at last, make the Soviet state so strong that all aggression against it would be deterred. In the hope of such a development he was cautious of provoking the Anglo-Americans against him—in Greece, in Czechoslovakia, and even in Poland. But the Anglo-Americans had nevertheless opposed him in Poland and elsewhere, and as the War drew toward a close circumstances had increasingly dictated events. The Red Army in eastern Europe, having to cope with the popular hostility provoked by its methods of administration, was impelled thereby to resort to still more brutal methods—until the victimized populations had been antagonized to such a degree that it would be dangerous to let go of them.

So the dynamics of the postwar situation produced an expansion of Moscow's tyranny that was not altogether voluntary. This expansion provoked, in the West, the reaction represented by the Truman Doctrine and the Marshall Plan. It, in turn, awoke Moscow's persecution-mania, which had, at best, been only momentarily quiescent.

If it had not been for this mania, the Western reaction to the Russian expansion might well have provided the basis for a settlement of the postwar issues.[1] Moscow, interpreting the Tru-

---

[1] In October 1962 the strong American reaction to the attempted Russian introduction of a nuclear armament into Cuba did provide the basis for at least a limited settlement.

man Doctrine and Marshall Plan as showing that the West was becoming increasingly strong to resist, might in traditional Russian fashion have adopted, at this point, a policy of retrenchment, accommodation, and appeasement. After all, it had its 'glacis,' and the West was not going to go to war over it. One may well suspect that Stalin's failure to adopt such a policy at this point was one of the charges in the indictment of him by his successors—even though it had to remain publicly unspoken. For the consequences confirmed the fact that his judgment had been wrong.

It is clear that in the summer of 1947 Stalin both underestimated the intrinsic strength of the West and overestimated its hostile intentions. He underestimated its strength because he counted on a general economic collapse that would involve the United States as well as the countries of western Europe. He saw them on the brink, needing only a push to go over. Throughout the second half of 1947 and 1948 the official statements of Moscow's attitude are full of references to the impending economic catastrophe which the United States will not be able to escape.

At the same time, he appears to have seen a likelihood of military attack by the United States that did not, in fact, exist. The United States, for a few years, had a unique atomic armament against which the Soviet Union was defenseless. Washington appeared to possess the means to destroy the Soviet state in one blow, and with impunity. In this moment, therefore, as never before, Russia stood naked to its enemies; and it must have been hard for its leaders to believe that those enemies would not now take advantage of its nakedness. To the Soviet mentality, only a fear of terrible retribution by the peoples of the world could deter the 'capitalist-imperialist ruling circles,' which dictated Washington's policies, from using America's atomic weapons, while they could still be used with impunity, to destroy the fatherland of Socialism. From this time on, then, an almost hysterical note of alarm characterizes Russian utterances. The whole world is repeatedly warned that the 'imperialist warmongers' intend to unleash a war against the Socialist camp, and that only the determined opposition of 'the people' everywhere can keep them from doing so.[2] The fear in Moscow that the United States would

---

[2] The atomic bomb was never mentioned, in this connection, as a reason for alarm, presumably because this would have drawn attention to the defenselessness of the Socialist camp. In fact, until Moscow had, by a gigantic effort, broken the American atomic monopoly, it pretended not to take atomic bombs seriously.

start an atomic war against it, before it could produce its own atomic deterrent to such a war, was surely genuine. It impelled the Soviet leaders to paint the United States in even more hideous colors than they might have otherwise. We cannot make sense of their behavior unless we appreciate the fact that they were desperate men.

*   *   *

In the face of what it regarded as a renewed campaign for the overthrow of the Soviet fatherland, Moscow now reacted, in much the fashion of 1939–1940, by moving to consolidate its hold on the newly captured states of eastern and central Europe. As had been true for a thousand years, danger from without called for centralization and absolutism within.

Perhaps Stalin had meant it when he had said, in 1945, that after the War the various Communist parties would become nationalist parties, giving the national interests of their respective countries priority.[3] Roosevelt had also meant it when he had said that the United States would withdraw from Europe after the War. But the threat posed by Russian expansion had brought the United States back to Europe, and now the threat that the American return seemed to pose impelled Moscow to tighten the bonds in which it held its satellites, attaching them more firmly to itself, suppressing within them any manifestations of national separatism.

What we see throughout this history is the dynamism of the self-fulfilling prophecy. Moscow, anticipating a threat from the West, expands its empire in that direction, thereby provoking a reaction that confirms its anticipation. Washington, reacting in fear of Moscow's spreading tyranny, provokes the spread and intensification of that tyranny by moving to contain it, thereby confirming the fear on which it had acted. This is not to say that dangers can always be averted by not acting upon their anticipation. We face, here, a condition of 'absolute predicament or irreducible dilemma.' The dialectic of conflict is in large measure unavoidable, although it can be mitigated by the manner in which it is conducted. It can be mitigated by a policy of speaking softly when one's own safety makes it necessary to show a big stick. This is where the practice of diplomacy as a peace-keeping art stands supreme. We have already seen an example in the con-

[3] See p. 73 above.

trast between the provocative proclamation of the Truman Doctrine and the unprovocative presentation of the Marshall Plan. We shall find others as we go along.

At the beginning of 1947 none of the countries that had fallen under the domination of Moscow had been transformed into Communist states on the model of the Soviet Union. Other political parties beside the Communist were tolerated in each of them, and in each case their governments were coalitions of several parties. Such a system could be made consistent with the 'friendliness' that was all Stalin had originally required in the postwar restoration of the eastern European states. It could not easily be made consistent, however, with the abnegation of nationalism in these states and their total subservience, under the discipline of Moscow, to the interests of the Russian empire. This further requirement, stimulated by the American return to Europe, coincided, moreover, with the beginning of a period in which the Communist parties—in Czechoslovakia, in Italy, in France, and elsewhere—were beginning to lose such popular strength as they had had in the moment of liberation from Hitler's tyranny. A disillusionment was beginning to set in, especially in eastern Europe, where the weight of the Red Army fell directly on the populations. This must have aggravated the anxiety that Moscow felt at the American return to Europe, provoking more extreme action on its part than it might otherwise have felt impelled to take.

Throughout 1947 and 1948 the agents of Moscow in Poland, Czechoslovakia, Hungary, Rumania, Bulgaria, Yugoslavia, and Albania resorted to the varied devices of terrorism, including faked trials and political purges, to reduce the non-Communist parties to false fronts for Communist intrigue, and to eliminate from the Communist parties themselves all such elements as might put national views and interests above their allegiance to Moscow.

This, however, was not enough. In the face of what it conceived to be a mortal danger from the West, Moscow now felt the need for a formal organization of Communist parties through which to direct, coordinate, and control Communist policy in Europe. Such an organization had existed from 1919 to 1943 in the Comintern, the international organization of Communist parties through which the Kremlin had, for a quarter of a century, directed the Communist conspiracy all over the world. The Comintern, however, had been discontinued by Stalin during the War in accordance with his ostensible abandonment of the conspiracy. Its discontinuance fitted in with his declaration that the Soviet Union no longer wished to Bolshevize Europe and that, after the War, the various Communist parties would become nationalist parties.

The Comintern had been created by Lenin in 1919, not to serve the national interests of the Russian state but, rather, to promote Communist revolution in other countries. In so far as the Russian Government was thereby involved in a conspiracy to overthrow the other governments on the international scene, this had been a bar to normal relations with those governments. Its abandonment, therefore, had removed one obstacle to the maintenance of the wartime alliance against the Axis.[4]

The problem that faced Moscow in 1947, with the inception of the Cold War, was different from the problem that had faced it in 1919. Now the Communist parties in seven European states outside Russia had achieved governmental power, and others elsewhere were close to achieving it. This meant that, in varying degree, Communist parties outside Russia had lost some of their former dependence on Moscow. In the face of what seemed mortal danger from the West, Moscow now felt the need to devise some organizational machinery for uniting them all in a common defense—in the defense, that is, of the Soviet state. They had all to be kept in a condition of obedience to Moscow. Otherwise, as had almost happened in Czechoslovakia after the announcement of the Marshall Plan, they might go their own way and end up in the enemy camp.

On September 22, 1947, representatives of the principal Communist parties of Europe were brought together at a conference in Polish Silesia. After listening to speeches by the Russian representatives alerting them to the danger, they dutifully proceeded to found the Cominform (Communist Information Bureau).

We may be sure that this Silesian conference, which lasted only two days, was not a deliberative meeting. It was a meeting called to hear the *ex-cathedra* decisions of Moscow on doctrine, policy, and action in the new circumstances created by the rallying of the West. The verbal formulations of Moscow's spokesmen were delivered to the others present as the formulations that they, in turn, were to use in communicating with others on the same problems. The auditors, under such circumstances, are not concerned with

---

[4] This is not to say that Moscow could not still direct the activities of foreign Communist parties by other means.

the literal truth of the words that are delivered to them. They listen as men under discipline receiving their orders as to the line that they are to take. They will then go forth and, at party meetings, at public gatherings, and in international conferences, repeat and repeat the line as the occasions for its use arise.

The principal spokesman for Moscow at the Silesian meeting was A. A. Zhdanov, the man whom Stalin had made responsible for bringing the foreign Communist parties under this discipline. Addressing them now, he referred to 'the aggressive and frankly expansionist course to which American imperialism has committed itself since the end of World War II.' The Truman Doctrine and the Marshall Plan, he said, 'are both an embodiment of the American design to enslave Europe.' The United States had launched 'an attack on the principle of national sovereignty.' By contrast, the Soviet Union 'indefatigably upholds the principle of real equality and protection of the sovereign rights of all nations, large and small.' It is a 'reliable bulwark against encroachments on the equality and self-determination of nations.' The speech referred to 'the desire of the imperialists to unleash a new war.' But —'the warmongers fully realize that long ideological preparation is necessary before they can get their soldiers to fight the Soviet Union.'

What were the implications of all this for Communist policy and action?

'The Soviet Union,' said Zhdanov, '. . . will bend every effort in order that [the Marshall Plan] be doomed to failure. . . . The Communist parties of France, Italy, Great Britain and other countries . . . must take up the standard in defense of the national independence and sovereignty of their countries.' Finally, 'the need for mutual consultation and voluntary coordination of action between individual parties has become particularly urgent at the present juncture when continued isolation may lead to a slackening of mutual understanding, and, at times, even to serious blunders.'

So Zhdanov set forth the basic line to be taken by the foreign Communist parties and the reasons for the establishment of the Cominform. G. M. Malenkov, the other representative of Moscow present, simply added a few embellishments.

The ruling clique of American imperialists . . . has taken the path of outright expansion, of enthralling the weakened capitalist states of

Europe and the colonial and dependent countries. It has chosen the path of hatching new war plans against the Soviet Union and the new democracies. . . . The clearest and most specific expression of the policy . . . is provided by the Truman–Marshall plans. [With regard to] such countries as Yugoslavia and Poland, the United States and Great Britain are pursuing a terrorist policy. . . . Plans of fresh aggression, plans for a new war against the Soviet Union and the new democracies, are being hatched. . . . Imitating the Hitlerites, the new aggressors are using blackmail and extortion. . . .

I exhibit this language here because from now on it is a mjaor feature of the Cold War. It will be constantly repeated, with vituperative ornamentation, by Communist speakers at meetings of the United Nations, over the Communist radio-stations, and in official Communist statements. It will wash over the whole world in wave after wave. This is the beginning of a massive and co-ordinated verbal assault on the United States and its allies.

There is a sense in which such language as this, used on such a scale, gives the Cold War a total character. The definition of a total war is not necessarily one in which every weapon and device is used without limitation. Such a war may be defined, rather, as a war for total objectives in which the parties are limited, in their employment of means, only by considerations of what is useful in staving off total defeat and producing total victory. We commonly think of World War II as a total war; yet both sides in that war were mutually deterred from using poison-gas. In the Cold War both sides are mutually deterred from using a far greater range of weapons. Nevertheless, the conflict becomes, in its essentials, as complete as in the case of the two World Wars that preceded it.

One criterion, here, is the rupture of communication between the two sides. In a limited war diplomatic contact continues between the opposing parties, and any fighting is related to the strategy of diplomatic negotiators, who keep it under control and use it only to serve their purposes in negotiation. Up to this point, Western and Communist negotiators had been in close if not amicable communication with each other—at Yalta, at Potsdam, and at other conferences that continued to take place up to the early part of 1948. Now, however, a time was approaching in which the very violence of the language to which the Communists resorted had the effect of breaking off diplomatic communication. The United States would continue to maintain an embassy in Moscow;

but its staff, like those of the other Western missions, would be virtually cut off from contact with the Russian Government and the Russian society, kept in isolation and under close surveillance. The Soviet Union would continue to maintain an embassy in Washington, but its members would keep to themselves and would, in any case, be shunned by the Americans in whose midst they lived. Mutual denunciation in public would for some years be virtually the only form of communication between the two sides.

In politics, as in all human affairs, words are deeds. A declaration of war, for example, while it is merely a form of words, has the effect of a blow stuck, and what follows is physical violence. An announcement by one side in a conflict that the other is about to start a war (which everyone must consequently prepare for) is bound to make the other apprehensive that the announcement is merely a prelude to the inauguration of a war by the side that made it. Alarmist language impells both sides to arm and prepare. On both sides, reasonableness and moderation are discredited; the representatives of extremism tend to achieve the seats of influence and power. Each side is impelled by its own fears to bemonster the other, cultivating the image of a ravening beast, called 'the Enemy,' that is bent on the enslavement of mankind. The situation is made to appear desperate, thereby justifying resort to measures of desperation.

The shouting abuse to which Moscow resorted, in its reaction to the Truman Doctrine and the Marshall Plan, made Churchill's bluntness at Fulton, which had seemed so shocking at the time, sound like the plaint of an apprehensive dove. Considering how dangerous such verbal excess was, for the Russians no less than for everyone else, one wonders what beside their own fears made the Russian leaders indulge themselves in it.

In the first place we have to bear in mind that, so far from representing the tradition of civility in terms of which the West was accustomed to conduct its affairs, the men in the Kremlin represented a rebellion against it. Like Hitler, who had also indulged in such verbal extremism, they had their roots in the unprivileged strata of society that had not shared, historically, this essentially aristocratic tradition. In their own dealings with one another coarse abuse was sufficiently common so that they would not expect others to be quite so shocked and angered by it as the people of the West now were.

Such abuse also belonged to the Marxist tradition, which was based on a total contrast between the mythical abstraction that represented capitalist wickedness and the mythical abstraction that represented proletarian virtue. Marx had invariably used it in his references to 'the bourgeoisie,' and Lenin had made vituperation the central element of a literary and oratorical style that had become exemplary in the Bolshevik tradition. We may well suppose, therefore, that in the world represented by Moscow this language, which now contributed to provoking so grim a reaction in the West, was not abnormal.

The tendency to go to these linguistic extremes was certainly aggravated by the psychological dynamics that characterize all societies, and especially their bureaucracies, in wartime. Men who are rivaling one another for advancement in a governmental bureaucracy become involved in the competitive manifestation of zeal for the cause, the competitive demonstration of their identification with it. In the atmosphere of wartime they all feel themselves under observation and under suspicion of not being perfect in their appreciation of the evil that the enemy represents. So a rivalry in demonstrative extremism gets under way. The composition of the speeches that Zhdanov and Malenkov made at the Silesian conference may not have been uninfluenced by an awareness of Stalin's increasingly suspicious disposition. Those speeches, in turn, set a standard that the other members of the conference would try to equal or surpass. This kind of thing occurs in all societies and in all governments. In Washington after 1949 it would take the form of a shrill and fanatical anti-Communism, increasingly divorced from real circumstances, that would approach if not equal the extremes exemplified by the Communist world.

This dynamism of conflict would immediately engender, now, another element of the totality that I have identified with the Cold War. Each side would insist, and would in some measure convince itself, that the other aimed to make itself master of the whole world. (In the same way, during the two World Wars all good Americans and Englishmen knew that, in the first case the Kaiser, and in the second Hitler, was aiming at the conquest of the world.) Each, in attributing this unlimited objective to the other, would thereby be led to the conclusion that the struggle could be resolved only by the total defeat of the one side or the other—as in the wars between Rome and Carthage. Western politicians, paraphrasing Lincoln, would announce that the world could not exist half slave and half free (although it always had). Communist leaders, citing Marx, would proclaim the inevitable doom of the capitalist world, its total defeat and destruction (which Marx had expected to take place not later than the end of the nineteenth century). The objective, once again, could be nothing less than unconditional surrender.

The concept of total victory or total defeat as the only alternatives was bound to appeal especially to many American military men, whose professional training and indoctrination disposed them to accept, uncritically, the view to which General MacArthur would later give expression, that 'in war there is no substitute for victory.' At the council-tables of government and on private occasions they would begin to manifest an unhappy impatience with the policies of the civilians under whose orders, nevertheless, they would continue faithfully to serve. I have no doubt that there were circles in Moscow where a like attitude was manifested.

*   *   *

The Declaration adopted by the Silesian conference, in connection with the founding of the Cominform, represents the official view of the Cold War, henceforth binding on all Communist parties and their members. It states that:

While the war was on, the Allied States in the war against Germany and Japan went together and comprised one camp. . . . [After the war] two camps were formed—the imperialist and anti-democratic camp having as its basic aim the establishment of world domination of American imperialism and the smashing of democracy, and the anti-imperialist and democractic camp having as its basic aim the undermining of imperialism, the consolidation of democracy, and the eradication of the remnants of fascism. . . . The Truman–Marshall plan is only a constituent part, the European subsection of the general plan for the policy of global expansion pursued by the United States in all parts of the world. The plan for the economic and political enslavement of Europe by American imperialism is being supplemented by plans for the economic and political enslavement of China, Indonesia, the South American countries. . . . Under these circumstances it is necessary that the anti-imperialist democratic camp should close its ranks, draw up an agreed program of actions and work out its own tactics against the main forces of the imperialist camp, against American imperialism and its British and French allies. . . .

A resolution of the conference charged the newly instituted Cominform 'with the organization of interchange of experience, and if need be, coordination of the activities of the Communist Parties on the basis of mutual agreement.'

One of the Cominform's first undertakings was represented by the strikes and disorders that began in France and Italy in November.[5] What their ultimate failure signified was the failure of Stalin's policy of pushing the West over the brink, on which it balanced, into economic disaster.

A few months later, on March 17, 1948, in a special Message to Congress, President Truman would say:

Since the close of hostilities the Soviet Union and its agents have destroyed the independence and democratic character of a whole series of nations in Eastern and Central Europe. It is this ruthless course of action, and the clear design to extend it to the remaining free nations of Europe, that have brought about the critical situation in Europe today. . . . The Soviet Union and its satellites were invited to co-operate in the European Recovery Program. They rejected the invitation. More than that, they have declared their violent hostility to the program and are aggressively attempting to wreck it. They see in it a major obstacle to their designs to subjugate the free community of Europe. . . . I am sure that the determination of the free countries of Europe to protect themselves will be matched by an equal determination on our part to help them do so.

The President would then ask Congress to enact legislation providing for universal military training and for the re-institution of conscription, which had been dropped at the end of the War.

On the same day that the President was to send this Message to Congress, the foreign ministers of Great Britain, France, Belgium, Holland, and Luxembourg, would meet together in Brussels to sign a treaty providing for a collective defense in case of an armed attack on any one of them. The project of such a treaty, establishing what was called 'Western Union,' had first been advanced by British Foreign Minister Bevin in the House of Commons on January 22 as a response to the creation of the Cominform.

So we see how, by a self-perpetuating dialectic, a process of action and reaction back and forth between the two sides, the Cold War grew rapidly in magnitude and intensity. This process would continue—toward what end no one, at the time, could foretell.

[5] See pp. 140–1 above.

CHAPTER XVI

*The real issue of the Cold War and its mythic formulations;
the Berlin Blockade and its failure*

IN ideological terms, the Cold War presented itself as a worldwide contest between liberal democracy and Communism.
Each side looked forward to the eventual supremacy of its system
all over the earth. The official Communist goal was the liberation
of mankind from capitalist oppression. Ideologically-minded
Westerners interpreted this as signifying that Moscow was trying
to impose its own authoritarian system on a world that it meant to
rule. Americans, for their part, had traditionally looked forward
to the liberation of mankind from the oppression of autocracy, and
to the consequent establishment of their own liberal system
throughout the world. To the ideologists in Moscow this meant
that 'the imperialist ruling circles' in America were trying to
enslave all mankind under the yoke of Wall Street.

The ideological view of human affairs has always had an
irresistible popular appeal because it conforms to the child's
image of a world divided between two species, the good (we) and
the wicked (they). According to this image, the essence of life is
the struggle between good and evil so represented. The two con-
testing species take many different forms but are always essentially the same. On one occasion they may take the form of the
cops and the robbers, on another that of the cowboys and the
Indians, on another that of 'peace-loving' and 'aggressor' nations.
In orthodox Marxism they take the form of the proletarians and
the capitalists. This is the universal fairy-tale of mankind, to
which we are all brought up. Any struggle cast in terms of it must
properly be total. It would be improper for the cops to negotiate
a compromise settlement with the robbers, or to limit the efforts
they make to overcome them by such rules of combat as would be
appropriate in a boxing-match, where the moral issue is absent.
Christians in the Middle Ages were limited by explicit rules of
chivalry and ecclesiastical law when they fought one another, but
not when they fought pagans. When they fought pagans the only

157

proper objective was that of eliminating them, or what they represented, from the face of the earth. Similarly, to the extent that the
Cold War was to be regarded as an ideological contest there
could be no geographical limitation to it, and it could properly
end only when one side had, at last, destroyed the other.

The ideological view, however, is in its essence mythical. The
grand eschatological objectives that go with it tend to have little
or no expression beyond the nominal. They are not, in any case,
objectives toward which the daily operations of government are
actually directed. At no time, after the first years of the Bolshevik
regime, was the operative policy of Moscow directed in any immediate or meaningful sense toward the objective of a single
classless and stateless society encircling the globe. This was,
rather, a nominal objective that pertained to a mythological
future. As such, however, it had a noble simplicity that made it
more real to the man in the street than such operative objectives
as that of acquiring the 'glacis' of secure territory along the
western frontier of the traditional Russian state.

This is not to say that the ideology, with its grand objective,
did not make a difference. It made a great difference. Not only
did it constantly threaten to draw the makers of policy into foolish
and dangerous adventures (for example, the 1920 march on Warsaw), it gave a mythic justification to the distrust of the outside
world that, in fact, had other roots; it provided its votaries with a
sense of mission; it furnished a cover of respectability for political
practices that, in their nakedness, would have seemed shameful; it
made those who were driven by terrible necessity to the perpetra-
tion of sinister deeds feel themselves morally justified. From the
first, however, the deeds themselves were directed toward more
limited and practical objectives that were not essentially different
from the traditional objectives of the Russian state. While the
nominal ideology had an influence that one could only regard as
dangerous, what was determinative for action was the complex of
considerations, representing power-politics, that stemmed from
the self-interest of the Russian state.

President Wilson's objective of making the world 'safe for
democracy' had, in a detached view, implications not altogether
unrelated to those arising from the ideological objectives associated
with the Russian state since 1917. The influence of that abiding
objective was, on occasion, dangerous—as in the ideological interventions that the United States undertook in Latin America

immediately after World War II, as in its commitment to the maintenance of liberal democracy in China. In the long run, however,
what was generally determinative for the operating policy of the
United States, as for that of Soviet Russia, was its own vital
interests in a world of power-politics.

In practice neither the United States nor the Soviet Union
was bent on establishing its rule over the earth. Each, however,
could be represented, with a certain show of plausibility, as seeking
to do so. The Cold War would tend to be intractable and un-
limitable to the extent that each side allowed itself to be entranced
by the nominal and ideological questions at issue, subordinating
the real, strategic questions.

All ideologically minded societies are given to a rhetoric of
generalization that, in its literal application, is absolute and universal. This rhetoric may not be intended for such application in
the practical world. The American founding fathers, for example,
did not intend to apply the saying that all men are created equal
to the status of Negro slaves in their society. Again, although the
immediate situation that caused the United States to enter World
War I was the torpedoing of merchant ships outside its Atlantic
harbors by German submarines, which made the menace of German expansion seem vivid as never before, when the nation responded by going to war against Germany the nominal cause that
it proclaimed was 'freedom of the seas'—a formulation that did
not distinguish the waters off its Atlantic harbors from the Sea of
Okhotsk. Again, the purpose of the United States 'to make the
world safe for democracy' did not put Europe ahead of Asia or
Africa. This rhetoric of World War I presented the American
people with generalizations of local situations that led them to
think in global terms, and that thereby strengthened the tendency
of all war to overspread geographical and other limits.

The proclamation of the Truman Doctrine represents the same
disposition. In 1947 it was the expansion of the Soviet Union in
Europe only that had upset the balance of power and that represented a mortal danger to the Atlantic community of which the
United States and Canada were the only undisabled members.
The immediate danger was in Europe, not in the Pacific or South
Asia or Africa. It was the situation in Europe that called for containment. Nevertheless, what the Truman Doctrine said was that
'it must be the policy of the United States to support free peoples
who are resisting attempted subjugation by armed minorities or

by outside pressures.' The concept this represented was simpler and grander than that of containing only Russia's expansion, and containing it from a particular point on the Baltic to a particular point on the Adriatic; but it was also less practicable. Taken literally, it covered the whole globe, applying to attempted subjugation of any free people anywhere by any armed minority or any outside pressure. So taken, it imposed an unlimited commitment on the United States, a commitment that might extend it far beyond its resources. Finally, it could only aggravate the fear of encirclement that had haunted Moscow for so many centuries. Who could say that it did not mean the use of the atomic bomb to enforce the American conception of freedom all around the globe? We Americans knew that we intended no such thing, but the Russians had a less benign picture of our character and our intentions.

We must distinguish, then, between the conflict represented by ideology and rhetoric, which was global and at best secondary, and the real conflict, which was over the balance of power that had its fulcrum in Europe. What the United States actually set out to do in 1947 was simply to defend what was left of Europe against an expanding Russia. If the resulting conflict was to spread to Asia, to Africa, or to Latin America, that would be an unfortunate development of later days which the statesmanship of the time might well have been seeking to avert.

*   *   *

We may compare the Cold War, as we may the two World Wars that preceded it, to an earthquake, which occurs in a particular locality but sends its tremors all around the globe. The epicenter was along a line that ran from Lübeck, below the Danish islands, to the head of the Adriatic. This was the line that Moscow's expanding power had reached by 1947, the line along which the rapidly developing Atlantic community now mounted its defenses. The policy of containment did not really apply to Outer Mongolia, Afghanistan, or Manchuria. In the years to come the radio-waves of the whole world would carry the noise of controversy, covert operations and propaganda would be conducted on all the continents, but the main confrontation would be along this line.[1]

This line did not correspond to any natural boundary,

---

[1] An important but secondary line of confrontation, where accidental circumstances would for a time cause the conflict almost to get out of control, was the 38th parallel in Korea. We shall, however, come to that in later chapters.

geographical or ethnographical. On the contrary, it not only divided
Europeans from Europeans, it divided Germans from Germans
and Austrians from Austrians. It cut families apart. In Berlin and
in Vienna it ran through the heart of a metropolis, through its
crowded streets, between its packed buildings, across its tram and
subway lines, across its electric-power lines, across its water and
sewage systems. The way the line was drawn is evidence in itself
that no one concerned with drawing it, on either side, had
thought of it as a line that, for at least a generation to come, would
divide from each other two great warring camps. The monstrosity
that it represented, as a line marking such a division, was com-
pounded by the fact that the Western zones of the two cities across
which it ran were enclaves in what was otherwise territory on the
Russian side of the line. Berlin, with its Western sectors of occupation, was 110 miles inside the Russian zone of Germany; Vienna
45 miles inside the Russian zone of Austria.

As we have seen, the intention on both sides was that Germany
and Austria should not be partitioned. Germany was to be administered as a single political and economic entity by a single
governing body, the Allied Control Council, sitting in its capital,
Berlin. The unanimous decisions of the Council—composed of the
representatives of France, Britain, Russia, and the United States
—would be administratively realized in each zone by the occupying authorities of that zone. Berlin, too, would be governed as a
unit, although divided into sectors for purposes of administration
as the City of New York is divided into boroughs.

Since everything depended, however, on unanimity in the Allied
Control Council, the development of the Cold War assured the
failure of the whole occupation plan. In the absence of unanimity
the occupying powers carried out, in their respective zones, what
policies seemed to them necessary or desirable, and this quickly
led to that partition of Germany which no one had planned. By
1947 the American and British zones had been merged; and by
1949 Germany had been definitely broken into two opposed
states—the Federal Republic of Germany, a liberal democratic
state tied to the West, and the German Democratic Republic, a
Russian satellite under the rule of Communist puppets who were
kept in power by the Red Army.

Because the two sides in the Cold War were deadlocked in
Germany from the beginning, the temporary line of administrative division between the Russian and the Western zones became a

line of national partition. It included, however, the boundary of that isolated enclave deep in Russian-dominated territory, the Western sectors of Berlin. Here the strategic position of the Western allies appeared to be one of extraordinary weakness. They had no formal agreement giving them rights of access to Berlin across what was to be enemy territory. Not anticipating the partition of Germany, they had relied on general and informal understandings regarding the use of certain limited routes to supply the small garrisons they had planned to post in Berlin. Their access to the city and the maintenance of their positions there were, in terms of the local military situation, at the mercy of Moscow, which had the local power to cut the routes and to capture or starve the Western garrisons whenever it might wish to do so. The Western position was militarily untenable. Yet, as the Cold War developed, the Western allies found themselves in a position in which they dared not and would not retreat from this indefensible outpost, even in the face of warlike measures by the Communists to force them to do so. Berlin would therefore become the principal center of tension in the Cold War. A series of Berlin crises would bring the world the closest that it was to come to all-out nuclear war.

The temptation that the Russians were under to take advantage of the West's weakness in Berlin must have been nearly irresistible. As the Communist rule was fastened upon the unhappy population of East Germany and East Berlin, the persistence of an island of freedom in the midst of the subjugated area created virtually insurmountable problems for those who were trying to maintain their despotism over it. For one thing, the contrast between the spiritual and economic misery of the East Germans and the relative well-being of the West Berliners was plain for all to see. The Westerners could see for themselves what conditions were in the prison-house of the East by simply walking into East Berlin, while the inhabitants of the prison-house could see what conditions were in the West by stepping across the open sector-boundary into West Berlin.

Churchill at Fulton had talked about an 'iron curtain.' Berlin constituted an open hole in that curtain.[2] The free speech allowed

[2] It is interesting to note that when Churchill gave his Fulton Address he described the line of the iron curtain as running 'from Stettin in the Baltic to Trieste in the Adriatic.' He thereby excluded what was still regarded, in March 1946, as 'eastern Germany' rather than 'East Germany.'

in the West flowed through that hole into the East by means of newspapers, magazines, books, radio-broadcasts, and Western visitors. As long as it remained, the 'closed society' imposed by Moscow could not be properly closed.

Worst of all, this opening in the curtain provided a route of escape for the East Germans who, if they could get as far as Berlin, had only to walk into the Western sectors and declare themselves to the Western authorities as refugees in order to be saved. From 1949, when the division of Germany was made definitive by the establishment of the two German states, until 1961, when the opening was sealed by cinder-block and barbed-wire, over 2,600,000 persons (out of a population, in 1949, of 17,500,000) had already escaped from the German Democratic Republic into West Germany. This loss of population threatened a complete breakdown in the social services and in the economy of the already shaky East German state. A substantial proportion of all its doctors, dentists, teachers, and policemen escaped during this period. Serious and growing labor-shortages developed in agriculture and industry.

Given these circumstances, it is not surprising that the leadership of the Communist camp should, throughout the Cold War, go to more dangerous lengths in order to prize the Western allies out of Berlin than they would for any other objective. In one of his graphic metaphors Mr. Khrushchev was to refer to Berlin as a bone in Moscow's throat. Only with respect to Berlin were the usually cautious Russians to show themselves, on occasion, desperate to the point of recklessness. But to no avail.

*   *   *

Efforts made at a series of four-power meetings to agree on what to do with Germany ended at last, in December 1947, with angry words between Russia and the Western powers. Thereafter the Western powers discussed the future of Germany without Russia, just as they had proceeded to discuss European recovery, after the middle of 1947, without Russia. Then, on March 20, 1948, the Russians withdrew their representative from the Allied Control Council in Berlin, declaring that it no longer existed. The Western allies went ahead on their own to deal with the problems of Germany and to prepare for its reconstitution as a self-governing state, thereby confronting Moscow with the specter of a rehabilitated and restored West German state, perhaps as dangerous as other German states had proved in the past, and allied with the West against it. Berlin, however, must have seemed to Moscow a useful hostage to prevent the West from carrying any such development through.

On June 18 the Western allies took their first major step to re-constitute the West German economy by instituting a currency reform that was long overdue. That evening the Russians, main-taining that the Western powers had no right to be in Berlin at all, inaugurated measures to stop all the surface traffic of the Western allies into and out of Berlin. Six days later they cut off all electric current, coal, food, and other supplies to West Berlin from territory under their control. The Berlin Blockade had begun. Russia had challenged the West, at what appeared to be its weakest point, to a test of strength.

On June 21 the Anglo-American powers launched a massive and desperate effort to supply the 2·25 million inhabitants of West Berlin by air. Within a few days a veritable bridge of transport planes from the West had been built. They flew one behind another in steady procession night and day, carrying heavy quantities of coal, food, and other necessary supplies.

While the Russians pretended, for the most part, that their stoppage of surface traffic was based on technical problems con-nected with the maintenance of the routes, they also took the position that Berlin was part of their zone of Germany, and that the Westerners were in it on sufferance rather than by right. Responding to this on June 30, Secretary of State Marshall in Washington and Foreign Minister Bevin in London announced that the Western powers were in Berlin by right and intended to stay.

We may if we wish regard this as the opening of the first great battle in what was now, in effect, an overt and declared Cold War. In prompt retaliation for Russia's blockade of West Berlin, the Western powers stopped all railway traffic in goods between the Western zones and East Germany. At the same time, sixty long-range bombers of the U.S. Air Force were quietly moved across the Atlantic to the British Isles. There was much fruitless diplomatic negotiation, on both sides efforts were made to limit provocation while yet standing firm, the Security Council of the United Nations became seized of the dispute, committees were set up and dissolved.

Meanwhile, as the months went by, Moscow was finding itself

in an increasingly embarrassing position. Before the eyes of the whole world it appeared to be trying to starve over two million men, women, and children in West Berlin, while the Berlin airlift, continuing month after month, provided a tangible demonstration of Western determination and competence. The population of West Berlin, moreover, stood solid in support of the Western resistance to the Russian challenge, accepting short rations and rejecting Russian offers to feed it in return for symbolic acts of submission. The success of the airlift, in particular, must have been unexpected to the Russians, since it was unexpected even to those who first set about organizing it. This spectacular undertaking, together with the attitude of the Berliners, caught men's imagination and invested the whole enterprise of resistance with an aura of heroic splendor.

By May 1949, then, Moscow had no choice but to recognize that its blockade was a costly failure, and to call it off with what grace it could. This concluded what was the first, but not the last, Battle of Berlin.

In challenging the West at Berlin Moscow had challenged it at what was ostensibly the weakest point along its whole front. The weakness was so conspicuous that anyone might have expected the West to accept the strategic impracticability of trying to hold so isolated an outpost in enemy territory. This, however, was to reckon without some of the factors in the strategic situation that were intangible or not locally apparent.

For one thing, the West had profited from the experience of the Munich surrender in 1938, which had led by way of catastrophic preliminary losses to the War that it had been designed to avert. There were 2·25 million people in Berlin for whom it had a responsibility that it would have been a scandal to shirk. If, to avoid the challenge that Moscow now offered, the West had simply abandoned these people to the Red Army and the secret police, then all the people in West Germany and beyond, wherever the protection of the United States and the West was counted on, would have doubted that they could count on it any longer. They would thereby have been given reason to sue for whatever terms of surrender they might obtain from Moscow. So the whole defense of the West might have crumbled away, and what remained of free Europe fallen under Moscow's domination. This was one of those situations in which each surrender makes a stand at each successive point of retreat less convincing and more dangerous—until all one's defenses are overcome or, more likely, until a desperate but belated stand brings on a catastrophe at least as great as what one had tried to avoid by the first retreat. These situations have their own dynamics, to which even the advancing side falls victim. In 1948 the West was able to recognize, if only instinctively, that such was the situation in Berlin, and it acted accordingly.

Another point to note, if we are learning the lessons that the experience offers, is that, although Moscow was overwhelmingly superior in local military strength at Berlin, in any ultimate test it would find itself effectively inhibited from the use of that superiority by the American possession of atomic bombs that, carried by bombers stationed in West Germany and Britain, might destroy Russian cities. If, then, the Western nerves were strong enough, what use was the military superiority of the Russians at Berlin?

Here, for the first time in this account, we confront the fact, which would become increasingly evident, that the advent of nuclear weapons had revolutionized classical strategy, drastically reducing or eliminating possibilities that, up to now, had always been functions of certain relationships of force. If nuclear weapons had not existed, and certainly if long-range air-power had not existed, Moscow would not have been deterred from using its local military superiority to take West Berlin by force.

At the time it was a general and altogether plausible belief that, not atomic power in itself, but the Western monopoly of that power, was what prevented this—that if Moscow had already had an equivalent atomic armament of its own, to deter and thereby neutralize the Western atomic armament, it could have taken Berlin as if atomic arms had never been invented. This, however, would be tested, after Moscow had acquired its own atomic armament, in other Berlin crises, which would show that the mere existence of such armaments, even though possessed by both sides equally, had a radically inhibiting effect on the use of conventional military forces.

Related to this is another lesson taught by this first great confrontation of the Cold War, to be confirmed by other confrontations that would follow. It was that, in a world of atomic armaments, the geographical *status quo* between opposing sides tends to be frozen. Even such an apparently untenable position as that of the Western allies in Berlin proved to be tenable, in spite of pressure that was sometimes brutal, throughout the Cold War. The first Battle of Berlin was a victory for the *status quo*, which would continue to win each time military force was invoked, whether by Russia or the West, to challenge it.

Throughout the first Berlin crisis the outbreak of a third world war, involving military combat on a vast scale all around the globe, seemed an imminent possibility. This produced, on both sides, a grim preoccupation with the implications of the general military situation. The time has come for us to look at what those implications seemed to be, and what they were.

CHAPTER XVII

The implications of atomic power; the reluctance of the West to re-arm

WITH the Berlin Blockade, the conflict between Russia and the West finally crossed the boundaries of an ordinary diplomatic contest and took on the semblance of a war. Barely dissembled force was being used. The military balance now became the dominant concern of both sides.

The military balance of the late 1940's was unique in history because nuclear weapons were included for the first time, and there was little basis of experience for knowing what weight should be attached to them. It was evident that they could not be casually used for limited objectives. Because their power was such as to destroy populations and crack the foundations of society, their use had implications of spreading anarchy over wide areas. It would, one felt instinctively, start something of which no one could foresee the end. Consequently, almost any decision to use them outside the context of a generalized conflict like World War II would be the desperate last resort of a state for which the apparent alternative was its own disappearance.

These considerations, instinctively apprehended, caused alarm among the governments and populations of the West no less in the days when the monopoly of such weapons was on their side than later. Perhaps nuclear weapons caused them more concern because they held them in their own hands, saw at close quarters how powerful they were, and did not know how to control them.

*　　*　　*

At the First Quebec Conference, in August 1943, Sir John Anderson, head of the Scientific Research Committee of the British War Cabinet, told the Canadian Prime Minister that the country which first succeeded in producing atomic bombs would have control of the world.[1] Two years later the United States did be-

---

[1] Quoted by Groom, p. 123, from Pickersgill, p. 532.

come the first country to succeed in producing atomic bombs. The result, however, was manifestly not to give it control of the world.

It is true that control of the world was not an American objective. Even for the attainment of more limited objectives, however, the atomic monopoly that the United States enjoyed for the best part of a decade did not serve.

Item. The United States was opposed to the Communist seizure of Czechoslovakia in 1948. Why didn't it simply inform the Soviet Government that, unless Czechoslovakia was liberated forthwith, Moscow would be blown off the face of the earth? The words of the Potsdam Declaration ('the alternative . . . is prompt and utter destruction') would have carried a more explicit meaning this time, after the examples of Hiroshima and Nagasaki.

Item. Why didn't Washington tell Moscow that its cities would be atomized unless it lifted the Berlin blockade immediately?

Item. Why didn't Washington require Russia to withdraw from the half of Europe it had captured, back into its traditional frontiers, on penalty of atomic devastation?

Item. Above all, why didn't the United States use its atomic monopoly to preserve its atomic monopoly? Why didn't it serve notice on Moscow that, if it ever tested a nuclear device of any kind, the United States would immediately destroy the Soviet Union? Or why didn't it, for that matter, tell Moscow that, unless it agreed never to make atomic weapons, and unless it allowed full American inspection of its territory to insure that the agreement was kept, the Russian society would be shattered?

In September 1949 the United States was alarmed and dismayed when the Soviet Union, some three years ahead of expectations, produced its first atomic explosion. Surely this was the time to deliver an ultimatum to Moscow, saying that, unless all work on atomic devices was stopped, and the stoppage confirmed by inspection, the United States would launch a massive atomic attack on the Soviet Union!

While the United States never wanted to control the world, there can be no doubt that it very much wanted to keep Russia from getting atomic weapons. Yet it appears to be the fact that the Government of the United States never gave official consideration to the possibility of waging, or threatening to wage, a preventive atomic war for the realization of this vital purpose. While individuals inside the Government, and any number of American military officers, as individuals, may have favored such a war, I believe it can be truly said that the Government never even raised the matter, within its own councils, for consideration; that no studies of what such an undertaking would entail were ordered; and that the matter never appeared on the agenda of the National Security Council.

Perhaps what we confront here is simply a default of will on the part of the United States. One may not doubt that, in an absolute physical sense, there was a period when it could have compelled the Soviet Union to retreat or surrender either by destroying its principal cities or by threatening to do so. There was a period when it had the physical power to do this, so that its failure to do it can be attributed to a lack of will—in which it may or may not have been justified.[2]

At the time, it was claimed that Moscow held West Europe as a hostage, thereby effectively deterring an atomic attack by the United States. It was said that, as soon as such an attack was launched, the Red Army would move, unimpeded, to occupy all the principal cities of West Europe, where it would maintain itself on the resources of the lands it occupied.[3] What would the United States do then? Would it atomize Paris, Brussels, Rome, Munich, and the other European cities in order to hurt the Red Army? To do so would have been unthinkable even for the most ruthless Americans.

[2] The facts are not available, but it is likely that the American stockpile of atomic bombs before the 1950's was so limited as to put in doubt the ability of the United States to destroy the Soviet society. Manned bombers were still the only means of delivery, and the Russian air-defenses would presumably have been able to prevent a large proportion of the bombs from reaching their targets. The smaller the proportion that could reach their targets, the larger the number that would be needed for a successful attack. Presumably Moscow had a fair idea of the size of the American stockpile, so that the possibilities of diplomatic bluffing would have been limited. It is unlikely, however, that the stockpile was negligible. Walter Lippmann has reported that 'in the late 1940's' a 'high official' of the Defense Department in Washington tried to persuade him 'to write articles in favor of launching a preventive [nuclear] war against the Soviet Union.' (*New York Herald-Tribune*, Internationl Edition, June 25, 1965.) The official presumably knew the size of the stockpile and the expert estimates of what might be done with it. In any case, we may be sure that in the 1950's the stockpile was growing rapidly to gigantic proportions. There was certainly a period when the capability of the United States was such that it could be reasonably sure of being able to destroy the Soviet Union without undue risk of direct damage to its own territory. (See Dinerstein, pp. 174-7.)

[3] 'In the spring of 1947 the famous Soviet historian, Eugène Tarlé, described in a public lecture the nature of a hypothetical war between the United States and the U.S.S.R. As soon as the war started the Soviet Union would occupy Western Europe.' (Dinerstein, p. 174.)

Whatever the weight to be attached to the consideration that Moscow had a hostage, there were powerful moral inhibitions, in the minds of military men and civilians alike, against killing in cold blood millions of men, women, and children for the sake of achieving even a vital political objective. The people of the United States would have been horrified and revolted. There would have been political turmoil inside the country that might have ended by destroying the authority of the Government.

This, however, was not all there was to the matter. I think that most persons felt instinctively, and with good reason, that the result of a nuclear attack even on a defenseless Russia would be a spreading chaos throughout the world, a chaos that would not fail to communicate itself to the United States.

Constitutional and other difficulties would have made it hard for the United States to issue an ultimatum in which it posed nuclear destruction as the alternative to the acceptance of its terms, and the reaction to such an ultimatum throughout the world, while incalculable, might well have been revolutionary in its impact. The terrible ultimatum itself would have loosened the bonds in which chaos is held. Then, if it had been acted on, perhaps the whole fabric of world order, such as it was, would have cracked and crumbled. The shock of horror at the scenes of piled-up death in the Russian cities, the collapse of the Russian state, the possible invasion of the West by the Red Army, the sudden vacuum of power and authority over half the world—one felt instinctively that these possible consequences, with their implications, would immediately make the situation of human civilization everywhere, not excepting the United States, desperate.

Sir John's statement that the first country to produce the atomic bomb would control the whole world provides a bench-mark from which to measure the progress of thought in the postwar period on the strategic implications of nuclear armaments. His statement, when he made it in 1943, was plausible if one could assume that whatever state first acquired atomic bombs would possess a power with which it could destroy any state or any combination of states that challenged or resisted it. Is this not supreme power? And doesn't the holder of supreme power control the world?

There is an abstract and theoretical sense in which Sir John was not wrong. The atomic bomb did confer the physical power to control the world on any country that, having the resources to produce it first, was determined to preserve its monopoly. It did confer this physical power. But conferred it on what specifically? Not on a man, because no single man could produce, load, and deliver the bombs to their targets. It conferred it, rather, on something called a government, which is an organization that can function only within certain limits.

The President of the United States, as commander-in-chief of its armed forces, has the constitutional authority, acting entirely on his own, to order the U.S. Navy to cross the Atlantic and attack the British Isles. But we may be sure that if he gave such an order today it would not be obeyed. All concerned in Washington would immediately conclude that he had gone insane, that therefore he was no longer in condition to exercise the duties of his office, and that this obviated the Constitutional requirement of obedience. We have to distinguish, then, between the President's theoretical power under the Constitution and the actual power he is able to exercise. We have to distinguish similarly between the theoretical power of the Government of the United States to use the atomic bomb for the control of the world and its actual power to do so. The actual power, overlooked by Sir John, is what counts.

In any case, real power is always something far greater than military power alone. A balance of power is not a balance of military power only: it is, rather, a balance in which military power is one element. Even in its crudest aspect, power represents a subtle and intimate combination of force and consent. No stable government has ever existed, and no empire has ever become established, except with an immensely preponderant measure of consent on the part of those who were its subjects. That consent may be a half-grudging consent; it may be a consent based in part on awe of superior force; it may represent love, or respect, or fear, or a combination of the three. Consent, in any case, is the essential ingredient in stable power—more so than physical force, of which the most efficient and economical use is to increase consent.

By using physical force in such a way as alienates consent one constantly increases the requirements of physical force to replace the consent that has been alienated. A vicious spiral develops that, continued, ends in the collapse of power. If the Government in Washington had undertaken to use the atomic bomb to control the world it would surely have ended by incurring the fanatical hostility of the world's peoples, with incalculable consequences. It would have found itself trying to dominate the world by terror alone; it would have found itself driven to ever greater extremes of ruthlessness; and the requirements of a totally ruthless policy would, at last, have compelled it to establish a tyranny over the American people as well as over the rest of mankind. At some point early in this progress, however, it would have fallen and been replaced.

The fact is, as we have all come to appreciate, that nuclear weapons are too powerful to serve as all-purpose weapons, or to be used as instruments of policy except where the issues of national life or death are directly in question. As a witty colleague of mine once put it, one does not use a hand-grenade to kill mosquitoes in one's living-room.

What I have been dealing with here are the principles that define the strategic use of nuclear weapons in terms of relative rationality. They can, of course, be used quite irrationally, and once a great war between major powers had broken out the danger that they would be so used would increase. This constitutes an effective deterrent to any direct resort to war by one major power against another.

To this I should add that, as both sides in the Cold War were to find out, the overt threat to resort to nuclear attack necessarily shares, in whatever degree, the limitations on the usefulness of such attack itself.

In the late 1940's the countries of the West were alarmed at the imbalance represented by the contrast between the vast strength of the Red Army and their own nakedness in the conventional instruments of military land-power. They felt themselves defenseless in the path of the Russian advance. At the same time, they had such a horror of the atomic bomb, even though their side had the monopoly of it, that its use could hardly be contemplated. This psychology must account, at least in part, for the fact that throughout the tense months of the Berlin blockade Washington refrained from any overt threat to use the bomb.

On the other hand, to the Russians the imbalance must have appeared the other way around, for they saw their society defenseless against an annihilating attack that the 'capitalist imperialists,' ruthless by definition, might launch at any time.

It is in its psychological effect only that the balance of power implies stability. This is to say that it exercises its restraint on political or military adventure only to the extent that it is believed to exist, whether it exists in fact or not. In 1948–1949 there was a psychological balance of sorts between utterly disparate powers—like a balance between a chimera that breathes fire and a dragon that lashes with its tail. In this case, the chimera would feel an urgent need to acquire a powerful tail for lashing, the dragon to acquire a fire-breathing capability. The West would set about rebuilding its conventional land-forces while Moscow would be working on a crash basis to develop an atomic armament.

The great fear in the West was of what would happen when, as was inevitable in time (assuming that a preventive war would not be launched), Moscow did acquire such an armament. Its acquisition, everyone supposed, would deter and thereby neutralize the Western atomic armament, leaving the Red Army free to advance once more. This logic seemed unassailable, and the fear it inspired in the West made us all contemplate the future with awful forebodings. For years one had the feeling that the time left for the enjoyment of a tolerable existence was running out. Thinking of the fate of the Carthaginians, one wondered what except tribal habit caused one to take such pains in the rearing of one's children. Historians may recapitulate the events of such times as these, but they can never recapture the emotion.

*   *   *

The atomic bomb, from the moment that its existence became known, inspired a panicky alarm among Americans by the geologic destructiveness of its power. This alarm was aggravated by a revolutionary new situation, in the realm of military geography, that accompanied its advent. American territory, having for generations been regarded as beyond the reach of any enemy, was suddenly about to be open to attack from other continents by foreign airplanes or missiles loaded with the means to make a city disappear under a mushroom cloud that would rise like a tombstone to mark the spot where it had stood. This new threat of surprise attack, moreover, had a particularly vivid reality for Americans because of the successful Japanese attack on Pearl Harbor in 1941, which left its traumatic and indelible impression on the national consciousness.

As early as November 1945, General H. H. Arnold, commander of the U.S. Army Air Force, issued an official report of an alarming nature.

With the continued development of weapons and techniques now known to us [he wrote], New York, Pittsburgh, Detroit, Chicago, or

San Francisco may be subject to annihilation from other continents in a matter of hours. . . . Future attack upon the United States may well be without warning. . . . Today many modern war devices of great destructive power can be built piecemeal and under cover. Sub-assemblies might be secretly made in underground laboratories, and assembled into an annihilating war machine. War may descend upon us by thousands of robots passing unannounced across our shore-lines. . . . The first target of a potential aggressor might well be our industrial system or our major population centers. . . . [The United States] must recognize that real security against atomic weapons in the future will rest on our ability to take immediate offensive action with overwhelming force. It must be apparent to a potential aggressor that an attack on the United States would be immediately followed by an immensely devastating air-atomic attack on him. The atomic weapon thus makes offensive and defensive air power in a state of immediate readiness the primary requisite of national survival.

This was not the confident language of a country that suddenly found itself with a monopoly of supreme power, in a position to control the world.

A principal source of spreading alarm, after the atomic bomb's existence had been revealed and demonstrated, was the American scientific community. Regarding the bomb as the monstrous progeny of their own hitherto honored profession, the scientists now felt a moral duty to apply their minds and their authority as scientists to the revolution in international politics that, as most of them saw it, was made necessary by the weapon they had created. It was natural that they should tend to address them-selves to the problems of politics, the difficulties of which they generally underestimated, in terms of formulations appropriate to the physical sciences with which they were familiar—above all, in terms of formulations that provided exact and final conclusions. Even before the close of the War one of the two most distinguished physicists living, Dr. Niels Bohr, was seeking acceptance by Roosevelt and Churchill for an arrangement by which Stalin, in return for the secret of the atomic bomb, would transmute the traditionally closed society of Russia into an open society—pre-sumably by issuing appropriate orders. Later, immediate world government was declared, by leading scientists, to be the only alternative to general annihilation. Eminent physicists and mathe-maticians issued statements in which they warned that either all war would be abolished forthwith (presumably by some single decision) or we would all die in the radioactive ruins of our cities.

Representative scientists, individually or through their associations, described how atomic bombs in small boxes would be smuggled into American cities, hidden under the city-roofs on which the unsuspecting citizen looked out, and detonated whenever a secret, anonymous enemy gave the order—unless a complete reformation of mankind took place immediately.[4]

The scientists, entering upon political prediction and prescription, were treading unfamiliar ground. Moreover, in undertaking to arouse the public by their reports, they gave up the scientific detachment on which the validity and authority of those reports depended. The result was a double failure: their predictions, happily, were not to be borne out; their alarmism intensified the Cold War and contributed to an atmosphere of latent panic in which extremist measures, directed at the dangers of espionage and subversion, were increasingly to debase the quality of American life. Again we see how the highest intentions, resting on a foundation of perfect sincerity, may lead to ends that are opposite to those intended. Dr. J. Robert Oppenheimer has remarked that if one tries to be, at one and the same time, an observer and an actor on the scene under observation, one will fail in both respects.[5]

I must not give the impression that there was no occasion for such alarm as was expressed by military men and scientists alike. The military men were not creating a bogus specter to frighten the American public into supporting rearmament and remobilization; the scientists were not expressing an alarm that they knew to be without foundation in order to stampede the American people into abolishing war or instituting world government. The alarm was not at all without foundation in the objective circumstances of the day, to the extent that they could be judged by contemporaries, and those circumstances required the urgent exploration of all possibilities for reducing or eliminating the danger they represented. These possibilities surely did not, however, include immediate world government or some act whereby war was abolished, both of these being abstract concepts from the nominal world of law without adequate correspondence to the real world in which the danger presented itself. (The legal abolition of war, for example, would not really abolish war any more than the legal abolition of crime, although supported by

---

[4] For specific examples, see Halle, 1958, pp. 18–25.   [5] Oppenheimer, p. 88.

sanctions, abolishes crime.) Their advocacy offered a psychological refuge to those who might otherwise have been overcome by their justifiable fears, but did not offer any realizable solution to the danger.

If one ruled out, as equally unreal, a preventive war, or the threat of such a war, and the subsequent rule of the world by Washington under the sanction of its atomic monopoly, then the only solution was the humdrum and partial solution of working to restore international stability through a balance of power in which mutual deterrence was an essential element. Once a sufficient degree of international stability had been restored, other measures of a more solid and permanent nature might progressively become possible. This, implicitly and to some extent explicitly, is what George Kennan was advocating in his article setting forth the policy of containment.

Among the requirements of such a policy was the rearmament and remobilization of the West, to be carried on with expedition but in such a manner as to give the least possible provocation to Moscow.

*   *   *

The total population of all the nations that, beginning in 1947, stood opposed to the continued westward expansion of the Russian empire greatly exceeded the population of that empire itself. They were not, however, organized to match the Russians in military manpower. In Russia all major decisions were taken by one man in the Kremlin and imposed on a population that was politically inert and obedient. The creation of a larger Red Army, any time the Kremlin might wish, would under these circumstances be essentially a matter of herding. The Army so created was a single army under a single command. It was, moreover, an army of such stalwart stock, so inured to hardship and discipline, that it could be kept effective on relatively short rations and with a minimum of amenities.

The far greater manpower of the West was, by contrast, scattered among a multitude of distinct sovereignties, and for the most part in countries in which major decisions were ultimately made by the people rather than imposed on them. Only a combination of the most extreme and immediate danger from outside, together with high morale inside, would bring these separate populations to accept large-scale and compulsory military mobilization—especially for indefinite duration in what was nominally peacetime. In the late 1940's the populations of the West were heartily sick of such military requirements, longing for the restoration of normal civilian life. Only the extremity of their plight in the years of World War II had brought them to accept, temporarily, such a derogation from their sovereign independence as was represented by putting their military forces under a foreign command for purposes of centralization. Finally, the European members of the group were all in a condition of economic distress, and some of them were in a condition of social turmoil.

Add to this that the greatest of the properly European countries, Germany, was divided, and that the Germans of the West at this time could not be allowed by the others to create a military force, being still regarded as a dangerous 'aggressor nation.'

There were other reasons as well, impalpable but profound, why with their combined resources the nations of the West could not be expected to match the Red Army, reinforced by the armies of the European satellites. The willingness to make sacrifices for the sake of a common future tends always to be proportionate to the degree in which one feels that such a future depends on the sacrifices one makes—the degree in which, consequently, one feels responsible. The people of the United States, for example, might well feel that the future of the West depended on the sacrifices they were willing to make for it, that the future of the West was thus their responsibility. But the people of Paraguay, although they had just as great a stake in that future, would know how far from decisive for it like sacrifices on their part would be. Therefore they would have less incentive to make such sacrifices for it. The fact that responsibility and authority, centralized in the Russian empire, were so widely scattered in the West, would in itself mean that the West could not, especially in times of nominal peace, match the military manpower of the former.

Nevertheless, an effort would be made to develop a multi-national force adequate to provide effective military deterrence, in the West, to any further advance by the Red Army. And the individual Western countries would try to keep up or increase their respective land forces with this in mind.

The United States, which felt the responsibility as others at this time could not, had a tradition of maintaining only token ground forces on a volunteer basis in time of peace. Nevertheless, it broke with tradition by enacting in Congress, on June 24, 1948, the

'Selective Service' bill, which provided for the continuing conscription of men from nineteen to twenty-five years of age for
military service of twenty-one months. March 1948 was to mark
the low point for the American military establishment, in terms of
manpower. After that it would expand.

A notable expansion of American air-power was undertaken at
the same time; massive support was given to scientific research and
development in nuclear weapons and delivery systems; civil defense was planned and organized to prepare for the contingency of
nuclear attacks on American cities. The United States and Canada
entered into cooperative arrangements for the establishment, in
the far north, of radar-systems providing early warning of air-
attack across the polar regions.

The British and French, still having at least the remnants of
overseas empires to police, and having to bear their respective
parts in the occupation of Germany, also instituted peacetime
conscription, although this was against the English as against the
American tradition.

A defense of West Europe, however, could not be made with
each country acting separately. After the urgent requirements of
economic rehabilitation, met by the Marshall Plan, the organization of a common Western defense made its claim to top priority.
This would be the task with which the crowded decade of the
1940's would end.

CHAPTER XVIII

The formation of the Western military alliance, culminating in NATO

THE winter of 1947–1948 was a winter of crisis for the nations of western Europe. Their economies had broken down, the Communist parties under orders from Moscow had embarked on an all-out effort to wreck their political structures, invasion by the Red Army seemed an imminent possibility. Economic restoration was now successfully undertaken, under the European Recovery Program, by a combined effort through the Organization for European Economic Cooperation. The internal Communist attacks were, after some anxious weeks, beaten back and finally put down. It remained for these war-crippled countries to re-habilitate themselves militarily so as to cope with the threat from the east.

The military defense of West Europe, like its economic rehabili-tation, required a combined effort through a common organiza-tion. On March 17, 1948, the day that President Truman asked Congress to re-institute military conscription, the representatives of France, Belgium, Luxembourg, the Netherlands, and Great Britain signed the Brussels Treaty providing that, 'if any of the Parties should be the subject of an armed attack in Europe, the other Parties will . . . afford the party attacked all military and other aid and assistance in their power.' Under this alliance, which bore the name of Western Union, the five West European states set up a Consultative Council through which to organize a common defense.

Just as the combined effort at economic rehabilitation through the O.E.E.C. depended on the American contribution, so the combined effort at defense through Western Union depended on whatever hand in the matter the United States might see fit to take. This posed a difficult problem for the Administration in Washington, since any military alliance with a European country, or any binding military commitment to the Old World in time of peace, would be in contradiction of the most revered of American

180

political traditions, however obsolete that tradition had been made by circumstances and by the Truman Doctrine. Nevertheless, the Administration had determined to make the break with tradition, and the Senate, alarmed at the Russian threat, would agree to its doing so.

*   *   *

I have already commented on the universalizing tendency of American idealism, represented by the Truman Doctrine and by the proclamation of such objectives as 'freedom of the seas' and 'making the world safe for democracy.' In the wartime consideration of postwar organization, Churchill had favored regional groupings of nations, but Roosevelt had insisted on the conception, realized in the United Nations Organization, of one universal organization without regional subdivisions.

This universalization, which manifested the American tendency to go from one extreme to the other, was at odds with that concept of two worlds, an Old World and a New, on which American policy had traditionally been based. During the 1930's and 1940's this concept of two worlds had been the matrix for the Latin American policy of the United States, called the Good Neighbor Policy. Under the Good Neighbor Policy the twenty-one American republics constituted one band of brothers, bound together by ideals peculiar to the New World, standing in opposition to the sordid politics of the Old World.

What this concept meant in the realm of security was that the American republics were bound together in a common defense against the Old World, a defense that they mounted on the beaches of their common Hemisphere. As the menace of Axis aggression assumed ever more frightening proportions in the 1930's, the United States had taken the lead to organize this common Hemispheric defense, no less in the political and economic fields than in the military. Beginning at the Conference of Buenos Aires in 1936, it had led the way to a series of agreements whereby all the American republics together assumed a common responsibility for maintaining the integrity of the Hemisphere in the face of threats from the Old World, a responsibility which the United States had hitherto borne alone under the Monroe Doctrine. Then, during and after the War, it had given the other American republics increasing assistance—economic, social, and military—in accordance with the concept of a special and exclusive family-relationship among them that distinguished them from the profane nations of mankind. All this was accompanied by those resolutions of inter-American conferences, couched in noble rhetoric and redolent of exalted sentiment, to which the Latin American nations were peculiarly addicted.

At the end of the War the United States did not lessen the attention that it gave the other American republics. In fact, it increased its material assistance to them. At the same time, however, it entered into those ties with the countries of the Old World that I have been chronicling here. Under the Marshall Plan it gave those countries assistance that quite dwarfed what it was giving the countries of its own Hemisphere, who felt that their claims were not only prior but exclusive. Washington's new policy of containment, which represented defense at a distance rather than defense on the beaches of the Hemisphere, appeared to them as a betrayal.

The Latin American republics did their best, as the War drew to its conclusion, to preserve the exclusive regional relationship, with its Hemispheric isolationism, in the face of all the circumstances that were drawing the United States across the Atlantic and impelling it to assume world leadership. Apprehensive at the provisions in the draft *Charter of United Nations* that made Hemispheric security dependent on the unanimity of Russia, Britain, France, China, and the United States (and thus on the veto of any one of them), leaving no place for such special and exclusive security arrangements as they had hitherto enjoyed in their relations with the United States, they took the initiative to have inserted into the Charter certain provisions for regional arrangements—including Article 51, which provided that 'nothing in the present Charter shall impair the inherent right of individual or collective self-defense. . . .' The word 'collective,' in this clause, opened the way for such regional security agreements as the American republics had already projected.

Since the universalism of the United Nations Charter would prove unworkable in the field of international security, Article 51 was to have an importance that Washington had not anticipated. It opened the door for the regional alternative when universalism failed. The Brussels Treaty was based upon it, referring to it explicitly, and it would provide the legal basis for the North Atlantic alliance that was now to be constructed.

The Act of Chapultepec, concluded at an inter-American

meeting on March 6, 1945, had recommended that the American republics enter into a treaty by which they would ally themselves in a common defense, and it was with a view to allowing for such a treaty that they had sponsored Article 51. The projected treaty, the Inter-American Treaty of Reciprocal Assistance, was concluded at Rio de Janeiro in September 1947. Its importance in this account is that it provided the precedent and the model for the North Atlantic Treaty. In it, the High Contracting Parties agreed 'that an armed attack by any State against an American State shall be considered as an attack against all the American States and, consequently, each . . . undertakes to assist in meeting the attack in the exercise of the inherent right of individual or collective self-defense recognized by Article 51 of the Charter of the United Nations.'

There is, in retrospect, a quality of unreality in the sense of historic accomplishment with which this Treaty was prepared and concluded. One who was present throughout the process of drafting it, in however minor a capacity, recalls how it seemed the culmination of the long development of its inter-American relations on which the United States had embarked some fifteen years earlier. What it represented, however, was the persistence of an old concept, that of defending the Hemisphere on its beaches, after a new concept, that of defense at a distance, had replaced it. This is not to say that it was worthless or meaningless. It was simply less important as a military alliance than it seemed at the time; and the North Atlantic Treaty, to be concluded a year and a half later, would be an additional reason why it was less important.

It must have been sometime in 1948 that Mr. Dean Rusk, then Director of the Office of United Nations Affairs in the State Department, called a meeting to consider an undertaking with which he had been charged by Secretary Marshall. The Secretary, he announced in opening the meeting, wanted the Department to address itself to the question of preparing a treaty, modeled on the Rio Treaty, that might be entered into by such countries all around the world as were disposed to resist the expansion of the Soviet Union.[1] The meeting is worth mentioning here simply because what eventuated from it after many months

---

[1] Since there is no public record of such matters I have only my own memory as a participant in the meeting to rely on. Earlier, Mr. Rusk, as a lieutenant colonel in the Office of the Secretary of War, had taken a hand in the drafting of the Rio Treaty.

was, rather than a worldwide alliance, the North Atlantic Treaty. The universalistic disposition of American thinking is illustrated by the fact that the initial conception, later narrowed down, was of one arrangement that would embrace, alike, the defense of Japan, of South Asia, of West Europe, and of any other threatened areas of the world. With the abandonment of the doctrine of the two worlds, the United States was powerfully moved, during these years, by the unattainable ideal of one world.

The Brussels Treaty had been concluded in the hope of that eventual American participation in the common defense without which it would, for the foreseeable future, remain ineffective. No one could be sure that such participation would be forthcoming, although the Truman Administration gave every encouragement, and no one could tell what form it might take. One form that it was to take was that of substantial military-assistance programs to help equip the forces that the West European countries were to develop. The other principal form that it would take, however, was that of the alliance formalized in the North Atlantic Treaty, which was signed at Washington on April 4, 1949, by the five Brussels countries plus Denmark, Iceland, Italy, Norway, Portugal, Canada, and the United States. (Greece and Turkey were to join in 1952, West Germany in 1954.) Like the Rio Treaty, it provided 'that an armed attack against one or more of [the Parties] in Europe or North America shall be considered an attack against them all; and . . . if such an armed attack occurs, each of them . . . will assist the Party or Parties so attacked. . . .'

*   *   *

The Americans who sponsored the North Atlantic Treaty in 1948 and 1949 did not see any immediate prospect that a barrier of ground forces on a scale to be effective in itself could be erected in the path of Russia's westward expansion. It was thought, rather, that without the American guaranty contained in the Treaty, with the atomic bomb behind it, the Europeans would feel so hopeless about their future, faced as they were by the unmatchable Russian might, that they would hardly have the heart for the effort that their own rehabilitation required. The American guaranty, rather than an actual build-up of forces, was the point of the Treaty—and its purpose was largely psychological. The strategic concept on which the common defense was now based did not vary essentially from the American recommendations as set forth by General Omar Bradley in a statement before the House Foreign Affairs Committee in July 1949.

First, [he said] the United States will be charged with the strategic bombing. We have repeatedly recognized in this country that the first priority of the joint defense is our ability to deliver the atomic bomb.

Second, the United States Navy and the Western Union naval powers will conduct essential naval operations, including keeping the sea lanes clear. The Western Union and other nations will maintain their own harbor and coastal defense.

Third, we recognize that the hard core of the ground power in being will come from Europe, aided by other nations as they can mobilize.

Fourth, England, France, and the closer countries will have the bulk of the short-range attack bombardment, and air defense. We, of course, will maintain the tactical air force for our own ground and naval forces, and United States defense.

This strategic concept made good sense in purely military terms, having regard for the resources and capabilities of the various countries concerned. Crudely stated, however, what it meant was that the United States, which would enjoy the commanding position in the organization of the common defense, would wear on its own shoulders the wings that would bear it into battle, if the occasion arose, while its European allies would provide the infantry that crawled over the ground or, in battle, was pounded into the mud. This would in time, although not immediately, cause many Europeans to look on it unfavorably.

In 1949 and 1950 a major concern of the European governments, still, was whether the United States would commit itself fully and permanently, and the terms on which it might so commit itself. The atom bomb, most authorities agreed, was all that deterred the Red Army from moving on to the Channel, and this would continue exclusively in American hands. What would make its use sure, and known to Moscow to be sure, in the event of Russian aggression against West Europe?

The discrepancy between the number of divisions facing each other at the Iron Curtain was understood to be of the order of 125 to 14 in favor of the Russians. Later estimates of total Communist divisions would range up to 263, the number facing the

West being commonly given as 175.[2] It was evident that, without the atomic armament, the conventional forces of the Atlantic Treaty countries would hardly suffice even to delay the Red Army, should it march. Nor was it believed practicable for the West to build conventional forces of a magnitude remotely approaching that of the forces at Moscow's disposal.

A conception tailored to these harsh circumstances was now developed. It was represented by the analogy of the plate-glass window in a jeweler's shop: the window is easily broken, but from a thief's point of view there is a world of difference between seizing articles of display for which he has only to reach out his hand, and having first to smash a sheet of glass interposed between him and them. He may be deterred by the presence of the glass simply because, in smashing it, he would raise an alarm that might produce the most drastic consequences. The fragility of the glass, therefore, does not make it useless as a deterrent, even though it would be better if unbreakable.

The purpose of NATO's conventional forces could hardly be to frustrate and repel a Communist aggression by themselves.[3] As a minimum, their purpose must be to make it certain that the Red Army could not advance, as Hitler's Army had advanced into the Rhineland in 1936, without fighting. The minimum purpose must be to make it clear to Moscow that it could not order the Red Army forward without starting a real war. There would be a window to smash. Presumably the American divisions in Germany, of which there were two in 1949, would be in the path of the Red Army, thus assuring the immediate involvement of the United States, with its atomic armament, in such a war. The smashing of the window might detonate the atomic bomb.

By another metaphoric analogy this conception came to be known as that of the shield and the sword. The West's conven-

[2] Sources that should be authoritative are not in agreement on the size of the forces that faced each other across the Iron Curtain. On the Western side, a distinction has to be made between divisions in readiness and divisions that could be put into the field after a period of time. Russian divisions were generally smaller in manpower than Western divisions. See Stebbins, 1950, p. 145; Stebbins, 1951, p. 121; Calvocoressi 1953, p. 87, fn. 10; U.S. Senate Armed Forces Committee hearings, February 19, 1951; Gen. Eisenhower's report to NATO Planning Committee, October 10, 1951; etc. In the 1960's it began to be understood in Washington that the estimate of 175 Russian divisions had been greatly exaggerated, that 75 to 85 would have been nearer the mark.

[3] NATO (the North Atlantic Treaty Organization) was established in late 1949 to plan and direct the common defense provided for by the Treaty.

tional forces constituted the shield that would receive the first impact of a Russian armed attack; the American atomic armament was the sword with which the return stroke would then be delivered. Without the shield, there might not be a chance to use the sword.

From an early stage Washington was preoccupied with the strength of the shield. A paper shield would not do. The NATO forces would have to be strong enough to require that any Russian military aggression be prepared and mounted on such a scale as to leave no doubt of what was intended; and strong enough to provide a pause, to delay a Russian advance until the terrible decision to wield the sword could be made clear and, if necessary, executed.

The American horror of the atomic bomb played its part here. This terror was heightened by the possible inadequacy of the American atomic stockpile and by the fact that Russia had just produced its first atomic explosion. It would be further heightened in 1952, when the United States would successfully produce the prototype of a hydrogen bomb (based on the fusion of atoms rather than their fission alone), thereby inaugurating the development, in which Russia would not be far behind, of bombs thousands of times more powerful than those that had been dropped on Nagasaki and Hiroshima only some seven years earlier.[4]

Finally, there was the established view that an atomic attack on Russia would immediately be followed by the Red Army's occupation of West Europe. The atomic bomb might deter Moscow from capturing West Europe but could not prevent it from doing so once hostilities had broken out. Only adequate ground forces—ninety divisions was a common estimate—could do that.

One might have thought that the European members of NATO would have been no less impressed than the Americans by the need to develop a strong shield. It is characteristic of Americans, however, as of no other people, to go all-out in any national effort they undertake. Moreover, the responsibility of leadership was theirs. A corollary of this was that the position of the Europeans on their own continent was humiliating and productive of cynicism. In any case, they were still undergoing wartime privations, they had not yet succeeded in recovering their feet, and they were weary. The building of huge ground forces, even with massive American assistance in equipment, was more than they could

---

[4] Russia's first hydrogen explosion was produced in August 1953.

afford without great strain and hardship. Moreover, half their fear of the Russian colossus was fear of provoking it. The view was widely held that the Red Army would not march except to forestall the rearmament of West Europe—especially that of West Germany, which was, as yet, hardly contemplated in these days. It is part of the ironic element that looms so large in the whole history of the Cold War that, at a time when the Russians undoubtedly lived in the greatest fear of a preventive attack by the West to forestall their acquisition of a nuclear armament, the West lived in fear of a preventive attack by the Red Army to forestall its own rearmament. On each side it was thought that the other had a vital interest in bringing about an early war. This is representative of the tendency, in any warlike conflict, for each side to regard the other as more purposeful, deliberate, and ruthless than it actually is.

Now, as the tensions of the Cold War mounted, Moscow developed what came to be called the 'Peace Offensive,' a propaganda campaign mounted on a massive scale, using all the resources of world Communism to persuade the public in all countries that the Soviet Union, its back to the wall, was waging a desperate struggle for peace against the imperialistic American ruling circles, who were organizing West Europe for an atomic war of aggression. At international 'peace congresses' held in cities all around the globe leading intellectuals were persuaded to serve Moscow's cause, in most cases unwittingly, by fervent public appeals for the disarmament, in effect, of the West.[5] The Dean of Canterbury, distinguished artists like Pablo Picasso, eminent scientists like J. B. S. Haldane, and a variety of other notables who were more at home in the world of the mind than in the world of affairs contributed an element of genuine passion and a semblance of sincerity by their participation. The Communists, under the discipline of Moscow, were able to produce hundreds of millions

[5] The sector of public opinion generally most vulnerable to ideological propaganda is constituted by that peculiar class, concentrated in the great cities, called the intellectuals. Their principal characteristic is a preoccupation with ideological formulations, a preoccupation that tends to blind them to what actually *is*, as opposed to what is *said*. They live in the Socratic world of ideas, a nominal world that is more real to them than the real world. Because of this the leaders of the Communist movement have been able to look hopefully to the intellectuals in non-Communist countries as potentially their most useful instruments. The widespread and innocent acceptance by intellectuals of the pretense that Lenin's regime and Stalin's represented the liberation of the people, the rule of the proletariat, and the triumph of peace is one of the embarrassing circumstances of twentieth-century history.

of signatures on the 'Stockholm Peace Appeal,' which called for the unconditional prohibition of the atomic weapon as 'a weapon of intimidation and mass extermination of people.'

This campaign, appealing to the poignant aspirations of people everywhere, was not without its effect in frustrating the effort to rebuild the defenses of the Atlantic world. Many persons who did not go in for the kind of analysis that involves counting divisions saw the Soviet Union, from now on, as on the defensive against a NATO, manipulated by Washington, that represented a threat of aggression against it. Just as many well-meaning persons had argued in the 1930's that a build-up of Western defenses against Hitler would pose a provocative threat for him, thereby leading to war, so many persons now saw NATO as a warlike provocation of an encircled Soviet Union that was bound to react in its own defense. Those who advanced this argument were by no means confined to the uneducated multitude.

NATO was to be successful in organizing itself, in the development of joint planning among its members, in the unification into one military force of the contingents contributed by each, and in the provision of an institutional framework on the basis of which common military action could be taken in such an emergency as might fall on the West at any moment. In the first months of its existence, however, any prospect of creating NATO ground forces capable of acting as more than a paper shield was hardly apparent.

Then, unexpectedly, on June 25, 1950, Communist armed forces attacked across the line that separated the two sides in the Cold War—not in Europe but in the Far East. The satellite Army of the Communist half of Korea, in a stroke that achieved complete surprise, invaded the non-Communist half. Immediately it became plausible that the same thing might happen at any moment along the line that divided the two Germanies. The whole situation was thereby changed, alarm was aroused, and the point of building an effective NATO acquired a more vivid quality than it had previously had.

It is, then, to the Far East that we must now turn.

CHAPTER XIX

The Far Eastern policy of the United States and its disasters up to 1950

M ISUNDERSTANDING, misconception, mistake—these are inevitable in all international controversy. In the history of the Cold War as it developed in the Far East, however, they are consistently predominant. Americans, Russians, and Chinese, time and again, completely mistook the situation with which they had to deal. Time and again they acted on false premises, often with catastrophic consequences from which they could not afterwards extricate themselves. Bloody conflicts took place that neither side had intended, that neither side wanted, and that neither side could end. The Korean War was the greatest of these.

This history of blindness and blundering did not begin with the Cold War. For the United States it began in 1898, with its entirely inadvertent and unwanted acquisition of the Philippines.[1] Then in 1900, in an offhand and unconsidered gesture, the United States made itself the champion of the independence and territorial integrity of China—thereby casually assuming a commitment, not based on its national interests, that it never expected to have to honor by any means more costly than diplomatic notes. Unable, however, to disengage itself from the commitment when its implications became increasingly clear, it finally was led by it into the conflict with Japan that, intensifying over the years, culminated in the Japanese attack on Pearl Harbor.

Again, from 1895 to the 1930's, when Japanese expansion was moving northeastward toward Russia, with the occupation of Korea, Manchuria, and Siberia, the United States pursued a policy of outspoken opposition that finally contributed to deflecting

[1] The established legend is that imperialistic Americans, of whom Theodore Roosevelt and Alfred Thayer Mahan were the most notable, engaged in a successful conspiracy to have the United States acquire the Philippines. The evidence, explicit and unambiguous, contradicts this. In fact, both Roosevelt and Mahan considered the acquisition of the Philippines a misfortune. See Halle, 1959, Chapters XV through XVII.

that expansion southward, toward the area of its own interests. All this was done under the impression, tacitly accepted by the American people, that the purpose of foreign policy was the defense of moral principle, even in distant and exotic lands, rather than self-defense or the safeguarding of one's national interest.

The Japanese blundered as badly, although for other reasons. They seized Manchuria in 1931 without anticipating the consequences in the form of an unappeasable Chinese opposition. Thinking to overcome this opposition by invading the north of China, they found that they only increased it. This involved them in ever-expanding military operations for the pacification of China, until they had become overextended and inextricably engaged in a war that they could not win, that they could not end, and that brought them into increasing conflict with the United States, committed as it was to the defense of China. At last, in blind desperation, they lashed out at the United States, inaugurating at Pearl Harbor another War that they could hardly have won even if their ally, Hitler, had succeeded in putting Russia and Britain *hors de combat*.[2]

I have already commented, in Chapter X, on how the United States ended the War with Japan, determined to smash its power and, thereafter, to keep it disarmed. In the Constitution which, in effect, it imposed on Japan, it even went so far as to proscribe the creation of any Japanese military establishment. Japan was to be permanently defenseless, a power vacuum.

Russian military power, entering the Far Eastern war only in its last week, spilled across Manchuria and into Korea, but never got as far as Japan. It was American power, with which the British had associated themselves, that now filled the Japanese vacuum.

What this meant was that the United States had now taken upon itself, for an indefinite future, the responsibility for the defense of Japan. Just as it had unwittingly assumed, in 1898, the liability of having to provide for the security of the Philippines, so it unwittingly assumed, now, the liability of having to provide for the security of Japan as well. The considerable burden that this represented in terms of material resources was dwarfed, however, by the political and strategic cost. For now the tradi-

[2] The Japanese themselves had no illusions about being able to defeat the United States, but they were so unknowing as to think that the United States might be brought to a compromise settlement.

tional enemy of Japan, its opponent in consequence of the strategic geography of the area, would become the enemy of the United States *qua* Japan. When Americans took over from the Japanese the burden of Japanese defense they took over, as well, the conflicts which that defense involved. For many centuries such a conflict had existed between China and Japan across the narrow waters that separated them. Throughout the twentieth century, the United States had sided with China in this contest, the final result of its participation being its defeat and occupation of Japan. Now, however, at one stroke it assumed all those Japanese security commitments that, as the successor power in the Japanese Islands, caused it to inherit the traditional conflict with China.

To such implicit political and strategic liabilities as these we Americans were blind at the time, if only because to appreciate them would have required a Bismarckian sophistication that was beyond our experience or education, a sophistication of which a representative democracy may not be capable in any case. We were governed by the mythic notion that threats to security came only from 'aggressor nations,' so that the disarmament of such nations removed such threats. 'Once Japan is destroyed as an aggressive force,' Ambassador Joseph Grew had said, 'we know of no other challenging power that can appear in the Pacific. . . . Once militant Japan is out of the picture, there should remain no threat of further war in the Pacific area. I say this advisedly. Japan is the one enemy, and the only enemy, of the peaceful peoples whose shores overlook the Pacific Ocean.'[3]

Add to this that it was a rare American who knew anything about Far Eastern history before the most recent times, and the history of the most recent times presented itself to Americans in terms of the mythic contest between good and evil, rather than in terms of strategic conflict. In their view, the greedy Japanese, in 1895, had seized Korea and Formosa, which thereafter constituted stolen property—to be restored, the one to independence and the other to China, by the sword of an avenging justice that it had been given to America to wield.

Perhaps if we Americans had been steeped in Far Eastern history we would have understood that, by its geography, the Korean peninsula had been for centuries, and was bound to be, a strategic point of the utmost sensitivity, at least as much so as the

---

[3] Address of October 10, 1942.

Rhineland or the Turkish Straits. A person wise in strategic matters could see by a glance at the map why this was necessarily so. If we think of China and Japan as, respectively, the two verticals of a capital H, the Korean peninsula is the cross-bar that connects them. It is the route by which either might invade the other, so that the security of each would seem to depend on having the military control of it. This was unfortunate for the Korean people, just as it was unfortunate for the Poles to find themselves caught between the Germans and the Russians, but it was a strategic fact that no one concerned with security and stability in northeast Asia could afford to overlook.

The endless contest between Chinese and Japanese over the Korean peninsula goes back to the beginnings of Japanese history, and it continues today with the Americans in the place of the Japanese. In the 660's, China and Japan were at war in Korea, the Chinese emerging victorious. A Korean War in the 1590's was remarkably similar in shape to the Korean War of the 1950's, the Japanese marching toward the Yalu River, which constituted the Chinese border then as now, only to be forced back below the 38th parallel by a massive Chinese counter-invasion.

In the 1890's the Japanese, growing in power while the Chinese state was crumbling, fought another and, this time, a victorious Korean War with the Chinese, as a result of which Korea became the Japanese dependency that it continued to be until 1945.

Of what this long history meant, however, we Americans were unaware when we made ourselves the successor power in Japan and, at the same time, occupied the southern half of Korea. One may doubt that the subsequent clash with China over the Korean peninsula, for which we were unprepared, was altogether accidental.

*   *   *

For half a century the United States had nourished a sentimental attachment to the Chinese nation, an attachment that reflected a pure idealism accompanied by a degree of simplicity. One hesitates to enter into the psychological elements of this attachment, as one must always hesitate to enter into the psychological elements of any self-conscious virtue.

At least part of the reason why we Americans loved the Chinese people was that we were allowed to patronize them. We made ourselves their mentor and protector. We offered ourselves as the model for their own reform and advancement, imparting to them our own religious enlightenment, educating them, showing them how to build for themselves such a democratic society as we enjoyed. In a word, our relationship to the Chinese made us feel godlike, as the relationship of ante-bellum whites to their devoted Negro slaves made them feel godlike, as the relationship of a man to his faithful dog makes him feel godlike. The feeling of being godlike generally prompts men to rise to a sense of moral responsibility and dignity. It may also, however, be corrupting in its effect. No moral risks are as great as those that missionaries run, and our relationship to the Chinese was predominantly that of missionaries to the heathen.

For half a century the Chinese had been our wards, upon whom we had lavished a parental beneficence. We had cherished Chiang Kai-shek, the leader of the Chinese, as a convert to Christianity, as one of us, and we had been swayed by the eloquence and charm of his wife, an Americanized graduate of Wellesley College who repeatedly visited our shores and spoke to us in moving terms of her land and her people. At moments, Chiang Kai-shek seemed to us like the George Washington of his people.[4]

This ingenuous and dangerous attachment that we felt to the China represented by Chiang Kai-shek and Mme. Chiang moved us to act as its sponsors in the postwar world. To the dismay of the British under Churchill, we insisted that this China, riven by weakness and corruption as it was, be considered, together with the United States, Great Britain, Russia, and later France, as one of the five great powers chosen to preside over the international order and security of the postwar world.

Ever since 1911, however, China had been in a state of chronic civil war. No government had at any time been able to establish its rule over more than part of the country, and usually there had been at least two governments contending with each other for supremacy. The generally predominant faction had been that of the Kuomintang or Nationalist Party, of which Chiang had become the leader. This faction had sometimes associated itself with the Americans and British, sometimes with the Russians.

---

[4] It was, however, George Washington who in his Farewell Address had said that 'the nation which indulges toward another an habitual hatred or an habitual fondness is in some degree a slave. It is a slave to its animosity or to its affection, either of which is sufficient to lead it away from its duty and its interest.'

The Chinese Communists had belonged to it until 1927, when Chiang had suddenly turned against them and driven them out.

Up to 1927 the Chinese Communists had accepted the tutelage of Moscow and had obediently followed its strategic direction. Now, however, Moscow ordered them to proceed with the Communist revolution by seizing the cities and basing themselves on the proletariat. In Moscow's detached view, the Chinese Revolution must be based on the proletariat because that was what the Marxist–Leninist scriptures, which had been addressed to a situation formerly existing in the industrialized countries of the West, had called for. But China in 1927 was still a peasant society and a peasant civilization. As well base a revolution in the United States on the street-cleaners as base a Chinese revolution on the proletariat. The Chinese Communists, nevertheless, obeyed orders, tried to capture the cities, and were thoroughly trounced by Chiang's forces for their pains. That was the beginning of the end of Chinese Communist obedience to Moscow.

A movement of peasant revolt, which was only nominally Communist, now developed under the direction of an agrarian leader, Mao Tse-tung, who called himself a Communist while disregarding Communist doctrine and discipline. Elements of China's peasant armies joined it. For the next dozen years one can hardly say more for the success of this movement than that it survived in the face of formidable dangers and difficulties. Essentially, this new movement, which was to govern all China after 1949, was born of rebellion against Moscow—the rebellion of men who, having identified themselves with Communism, had been led to defeat by following Moscow's directives. We may be sure that there was no time, from 1927 on, when Moscow and the so-called Chinese Communists under Mao did not regard each other with mistrust. To Moscow Mao's movement was a heretical movement with schismatic implications.

All this would have been better understood in the West, and perhaps the history of the world would have been different, if this peasants' movement had not called itself Communist. But the leaders of the movement had an intellectual formation in which the term Communism was equated, not only with a certain confused body of doctrine, but also with general enlightenment and a better world to come. It stood for an inevitable salvation that was approaching for all mankind. Whoever enlisted under it was putting himself on the side of a noble future and turning his back on a sordid past. By calling their movement Communist Mao and his associates, in line with a Confucian semantic tradition represented by the phrase 'rectification of terms,' were endowing it with this credit and this assurance of victory in the eyes of intellectuals everywhere. It appears certain, however, that Stalin and his associates did not regard it as representative of true Communism.[5]

The fact remains, and it is central to this whole history, that the nominal is always more real to us than the real. The identity of names between Moscow's movement and Mao's, together with other nominal factors, tended to persuade all except those in the respective leadership of the two movements that they were one movement, and even those in the respective leaderships must have felt that their real difference represented an abnormality.

Just as is the case in Russian history since 1917, there is more continuity of tradition in Chinese history since 1949 than the nominal situation shows. Just as there is a real sense in which Stalin was a new czar of all the Russia's, so there is a real sense in which Mao was the founder of a new dynasty in China—in succession to the Han, Chin, Sung, Yüan, Ming, and Ch'ing dynasties. The Communist élite, with its special training in the Marxist scriptures, is equivalent to the Mandarin élite, with its special training in the Confucian scriptures. After the Communist revolutions in the two countries what we have still is two countries, Russia and China. This has nothing to do with anything that either Marx or Lenin foretold.

*   *   *

When the Far Eastern war ended, on August 14, 1945, China had declined into a condition of increasing chaos. It was in the grip of a disastrous inflation, its foreign trade had stopped, its railways had almost come to a standstill, other communications

---

[5] Both Stalin and Molotov, talking informally to Americans on various occasions, referred to Mao and his followers as not real Communists. In June 1944, for example, Stalin said to Ambassador Harriman: 'The Chinese Communists are not real Communists. They are "margarine" Communists.' In August of that year Molotov told General Hurley that the so-called Chinese Communists were Communists in name only. (Quoted by Feis, 1953, p. 140, and 1957, pp. 408–9. See also Schwartz, especially pp. 187–204.) The time would come, after 1949, when feeling ran so high in the United States that Americans would be hounded from public life for taking a like view. At the end of the War, however, this was still not so. Secretary of State Byrnes, testifying before the Senate Foreign Relations Committee on December 7, 1945, spoke of 'the so-called Communists' in referring to Mao's party.

had broken down, food-production was falling, Chiang's Government had increasingly degenerated into an arbitrary and corrupt despotism, in large parts of the country its authority was flouted, over important areas it was not in a condition to accept the surrender of the Japanese forces, and civil strife was threatening widespread bloodshed. This was what the United States, as China's mentor and its sponsor in the international community, had to deal with.

This condition had existed, and had been getting worse, throughout the War. Throughout the War a three-cornered struggle had been going on between the forces of the central Government under Chiang, the Communist forces under Mao, and the Japanese forces. While both Chinese groups fought the Japanese, each kept substantial portions of its forces back to block the other. Nothing could have been more exasperating to the United States, which was making extraordinary efforts to supply the Government forces (chiefly by the dangerous air-routes over the 'Hump' of the Himalayas from India) while a substantial portion of those forces were being deployed, not against the Japanese but against other Chinese.

We can now see that the situation which existed in China during the 1940's represented a repeated pattern in the long millenia of Chinese history. In this pattern a ruling dynasty would gradually decay, becoming ineffective, feeble, and corrupt; in its decadence it would lose what was called the Mandate of Heaven —that is, in effect, its legitimacy and consequent authority in the eyes of the ruled. At some point in this process a commanding figure would arise to lead a rebellion that resulted in the foundation of a new dynasty possessed of the Mandate of Heaven. Mao Tse-tung represented the latest in this succession of commanding figures who became the founders of dynasties. It was to him that the Mandate of Heaven was being delivered in the aftermath of the War.[6]

---

[6] It was the Ch'ing Dynasty, the Dynasty of the Manchu invaders, founded in 1644, that had last had the Mandate of Heaven. By the beginning of the twentieth century this Dynasty, like its predecessors, had fallen into decay. After its overthrow in 1911, a generation of turmoil ensued, as so often in Chinese history, to be resolved at last by the triumph of Mao in 1949. Both Sun Yat-sen and Chiang Kai-shek had, in turn, been candidates for the Mandate, but the first had died before he could achieve it and the second, after a promising start, had failed. It is interesting to note that, in the deceptive game of ideological labels that has bemused so many observers, Sun was sometimes a Jeffersonian Democrat, sometimes a Communist. The one thing we can be sure of is that, like Chiang and Mao, he was first of all and at all times a Chinese.

What, in these circumstances, was the United States to do? Formally and officially it recognized Chiang's regime as the legitimate Government of China. It was, in fact, tied to that regime by bonds of obligation and of what we may call putative ideological association. At the same time, by the end of the War the decadence and progressive failure of that regime had reached an advanced stage. To the extent that the United States was bound to it, therefore, it was bound to a sinking ship.

It is probably no coincidence that most if not all of the professional experts on China in the American Foreign Service were in favor of a policy that tended toward disengagement from what they recognized as a doomed regime. They knew Chinese history well enough to have a sense of what was happening. On the other hand, the American military men, while recognizing the weakness of the Nationalist regime, were disposed to regard any regime that bore the name Communist as an instrument of Moscow and, by virtue of this nominal identity, as the enemy. They tended, by their training, to regard international relations as a life-and-death combat between totally opposed forces in which no compromise was possible, the only alternative to total victory being the unacceptable one of total defeat. As for American politicians remote from the scene, and the American public, it was a foregone conclusion that they would hardly see a difference between the Chinese Communists and, let us say, the Bulgarian Communists, in terms of their relationship to Moscow. To them the triumph of the Chinese Communists would represent the capture of China by Russia, precisely as the triumph of the Bulgarian Communists, who were mere agents of Moscow, represented the Russian capture of Bulgaria. And with the development of the Cold War this became an intolerable prospect.

What President Truman's Administration undertook to do, in the situation, was to resolve the developing Chinese civil war by bringing the two sides together in a coalition government. At the same time, being already so committed to the Nationalist side, Washington helped it to forestall the Communist acquisition of territory relinquished by the Japanese, providing air-transport for Nationalist troops and continuing its wartime assistance. In both these enterprises—the effort to bring the Nationalists and Communists together, and the support of the former against the latter —it failed. It failed, if I may speak figuratively, because the Communists had the Mandate of Heaven. They had, increasingly, the support of the Chinese peasants and scholars, and this was more important than weapons and ammunition, of which they had little.[7]

This American failure was far from dishonorable. The United States had had an obligation to its wartime ally, Chiang, however much cause for dissatisfaction he gave, and it did not shirk that obligation. The attempt to bring the two sides in the civil war together was at least well intentioned. But Mao's forces gathered strength from the source of all strength in China, the peasants and scholars, and toward the end that strength grew like an avalanche. By 1949 they had taken over the whole of mainland China, driving the Nationalists across the water to refuge on the island of Formosa, and had established the new Government of China in Peking.

In the face of the Communist victory there was only one thing for the United States to do. The rules of international relations, such as they are, prescribe that, when a civil war ends in the replacement of one governing regime by another, then the new governing regime is normally to be accepted and recognized by the members of the international community. Whether one likes that regime or approves of it is irrelevant. Official international business has to be done between the authorities actually governing in the respective countries simply because there are no other authorities with which to do it. The moral test, aside from being presumptuous in most cases, is unworkable. Regimes that represent, among them, differing premises of moral judgment have to deal with one another if there is to be any hope of peace and order in the world. Plain realism compels one to add that the great majority of the governments of mankind today are, by the standards of Western democracy, disreputable in greater or lesser degree.

The United States had discharged its obligation to Chiang Kai-shek's regime. When that regime lost the civil war nevertheless, the time had come to recognize and enter into official relations with the winner. In addition to the propriety that this would have represented, there were good reasons of political strategy for it. It was not a foregone conclusion that, because the

[7] Traditionally, the political base on which any Chinese dynasty depended for its achievement of or continuance in power was the support of the peasants and of the Mandarin civil service composed of Confucian scholars. In our time, the Communist intellectuals correspond to the Confucian scholars of earlier times.

new regime called itself Communist, it would not continue, after whatever period of uncertainty, along the established course of Chinese foreign policy, which included friendship with the United States. It was not a foregone conclusion that it would wed itself to Russia, with which it was in constant or, at least, potential conflict along the frontiers of Sinkiang, Outer Mongolia, and Manchuria—after Mao's advent to power as before. By refusing to recognize it or deal with it, however, the United States was sure to drive it into the arms of Russia, thereby providing one more example of the self-fulfilling prophecy.

Contrary to accepted belief in the United States at this time, relations between Moscow and the Chinese Communists appear not to have been cordial. More than we were willing to credit, Moscow at the end of the War had found itself in the same essential position as the United States with respect to China. It recognized and supported Chiang's Nationalist regime, while knowing full well its weakness; it mistrusted Mao's Communist regime and apparently gambled on its not winning the civil war. When Mao's regime did win, and as its approaching victory became clear, Moscow found itself, like the United States, in the position of having to adjust itself to an accomplished fact. It recognized the new regime and undertook, by giving it indispensable cooperation, to make it dependent and thus subservient. The policy of the United States, as it developed, insured the success of this Russian undertaking for a decade after the inauguration of the new regime.

The difficulties in the way of the adoption by the United States of a policy based, like that of Russia, on recognition of the accomplished fact were immense. They precluded the immediate establishment of normal relations with Mao's regime, and in fact an opportunity for establishing such relations was never to arise. There was no moment when it was possible. For one thing, Mao's new regime regarded the United States as the enemy, partly because of its identification with Chiang's side in the civil war, partly because it represented the Chinese past against which it was conducting a revolution, partly because Mao and his associates needed the putative threat of a monstrous external enemy as a basis for invoking or compelling domestic discipline in the nation over which it was about to establish a ruthless rule. It would at the least have been unseemly for the United States to have recognized the new Peking regime at a moment when it was inflicting death and torture on American (but not on British) missionaries, and when it had arbitrarily jailed the American Consul General in Mukden.

Another impediment to the acceptance by the American people of the new regime's legitimacy as the successor government in China was the Communist label that it bore, a label that was bound to subsume the whole of reality as mythically conceived by people of limited intellectual sophistication.

Nevertheless, under the informed if unpopular direction of the State Department, the Government of the United States began to prepare for the time when it would be possible to transfer its recognition to the new Chinese regime and establish official relations with it. The hope of doing this was suddenly foreclosed, however, by a wholly unforeseen contingency, the outbreak in Korea of a War in which the Chinese would find themselves on one side, with the Americans in place of the Japanese on the other.

CHAPTER XX

Surprise attack in Korea and improvisation by the
United States to meet it

ON December 1, 1943, after Roosevelt, Churchill, and Chiang
Kai-shek had conferred together in Cairo, they issued a
declaration in which they said that their three nations, 'mindful
of the enslavement of the people of Korea, are determined that in
due course Korea shall become free and independent.' Later
Roosevelt proposed to Stalin, who agreed, that the victorious
allies, Russia included, should for perhaps twenty or thirty years
exercise over Korea a joint trusteeship that would have the objective of preparing the Korean people for self-government. Stalin
also agreed with Roosevelt that no foreign troops should be
stationed in Korea. (What Roosevelt presumably did not know was
that there were one or two Korean divisions, indoctrinated and
trained in Russia, that Stalin could send in to take over.)

Looking back on these offhand exchanges, we may note with
irony and pity how casually the looming dilemmas of the postwar
world were disposed of by the harassed and exhausted statesmen
of 1945.

In any case, the future of Korea did not figure in American
thinking as one of the great matters at issue. To the Americans of
the day Korea was a faraway and legendary land of quaint people
with conical hats who would now have to be taught (by the
Americans, the Chinese, the British, and the Russians) to govern
themselves in accordance with the principles of Jeffersonian
democracy.[1] It is clear that few Americans, civilian or military,
regarded this land as having any strategic significance for the

---

[1] I recall a school-geography of my childhood that reported how, in the cold
Korean winters when noses might freeze before their owners knew it, any pedestrian
in the streets, noticing the whitened nose of a passer-by, would politely warn him by
crying out: 'Your nose, your nose, Sir!' This pleasant custom constituted my principal
knowledge of Korea. At a meeting in the State Department in 1945, Secretary of
State Stettinius is said to have asked one of his subordinates to tell him where Korea
was. The possibility cannot be dismissed that he did not have even my knowledge of
matters Korean.

United States. The American Government had not yet learned to think in terms of the new responsibility it was about to assume for the defense of Japan. Indeed, it was unaware of incurring any such responsibility at all.

When it came time to prepare for the Japanese surrender, the American and Russian chiefs of staff agreed that the line on each side of which Russians and Americans, respectively, would accept the surrender of the Japanese forces in Korea should be the 38th parallel of latitude. The Red Army entered Korea in the first half of August, accompanied by one or two divisions of Koreans already trained in Russia. It was not until almost a month later that the American commander in the Far East, General MacArthur, felt able to spare one regiment for dispatch to Korea.

While the Russians appear to have made plans for the administration of northern Korea, the American military command found itself quite unprepared for the political problems that took it by surprise when it entered the zone reserved to it. It discovered that the Koreans were not disposed to accept trusteeship. They did not consider that they needed a period of preparation for self-government. They were a liberated, not a conquered nation, and they intended to exercise their national sovereignty forthwith.

The question that arose for the American command was that of which, among the rival political groups in Korea, spoke for the Korean people. The same question did not arise for the Russians, who considered that the Communists spoke for the people, and that those who opposed them spoke for the enemies of the people. There was, consequently, no basis of agreement on which the Russians and Americans could act jointly, as had been projected, to bring into being a Provisional Korean Government for the whole country. After a period of muddle and frustration, therefore, the Russians set up and armed a Communist Government in the north, while the Americans, on the basis of free elections, set up and armed an anti-Communist Government in the south. So, like Germany, Korea was finally divided along the line that had been drawn in 1945 to demarcate the respective spheres of the Russian and Western military forces.

As in the case of Germany, the Korean *status quo* of 1945 would become permanent in spite of all attempts to change it. Moscow would make a more violent attempt to change it in Korea, however, than in Germany; and the attempt itself, although unsuccessful, would change the whole character of the Cold War. It would alarm the West, provoking it to far-reaching measures of military preparation that would now give the political struggle the character of an overt contest for military supremacy. Henceforth, military considerations would predominate in Washington as in Moscow. As always happens when the military element becomes dominant in government, the thinking on which Washington based its policy would now become progressively coarsened. The men of sensitivity and insight would tend to be displaced by the rough commanders who see things in simpler terms. Thucydides had given the classic account of such a development twenty-four centuries earlier, observing that what had happened in his Athens during the long course of the Peloponnesian War would 'according to human nature happen again in the same way.' It was inevitable that the Cold War, intensified and prolonged, would entail a degeneration of government.

*   *   *

While the Cold War may in itself be regarded as an historical necessity, if only in view of the mistakes that had accumulated over the two generations that preceded it, the outbreak of fighting in the Korean theater appears to have been essentially accidental, the product of misunderstanding. Moscow, frustrated in the West by European recovery and allied firmness in Berlin, frustrated in the East by the position of the United States in Japan, and feeling the loss of momentum that its cause was suffering throughout the world, was tempted to advance at the one point where a notable victory seemed to be offered for the taking. Washington had repeatedly given the impression that its military protection did not extend to South Korea, which it regarded as more of a strategic liability than an asset. This seemed to imply impunity for the Communists if they should now move to add it to their empire.

What led Washington to give this impression?

In the first place, as we have seen, Washington had indeed failed to appreciate the strategic importance that the Korean peninsula had suddenly acquired for the United States with the occupation of Japan, and it did not appreciate the inescapable moral responsibility that it had incurred by setting up the South Korean Government under its sponsorship and protection.

By 1947–1948, moreover, the United States had reduced its ground forces to such a point that it simply did not have men to spare for the continued occupation of Korea. It therefore took the initiative to negotiate an agreement whereby Russian and American troops alike would be withdrawn from Korea. The Russians agreed the more readily because they had already trained and equipped North Korean forces to a pitch of efficiency that made them clearly the superiors of such native South Korean forces as the Americans would leave behind them.

The most important factor of all, however, was a peculiar limitation to which American war-planning in these days was subject. The unique contingency to which it addressed itself was that of a third world war, with Communist Russia in place of Nazi Germany as the enemy. In other words, the war-planners were, as usual, preparing to fight the last war. General Marshall had said in 1945: 'We can be certain that the next war, if there is one, will be even more total than this one. The nature of war is such that once it begins it can end only as this one is ending, in the destruction of the vanquished.'[2] The term 'limited war' was not yet in the American military lexicon. All our fighting men had been brought up on the principle that, once a nation goes to war, it must properly go all out, not limiting its effort in any way until total victory has been achieved. They had been taught that this was, in General Marshall's words, 'the nature of war.' This prevented them from preparing for the kind of war that actually did break out in Korea.

In the contingency to which the planners were addressing themselves, that of a third world war, it would be strategic folly for the United States to try to hold the Korean peninsula or any other part of the Asian mainland. Consequently, the decision was made in Washington not to attempt the defense of Korea in case of such a war. This decision, as we shall see, became publicly known, but without the limiting context in which, alone, it made sense.

It was because its moral and strategic commitment to the defense of South Korea was unappreciated by Washington that it could withdraw its military forces with so little misgiving. And it was because of the assumption that another war would be World War III that Washington, faced with a popular demand for economy, reduced its Army to hardly more than half a million men by 1948. A third world war, it was believed, would be fought by long-range air-power with nuclear weapons. Ground forces, if

---

[2] Marshall, p. 229 . . . quoted in Higgins, p. 4.

not obsolete in the circumstances of such a war, would have only an incidental role.

By December 1948 Moscow had carried out the agreed withdrawal of its forces from Korea. The evacuation of the American forces, begun at the end of the summer of 1948, had been delayed by disturbances in South Korea, but was completed in June 1949.

In Tokyo on March 1, 1949, General MacArthur gave an interview to a British journalist in which he implicitly placed Korea outside the American line of defense in the Pacific, saying that the line 'starts from the Philippines and continues through the Ryukyu Archipelago. . . . Then it bends back through Japan and the Aleutian Island chain to Alaska.' One supposes that this interview, which appeared in *The New York Times*, did not go unnoted in Moscow.

Then, on January 12, 1950, Secretary of State Acheson gave an unprepared address before the National Press Club in Washington in which he said that 'the defensive perimeter runs along the Aleutians to Japan and then goes to the Ryukyus.'[3]

The virtually identical statements of the General and of the Secretary could be interpreted by Moscow in the light of the eagerness Washington had shown to get the American military forces out of Korea.

* * *

A few minutes before 9.30 p.m. on Saturday the 24th of June 1950, a cable reached the State Department that caught Washington as completely by surprise as it had been, eight and a half years earlier, by word of the Japanese attack on Pearl Harbor North Korean forces, the cable reported, had crossed the 38th parallel to launch an all-out armed invasion of South Korea.

The Assistant Secretary of State for Far Eastern Affairs, Mr Dean Rusk, telephoned the bad news to Secretary Acheson at his farm in Maryland, and Secretary Acheson telephoned it to President Truman in Missouri.

The following afternoon at two o'clock the Security Council of the United Nations met in New York, at the initiative of the

---

[3] The reader may reasonably suppose that General MacArthur and Secretary Acheson, alike, were referring to the contents of a classified policy document dealing with the contingency of a third world war. The accidental circumstance of bureaucratic confusion inside the State Department had put the Secretary in the position of having to deliver his address without a prepared text.

United States, to take action on behalf of the international community in the face of what was identified as a threat to the peace. This time it was the turn of Moscow to be caught unprepared. Having refused since January to attend meetings of the Council (in protest at the continued occupation of China's seat by the Nationalist regime that had been defeated in the civil war), Russia was now without a representative in its own seat to veto such action as might otherwise be taken for the purpose of countering the North Korean aggression. Therefore the Council, in successive meetings, was able first to recommend that the members of the United Nations come to the aid of the South Korean forces, then to establish a unified United Nations Command under General MacArthur with the mission of repelling the North Korean attack and restoring peace and security to the area.

Decisions in Washington and at MacArthur's headquarters in Tokyo were necessarily taken pell-mell in these days, and at least one of them was to have historic consequences that would impede the achievement of a true peace in the Far East, perhaps for generations to come. Washington had already sent American air and naval forces into the fighting before the Security Council explicitly authorized it. General MacArthur had already sent American air forces into North Korea before Washington authorized it.

The great decisions were made at two successive meetings, on the nights of June 25 and 26, in Blair House, which was the President's temporary residence in Washington while the White House was being reconstructed. Confronted with the unexpected emergency, everyone now saw that the United States had no practicable choice but to take its stand alongside the South Koreans in resisting the invasion. The 'defensive perimeter' of the planners was clearly inapplicable to the actual situation.

The reason why the United States obviously had to come to the rescue of South Korea had little to do with such considerations of strategic geography as bore on the defense of Japan. To the men in Blair House it was suddenly clear, in this 'moment of truth,' that the United States was deeply, if tacitly, committed to the defense of South Korea, just as it was committed to the defense of Japan.

The fact is that one cannot liberate a country, or take a temporary responsibility for it (as in the case of Japan), without involving oneself in continuing responsibility for its future. Having liberated the Philippines from the Spanish Empire in 1898, the United States found that it had incurred a moral obligation not to let them fall to the Kaiser's German Empire. Now it could not allow its own ward, South Korea, to fall to the Communist empire, any more than it could allow West Berlin to fall to it. Everyone in Washington saw right away that this was so.

Everyone saw, now, that the moral obligation was a practical one as well; for a failure to discharge it would surely involve the United States and its allies in mounting disaster. The leader of the free world would be identified with a craven act of desertion. All those who had put their trust in the protection of the United States, from Japan to Germany, would feel betrayed and would be disposed to make the best terms they could with a Communist empire now destined, as it would appear, to inherit the earth. In every country, the Communist parties and their supporters would be strengthened.

The obligation, as everyone now saw, had to be met. But the problems that were posed by the lack of military preparedness in the Far East, and the urgency with which they had to be met, were not conducive to a spirit of detached contemplation and a cultivation of the long view among those who came together in Blair House. The meetings concentrated on the emergency of the moment.

Every report that came from across the Pacific was of the imminent complete collapse of the South Korean forces, so that even a prompt rescue might come too late. The ground forces that the United States had in Japan for occupation duties, consisting of four divisions, were largely composed of service troops (cooks, jeep-drivers, etc.) and combat formations made up of inexperienced boys. The prospect of committing large forces to Korea, and in particular that of committing these particular forces, aroused alarm on two scores. One was that, if hostilities should widen into a World War, any considerable forces engaged in Korea would be needed elsewhere. The other was that, by taking all military forces out of Japan for action in Korea, Japan would be left wide-open to any hostile expedition that might cross the narrow waters from a China that had just been engulfed by the expanding Communist movement. Communism, in the shape of a Chinese expedition, could take over a defenseless Japan virtually without firing a shot.

It was in response to this latter cause of alarm that, at the second night-meeting in Blair House, the decision was made to intervene with force, at this particular moment, in the Chinese civil war. The decision to interpose the U.S. Seventh Fleet between the victorious regime of Mao Tse-tung on the Chinese mainland and the defeated Nationalist regime in its last refuge on the island of Formosa was, in effect, a commitment to the losing side. It was a far-reaching political decision made by the President without due consideration of its political implications, on the word of the military representatives at Blair House that it was a military necessity in the emergency of the moment. Here we have a demonstration of the increased role played by the military in Washington now that the Cold War had eventuated in fighting.

If Japan was to be left defenseless, the military argued, then the Chinese would have to be restrained from taking advantage of the situation by a diversionary threat on their flank, in the Straits of Formosa. This argument was plausible only in terms of the principle that military preparations must be based on a possible opponent's capabilities rather than on his intentions. For a variety of reasons it was virtually inconceivable that the new regime in Peking would actually undertake the conquest of Japan, but the fact was that it would have the capability of doing so. If, then, one considered only the capability, the security of Japan made it necessary for the United States to pose its deterrent threat on the Chinese flank.

What was wrong, in this instance as in all such instances involving decisions of political consequence, was the principle that only capabilities, not intentions, are what count. On this principle I once heard it argued by men in high position that the United States had to take drastic measures against Guatemala because the Guatemalans had the capability of bombing the oil-fields of Texas. If any great state actually allowed itself to be governed by this principle it would soon find itself at war with the whole world. Late at night in Blair House, however, was a poor occasion for considering the philosophical weakness of the principle traditionally invoked by the military as a basis for the definition of what constitutes military necessity.

We may suppose that the President and his civilian advisers had some misgivings about this move. They allowed themselves to believe, however, that it was for the duration of the military emergency only, that they could engage the country in the Chinese civil war only temporarily, disengaging it as soon as the immediate emergency was over. In announcing the move President Truman said: 'The determination of the future status of Formosa must await the restoration of security in the Pacific, a peace settlement with Japan, or consideration by the United Nations.' On July 19 he told Congress that the action with respect to Formosa was 'without prejudice to the political questions affecting that island.' He believed that the United States could, in the name of 'neutralization,' temporarily undertake the defense of Formosa against the new Chinese regime without committing itself on the issue of Formosa's future.[4]

To this belief, which made the decision seem so much less consequential than it proved to be, we must add, as an explanation of the fact that it was taken, the psychological disadvantage under which civilian political leaders labor when they confront the military on an issue of military necessity. Military necessity must, by definition, be governing. Almost no political leader feels that he dare take the responsibility before history of opposing what has been certified to be such a necessity by the only authority that counts. The military commanders represent, in his eyes, a recondite profession that they have spent their lives in mastering, a profession in which he has no competence. Moreover, they are traditionally identified with a more complete patriotism than politicians are thought to possess. At the first Blair House meeting there were present, in addition to the President, five representatives of the State Department and eight representatives of the military departments and services, including three generals and an admiral. At the second meeting the proportion was five to seven. Those who spoke for political considerations, as opposed to military considerations, were in a minority; and from now on this would tend to represent the balance of power within the Executive Branch of the Government when the great decisions of foreign policy were under consideration.[5]

Finally, domestic political considerations of the most pressing kind would have made civilian opposition to the military view

[4] The official mission of the Seventh Fleet was to prevent any assault by either side against the other in the Chinese civil war. The actual effect was to protect the losing side by preventing the winning side from completing its victory.

[5] In fact, this military preponderance dates back to the creation of the National Security Council in 1947 as the chief advisory body on foreign policy to the President. About the same time, the term 'foreign policy' itself tended to give way to the term 'national security policy,' a verbal change that was not without significance.

difficult and dangerous in the extreme. The victory, a few months before, of the Chinese Communist leader, Mao Tse-tung, over America's ally and protégé, Chiang Kai-shek, had not been understood by the American people. In their mythical view of the situation, Chiang represented the Chinese people, who gave him all their allegiance and support. Mao Tse-tung, by contrast, was the agent of the international Communist conspiracy with its headquarters in Moscow. He represented the conquest of China and the enslavement of the Chinese people by the foreign empire under Moscow.

How could such a thing have happened? How could a foreign conspiracy, with such limited means as it had, capture a nation of six hundred million people who gave their allegiance to their own native government?

There were demagogues on hand who were ready to explain how it had happened. Their explanation was that the State Department had fallen under the control of Communists who had secretly conspired with Moscow against Chiang Kai-shek and the Chinese people. In January Mr. Alger Hiss, a former officer of the State Department now supposed to have been one of its top officials, had been convicted as a Soviet spy. On February 9 a Senator Joseph McCarthy had opened Pandora's box by a speech in which he claimed that he held in his hand a list of 205 employees of the State Department whom Secretary Acheson knew to be 'card-carrying' members of the Communist Party.[6] Secretary Acheson, himself, was accused of siding with Communism. Had he not invited the Communists to attack South Korea by his speech referring to the American 'defensive perimeter' in terms that excluded it? Had he not, as was falsely alleged, been close to Alger Hiss?

Chiang Kai-shek and the Chinese people, it followed, had been betrayed by the Communists who had gained such a large measure of control over the Government in Washington. It also followed that the Chinese people stood ready to throw off the yoke of Moscow, represented by Mao, and welcome Chiang back to the mainland. All that was needed was for Washington to stop with-

---

[6] The technical charge on which Hiss was convicted was perjury, the statute of limitations having expired on espionage. It made no difference that McCarthy had to abandon his position when asked to give detailed information, confessing at last that he had no list at all. The gates had been opened to a havoc that could no longer be controled. A large part of the American people now believed that their own Government was conspiring with the enemy against the nation.

holding its cooperation from the Chinese, to place itself on their side once more.

Under these circumstances, with the country becoming more and more impassioned against Washington, with Secretary Acheson and the State Department daily reviled in increasingly wild terms, the Truman Administration had for months held out, with increasing difficulty, against any intervention in the Chinese civil war, which Chiang had now, in effect, lost irretrievably. Its expectation was that Mao Tse-tung's new regime would inevitably complete its victory by the conquest of Formosa, and that in due course it would be proper for the United States to recognize the accomplished fact. In the face of a mounting popular outcry it had nevertheless moved to prepare for these developments. With the outbreak of the Korean War, however, the Administration at last lost control. The domestic political situation made it that much harder to oppose the military demand for intervention.

From the point of view of the military commanders, now that fighting had broken out between the two sides there was a war that was more than a cold war between the Communist world and the free world. In that war, Chiang was an ally, Mao an enemy. The choice was between victory and defeat. The dispatch of the Seventh Fleet to the Straits of Formosa was a logical move in the worldwide war between Communism and freedom, rather than an unwarranted intervention in a Chinese domestic feud. They testified that it was a military necessity, and the civilians at Blair House accepted their testimony in good faith. The consequent intervention in the Chinese civil war meant the abandonment, at last, of a course of action that, in the face of mounting domestic opposition, had become increasingly hard to sustain. In politics what is right has always to give way, at last, to what is possible— especially when, under the stress of the moment, those who make the decisions are no longer quite sure what is right.

Those who met in Blair House on the two successive nights made a series of decisions that were brilliantly right. Perhaps they made only one that was wrong.

CHAPTER XXI

*The Korean War to the point where Western success
provokes Chinese intervention*

No government ever has as much control of events as it pretends to have. At the best, its control is little enough. From June 25, 1950, however, the Truman Administration lost most of such control as it had previously had. Less and less able to shape public opinion as the country lost confidence in it, it was more and more limited in the choices it could still make. And such choices as it made, in meeting the unforeseen contingencies that confronted it in the Far East, increasingly foreclosed further possibilities of choice. It found itself funneled by circumstances into a narrow course from which it could neither retreat nor turn away.

This is what happens when international conflict reaches the pitch of war. It had happened to the Roosevelt Administration, which had nevertheless retained the confidence of the country on the basis of appearing to master the events that, in fact, mastered it. Now, however, the country itself turned against the Truman Administration, showing itself increasingly willing, in its fears, to listen to the fantastic counsels of the ignorant and the unscrupulous. Mr. Truman, as valiant a President as ever served, did not represent those elements of personal superiority to the common man that the people look for in their leaders when great troubles are upon them. He could not stand before the crowd in the mythic mantle of a higher authority, a father to his people. His speech could not uplift and reassure them because it was nothing more than the common speech of the streets. He represented the people too well to wear the distinction of leadership.

Secretary Acheson, on the other hand, by the aristocracy of his intellect, his character, and his behavior, was too unrepresentative to be trusted. He seemed foreign to the people. Like Coriolanus in Rome, he was the perfect target of the demagogues who now set themselves up as Tribunes of the People. A scapegoat had become a psychological necessity for the nation and, by his refusal to compromise with what he considered to be right, by his contempt

213

of the little hypocrisies and demagogic devices in which every politician has to indulge, he virtually offered himself for the role. No man in American history, before or since, has remained erect, and has continued to do his duty as he saw it, under such a barrage of villification as was directed at him by the craven and the unscrupulous from the end of 1949 until the Truman Administration finally went out of office in January 1953.[1] This, in its way, is as honorable a record as has ever been made by a public servant. History owes him a debt, as much for the example he gave as for the record of his intellectual leadership in shaping the new postwar policy of containment. If he had resigned under the barrage, as he was pressed from all sides to do, the forces of ignorance and evil would have won a victory that would have permanently weakened the body politic. He had the sense and courage, in a lonely hour, to know that for the country's sake he must not do it. Fortunately, the President knew this too, and stood by him.

Secretary Acheson's power to grapple with the external events that confronted the nation was, however, impaired. And the Administration itself became paralyzed—like a tightrope-walker who, under a rain of brickbats from the spectators, can no longer move forward or back.

In the period immediately after June 25, 1950, the demoralization of the American people was temporarily mitigated or put off, first by the initial emotion of being in a fight, and then by military success of the most dramatic kind. During the first two and a half months the defending forces were driven down to the tip of the Korean peninsula and almost off it altogether. By September 15 they had left to them a mere foothold around the port of Pusan on the southern coast, from which the Communist forces were now only thirty-five miles distant. On that date, however, General MacArthur carried off successfully a military gamble that, by the best reckoning, had the odds heavily against it. He made an amphibious landing at Inchon, the port of Seoul, far behind the enemy lines. By the 27th he had captured Seoul; the Communist forces, cut off from behind, were in collapse, their disordered remnants streaming back north across the 38th parallel. In those few days their estimated losses included 335,000 men. Apparently

[1] There is some parallel with the ordeal that President Washington went through in 1793, when he issued the 'Proclamation of Neutrality' in the war between England and France; but his trial, great as it was, did not come up to Acheson's.

less than 30,000 were able to make their way back to North Korea.

Victory was virtually complete now. The mission of the forces under MacArthur's command, as set forth in the United Nations resolution, had been 'to repel the armed attack and to restore international peace and security.' Now the armed attack had been repelled. The restoration of international peace and security was not a precise objective, but a prudent interpretation would have it that what remained was to conclude a settlement with the utterly defeated North Koreans. Secretary Acheson had stated in June that the United Nations action was 'solely for the purpose of restoring the Republic of Korea to its status prior to the invasion from the north.'[2]

Now, however, an irresistible temptation presented itself to the victors. Ever since 1945 the objective of the United States and the United Nations had been a unified Korea under a freely elected and representative government. The Government that had been established in Seoul, South Korea, under President Rhee, had been the product of free elections supervised by the United Nations in the only part of Korea in which it had been allowed to hold them, the part south of the 38th parallel. This Government had been accepted by the United Nations as the legitimate Government of all Korea, North as well as South, but it had been excluded from the North by the satellite Government that Moscow had installed there. Now at last, with the North Korean Army shattered, the opportunity seemed to present itself to unify the whole country under the Seoul Government. All that was needed was for MacArthur's forces, in hot pursuit of the fleeing Communist remnants, to liberate Korea north of the parallel as well as south.

How could the Administration in Washington justify itself before history if it now ordered General MacArthur to stop his pursuit at the parallel, to desist from exploiting the logic of his victory to encompass by a notable act of self-restraint the security of the Communist regime in North Korea?

There was just one argument for stopping the pursuit, for preserving the division of Korea: that an invasion of North Korea would have the effect of bringing the Chinese, and perhaps the Russians as well, into the War on the North Korean side. If this

---

[2] Quoted by Rees, p. 101, from State Department *Bulletin* of July 10, 1950.

should happen, the War could never be won in Korea. Once it happened, the War could be won only by attacking China directly, in which case Russia, having a treaty of alliance with China, would find itself under obligation to come to its aid. The choice would be between a general war, almost surely World War III, and the frustration of the United Nations forces. All this was clearly seen at the time as the consequence to be expected of a full-scale Chinese intervention.

Among the alternatives that confronted the West, in the last days of September, was that of halting its forces at the 38th parallel, that of halting them at the narrow waist of the Korean peninsula above the parallel, and that of allowing only Korean troops to move north toward the Chinese frontier. The choice would represent a judgment of how far the West could go without provoking Chinese intervention.

The Chinese, for their part, must have felt themselves confronted with an equally delicate situation. One may suppose that the advance of an essentially American Army toward the Yalu River, their frontier, would make them feel that their survival was in balance. Consequently, they would no more wait for it to reach the Yalu, before intervening against it, than the United States would wait for a Communist army marching north through Mexico to reach the Rio Grande before intervening against it. On the other hand, only desperation could justify them in starting a war with the United States that might well end in the devastation of their cities and the decimation of their population by atomic attack. They would therefore be tempted to delay an intervention for as long as other alternatives to such a risk of disaster remained. In the event, they were to delay it too long for the good of either side.

We do not know to what extent the Chinese Communist regime had been privy to the plans that eventuated in the North Korean attack on South Korea. Mao Tse-tung had been in Moscow, consulting the Russian leaders, the previous December and January. If one takes the view that the relations between Moscow and Peking were those of mutual confidence—a view that goes against the real as opposed to the nominal circumstances—then one must suppose that, either then or later, Mao was made privy to Moscow's plans for Korea, since those plans were of such vital strategic concern to him. If, on the other hand, one takes account of the strained relations that had existed between Moscow and Mao since

1927, and of all the circumstances that must have tended to divide them in 1949–1950, then the matter is less sure.

Moscow did not regard Mao and his cohorts as true Communists, and did not trust them. It is, then, plausible that Moscow's policy in Korea had, at least for one of its objectives, an encirclement of China that would limit the independence of its new regime. Given habitual Russian secretiveness, it seems possible that Moscow would not have taken Mao into its confidence on decisions, having to do with Korea, with which Mao might be expected to disagree.

It is hard to believe that Mao could have been happy about the status of North Korea as a satellite of Moscow. When he came to power he found the Russians (who had refrained from helping him until his success was clearly foreseeable) in domination of Outer Mongolia, Manchuria, and North Korea. Surely he must have regarded this as a situation to be remedied. We have seen how sensitive China had been for over a thousand years about the control of the strategic Korean peninsula. It is unlikely that a Chinese nationalist, as Mao surely was, would now have agreed to having Russia add South Korea to its satellite empire.

Mao's forces had effectively won the civil war, having driven Chiang's forces off the mainland by the beginning of October 1949. In December and January, as we have seen, Mao was negotiating in Moscow. In April there began a redeployment of the Chinese Communist Army to the north—to Manchuria and to Shantung. One could make the argument that the purpose of this redeployment was to backstop the North Koreans in the adventure on which they would embark, under Moscow's direction, at the end of June. It seems more plausible, however, that the intention was to assert Chinese sovereignty and influence in an area that Russia had been dominating.

If this is so, then the North Korean attack on South Korea may have come to Peking as an unpleasant surprise. Its success would mean an extension of Russian influence in the zone of China's traditional interests, while its failure could mean an alarming build-up of American power on the Asian mainland, along the most sensitive part of the Chinese frontier.

Now, after the Inchon landings, Moscow's Korean adventure had failed disastrously. But it was China rather than Russia that appeared likely to bear the brunt of the disaster. One can imagine that there was consternation and bitterness in Peking, and that such regard as there had been for Moscow's wisdom was impaired.

Matters moved at an almost uncontrolable pace after September 15, too fast for all concerned, and we may regret that the Chinese, if they were going to intervene at all, were not more forehanded about it. Chinese military intervention before the West became committed to the liberation of North Korea, or an unambiguous warning of such intervention, would almost surely have forestalled the commitment. But when the intervention came, at last, the United Nations forces were already across the parallel, sweeping toward the Yalu at full tilt.

The one thing that is consistent about this history from its beginning is the succession of misunderstandings between the two sides at every juncture. How many lives, what widespread damage and what grief could have been saved, if only there had been channels of mutually intelligible communication between them! Understanding between enemies, in a dangerous conflict, may be even more important than understanding between allies.

*   *   *

General MacArthur, flushed with a sensational victory, was determined to complete it by the conquest of North Korea. If this had not been his disposition he would have lacked the qualifications of a successful military commander that he did, in fact, have. Over every great military commander, however, there should be an authority that represents something more than the qualifications that make for victory in battle. The decision whether to advance into North Korea was a political decision quite beyond the competence of the local military commander. It had to be made independently by the civilian political leaders at the seats of government.

The political position of the leaders in Washington, however, was much too weak in this moment of crisis. MacArthur had, over the years, shown an increasing disposition to be insubordinate, to take matters into his own hands. He had conspired with the political opposition in the United States to discredit his successive commanders-in-chief in the White House, first Roosevelt and then Truman. He issued statements designed to diminish their authority and to frustrate them in the policies they were pursuing. He engaged in independent actions contrary to those policies. He defied and disobeyed orders—as when, on June 29, he ordered the American Air Force to bomb North Korean targets in spite of the fact that, at the time, he had been authorized to use air and naval forces south of the 38th parallel only. He could be expected, now as in the past, to make public his disapproval of orders from Washington to which he objected, to arouse powerful political opposition to them, and perhaps to find ways of disobeying them. As the effective ruler of Japan and as Commander-in-Chief of American forces in the Far East, he had already invested himself with some of the attributes of an independent sovereign.

MacArthur was able to assert this independence because he had become the gleaming symbol of the heroic life for the American people. He was the bronze image on horseback, as Mr. Truman was not. The myth of his exalted statesmanship radiated from him to the remote corners of the earth. Whatever the Constitution of the United States said about the relations between the President and an American military commander, in a test between MacArthur and Truman it seemed likely that the majority of the American people would support MacArthur. Already the majority of Congress was behind him. The President had reason to believe that, if he attempted to discipline his subordinate by asserting his full constitutional authority, he would be committing political suicide.

President Rhee of South Korea was also in a rebellious mood. 'Where is the 38th parallel?' he asked. 'It is non-existent. I am going all the way to the Yalu, and the United Nations can't stop me.'[3]

Under these circumstances it was hardly possible for Mr. Truman to stop MacArthur in his hot pursuit of the fleeing North Koreans on the grounds that for him to continue toward the Yalu would invite the disaster of Chinese intervention. MacArthur asserted that there was 'very little' risk that the Chinese would intervene, and since he was widely regarded as infallible his word on a matter of this sort carried more authority than that of the President.[4]

This was, moreover, at a time when the American people were becoming convinced that the foreign policy of the United States had fallen into the hands of Communist conspirators, agents of Moscow, who had infiltrated the Government under Truman and virtually captured the State Department. For the Government

[3] Quoted by Higgins, p. 55, from Baille, pp. 267–8.
[4] Quoted by Rees, p. 119, from the transcript of the Wake Island meeting between Truman and MacArthur on October 15, 1950, reprinted in Rovere & Schlesinger, pp. 253–62.

now to have ordered MacArthur to desist from giving the beaten Communists the *coup de grace* would have appeared to confirm this view. Without the actual test, the people, having MacArthur's word for it, would never have believed that Korea could not have been quickly unified under a friendly democratic regime if he had not been wantonly held back by those who secretly took their orders from Moscow. Truman's action would have gone down in history as the great betrayal.

In the Inchon landings, moreover, MacArthur had just given an example of what might be accomplished by superb daring in defiance of the counsels of prudence. The Joint Chiefs of Staff had opposed the landings because the apparent odds against their success made a total disaster probable, and we have no reason to doubt that they were right; but MacArthur had gone ahead on the basis of his own intuition and self-confidence alone, and the long chance had paid off with spectacular results. No one was in a position, after that, to tell the triumphant Proconsul of the East that the risks of what he intended next were too great. A noble boldness, rather than a craven timidity, became the order of the day—and everyone wanted to be identified with it.

Finally, the political leaders in Washington, in London, and elsewhere were themselves in a state of *hubris* brought on by success after long failure. They were themselves swept along by the momentum of victory, and they allowed themselves to be swept along the more readily because anything else was politically impossible for them.

However, one who recalls the corridor-discussions in the State Department, during these dramatic days, recalls the misgivings of men who could not get it out of their minds that, if MacArthur's forces continued pell-mell toward the Yalu, the Chinese were bound to come in. These men, since they were not on the political firing-line, could still think with some detachment. George Kennan, an advisor rather than a man responsible for decision, represented their point of view. He opposed the advance. But the influence of the reasonable, the prudent, the sensitive, and the moderate men was now in sharp decline. Control of events had been lost. Either one went along with them or one was spilled off into the roadway of history, to be left behind. Many were spilled off in the months and years to come.

On September 15, the day of the Inchon landings, MacArthur was authorized by the President to extend his operations north of

the 38th parallel and to plan the occupation of North Korea—
except that no ground operations should be conducted north of
the parallel if there was Russian or Chinese military intervention.
The confusion implicit in this order, which forbade certain operations in a contingency that would be realized only after they had
been undertaken, represents the efforts of the men in Washington
to control the events that, in fact, controled them.

Acheson had originally been opposed to intervention in the
Chinese civil war but, as we have seen, he had been carried away
by the strong flow of events. At the Blair House meetings he had
accepted the word of the men in uniform that such intervention
was a military necessity. Now he abandoned his previous position
that the United Nations action was properly limited to the restoration of the *status quo ante* south of the parallel. He rode with the
irresistible current, identifying himself with the objective of
unifying Korea by conquest of the North. In politics men do, not
what they had originally intended, but what they find they must.

The British Government, too, rode with the current, and not
without enthusiasm. Foreign Minister Bevin stated on September
26 that 'there could no longer be a North and South Korea.'
Like Rhee, he refused to attach once more to the 38th parallel a
significance that the Communists had themselves repudiated by
their invasion.

Surely MacArthur, Acheson, Bevin, and the rest were right
in terms of justice. It was proper, now that the bounds of peaceful
procedure had been broken by the Communists, to liberate the
North Koreans from an authoritarian regime that had been imposed on them by a foreign invader, and to give them the opportunity to choose their own government. The only question that
arose was one of prudence—the question whether, by attempting
to liberate the North Koreans, the United Nations would not
transform victory into defeat or, alternatively, detonate a third
world war. The question, in its most immediate aspect, was that
of whether the Chinese would come in, and there was every reason
to believe that they would if American forces crossed the parallel
for the liberation of North Korea and drove on toward the Yalu.

On September 27 Washington instructed MacArthur that he
was to undertake the destruction of the North Korean armed
forces. To this end he was authorized to conduct military operations north of the parallel—if, at the time such operations were
undertaken, 'there had been no entry into North Korea by major

Soviet or Chinese Communist forces, no announcement of an intended entry, and no threat by Russian or Chinese Communists to counter our operations militarily in North Korea.'[5] Moreover, only South Korean ground forces were to be used in the provinces bordering Russia or China.

While the element of prudence is not inconspicuous in these instructions, MacArthur was being encouraged to interpret them loosely. For example, on September 29 General Marshall, now Secretary of Defense, cabled him: 'We want you to feel unhampered strategically and tactically to proceed north of the 38th parallel.' This sentence virtually authorized him to interpret his instructions so widely as to nullify them.[6]

On October 1, South Korean troops of General MacArthur's command crossed the parallel and entered North Korea.

Throughout August, Peking had been conducting a 'Hate-America' campaign of mounting violence among the Chinese people, preparing them for intervention against the United Nations forces, which were so overwhelmingly American. On September 22 the Foreign Ministry in Peking issued a statement in which it said: 'We clearly reaffirm that we will always stand on the side of the Korean people . . . and resolutely oppose the criminal acts of American imperialist aggressors against Korea.' This was much too vague a warning to provide a basis for restraining MacArthur's forces.

On September 30, Chinese Prime Minister Chou En-lai said in a public address that the Chinese people will not 'supinely tolerate seeing their neighbors being savagely invaded by the imperialists.' Again, the warning lacked precision, and the next day the first troops under MacArthur's command, Korean contingents, crossed the parallel.

Finally, on October 2 Chou En-lai summoned the Indian Ambassador, Mr. K. M. Pannikar, and told him, for communication to Washington, that while Peking did not take a serious view of an incursion into North Korea by South Koreans, such as had occurred the day before, if American troops should cross the

[5] Rees, p. 103.

[6] Higgins, p. 54. A State Department officer who participated with the representatives of the Defense Department in drafting the basic instructions that it was sending MacArthur at this time, later told me that such restrictive provisions as, in accordance with policy decisions, were put into the instructions were generally surrounded by qualifying phrases, advanced by the military on military grounds, that tended to nullify them.

parallel China would enter the War. This, at last, was an un-equivocal statement of intention. In itself it should have allowed little room for doubt in Washington of what would happen if American troops entered North Korea.

By this date, however, the whole movement of policy on the United Nations side had gained too much momentum to be stopped. Mr. Pannikar, it was said, was untrustworthy, a Communist sympathizer—although it is not clear what relevance this had. Then the convenient term 'propaganda' was applied to Chou's precise and explicit warning as an excuse for disregarding it. He was trying to 'blackmail' the United Nations. There was a general breast-beating in Washington and New York. Two days later the Political Committee of the United Nations General Assembly accepted a resolution that was passed in plenary session on October 7 and that enlarged the original objective of the United Nations forces. 'All appropriate steps' were to be taken 'to insure conditions of stability throughout Korea'; all constituent acts were to be taken, 'including the holding of elections, under the auspices of the United Nations, for the establishing of a united, independent and democratic government in the sovereign state of Korea.' This could only mean that Korea was to be unified by the forces under General MacArthur's command.

On the same October 7, the first American troops crossed the 38th parallel, driving north.

A week later, President Truman and General MacArthur met at Wake Island in the Pacific as if they were two equal sovereigns negotiating an understanding. President Truman, in fact, appeared as the suitor for MacArthur's agreement—which he reported that he had obtained in certain matters, although the General was later to deny it.

It was at the Wake Island meeting that MacArthur discounted any danger of Chinese intervention, stating that all formal resistance in Korea would be over by Thanksgiving (November 23). Even as he was saying this, however, the first Chinese units were secretly crossing the Yalu into Korea, where their numbers would have grown to at least 300,000 a month later.

On the 24th of October General MacArthur, still not knowing of the Chinese entry, ordered all the forces under his command to drive forward at full tilt, in disregard of the instruction of September 27 that only Korean forces were to be allowed in the vicinity of the Chinese and Russian frontiers. When Washington called his attention to this, as it immediately did, he replied by citing Secretary Marshall's cable of September 29 telling him to 'feel unhampered strategically and tactically' in his northward advance. He also cited 'military necessity'—as he would on other occasions over the next few weeks to frustrate such efforts as Washington would make to keep him within bounds.

On October 26 the first of his troops reached the Yalu and the first encounter with the Chinese took place. On November 6, recognizing the fact of Chinese intervention, MacArthur cited it as 'one of the most offensive acts of international lawlessness of historic record.' In this he would be followed by the Government in Washington and by the General Assembly of the United Nations in New York, which would officially brand the Chinese intervention as wanton aggression.

Beginning on November 7, there was a lull in the fighting, and on the 21st American troops reached the Yalu. Their stay was to be brief. On the 24th MacArthur announced a great 'end-the-war' offensive. On the 26th the Chinese counter-attacked along the entire front. By the 28th, MacArthur's forces were fleeing south, toward and across the 38th parallel, and he announced that 'we face an entirely new war.' Once again the question was whether the Western forces could keep a foothold in South Korea.

*   *   *

The disaster that had been dreaded, even while its possibility had been discounted, had now befallen. From this moment on, the Western forces faced the choice between defeat or frustration, and an extension of the War into China (which had a defensive alliance with Russia), thereby risking its escalation into a third world war in which the West would depend on its capacity for nuclear destruction while the Red Army, perhaps, overran West Europe.

Now, however, a new determination manifested itself in Washington. With the full concurrence of the Joint Chiefs of Staff, and under pressure from the other Western governments, the President would re-establish a firm political control, even though this meant the acceptance of military frustration by keeping the War limited. When MacArthur continued rebellious, giving public expression to his sense of outrage at the political restrictions upon him and practising a kind of oblique insubordination, the President finally relieved him of his command—thereby resolving (at the cost of political disaster to himself, as he then thought) what had become a constitutional crisis for the American democracy over which he presided. The General, now a more heroic figure than ever in the eyes of the people, returned to the land from which he had been absent fourteen years like a Caesar returning in triumph to Rome. As he crossed his native country to the plaudits of the people, the President appeared diminished and humiliated, cast aside by his own countrymen. Arrived in Washington, the General addressed a joint session of the Congress assembled to do him honor. The nation listened on the radio to the words of the stricken hero and, listening, wept.

Meanwhile the United States, with its allies, was trapped in a War that went on claiming its daily hecatomb, a War that it could no longer either win or end.

*   *   *

Thucydides wrote his history of the Peloponnesian War twenty-five centuries ago in the expectation that the events he recorded 'will according to human nature happen again in the same way.' His history testifies to the fact that the events recorded in the above chapter had happened before and in the same way.[7]

[7] See *History of the Peloponnesian War*, III, 82 and IV, 18 *inter alia*.

CHAPTER XXII

The defection of Yugoslavia;
the image that Americans developed of Stalin's empire;
deadlock and arms race

B Y the summer of 1951 the line between the two Koreas had been stabilized in the vicinity of the 38th parallel. It stood again where it had been from 1945 to June 25, 1950. The attempt of the Communists to eliminate it by striking south across it had failed. The counter-attempt of the West, striking north across it, had also failed. A final drive southward by the Communists, with their massive Chinese reinforcements, had produced the final failure. No further attempt would be made by either side. At the risk of a third world war, and at an unimaginable cost in human life, in suffering, and in destruction, both sides learned, during the year and fifteen days of fighting until truce negotiations were opened on July 10, 1951, that the Korean *status quo* was unalterable—at least for the time being. Everything was back where it had been— except for the dead and the maimed, except for the blackened land, except for normal civil activity. The frustrated armies, pushing against each other, had come to a standstill, but could not disengage.[1]

The Cold War, which had begun in the summer of 1947, had now come to a point of culmination in the West and the East alike—with the abortive Berlin blockade, with the abortive invasion of South Korea. The lesson, in both cases, was that the *status quo* of 1945 could not be changed by sudden, forceful action

[1] From June 25, 1950, until the end of 1951, over 47,000 members of the United Nations forces were killed, over 182,000 were wounded, over 76,000 were captured or missing. The American estimates of Communist casualties to April 1952 ran to about a million and a half, and the number captured was given as 170,000. Most horrible, however, was the slaughter and crippling of the Korean civilian population—men, women, and children who found themselves in the line of fire. Seoul, for example, was captured by the Communists, recaptured by the United Nations, recaptured by the Communists, and recaptured by the United Nations in the course of the year's fighting. Upon its first recapture by the United Nations in September 1950, the advancing forces subjected it to artillery fire that, according to one observer, 'blotted out' whole areas. The real suffering is beyond statistics and cannot be reported in the official histories.

—at least within the limits of what either side regarded as acceptable risk. If it was to be changed, then, it would have to be by a
sort of political erosion, or by an evolution of basic circumstances
such as could hardly occur except with the passage of years. After
the two tests of force, the first half of the 1950's was to be a period
of deadlock between the two sides. In the second half of the decade, when the Western nuclear monopoly had been broken, there
would be renewed attempts to force a change in the *status quo*—
with what consequences we shall see.

*   *   *

Meanwhile, the slower and largely hidden forces of political
evolution were constantly at work. The Soviet empire had become overextended in the rush of its expansion into the power
vacuums on either side. Yugoslavia would re-assert its independence at an early stage, and Russia would find itself displaced in
Korea and Manchuria by its increasingly alienated Chinese ally.
By the middle 1950's the need for some retrenchment on the
European front would be felt in Moscow, and the problem it faced
would, increasingly, be that of how to disengage. This, whether
recognized or not, would also be the problem of the West.

The West, too, would find itself conducting a rearguard action,
although not along the front lines of the Cold War. It would be
disengaging itself—sometimes unwillingly, sometimes at heavy
cost—from the remains of empire in Asia and Africa. At some
points (e.g., India) it would succeed; at others (e.g., Indo-China)
it would flounder and fail. The Cold War would be involved in
this process because the two sides would compete for influence in
the newly liberated nations.

*   *   *

No sooner was the zone of Russian domination in Europe established, with the Prague *coup* of February 1948, than a disintegrating tendency began to manifest itself. In March a breach began
to open between Yugoslavia and the rest of the zone. Because the
Yugoslav Communists, led by Tito, showed themselves insufficiently subservient, Moscow undertook to discipline and repri-
mand them. Although the Yugoslavs responded by protesting
their loyalty, they defended themselves in terms that were not as
obsequious as Moscow deemed proper. So a contest got under
way, which quickly became a test of Moscow's power to enforce

upon Belgrade the unquestioning conformity that, in its conception, ideological purity and the exigencies of the Cold War alike required of the states grouped under its command.

The outcome of this contest confirmed the principle that real circumstances must ultimately prevail over ideology where the two conflict. Tito and his associates, although devout in their attitude toward the official doctrine for which Moscow spoke, were nationalists first.[2] They had achieved power in Yugoslavia on their own, by what was more a peasant than a proletarian movement, and they now had a power-base that was in substantial degree independent of Moscow. Having to deal with the actual Yugoslav society, rather than with the mythical society of the ideologists, they were bound to find the directives of Moscow frequently irrelevant. And they had reason to lose their naïve faith in the supreme wisdom and moral elevation of Stalin and his associates when, confronting them face-to-face, they found that, so far from being of heroic mold, they were petty, brutal, and uncomprehending.[3] Since real circumstances made Tito and his associates independent of Moscow, they could hardly fail, at last, to defend the society over which they ruled against the pretensions of the alien Russians who, while nominally representing Marxist–Leninist authority, were in their barbaric crudeness far from representing any innate superiority, intellectual or moral.

On June 28, 1948, the Yugoslav Communist Party was at last expelled from the Cominform for its independent attitude, and the Communists in Yugoslavia were invited to rid themselves of their delinquent leadership if it persisted in the error of its ways. Thus a cold war was declared against Tito and his associates with the objective of either bringing them to heel or replacing them by more tractable servants of Moscow. Economic boycotts, internal subversion, incitements to assassination, public denunciations, and threats of military action were used. Tito and his followers, by holding their own against these heavy attacks, at last brought worldwide humiliation on the Russian Goliath who could not overcome them. So Yugoslavia escaped from Stalin's dominion.

[2] Anyone who reads Tito's own words and those of his associate, Vladimir Dedijer, in the latter's *Tito Speaks*, will be impressed by the fact that Tito was not a Marxist intellectual so much as he was a nationalist whose single purpose was to liberate the Yugoslav peoples from tyranny, whether domestic or foreign.

[3] The resulting disillusionment has been poignantly expressed by Milovan Djilas, member of the Yugoslav Politburo and one of Tito's close associates at the time, in his *Conversations with Stalin*.

The line of the Iron Curtain fell back from the Adriatic—not by any push from the West but by the intrinsic weakness of Moscow's overextended empire.

Tito's successful defiance had a significance for Moscow's cause more fateful than that of merely entailing a recession of the Iron Curtain. It exposed, for those who had eyes to see, the implications of the national Communism that had been adopted by the Bolsheviks, in place of the original anti-national Communism, when their seizure of power in Russia failed to detonate Communist revolution elsewhere.

The reader will recall that the international boundaries by which separate national jurisdictions were marked off in the bourgeois world were not expected to survive in a world under the dictatorship of the proletariat. The proletariat, Marx had declared, knew no country. Nation-states and nationalism were devices of the proletariat's class-enemies. Lenin and his Bolsheviks had thought, in 1917, that they had abolished Russia, that the name would survive in the proletarian era merely as an ethnic term. What had been Russia, Poland, Hungary, Germany, etc., would become all one fraternal community as the Communists assumed power in each. However, after the unexpected failure of the Communists to achieve power outside Russia, the Bolsheviks had, perforce, fallen back on the doctrine of 'socialism in one country,' with its nationalistic implications. The 'Mother Russia' of the czars remained in being as 'the Fatherland of Socialism,' and under Stalin's increasingly counter-revolutionary rule allegiance to it superseded, in official doctrine, allegiance to the international proletarian cause.[4]

The greatness of Russia became, in effect, the objective of the Communist Party of the Soviet Union. Through its control of the Communist parties in other countries, Moscow imposed the same objective on them. It was for the sake of Russia that the Cominform was created, for its defense and its triumph in the Cold

[4] In 1939 the soldier's oath, which had to be taken by every member of the Red Army, was changed. 'The original Red Army oath, phrased in the early years of the Revolution, characterized the soldier as a "son of the toiling people" and pledged him "to direct my every act and thought toward the great aim of the emancipation of the toilers." The new version of the oath describes the soldier as a citizen of the Soviet Union. The soldier vows "to come to the defense of my fatherland, the Union of Soviet Socialist Republics, to defend it courageously, skillfully, with dignity and honor, not sparing my blood or life itself to win full victory over the enemy." ' (Chamberlin, pp. 243–4.)

War. So the Communist parties all around the world became 'fifth columns' of the Socialist Fatherland. The intellectuals and workers who placed themselves under their discipline were expected to give all their allegiance to that Fatherland, rather than to their own countries.[5]

In the days when the leaders of international Communism ostensibly represented the interests of the masses in all countries, and stood opposed to the particular interests of any nation-state as such, they had an ostensible claim on the allegiance of men everywhere. This was the basis on which Tito and Djilas, as young men, had given their allegiance to the original Bolsheviks and their successors. It was another matter, however, to demand that Communists outside Russia prefer the interests of the Russian nation to those of their own. The adoption of nationalism by the Communist movement inevitably implied the adoption of a different nationalism in each country. It implied what was to become known as 'Titoism.' What Tito's defiance represented was the national separatism that would eventually fragment Stalin's postwar empire—even though the threat of it was, as yet, a cloud no bigger than a man's hand.

All great centrally organized movements based on doctrinal authority pay the penalty of their success, as they grow, in fragmentation. As Christianity spread, Rome was unable to maintain its rule over the more distant churches. Schisms occurred. New centers of authority, independent of Rome, arose to challenge its primacy. Islam, as it expanded, split into rival caliphates. Even without the Bolshevik reversion to nationalism in the 1920's, the authority of Moscow could not long have been maintained beyond the area that the Red Army was able to dominate. All the evidence shows that Stalin, who understood the exercise of power and its limits, was so well aware of this that he preferred not to have Communists come to power in areas beyond his reach; for a Communist state beyond his reach was only too likely to become a rival center of authority, providing Communists the world over with an alternative leadership. This is why he had been so reluctant to support Tito's movement in Yugoslavia and Mao's in China.

---

[5] In March, 1948, when it appeared that the Red Army might soon be advancing into western Europe, the Communist parties of Norway, Denmark, Finland, Belgium, Great Britain, Austria, Italy, the United States, Canada, Cuba, Mexico, Colombia, Argentina, Uruguay, Australia, and Japan were brought to declare that they would not oppose Russia in war.

This is why he opposed Yugoslav support of the Communist guerillas in Greece. A Communist Yugoslavia, a Communist China, or a Communist Greece would constitute a threat to Moscow's authority that would not exist if those countries remained anti-Communist.[6]

Over the years that followed Moscow's humiliation at Tito's hands, evidence of the embarrassment and strain it suffered in trying to maintain control of its overlarge empire was not altogether lacking, despite the secrecy that was maintained behind the Iron Curtain. In June 1953 mass uprisings against the Communist rule, beginning in East Berlin, spread to cities all over East Germany. The whole of East Germany had to be sealed off by Russian forces, and the rebelling German people were put down by Russian troops and tanks when the German 'People's Police' proved inadequate to cope with them. From Poland to Bulgaria, it is clear, the governments of the new 'people's republics,' in the service of the Russian state, were able to maintain their rule over the overwhelmingly resentful peoples only by their monopoly of force, which depended on the backing of the Red Army.

The hostility of the captive populations must surely have had major military implications as the Cold War developed into a confrontation of rival military forces. If war should break out in Europe, if the Red Army should march westward, it was across these rebelliously disposed countries that its lines of communication would pass. This could not have been other than a major inhibiting factor in the minds of the Russian high command.

By February 1948 Stalin's postwar empire had reached its greatest extent. By the end of June, with the separation of Yugoslavia, it had begun to recede. What this shows is that, although the postwar *status quo* could not be changed by the application of force, it was subject to erosion. Given a long period of reasonable calm in which the erosive forces might operate, one could expect the slow

[6] Like all rulers, Stalin had to be preoccupied with the immediate threats to his power rather than with abstract objectives to be attained in a hypothetical future. Mao had been a rebel against his authority for twenty years, and would not become less so when he had captured an independent power-base sufficient to rival his own. Tito had already opposed Moscow's control of the Yugoslav Communist Party in the 1930's. A Greek Communist regime brought to power with Yugoslav support would be bound to Belgrade more than to Moscow. If, through the Cominform, Stalin gave the word for the strikes and disorders that the French and Italian Communists fomented in November 1947, his purpose was surely to defeat the Marshall Plan rather than to effect the Communist revolution in France and Italy. The primary mission of the Communist parties throughout the world, from Moscow's point of view, was to weaken the United States and its allies rather than to capture power for themselves.

development of renewed independence among the eastern European countries that, in the catastrophic aftermath of the War, had fallen under the yoke of Moscow. In time, Moscow would welcome accommodations, with the captive peoples and with the West, that relieved it of the danger and strain involved in holding down, over any extended period, explosively rebellious populations.

This, however, is not the way the American people and their Government saw matters. The psychological dynamics of wartime now possessed them, and indeed possessed half the world on both sides of the Iron Curtain. The demonizing of the enemy, the disposition to attribute to him superhuman determination and power in the service of an unlimited ambition—the same disposition that, only a few years earlier, had blinded us to the fact that Japan was ready to surrender—this disposition now caused us to see Russia as a monolithic empire, growing in power as it grew in extent, advancing inexorably, carrying out with unerring craft a master plan laid down by Lenin generations earlier for the conquest of the world. Just as, five years earlier, anyone tended to be discredited if he doubted that every last Japanese would die fighting rather than give himself up, so anyone tended to be discredited now if, indulging in 'wishful thinking,' he underestimated the demonic power, the insatiable ambition, and the accelerating progress of the new enemy. (No one should be lulled into complacency by an incidental minor setback like the Yugoslav defection.) Again, in Washington and in the nation men competed in demonstrations of their 'realism', their capacity to appreciate the menace that now loomed over the world, requiring desperate measures to save the freedom of mankind.

Tito's defection occurred before this wartime psychology had reached its pitch in the West. Washington welcomed it and, overriding those who were opposed to dealings with any Communist, cooperated in it by giving Tito economic support.[7] But it was generally regarded as a self-contained incident, without wider significance.

---

[7] Tito's Government had asked Washington to license the exportation to Yugoslavia of an American steel mill. This posed a basic policy issue for Washington. Those who saw the Cold War as simply an ideological struggle were unwilling to have the United States compromise its ideological purity by doing business with any Communist. On the other hand, those who regarded the Cold War as a power-struggle in which the enemy was Russia rather than Communism favored a positive response to Tito, and they won out. It is not certain that they would have won out a year later, when ideological passion had risen.

When, the following year, Mao Tse-tung and his followers won the civil war in China and set up their Government in Peking, the whole country interpreted this as the conquest of China by 'the Communist conspiracy.' It saw it as the capture and enslavement of the Chinese people by the little group of Lenin's successors in Moscow who, in the extreme view, were carrying out, in this as in everything they did, his plan for the conquest of the world. If anyone had suggested, at this point, that Moscow's empire had reached its greatest extension in February 1948, and would not expand thereafter (that it would, in fact, recede), he would quickly have been silenced by this overwhelming evidence to the contrary. Those who thought of themselves as hard-headed realists knew that Moscow's master plan had called for Stalin to switch suddenly to the East, in his march to world conquest, after having completed his first postwar stage in the West.[8] (One heard a great deal about the Communist 'blueprint' for world conquest, and the Communist 'time-table.') Virtually every Far Eastern expert in the American Foreign Service now found himself in serious trouble because he had been so soft-headed as not to have seen that Mao was a disciplined and obedient agent of Moscow. Social pressure in the United States began to impose a severe limitation on freedom of speech, and this limitation, tending to exclude the expression of all but one view of the international situation, isolated the American people from reality. This is what happens in a democracy under the stresses of wartime, as Thucydides had recognized in his account of the Peloponnesian War.

What now came to be the only acceptable view was well expressed by Secretary of State John Foster Dulles in a television address to the American people on January 27, 1953, six days after he had assumed office. Behind him, as he spoke, was a map showing what he identified as the 'area which the Russian Communists completely dominate.' On it, everything from the Elbe in Europe to the Straits of Formosa was one color, representing Moscow's empire. The boundary between Russia and China was no more.

The Soviet Communists, [said the Secretary of State] are carrying out a policy which they call encirclement. . . . They said they don't want to start an open war against us until they get such overwhelming power

---

[8] Lenin was widely quoted, in these days, as having said: 'The road to Paris lies through Peking.' There is no reason to believe that he ever said it. See Fischer, p. 668.

that the result will not be in doubt. . . . And they have been making very great progress. At the end of the Second World War, only a little over seven years ago, they only controlled about 200,000,000 people, and today, as I say, they control 800,000,000 people, and they're hard at work to get control of other parts of the world.

'Stalin,' he said, 'has boasted that with Japan the Soviet Union would be invincible. . . . Now the Soviet Russians are making a drive to get Japan.' If the Russian Communists once 'largely completed their encirclement of the United States' they would 'be ready for what Stalin has called the decisive blow against us with the odds overwhelmingly in their favor.' [9]

At the time of Mr. Dulles's address the United States had bases, from which it could deliver nuclear bombs upon Russian targets, in the British Isles, in Morocco, in Libya, in Saudi Arabia, in Turkey, and in Okinawa; and it would soon conclude an agreement to establish such a base in Spain. It had a military-defense alliance with fourteen European countries; it was about to enter into relations of political and military cooperation with the states to be grouped in the Baghdad Pact, including Iraq and Iran; it was about to conclude a military-defense alliance with Pakistan, Thailand, the Philippines, and Australia; it was supporting the French military forces in Indo-China; its own military forces were in Korea and in Japan. The actual strategic situation, then, was that the military power of the United States and its allies, including Canada, had Russia encircled. If Moscow had any designs on Japan, one must suppose that the objective was not so much to encircle the United States as to break out of its own encirclement.

Again we see, here, the dynamics of conflict. Neither Moscow nor Washington was aiming to conquer the world. But the abrupt and largely unpremeditated expansion of Russian power at the end of the War had provoked the defensive expansion of American power, which had provoked a similar Russian reaction. As in the Punic Wars, both sides were moved primarily by defensive considerations, and both sides suspected or at least accused the other of wishing to conquer the world.

[9] This address, delivered immediately after the Eisenhower Administration succeeded that of President Truman, was a bid to restore confidence in the Government by showing how alert it was, under the new Administration, to the Communist danger. We may suppose that the citations of what Stalin was said to have said had their basis in the myth that was now accepted as representing realism. The new Secretary was consciously and even ostentatiously identifying himself with the 'realists.' So Cleon had done in Athens twenty-four centuries earlier.

At the end of the 1940's the problem for both sides was twofold. First of all, there was the abnormal situation of East Europe, where the Russians were holding down by force populations of which they dared not let go. Communism had been a failure throughout this area. The proletariat had not really risen up to overthrow capitalist oppression and establish its dictatorship; the people had not really welcomed the military forces of the Soviet Union as liberators; the governments were not really 'people's' governments. Economically as well as spiritually, the masses were worse off under the nominally Communist regimes of East Europe than under the nominally capitalist regimes of West Europe. They continued in misery and stagnation while the masses in West Europe were enjoying a rising prosperity without precedent. Before the hostile and growing powers of the West, however, the Russians dared not release their helots, whom they had now profoundly antagonized. The West, on the other hand, could not liberate them without a devastating war in which, one could predict, the objects of their rescue, and perhaps the rescuers as well, would be consumed.

The other part of the problem was that of how to disengage. The two sides were like wrestlers locked in each other's grip: each thinks the other is trying to kill him, and the first to relax his hold may be sure that he will immediately be overcome by the other. In any case, on both sides a preponderance of opinion, presumably, still thought of the struggle as one to be concluded by a clear-cut decision that identified one side as the victor. To most simple Americans, and to all who represented the traditional military attitude, the Cold War could end only with the total victory of the one side over the other—as World War II had ended. This meant, on both sides, that one had to kill simply to avoid being killed; so that, to the extent to which this view prevailed, each side was right in believing that the objective of the other was to kill it.[10]

So we see, at the beginning of the 1950's, a deadlock in the Cold War. Neither side could advance, neither could retreat, and no disengagement was possible. But Russia had produced its first

[10] Some of my readers will be tempted to conclude, from what I have said here, that the United States should have proceeded to dismantle the bases and alliances with which it encircled the Soviet Union, and that it should have embarked on a program of disarming itself, thereby initiating the removal of the mutal provocation on which the Cold War was based. A careful reading, however, will show that this conclusion is not warranted.

atomic explosion in 1949 and would explode its first hydrogen bomb in 1953. By 1957 it would have created a nuclear panoply, including delivery systems, with which it could threaten the cataclysmic destruction of every country that harbored American overseas bases, and with which it could neutralize, by the threat of retaliation, the American nuclear panoply. It would then embark on a new attempt to break the deadlock by a diplomacy of menace backed by the ostentatious display of its new power.

At the same time the United States would be exerting itself to stay well ahead of the Soviet Union in nuclear technology and the development of delivery systems, as well as building up its conventional forces.

The chief feature of the Cold War in the 1950's, then, was to be the arms race. Both sides appeared to be advancing toward a final clash, which would be set off either by an accidental event or by the decision of either side, acting out of a desperate fear that it was doomed if it waited to strike.

CHAPTER XXIII

Remobilization, rearmament, and McCarthyism in the United States

W E may be sure that the North Koreans, when they launched their surprise attack on South Korea, were not acting on the basis of an established time-table for world conquest. They were moved, rather, by opportunism based on misconception. In his announcement of the American reaction to the attack, however, President Truman said: 'The attack upon Korea makes it plain beyond all doubt that Communism has passed beyond the use of subversion to conquer independent nations and will now use armed invasion and war.'

This single sentence, generalizing from what had happened in Korea, constituted the official American interpretation of the attack. The picture it presented was frightening. The Kremlin appeared as supreme master of the initiative, moving from one stage to the next in its inexorable and accelerating progress toward the conquest of the world. Now the hour had struck when, in accordance with its time-table, it had moved to the stage of armed invasion and war. Just as Japan's expansion, beginning in 1895, had culminated in the surprise attack on Pearl Harbor, so the expansion of the Communist empire had now reached a similar culmination in the surprise attack on South Korea.

One implication of the aggression in Korea, so interpreted, was particularly frightening. Everyone had in mind the similarity between divided Korea in the East and divided Germany in the West. In Korea the Russians, like the master chess-players they were, had succeeded in engaging the military forces of the United States while keeping their own free. They had committed aggression 'by proxy' (as everyone put it), using North Koreans to draw the military forces of the United States away from a more important theater of operations. Was it not logical that their next move would be in Europe? Either they would again attack by proxy, sending East German forces to invade West Germany while keeping their own forces free, or the Red Army itself would move into

West Europe while the American forces were helplessly entrapped in faraway Korea.

This view played its part in the historic crisis of confidence that now developed in the United States, threatening the whole structure of the society. Most Americans, in their hearts, must have felt that their Government was no match for the conspirators in the Kremlin. In Washington, and throughout the American society, the tremors of a suppressed panic could be felt.

Fear now brought to a culmination the need of the American society to relieve itself of the blame for what appeared to be mounting failure by finding within its ranks individuals or groups upon whom that blame could be cast. Then, by destroying such individuals or groups, in one way or another, the society could consider itself purged of an evil identified as the cause of its plight. The American nation, like any other nation in such circumstances, was irresistibly tempted to believe that its failures were not its own, that they were, rather, the product of alien forces in its midst. By dealing summarily with those forces it could feel that it was achieving its moral salvation, re-establishing its innate invincibility, restoring the complete security that it regarded as the normal condition of affairs. So the Nazis had brought moral relief and reassurance to the German society by putting the blame for its failures on the Jews, and by embarking on a course of extermination that would, accordingly, restore it to its former purity and invincibility. So the evils of other societies had, in all ages past, been symbolically drained from their own bodies into the bodies of witches, who were then ritually destroyed by burning, by driving a stake through the heart, or by other conspicuous acts of obliteration.

Throughout the West, but especially in the United States, men now accorded to the conspirators in the Kremlin the awe and the secret admiration that are the devil's due. Stalin was Satan, supreme in his craft and power, an adversary fit to grapple with the Good Lord himself, and perhaps to triumph.[1] Just as witches were Satan's agents, their supernatural power being his power, so the sinister conspirators for whom the whole American society was now combed were the agents of Stalin and his satanic court in the Kremlin.

---

[1] This is one of the repeated themes of the Bible. If one reads *Job* with an eye innocent of the exegesis with which the schoolmen have overlaid it, the explanation it offers of ubiquitous injustice in God's earthly kingdom is that God is no match for Satan, who outsmarts him, imposing on his vanity and his simplicity.

The American witch-hunt of the 1950's has acquired the name 'McCarthyism' from its leading practitioner. By 1953 Senator McCarthy, with the backing of a major portion of the nation, had gained substantial control over important parts of the Executive Branch of the Government, including the State Department, where those who were informally his agents, reporting to his organization, came to occupy positions that gave them a sinister power over the members of the Civil Service and the Foreign Service. One who saw this from the inside; who saw the procedures of organized blackmail, including the threat of public accusations privately admitted to be false; who saw the efforts of those who, fearing persecution, hurried to identify themselves with the views of the persecutors; who saw the demoralization in which men try to save or promote their own careers by turning on their colleagues; who saw good men broken in nerve and distinguished men broken in their careers; and who also saw the quiet heroism of the few— such a one knows that this episode in the life of the nation, as it really occurred, can never be made of historic record. The books that are written on McCarthyism can tell only a small part of the story, because shame has closed the mouths of its victims, as well as of those who practised upon them. Perhaps this is as well. 'Man, in the ideal,' said Herman Melville, 'is so noble and so sparkling, such a grand and glowing creature, that over any ig-nominious blemish in him all his fellows should run to throw their costliest robes.'

State Department and Foreign Service were now reduced to a morally crippled condition from which they could hardly be ex-pected to recover in less than a generation, and this would not be without its effect on the conduct of American foreign relations.[2]

*   *   *

The general alarm caused by the Korean War, interpreted as one move in an established strategy for world conquest, was not unwelcome to the Truman Administration in the summer of 1950; for it had been suffering from a frustration that would now be relieved.

The military forces that the people and the Congress had been willing to provide had been far less than what was needed for the

[2] Thucydides had predicted this too, in his way, when he foresaw that what had happened in Athens under the stress of war would, human nature remaining unchanged, happen again. See especially Book III, 82–4.

containment of Communism. The prevalent belief that any future war would be fought with atomic bombs delivered by air over intercontinental distances, rather than by armies locked in battle on the ground, had combined with popular reluctance to make, in time of peace, the sacrifices necessary for the maintenance of a large army. The consequence was that, at the outbreak of the Korean War, the Army of the United States, so recently over eight million strong, consisted of hardly more than half a million men, who had to be spread thin for the occupation of Germany and Japan as well as for service at home. Contingency planning, to implement the policy of supporting 'free peoples who are resisting attempted subjugation by armed minorities or by outside pressures,' was repeatedly frustrated by the dearth of military means. As happens in every democracy, the people were more ardent for the adoption of great objectives than for paying the cost of their achievement. The National Security Council drew up estimates of military requirements, but its members and staffs were sunk in hopelessness, knowing that nothing approaching those requirements could be met in the postwar mood that the country was still in.

The surprise attack on Korea, represented in the most alarming possible light, now changed all this. A month later an immediate and large-scale expansion of the American military establishment was announced to a Congress that had abandoned its preoccupation with budgetary economy. The process of closing down American bases overseas was stopped. The American Air Force establishment in Britain was tripled. In the year that followed, the Army of the United States underwent a three-fold expansion, while Navy and Air Force personnel were almost doubled. This, one supposes, was not a reaction that Moscow had intended to produce when it decided on the invasion of South Korea.[3]

After the Chinese entry into the Korean War, and the consequent rout of General MacArthur's forces, President Truman proclaimed a state of national emergency. He thereupon put the country on a wartime basis, instituting price-controls, wage stabilization, and restrictions on consumption, setting up an Office of Defense Mobilization. Within a year, he said, 'we will be turn-

---

[3] Leaders of the conservative opposition in the United States would insist, however, that the real purpose of the Communist conspiracy was to bankrupt the United States; and this would be the dominant view of the Eisenhower Administration when it came to power in 1953.

ing out planes at five times the present rate of production, combat vehicles will be coming off the production line at four times today's rate, and the rate of production of electronics equipment for defense will have multiplied four and a half times.' 'Our homes, our nation, all the things we believe in, are in great danger,' he said. 'This danger has been created by the rulers of the Soviet Union.' He then recounted how, when the United Nations 'had all but succeeded' in putting down the act of aggression in Korea, 'the Communists threw their Chinese armies into the battle against the free nations. By this act, they have shown that they are willing to push the world to the brink of a general war to get what they want. . . . That is why we are in such grave danger.'

Civil defense, for the contingency of an atomic war, was now organized on a crash basis. In New York State an air-raid warning system was instituted, fourteen thousand watchers of the skies were recruited, six hundred observation posts were established. The State of New Jersey got ready to receive a million evacuees from New York City. Along the highways of Virginia service-station attendants stopped scanning the sky for Russian bombers only long enough to scrutinize their customers suspiciously. Everywhere, notices of what to do in case of enemy attack sprang up. Before the end of the year a Federal Civil Defense Administration had been set up and Congress had been asked to authorize a plan for civil defense that would cost 3,000 million dollars.

It is hardly conceivable that the Soviet Union in 1950 had the ability, as yet, to engage in an exchange of atomic blows with the United States, although the President warned Congress in September that it had 'the power to attack our cities in force.' The accepted view was that the new measures of civil defense, to the extent of their effectiveness, strengthened the United States in its policy of containment by reducing its vulnerability. It is probable that their chief value was symbolic, providing evidence of American determination (and excitability) for the Russian leaders to contemplate. If they had had any thought of conquering West Europe, these measures would surely have given them pause.

*   *   *

In the address of December 16, 1950, in which he announced the national emergency, President Truman said:

The danger we face exists not only in Korea. . . . The same menace —Communist aggression—threatens Europe as well as Asia. . . . The

United States, Canada, and the nations of Western Europe united with us in the North Atlantic Treaty, have already begun to create combined military defenses. Secretary of State Acheson is flying to Europe. He and representatives of these nations will complete the arrangements for setting up a joint army, navy and air force to defend Europe.

On December 19 the North Atlantic Council announced the establishment of a single defense force for West Europe, to be composed of contingents contributed by the member states of the North Atlantic Treaty Organization, and to be under a single supreme commander. That supreme commander was to be General Eisenhower, the American who had exercised the supreme allied command against the Axis so recently. The next day, the decision was made to absorb the military forces of Western Union[4] into NATO. It was also decided that the American, British, and French occupation forces in Germany and Austria would be brought into the single defense force.

So western Europe rose up once more to man its defenses jointly with its American and Canadian neighbors in the community of the Atlantic. For the great ocean, once a barrier, now assumed the guise of a lake that drew the settlements around its shores together into a single society.[5]

The organization of a unified defense for West Europe, however, confronted a difficulty in that the divisions of World War

---

[4] The Brussels Treaty powers. See p. 180 above.

[5] Geography is conceptual as much as physical. For centuries Americans and Europeans had conceived the Atlantic as a gulf of wilderness, a terrestrial equivalent of outer space, that separated two 'Worlds,' the Old and the New. Now maps based on novel projections came into fashion to replace those, based on Mercator's projection, that had represented this separation. By contrast with the old, they showed how the encircling shore of the Atlantic was almost continuous between Europe and America, broken only by the Norwegian Sea, the strait between Iceland and Greenland, and the strait between Greenland and Canada. For centuries the differences between the two 'Worlds,' not only in society but in nature as well, had been emphasized. Now their similarities were emphasized. To take one example, it is hardly a coincidence, although it represented no conscious intention, that ornithological taxonomists, in their constant revisions of the official classification of birds, now tended to combine in one species European and American varieties that had hitherto been classified as separate species. It was decided, for instance, that the European and American goshawks were merely geographical varieties of one species, rather than two distinct species; that the European willow tit and the American black-capped chickadee, formerly considered two species, were one and the same. Zoological classification is, at best, subjective in some degree, and now, to use the language of Immanuel Kant, the principle of homogeneity became dominant over the principle of specification in the minds of those who occupied themselves with the classification of the avifauna that occurred along the shoreline from Florida to Gibraltar. (See Kant, pp. 379–80, 386.)

II had hardly time to heal, in five years, so as to give way to the new divisions of the Cold War. If the Atlantic peoples had had some initial difficulty in overcoming the notion, so recently impressed on them, that the Soviet Union was a 'peace-loving' power, they experienced greater difficulty, now, in dismissing the notion that Germany was a dangerous beast, bent on aggression whenever it should recover the means. Eliminating and replacing myths is a process that, in a democracy, cannot be accomplished overnight.

The decision had been made at the end of the War that Germany should be permanently disarmed. The defense of West Europe, however, as a glance at the map would show, was in the first instance the defense of West Germany. It was across West Germany that any invasion would be launched. The security of West Europe could hardly be achieved without the defense of West Germany. It was a foregone conclusion, moreover, that by occupying West Germany the Americans, British, and French had made themselves responsible for its defense—just as the American forces in Japan had made themselves responsible for the defense of Japan. Why, however, should the occupying powers have to bear, without any participation by the Germans, a burden that properly belonged to the Germans? Why should American, British, and French manpower stand guard over West Germany, thereby releasing German manpower to engage in the peaceful pursuits by which West Germany was already on its way to achieving a prosperity such as it had never known before?

The question of a German contribution to the common defense was raised most insistently by the United States, which was assuming the principal part of the burden. Moreover, since America was so distant from Germany, and had not itself been directly touched by Hitler's aggressions, Americans did not feel the same fear of the Germans as was felt by their European neighbors, who had so recently been ravaged or occupied by German military forces. On the contrary, Americans in occupation of Germany found a favorable contrast between the docile and cooperative attitude of this conquered people and the stiff-necked pride of the liberated French, for example, who did not have the same reason for docility and, while necessarily accepting American leadership, were disposed to question whether the immensely energetic and aggressive Americans who swarmed all about them always knew best. The Germans were so easy to get along with that Americans began to regard them with a sympathy that they did not feel for most foreigners.

Since the middle of the nineteenth century the dominant international problem for the French had arisen from the fact that their German neighbors had come to exceed them decisively in the resources that make for national power. When, in the second half of the century, the Germans had joined together to form one nation-state under one Government that represented the Prussian tradition, and when they had set out to make themselves the dominant European power, then the French faced the problem of how they could keep even their national independence, let alone the status as a first-class power that they had enjoyed for five centuries. They saw themselves in danger of becoming the helots of a German Sparta. In 1871 they had been overborne by the Germans, and had been left permanently weakened in the face of any renewed German attack by the loss of Alsace and Lorraine. In 1914 they would have been finally overborne by a renewed German assault if the British had not stood with them and if the Americans had not come to their side at the last hour. After that desperate experience, they had tried to keep the Germans disarmed, and to restrain them by the threat of international sanctions. This effort had failed completely, and in 1940 the Germans under their Nazi rule had captured France and established themselves over the French as a master race. Again it was Anglo-American power, this time in association with Russian power, that rescued them and restored them to national independence. But the old problem remained, that of living on the same continent with a potentially stronger neighbor who had in the past, at least, been ambitious for supremacy. France could not take as detached an attitude as the United States toward a proposed rearmament of West Germany for the purpose of enabling it to share in the containment of Russia.

The fears that this proposal aroused everywhere, not only in France, were aggravated by other considerations of weight. One was that the Russians, having twice in a generation had even more terrible experiences of German aggression than the French, having just lost some 1·7 million men in battle with invading German armies, might resort to desperate measures to prevent the rearmament of a West Germany that constituted by far the major part of the traditional Germany—of a West Germany that, it seemed, must inevitably be moved to attempt first the liberation of East Germany, and then, perhaps, of western Poland. It was conceivable that Moscow would order the Red Army forward to forestall such rearmament. The position was delicate and dangerous.

The assumption of the best informed minds in America and Europe was that a militarily rehabilitated West Germany would, in fact, be disposed to go to war for the recovery of East Germany. If, then, a rearmed West Germany came to be joined to NATO, would it not involve its unhappy NATO allies in a war against Russia for German reunification? Such a prospect was the more intolerable because the members of NATO had, for the most part, no reason to desire the restoration of a great and unified Germany. In fact, they dreaded it. The most respected voices on both sides of the Atlantic were raised in alarm now, crying out that the rearmament of West Germany would be an act of recklessness which was likely to precipitate the nuclear cataclysm that it must be the overriding objective of statesmanship to avoid.

It is possible that in this instance the best informed minds were not the soundest in their judgment of the future. Being steeped in the history of Europe for a century past, they assumed the persistence of the patterns of behavior that had characterized that period. It had been a period in which Europe as a whole had been sacrificed for the pursuit, by its component states, of purely national ends. The fierce and exclusive nationalism by which the European states had been dominated during this period had found one expression in irredentism, the determination of the nation-state to extend its boundaries until it has brought within them all the communities that share its nationality. In the period from 1870 to World War II the existence of large communities of one's fellow nationals beyond the national frontiers, under foreign rule, was widely regarded as an intolerable wrong and a dishonor, to be rectified and redeemed even at the cost of tearing apart the fabric of European civilization by military violence. This irredentism had been manifested as late as 1938 by Hitler's insistence on bringing the Sudeten Germans, who inhabited Czechoslovakia, within the borders of the German Reich. To those whose minds had been formed on this history (including, surely, all knowledgeable Russians) it was to be assumed that the West Germans would spare nothing in their determination to reunite the sacred Fatherland, perhaps as a preliminary to a renewed attempt to realize the persistent dream of a great German Reich supreme in the world.

The second half of the twentieth century, however, belonged to a different era from the first. The two Wars that had ravaged and wrecked Europe had left behind them a revulsion against the exclusive nationalism that had produced them. In addition, every European, the ignorant along with the sophisticated, now knew that in the nuclear age such nationalistic self-indulgence promised to transform their continent, by one spasm of violence, into a radio-active desert. Any Hitler who now offered national aggrandizement by force of arms would be quickly suppressed by his alarmed countrymen.

As the postwar years went by, moreover, the West Germans, by contrast with the East Germans, were beginning to do so well for themselves that people in England, which was recovering less readily from the War, began asking who had really won it after all. Their cities and their industries, wound up again, now began to hum. As the shattered life of the community was restored, in terms of a freedom that Hitler's Brown Shirts had prevented, the future seemed to hold the promise of a growing happiness that was not dependent on national grandeur. Few Germans were disposed to sacrifice this promise, and to plunge themselves once again into the horrors they had endured for twenty years past, in order to pursue mystic national goals that now represented shame rather than honor. Although they did not admit it publicly, the largest political and business interests, as well as many others, would have been embarrassed if an impoverished and increasingly alienated East Germany had suddenly presented itself for the joyful celebration of a reunion.

This attitude, however, because it seemed less than creditable, was not made outspoken. Instead, the West Germans said what was the conventional and respectable thing to say, and expected their political leaders to say it as well. Reunification became a proclaimed goal, its proclamation as such constituting the principal item in such political cant as politicians in every country feel obliged to include in their pronouncements. This tended to confirm the assumption, in the minds of those who made it, that the West Germans might go to desperate lengths to achieve reunification.

Since only Moscow was in a position to offer them reunification, this assumption led to a fear that they would turn away from the West and its ideology to accept such terms as Moscow might offer for reunification. Another Rapallo [6] was one of the nightmares,

---

[6] At Rapallo in 1922 Germany and the Soviet Union, both treated as outcasts by the victors in the recent War, administered an unpleasant surprise to the victors by concluding a treaty of mutual association and cooperation.

with which the Atlantic world lived in these days, that proved baseless. The West Germans were not going to retire from the sunlight of their newly achieved freedom into the prison-house of East Europe so as to be rejoined, there, to their separated brothers. And it was certain that Moscow would not agree to a reunified Germany that was also independent.

The argument can be made that the military undertaking represented by NATO was unnecessary, that it could only intensify the Cold War by giving provocation or alarm to Moscow. However that may be (and I, myself, can go no further than to say that I respect the persons who make it), the undertaking could hardly be realized without a military contribution from West Germany. This was the more true because the European members of NATO, for whom economic recovery had to come first, were unwilling to raise even remotely adequate contingents out of their own resources. The problem at the beginning of the 1950's, then, was how to rebuild German military power, needed for the containment of Russia, while insuring that it would not be used to make Germany dangerously great again or to serve an exclusively German ambition.

The approach that was now made to a solution of this problem represented a creative statesmanship comparable to that which had produced the Marshall Plan.

CHAPTER XXIV

*The movement toward West European unification,
and the restoration of German sovereignty*

FUNDAMENTAL to European disunity for a century past was
the established antagonism between France and Germany.
Now, in the shadow cast from the east by the expanded Russian
empire, the repair of this traditional breach became urgent. German strength was needed for the strength of the Europe that still
remained free.

But how could the revival of German strength be accomplished
without thereby also reviving the menace for so long associated
with it?

Statesmanship now found a way. As in Washington in 1947, so
now in Paris and Bonn, there were men of vision. These men saw
that the fear of Germany, which stood in the way of reviving
German strength, could be rendered baseless by combining the revival with European unification. If a major portion of West Europe should be integrated into a single economic and military community, which included West Germany, then the power of any
single member of that community, integrated with the power of
the others, would be incapable of independent action. At the same
time, West Europe, and West Germany itself, would be stronger,
more prosperous, more tranquil, and greater in the world at
large.[1]

In March 1950 the Chancellor of West Germany, Dr. Konrad
Adenauer, publicly proposed that the historic conflict between
France and Germany should at last be ended by a Franco-German
union that might come to include other European countries as
well. He suggested economic union between the two as the first
step to political union. Italy, the Benelux countries (Belgium, the
Netherlands, Luxembourg), and the Scandinavian countries

---

[1] A united Germany within a united Europe was the ideal. All that was possible at
the time, however, was a West Germany within a united West Europe. The decision
to move toward the latter objective was severely criticized, by men whose minds I
respect, for creating a virtually insuperable obstacle to the realization of the former
objective.

might, he said, join in; and 'if Great Britain really regards herself as a European power she could take a place commensurate with her position within the framework of the United Nations of Europe.' Dr. Adenauer made it clear that what he had foremost in mind was the salvation of West Europe from Russia.

This proposal was supported, from his temporary retirement, by General Charles de Gaulle, in terms that pressed history (with some violence) into the service of the cause.

One is almost dazzled [he said] by the prospect. . . . It implies the recommencement, under modern conditions, of the work of Charlemagne. No victory has ever been greater than that in which the Franks and the Germans together put Attila to rout. . . . I am convinced that the Soviet menace makes this task the more urgent.

The French Government then issued a statement of its conviction 'that a lasting settlement of Franco-German relations must be sought within the framework of the collective organization of Europe.'

Less than two months later, on May 9, the French Government publicly proposed the creation of a single authority to control the production of steel and coal in France and Germany, such an arrangement to be open to the other European countries as well. 'The uniting of the nations of Europe,' said Mr. Robert Schuman, the French Foreign Minister, in announcing what was to be known as the Schuman Plan:

requires the elimination of the age-old opposition of France and Germany. Any action taken must in the first place concert these two countries. . . . The pooling of coal and steel production should immediately provide for the setting up of common foundations for economic development as a first step in the federation of Europe, and will change the destinies of those regions which have long been devoted to the manufacture of munitions of war, of which they have been the most constant victims.

To this he added that the common production of these raw materials of war would make the waging of war between France and Germany 'not merely unthinkable, but materially impossible.'

The first great act of creative statesmanship in the years after the War had been the promulgation of the Marshall Plan, which had been based on a noble vision of peace and happiness to be achieved by a common enterprise of construction—an enterprise from which the nations behind the Iron Curtain were excluded only by Moscow's fateful decision. Now, three years later, with the foundations of civilization re-established in western Europe, we see a like act of statesmanship. The Schuman Plan belongs alongside the Marshall Plan on the record of history, testifying to the quality of vision that, more than coal or steel, restored a world so recently fallen into chaos, opening up to it, once more, a future of unlimited promise. Following a magnanimous precedent, Mr. Schuman, too, announced that the countries 'on the other side of the Iron Curtain' were not excluded. Now, however, it was a foregone conclusion that Moscow would, following its own precedent, exclude them.

Just as the Marshall Plan produced the Organization for European Economic Cooperation (O.E.E.C.), so the Schuman Plan now led to the creation of the European Coal and Steel Community (E.C.S.C.), comprising what would come to be known as 'the Six'; France, Germany,[2] Italy, and the Benelux countries.

Before the War, Europe's richest iron deposits had been on the French side of the Franco-German frontier, in Lorraine, while Europe's greatest coal deposits had been on the German side, in the Ruhr and the Saar. So, because of the political frontier between the iron fields and the coal fields, France's industrial strength had depended, to an important degree, on German coal for which, in effect, the French had to pay a tribute in the form of a price above that paid by the German competitors of French industry. Now, however, national identifications were to be removed from the coal, the iron, and the steel resources of the Six, which would come under the common ownership and management of the community as a whole. This was one of those triumphs of good sense that showed how fast Europe was moving away from the grim and impassioned nationalism that had prevailed, to its loss, for a century.

Moreover, the denationalization of the steel industry, its transference with the iron and the coal mines from the individual member states to the High Authority that was to rule their economic community, would virtually deprive the individual member

---

[2] From here on I shall allow myself to refer to the Federal Republic of Germany (West Germany) simply as Germany. Not only does it contain over three-quarters of the German population and over two-thirds of the German land, by its free and self-governing status it now becomes, as the German Democratic Republic (East Germany) by its captive status cannot be, the true successor to the traditional German nation.

states of the means to make war on one another. They would no longer be able to extricate their war-making resources from the common pool.

So the great work of European construction, begun in 1947, was carried forward for the double purpose, and with the double effect, of enhancing the general welfare and holding back the Russians. And so the acceptance of Germany as a respectable power in the European family of nations was made possible.

On April 18, 1951, the Six signed the treaty establishing the E.C.S.C. Then, after ratification had been completed by all, in the first half of 1953 the production and marketing of the coal, iron, and steel held in common came under the supranational High Authority. The whole area occupied by the Six now constituted a common market for these essentials of heavy industry, without internal frontiers. The next radical step for the Six, to be initiated in 1957, would be to create a common market over the whole range of their economic life, and this in turn would, by its own dynamics, propel them in the direction of political unification. This was the vision of the Schuman Plan, which would go so far toward realization in the years that followed.

*   *   *

The domestication of Germany's industrial strength by integrating it into the strength of a unified European community could, in theory, be applied as well to the German military forces that would have to be raised for the containment of Russia. Again, it was the French who proposed this.

The Schuman Plan had been announced on May 9, 1950. Less than two months later came the surprise attack on South Korea that aroused, especially in the United States, such alarm at the prospect of a similar aggression in Europe. So American rearmament and the creation of a NATO force were set afoot. There could have been little question now of not drawing on German military manpower, unless the other West Europeans, still struggling to regain their feet economically, had been willing to weigh themselves down with military burdens far greater than, in fact, they found acceptable. Although the Germans themselves, still tasting the bitterness of recent experience, were more than content never again to bear arms, and although the other West Europeans, not excluding the British, were filled with misgivings at the thought of any German rearmament whatever, the United States would not agree to have the Germans exempted from carrying a part of the burden, of which it was itself carrying such a large share. Therefore, when the North Atlantic Council met in September 1950, to provide for the creation of an integrated Atlantic defense force under centralized command, a reluctant agreement was reached 'that Germany should be enabled to contribute to the build-up of the defense of Western Europe.'

As the French saw it, the problem now was to devise means for the provision of German soldiers without, at the same time, creating a German war-machine, a German Army, or self-contained German military forces of any sort. On October 24 the Prime Minister, Mr. René Pleven, submitted to the French Assembly certain proposals for a European Defense Community (E.D.C.) that became known as the Pleven Plan.

On May 9, 1950 [he said] the French Government proposed that all European countries should place their coal and steel production under a common authority. . . . It believed that the realization of the coal–steel plan would accustom people to think in terms of European unity before such a delicate question as that of common defense was broached. . . . It now proposes that this question should be regulated by the same methods and in the same spirit.

Opposing the creation of a German Army, or even of German divisions, he then called for 'a European army linked to the political institutions of a United Europe.' Such an army should not be merely a coalition force but should involve, 'to the greatest possible degree, a complete fusion of all its human and material elements under a single European political and military authority.' There should be a European Minister of Defense responsible to a European Assembly. This European army would, in effect, be part of the NATO defense forces, although Germany, which was not a member of NATO (and, indeed, had not yet had its sovereignty restored), would be contributing to it on the same basis as the others.

The French Assembly faced an unhappy dilemma. In the debate that followed one speaker after another expressed alarm at what he foresaw if the Germans should again find themselves with arms in their hands, even though those arms bore a European label. No matter what kind of supranational control was instituted, the speakers insisted, the Germans, once they again had arms, would again turn them upon France. They would undoubtedly do so in alliance with the Russians, for whose containment the arms had been supplied, and there would be no counting on the British or the Americans. Everything would happen again as it had before. So the arguments went. On the other hand, with a vast movement of Western rearmament under way, with the defense of the West being erected along the line of the Elbe (the line dividing the two Germanies), the North Atlantic Council had already taken the decision, in principle, to enlist German manpower. The National Assembly therefore felt compelled to accept the Pleven Plan as a basis for negotiation that represented the least of alternative evils. It was clear, however, that the French were in no mood to accept the creation of German military units large enough to amount to fighting forces in themselves. If Germans were to be used, the effort would be to have them diffused as thinly as possible through the ranks of the other nationalities that were to make up the European army. But the more this conception was studied by the military experts of the Atlantic nations, in the months and years that followed, the less practicable it seemed.

The Pleven proposal inaugurated a laborious and protracted course of negotiation among the Governments of the Atlantic nations. It was not until May 1952 that a Treaty providing for the establishment of a European Defense Community was ready for signature. On May 26, by way of preparing the ground for its signature, the United States, Britain, France, and Germany signed a Convention providing that the occupation of Germany would end, and the essential sovereignty of Germany would be restored, upon the entry into force of the Treaty. The Convention provided that the common aim of the signatory states was 'to integrate the Federal Republic on a basis of equality within the European Community, itself included in a developing Atlantic Community.' They recognized

that both the new relationships to be established between them by the present Convention and its related Conventions, and the treaties for the creation of an integrated European community, in particular the Treaty on the European Coal and Steel Community and the Treaty on the European Defense Community, are essential steps to the achievement of their common aim for a unified Germany integrated within the European Community.

The day after this Convention was signed in Bonn, on May 27, the E.D.C. Treaty was signed in Paris by the representatives of the European Six: France, Germany, Italy, and the Benelux countries. It provided for the establishment of the E.D.C. as a supranational community with common institutions, common armed forces, and a common budget. Its armed forces, contributed by the member states, would wear a common European uniform and be under the supreme command of NATO. There would be a Council of Ministers, a Board of Commissioners, an Assembly, a Court of Justice. However, the conception of the Pleven Plan, that the national components of the European Defense Forces would be organized in units so small as to be incapable of any independent standing, was not to be found in the Treaty, which provided that the national units should be, in the case of the ground forces, on a divisional scale—13,000 to 15,600 men each in the case of infantry, 12,700 to 14,000 in the case of armored forces. The creation of German divisions was not what the French Government had had in mind, although it now signed the Treaty, which remained subject to approval by the French Assembly.

The French had also attached first importance to guarantees that British forces would not, at some future time, withdraw from the continent, thereby reducing the balance against the German forces. Accordingly, in an attempt to reassure the French without committing themselves in specific terms, the British solemnly gave once more guarantees that they had already given to respond to an attack on any of the Six or on West Berlin as an attack upon themselves,[3] and solemnly repeated, what they had previously avowed, 'their resolve to station such forces on the Continent of Europe, including the Federal Republic of Germany, as they deem necessary and appropriate. . . .' The French hardly needed a lawyer to advise them on the worth of this last undertaking.

All these designs and efforts were based on the conception of two developing communities, a North Atlantic community and within it, as a subdivision, a European community. From the time that the Schuman Plan was first broached, the choice was Britain's whether she would consider herself a European power and, accordingly, join the European community, or identify herself as belonging to that part of the North Atlantic community which, like the United States, Canada, and Iceland, lay outside Europe. The lingering influence of her Commonwealth ties (although they were increasingly tenuous) and of her position as a world power (although it was almost gone) made her decide that she could not join Europe. This choice would be decisive for the French, who

[3] They had already given these guarantees in the Brussels Treaty, in the North Atlantic Treaty, and in a Declaration of September 1950 that they would consider an attack upon West Germany or West Berlin as an attack upon themselves.

lived in such fear of German hegemony on a continent from which Britain was absent. A decade earlier, in the terrible spring of 1940, the British had proposed to France the establishment of a common Anglo-French state with a common Anglo-French nationality.[4] A decade later, a change of mind would lead them to apply for membership in the developing community of the Six, whereupon the French would veto any acceptance of their application.

The laboriousness of the negotiating process that had culminated, at last, in the signing of the E.D.C. Treaty on May 27, 1952, was exceeded only by the agony of what followed. The French National Assembly, asked to agree to the ratification of what the French Government had signed, responded as the American Senate had responded when asked to consent to the ratification of the Versailles Treaty, which President Wilson had signed. It balked, it temporized, it urged revisions—while the months turned into years. In a series of attempts to give the satisfaction required, the British renewed previous undertakings—as in a declaration of April 13, 1954, that they would continue to maintain on the continent 'such units of their armed forces as may be necessary and appropriate to contribute its fair share . . .,' etc. Or they made gestures, such as offering to place a British armored division within an E.D.C. army corps. Washington, too, promised, on April 16, that it would continue to maintain in Europe 'such units of its armed forces as may be necessary and appropriate to contribute its fair share . . .,' etc. It also promised that it would keep its promises, that it would honor a long list of commitments into which it had entered since the War.

The new Administration of President Eisenhower, which had come into office in January 1953, and which had promised to be more forceful than its predecessors, also undertook, in the person of Secretary of State Dulles, to put pressure on France by threatening dire consequences if she should fail to ratify the E.D.C. Treaty. Addressing the North Atlantic Council in Paris on December 14, 1953, Mr. Dulles referred to the 'vast material contributions for economic aid' that the United States had made to Europe, and its military contribution to the common defense. However, he

---

[4] It must be remembered that this proposal was made by Churchill in desperation to prevent the French from surrendering to Hitler, and without time to determine whether it was constitutionally realizable. We must therefore avoid the temptation of taking it too seriously in order to make a point with respect to events a decade later. Nevertheless, it is at least symbolic of the disposition nations have to take radical steps in an emergency, but not otherwise.

added, if the E.D.C. should not come into effect, 'that would compel an agonizing reappraisal of basic United States policy.' He foresaw, in the event of failure to realize the E.D.C., the possibility that the United States would withdraw its support and 'that Western Europe would be unified, as Eastern Europe has been unified, in defeat and servitude.' [5]

Neither the assurances of resolution in remaining by the side of France nor the threats of abandonment availed. On August 30, 1954, in a vote from which the members of the Government abstained, the French Assembly rejected the E.D.C. by 319 votes to 264. The project of a European armed force, under supranational command and wearing a common uniform, was dead, killed by the country that had brought it to birth. [6] With its demise, the contingent arrangements for ending the occupation of Germany and restoring German sovereignty lapsed as well.

So intent had Washington been on the realization of this project that no alternative to it had been contemplated or even considered possible. [7] There is always an alternative, however, to what may not happen—even if it is only what, when it fails, actually does happen instead. In presenting the E.D.C. Treaty to the Assembly for its final consideration Prime Minister Mendès-France had told it to expect that, if it rejected the Treaty, the British and Americans would still be prepared to restore full sovereignty to Germany. However, he said, 'this decision of our Allies seems to me inevitable whether the Treaty is ratified or not. When a country has been defeated, whatever conditions may have been imposed on her in an armistice, no one can imagine that she can remain indefinitely in a condition of tutelage.' Continuing, he said that the question of German rearmament would also remain after rejection of the Treaty, and that the British and Americans would not renounce 'their attempt to obtain a German contribution to Western defense.' However, there were alternative

[5] Mr. Dulles's strong statement was more effective with American voters who had been promised the spectacle of forceful American leadership than in promoting the end to which it was ostensibly addressed. The French of all parties were for the moment unified in their resentment, a resentment that was to grow into a bitterness against American leadership that would not diminish as, regaining her strength, France also regained the means to avoid such humiliations.

[6] It was an embarrassing fact for the French that a decisive 99 of the 319 votes against the E.D.C. had been cast by Communists under the orders of Moscow.

[7] This was the position taken inside the State Department under the direction of a Secretary of State so strong-willed that he found it impossible to contemplate defeat in anything he had set himself to accomplish.

ways of doing this, he said, that could not be explored before France had made her decision on the E.D.C.

* * *

The French rejection of the E.D.C. created a crisis throughout the Atlantic world, where it was generally held that the whole movement toward European unification, with all its promise, had been wrecked by a combination of nationalism and Communism within France. The disappointment and bitterness of the Germans, who by this act seemed to have been deprived of their promised sovereignty, were intense. The disappointment and bitterness in the United States were hardly less.

A month of agitated diplomatic consultation ensued, culminating in a conference of nine powers (the Six plus Britain, the United States, and Canada) in London from September 28 to October 3. At this conference the British Foreign Secretary, Mr. Anthony Eden, created a sensation by making, on the part of his country, the saving commitment that it had not been willing to make before the crisis.

The United Kingdom [he announced] will continue to maintain on the mainland of Europe, including Germany, the effective strength of the United Kingdom forces which are now assigned to the Supreme Allied Commander, Europe—four divisions and the Tactical Air Force—or whatever the Supreme Allied Commander regards as equivalent fighting capacity. The United Kingdom undertakes not to withdraw those forces against the wishes of the majority of Brussels Treaty Powers.

This commitment was what the French had needed all along to give them a sense of at least the minimal security acceptable before the prospect of again sharing the continent with a sovereign and armed Germany. It cleared the way for a constructive alternative to the E.D.C., as perhaps it would have cleared the way for the E.D.C. itself. However, as Mr. Eden observed, it was for Britain 'a very formidable step to take.'[8]

[8] To this he added a remark of appealing candor. 'You all know,' he said, 'that ours is above all an island story. We are still an island people in thought and tradition, whatever the modern facts of weapons and strategy may compel.' Mr. Mendès-France had been equally candid when, nine days earlier, he had given as one of the two principal reasons for the French rejection of the E.D.C. its supranational character, to which, he said, French opinion was extremely sensitive. (The other principal reason he had given was the absence of Britain.) We should not forget the difficulty these ancient powers had, and would continue to have, in adapting themselves so radically and at such a headlong pace to a world in revolution.

When the London conference ended on October 3, France, Britain, and the United States had formally agreed that they would, as soon as possible, end their occupation of Germany and restore German sovereignty. It had also been decided to invite the adherence of Germany and Italy to the 1948 Brussels Treaty that had, in the days before NATO, created Western Union as the organization of West European states for their common defense, and to strengthen Western Union as the organization that would now discharge the responsibilities which had been projected for the E.D.C. Since Britain was a charter member of Western Union (now to be called Western European Union), this automatically brought her into the European defense association with what would, when Germany and Italy had gone through the formalities of joining, be the European Six.

Finally, the conferees decided to recommend to the North Atlantic Council the admission of Germany—which, accordingly, became the fifth member of NATO on May 9, 1955. By the intimate association of the refurbished Western Union with NATO, the armed forces contributed to it, including the German, would in effect be contributed to NATO and would come under the Supreme Allied Commander for Europe. Such forces were to be 'integrated [with one another] as far as possible consistent with military efficiency.'

Never was there quicker recovery from failure and hopelessness than in the month and four days that followed the French rejection of the E.D.C., an act of negation that had followed four years of futility and frustration. According to Secretary Dulles, who had so recently predicted the fall of West Europe if France rejected the E.D.C., the London conference was 'without doubt one of the greatest conferences of all time.'

So, at last, Germany was reprieved from the captivity that had ensued upon her defeat in World War II, and was enlisted in the ranks of the Western powers who had organized themselves for the containment of Russia. But the plans for a single European defense force, belonging to a single European community, which we now know to have been too ambitious, had failed. It was into a coalition, rather than into a single military force, that the German contribution was brought.

CHAPTER XXV

The situation at the beginning of the 1950's

Looking back on these years, during which Western statesmen exhausted themselves in wrangles over proposals that ended, so often, in frustration and bitterness, we may now see what was less clear at the time. The plans of economic construction, and the plans of political construction associated with them, elicited a general support that was not to be had for the plans of military construction. Whatever arguments the military analysts might make, the nations on the European side of the Atlantic were unwilling to bear the burden of providing ground forces that, in association with American and Canadian ground forces, would be even remotely adequate to hold their own against those that they faced across the Iron Curtain. We also know now that ground forces of such magnitude were not indispensable, since West Europe remained unconquered in spite of the failure to raise them.

Looking back, we must conclude that by the end of 1950 Moscow had, at least for the time being, lost any appetite it might have had for expansion. It may be that in 1947–1948 the expectation of imminent economic and social collapse in the West had tempted it to think in terms of occupying what would shortly be the ruins of Western civilization. But any such expectation, so far from being realized, would have been mocked by the great recovery that, beginning in 1948, eliminated these grounds of temptation.

Looking back, on the basis of our present knowledge that we would survive, we can see that the expanded Russian empire was made to appear more fearsome than it actually was by the illusion that empire in itself represents strength, that the more lands and peoples a power has under its sway the stronger it is. In modern times, however, this has been true only under special circumstances. The revenue from most subject territories in modern times has been far less than the cost of governing and defending them. Where the peoples of such territories are actively antagonistic to their rulers, so that force and intimidation are necessary to hold them down, then the costs of such rule, tangible and intangible, as well as the constant dangers that it entails, can become a source of the gravest weakness (as the Emperor Hadrian knew). It is clear that by the end of World War II India, Burma, Indochina, and the East Indies had become liabilities to the British, the French, and the Dutch states, compelling them to dissipate the strength they needed at home. Their real problem, although they did not always recognize it, was to disengage themselves from such distant empires.

Whatever advantages Moscow gained from the satellite empire in eastern Europe were surely balanced by expenses and dangers entailed in its possession that must have constituted a dire problem for it. There was all the apparatus of suppression to maintain, the conspiracies within conspiracies to watch and counter. There was the problem of demoralization that afflicts troops quartered for an indefinite time on populations with which there can be relations of hostility only. There was the constant danger of explosive uprisings in the subject populations (such as occurred in East Germany in 1953) that might set off other uprisings, and so spread out of control. There was the bad name that a power got throughout the world by the impositions that it had to practice on captive populations to keep them captive. Finally, there was the knowledge that, in case of a European war, perhaps as many men would be needed to keep the rear areas under control and guard the lines of military communication as were sent to, the front; that, even then, the rear areas might heave themselves up in civil strife, with disastrous consequences for the Red Army in West Europe.

It was plausible that the possession of a 'glacis' of states immediately on its western frontier contributed to Russia's military security. But to have to hold down the whole of Europe for over a thousand miles beyond the 'glacis' could hardly have been an enticing prospect to the realists in the Kremlin.

These factors, however, had no weight in Washington. Any suggestion advanced in the councils of the State Department that they might exist, to be taken into account, was immediately dismissed on the grounds that the new technological means available to a sufficiently ruthless police government made the control of hostile populations no problem at all. Looking back, one can see why Washington was unable to take these factors into consideration. Anyone who had showed himself prepared to weigh them would have tended to be discredited as a wishful thinker who under-estimated the enemy. The same psychology was operative here as on the question of Japanese surrender.

In this case, however, it was aggravated by special budgetary and political considerations. The Truman Administration was asking Congress and the nation to support an immense expansion of the American military establishment, and it was pressing its NATO allies to expand their own contributions to the common defense. All this it justified by the magnitude of the danger, which was associated with the image of the Soviet Union as an insatiable and unchecked monster that, in accordance with the President's interpretation of the Korean aggression, was about to swallow what was left of Europe. Any suggestion that what the monster had already swallowed was sufficiently indigestible to spoil its appetite for more tended to undermine this justification—which is to say that it tended to threaten the whole American policy. Inevitably, Washington was acquiring the equivalent of a vested interest in the Soviet menace.

Add to this that the Truman Administration was now under the fiercest kind of political attack from the domestic opposition on the grounds of disregarding the magnitude of the Communist danger. It was under compulsion to hold its own in what had become a national competition in exaggeration.

Looking back, these psychological pressures must also explain a failure to give weight to the deterrent effect, at least for the moment, of the American atomic capability—which made the prospect of any imminent aggression by Communist ground forces in Europe, as part of a supposed strategy inaugurated in Korea, implausible. Such an aggression would immediately have encountered American troops, thereby providing occasion for atomic retaliation. Short of some development that made Moscow desperate, it would presumably wait to carry out any aggression it intended until it had developed an atomic capability of its own to deter and thereby neutralize the American atomic capability. Although the Russians had produced an atomic explosion in 1949, it was not likely that they would have an effective atomic deterrent against the United States for several years.

On the other hand, because events command governments as often as governments command events, the danger of war in Europe could not be measured by Moscow's intentions only. Greece, as we have seen, had almost been added to the Communist camp against Stalin's will. If Italy and France had not recovered from their postwar crises they might have been added to it against his will. The dynamics of a developing situation might draw the Red Army into positions beyond those that Moscow had wished it to occupy. Sometimes the only option open is to go forward, although one had wished not to do so—as in the case of the American military involvement in Viet Nam in 1965. A miscalculation may eventuate in a loss of control. Under the circumstances, it was important (surely for the Russians as well as the West) that there be effective ground forces on hand for the defense of Europe. The twenty-one divisions, more or less, that were all the NATO countries ever provided seem to me to have been too few for safety, especially as the American atomic monopoly was approaching its end. In the event, however, they sufficed.

*   *   *

In 1947 the United States had at last addressed itself in a deliberate fashion to the objective of containing the Russian expansion. Looking back, we can now see that the end of that expansion had already come by 1948, and that by early 1951, with the frustration of the Korean aggression and the increasing recovery of West Europe, the objective of containment had, in itself, been achieved. The containing power had been restored, and was in process of reinforcement, around the borders of the expanded empire.

The success of containment, however, could not mean an end, now, to the Cold War. For one thing, the only way of knowing that containment had really been achieved would have been to see, over a period of time, whether the empire had stopped expanding. A retaining wall of sorts had been built, was still abuilding, but no one as early as 1951 could possibly know that it would hold. In fact, as we have seen, the universal opinion in the United States was that Moscow had just added 600 million Chinese to its empire, that it was going from success to success in carrying out its plans for world conquest. Anyone who had suggested, as early as 1951, or for years thereafter, that containment had been achieved would have been discredited in terms of his mental endowments.

For another thing, the arms race between Russia and the West had just got under way. The period from 1947 to 1950 had been a period of economic and political construction in the West. This, as we have seen, had been successful beyond the best hopes.

Beginning, however, with the outbreak of the Korean War, the emphasis in the West had shifted, under American leadership, to the military construction that encountered such substantial resistance within the alliance.

At the same time, Russia, giving top priority to the achievement of a nuclear capability that could deter and neutralize the American nuclear capability, while intimidating America's allies, appeared in process of radically upsetting, once more, the balance of military power. The accepted logic of the best minds, in these days, was that once Russia had matched the United States in the magnitude of its nuclear power, even if only roughly, it would accelerate its imperial expansion; for then, with the American nuclear armament neutralized, the immense superiority of the Russian ground forces would come into play. As we shall see, in the second half of the 1950's, when it had acquired the necessary nuclear capability, Moscow would, in fact, undertake to break through its containment. No one in 1951, or for years thereafter, could possibly have known that its attempt to do so would fail.

In the 1950's, then, the Cold War comes to be dominated by the arms race, the outcome of which no one can foresee. The race is not primarily in what are called, at this time, conventional forces; in armies and navies with their tactical equipment and air support. The West will decline the challenge of the Russian ground forces in the sense that it will not undertake to match them. In sea-power the United States and Britain, with their vital oceanic communications, will continue predominant. Russia will develop a submarine fleet designed to cripple that sea-power in case of war, and to be a carrier of strategic nuclear power, but otherwise will not seriously compete on the seas. The real arms race will be in nuclear armament. It will begin with the competitive development of explosive power, but by the end of 1954 both the United States and Russia will have mastered the production of thermonuclear weapons that can be made to yield as large a quantity of explosive power as would serve any conceivable military purpose and will have accumulated adequate stockpiles of such weapons; so that in this field the competition will shift to the production of smaller warheads and lower-yield weapons for tactical use in ground battles.

The central preoccupation of the arms race in the 1950's will be, increasingly, with devices for delivering the nuclear weapons to their targets. During the first half of the 1950's the United States had a fleet of long-range bombers capable of carrying nuclear explosives from its own territory to the major cities of Russia, and then returning; and it had air-bases around the periphery of the Eurasian Continent from which medium-range bombers could deliver nuclear explosives to Russian targets. Russia, during these years, had only bombers capable of delivering nuclear weapons to targets in the United States on one-way missions. In the second half of the 1950's, however, missiles up to intercontinental range (6 to 9 thousand miles) were being rapidly developed and produced by both powers for the delivery of nuclear warheads.

To an extent that had never been true before, the arms race of the 1950's was not a race in the mobilization of human and material resources, in recruitment and production, but in scientific discovery and technological invention. Its progress on both sides was such that, by the 1960's, the world's major armaments were radically different from any armaments that had ever been available before; and there was a total absence of experience in their actual use for waging war. Consequently, military strategy, as it related to the use of these revolutionary armaments, became largely imaginary. It became entirely the application to strategic planning of an abstract logic based on the fictional imagination of what a nuclear war would be like. No one had any sound basis for knowing what would really happen to the international world and civilization if the great new armaments were ever used in war.[1] Military forecasting, which had almost always been belied in the past by the actuality of experience when it came, now was virtually impossible. The consequent uncertainty in the governments that possessed the great armaments was a powerful factor inhibiting the initiation of their use.

During the 1950's the arms race was never at a stage, in technological terms, where it could be brought to a close by a stabilization of the balance between the contestants. The possibilities of imminent developments on either side that would completely upset the balance of power compelled each to apply itself with all its skill

---

[1] Everybody assumed that a third world war would be a war of nuclear devastation in which the societies of the West were virtually destroyed. But then, everybody in the 1920's and 1930's had assumed that a second world war would be a 'poison-gas' war in which the populations of the principal European cities would be destroyed. The ingenuity and technical elaboration of the studies that were made in the 1950's and 1960's on the nature of a nuclear war should not blind us to the fact that, even if the great nuclear panoplies were to be brought into play, no one really knew how many nuclear weapons, in such circumstances, would reach their targets or go off at all.

and all its means to forging ahead in the race. It was not until the end of the decade, as we shall see, that technological developments would produce a more stable situation.

The instability that kept the arms race going through the 1950's, and the mutual fears associated with it, obviated any possibility that, with containment achieved (if it was achieved), there could be a mutual disengagement and a settlement that brought the Cold War to an end.

There were other obstacles as well to ending the Cold War at the beginning of the 1950's. The issues that kept Germany divided, and Berlin a precarious island of freedom behind the Iron Curtain, were too intractable for settlement in the circumstances of the day. Above all, the West could hardly agree to make permanent the postwar extension of Moscow's rule to include all but the west and south of Europe. In 1947 the urgent immediate need had been for containment, for preventing any further expansion of Moscow's empire. When containment was achieved, however, the question was bound to arise whether it was, in itself, enough. Few persons in the West found it possible to believe that security and stability could be restored to the international world until the Russian flood had drained back into something approaching its traditional confines. The achievement of containment could hardly, by itself, be the basis for a final settlement.

We must bear in mind that, while there is a sense in which containment had been achieved by 1951, since the Russian empire would expand no farther, there is a sense in which it had not been achieved, for one might plausibly suppose that Moscow, having made such immense advances in so few years, was simply pausing while it summoned up its strength for new advances. Indeed, to the great majority of Americans, and probably of West Europeans as well, their plight seemed desperate. The Russian cause seemed to be advancing in the world. Russia was about to add a full nuclear panoply to its arsenal, and the most optimistic observers could hardly see how the eventuality of a nuclear war, toward which all developments appeared to be moving, could be avoided. The whole world lived, as it thought, under the sword of Damocles, its days numbered.

All the time, however, beneath the turbulent surface of current events, historical evolution was proceeding. Vast secular changes were altering the great societies that menaced each other, so that even while the Cold War remained deadlocked its context and setting was in constant transformation. Although their names remained unchanged, and their places on the map, the contestants who maneuvered in the Cold War of the 1950's were no longer quite the same as those who had maneuvered in the Cold War of the 1940's.

It is an old observation that opposing societies, by a natural process, take on each other's qualities and come to resemble each other, if only because their rivalry is half admiration. The conclusion of the dispatch that George Kennan had sent from Moscow in February 1946 was: 'the greatest danger that can befall us in coping with this problem of Soviet Communism is that we shall allow ourselves to become like those with whom we are coping.'

CHAPTER XXVI

The new Administration in the United States and its adjustment to responsibility

IN 1952 twenty years of Democratic rule in Washington were at last coming to an end. The Republican Party, beginning in 1932, had lost five successive Presidential elections. Its unexpected loss of the fifth, in 1948, had finally discredited the moderate leadership that had been associated with this record. The influence of demagogues and extremists grew. McCarthyism was embraced, overtly or covertly, as a means of identifying the twenty years of Democratic rule with a treasonable or irresolute attitude toward Communism.

During the period when any political party is out of power the objective that necessarily preoccupies it is that of returning to power. What this entails is an exclusive concentration on the domestic scene where the voters reside. A party out of power therefore tends, with the passage of time, to lose touch with the foreign scene, and to think of foreign relations only as offering possible opportunities to appeal to the voters at home.

Again, when a party has been out of power for twenty years the leadership that had been disciplined by the experience of responsibility will have passed away. A new generation of leaders who have not been matured by this discipline will have taken its place. This new leadership will, moreover, be made up of men who have risen to the top by preoccupying themselves exclusively with the domestic scene.

The man who in 1952 became the Republican Party's nominee for President was, however, an outsider to the Party. General Eisenhower was not himself an extremist, and he was far from inexperienced in foreign affairs. As a career officer he had always been politically neutral, so that until he entered the running for the Republican nomination in January 1952 no one had known whether he was a Democrat or a Republican. As a personality involved in national or international political situations, moreover, he had always displayed the virtues that go with a neutral

267

disposition of mind. His greatest public usefulness had been as a conciliator of opposing factions, a harmonizer. During the War he had done a notable job of harmonizing the American and British military elements under his command, and he had done the same kind of job as commander of NATO's international forces. When, in the late 1940's, rivalry between the American Army, Navy, and Air Force had reached a dangerous pitch, he was the man who was sent for to effect a reconciliation. It was in situations like this that Eisenhower manifested his genius. The essential characteristic of any great harmonizer, however, is that he is himself detached in his view of the issues in conflict. For if he had strong convictions of his own, on one side or the other, he could not play the mediating role.

The neutrality or indifference that was native to Eisenhower's mind had been strengthened by his training and experience as a general officer. He was at home with staff procedures whereby an organized team of subordinates prepares the decisions that the commanding officer then adopts as his own.

General Eisenhower, as the chosen leader of the Republican Party in the 1950's, was a moderating influence among the extremists who had been rising through its ranks. Taking his opinions, as always, from the environment in which he found himself, he neverthless spoke in terms of moderation himself, proclaiming principles that his Administration did not feel compelled to follow in practice. The result was that extremists who formed part of his 'team,' under his direction, tended to have their way while he, himself, was able in a remarkable degree to avoid association, in the public mind, with the discreditable if politically profitable aspects of their extremism.

The element of play-acting, which is essential to all politics, was particularly dominant in the Eisenhower Administration. A Hollywood actor was retained to coach the President and Cabinet members. At one point a televised Cabinet meeting, based on a prepared script and redolent of drama, was broadcast as if it had been a normal meeting with spontaneous discussion. Throughout the Administration the President, the Vice President, and the Secretary of State, in particular, played parts that had been as carefully conceived as the creations of any playwright. The President was cast in the role of the wise father who upholds the old-fashioned virtues, the Vice President in that of the young hero who is out to round up the enemy gang and bring its members to justice. The Secretary of State was the master strategist who at every turn foils the villains in their despicable devices.[1]

John Foster Dulles, who became Secretary of State in the Eisenhower Administration, was a New York lawyer of determined purpose who let nothing stand in the way of its realization. His habit was to concentrate on one particular goal at a time, and to concentrate on it so exclusively as to be genuinely incapable of comprehending, for the time being, any larger considerations. This made him unaware of the sensibilities and interests of others, so that to the end he would remain a better lawyer than he was a diplomat or statesman. From an early stage of his career he had set himself to become Secretary of State. In pursuit of this goal he had cultivated a public legend of his competence in the field of international relations that hid the actual paucity of his experience and the consequent limitations of his knowledge. Given the respective characters of the President and his Secretary of State, it is no wonder that American foreign policy under the Eisenhower Administration was identified more with the latter than with the former; so that, where one had referred to Roosevelt's foreign policy or Truman's, one now referred to Dulles's foreign policy.

The objective that Dulles set himself in the spring and summer of 1952, with his usual single-mindedness, was a Republican victory in the Presidential elections scheduled for November. One requirement of such success would be to assure the country that a Republican Administration would, by boldness and purposeful action, relieve it of the increasing frustration from which it had been suffering in the Cold War, and particularly in the Korean War, under the Democratic Administration of President Truman. So Dulles, in his campaign, promised that under the Republicans the Government would seize the initiative that the Democrats had allowed the Communists to retain. A Republican Administration, he said, would see to it that it was Russia rather than the United States that found itself on the defensive.

In this connection, Dulles denounced the containment policy

[1] For a notable early example of this see the incident in which, in September 1952, Vice Presidential candidate Richard Nixon was accused of improperly accepting and using certain funds. After an emotional television broadcast to the nation in which, his wife by his side, he recalled his service as a naval officer amid the falling bombs in the Pacific during the War, and pictured himself as the target of a conspiracy by the Communists and crooks in Washington whom he had set himself to get, he appeared for judgment before General Eisenhower. The General, in the role of father and judge combined, thereupon delivered a verdict of exoneration and rehabilitation so poignant that a large part of the nation was in tears at it.

of the Truman Administration for its essential passivity. The Republicans, he promised, would replace the objective of containment by the objective of liberation. They would, specifically, address themselves to the liberation of the East European nations and China from Moscow's grip. The plank on foreign policy that he wrote for the Republican platform said that a Republican victory would 'mark the end of the negative, futile and immoral policy of "containment" which abandons countless human beings to a despotism and Godless terrorism which in turn enables the rulers to forge the captives into a weapon for our destruction.' In the ensuing campaign, both he and Eisenhower promised that under their Administration the Government would never rest until the peoples of East Europe had been restored to freedom. By 'a policy of boldness' that wrested the initiative from Russia, the United States would achieve their liberation—albeit, as they always added, by peaceful means.

The objective of liberation, which Dulles proclaimed, was surely a proper, even an essential objective of American policy; for mere containment, once achieved, would still leave unrepaired the dangerous situation that had been created by the advance of Russian power so far beyond its proper and traditional bounds in Europe. It could hardly be denied that containment, in itself, was not enough.

In point of fact, the policy that George Kennan had first conceived and formulated had made containment merely preliminary to an ultimate retraction of Russian power. If containment were effectively applied 'over a period of ten or fifteen years,' he had written in his article in *Foreign Affairs*, the Russian power might, within that time, decay and crumble. 'The possibility remains,' he had written '(and in the opinion of this writer it is a strong one) that Soviet power . . . bears within it the seeds of its own decay, and that the sprouting of these seeds is well advanced.' It is true, however, that in the conception of 1947 the retraction of the Russian empire was something that would occur naturally rather than something that would be achieved by positive action to liberate the captive nations.

The containment policy had, from the beginning, been attacked for its essential passivity, which left the initiative to Moscow, and which also failed to foresee, in more explicit terms than those I have cited, any end to the necessity of continuing it along the frontier at which the opposing forces stood in 1947. In 1952, it was, therefore, eminently proper to ask what came after containment.

The proposed objective of liberation, however, as Dulles advanced it, raised questions of its own. Associated with the promise of a bold and dynamic policy, it aroused alarm that it would bring military force into play, detonating a third world war in which Western civilization would be finally consumed—in spite of Dulles's assurance that what he and Eisenhower proposed was the liberation of the captive nations by a moral and spiritual crusade, not a military crusade. (Especially in the first part of its career, the Eisenhower Administration would repeatedly declare its intention of achieving the national objectives abroad by means of the moral and spiritual power that the President and the Secretary of State represented so outspokenly. The translation of this conception into reality, however, was never achieved. It was less effective in the foreign field than on the home scene, where the parable of the Pharisee and the Publican was not the best known chapter in the Bible.)

It must be understood, however, that when Dulles proclaimed the objective of liberation nothing was further from his mind than the international scene. He was concentrating exclusively on the domestic scene and on the objective of winning the forthcoming election. He had been deeply impressed by Samuel Lubell's analysis of the American political situation, *The Future of American Politics*, from which he had concluded that the Republicans could never win a national election unless they succeeded in detaching certain specific groups in the voting population from their normal Democratic allegiance. Notable among such groups were Americans of East European descent concentrated in certain key industrial and urban areas. These groups, who still had relatives in the countries of their origin, or sentimental ties to them, would be moved to vote for the Party that promised to replace containment by liberation. Persons who were close to Dulles at the time, in a position to speak to him candidly and in private, found that they could not get him to turn his mind from the electoral implications of liberation to its implications for the conduct of foreign affairs. Foreign affairs, at the time, were beyond his horizon. When he became Secretary of State he would, at least in a perfunctory way, ask the bureaucracy under him to see what could be done to liberate the satellites by psychological devices. In fact, however, the new Administration, while continuing the policy of containment, would do nothing to put the proposed new policy of liberation into effect.

Even after the Eisenhower Administration took office in January 1953 and Dulles became Secretary of State, the twenty-year habit of thinking only of the domestic scene persisted. The new Secretary concentrated on the objective of gaining for the new Administration, by appropriate words and attitudes, the confidence that its predecessor had lost; and he was prepared to go to the greatest lengths, by cultivating his own public image as the strong man of anti-Communism, to avoid the fate of Dean Acheson, who had disdained any such resort. This propensity on the part of Dulles explains certain difficulties that arose for him in his conduct of American foreign relations. It also explains, however, how he managed to retain the confidence and respect of the American public, regardless of those difficulties, until the day of his death in 1959—when the entire country mourned for the man who had, by his public attitudes, seemed such a tower of strength in the cause of Godliness and morality against Godless and immoral Communism.[2]

*　　*　　*

The gravest problem that the new Secretary of State faced, throughout his first year in office, was not directly in the field of foreign affairs. The State Department and the Foreign Service, through which he had to conduct the foreign relations of the United States, and on which he had to depend for information and professional advice, were being corrupted by Senator McCarthy and those who made themselves his instruments. The Secretary found himself helplessly confronted with the appointment of a former police-agent and McCarthy henchman, Scott McLeod, to a post in the Department in which, under the guise of being charged with the maintenance of security, he was able to assume control of the entire personnel of the Department and

[2] I would not give the impression that John Foster Dulles was not a man deserving of sympathy. (I have treated his character more fully, and therefore more sympathetically, in *The New Republic*, December 8, 1962.) Whoever believes that he is fighting the Lord's fight against the forces of Satan is likely to feel himself justified in using the devices of Satan in such a cause. Practising hypocrisy, he is still not a hypocrite. Those who do the Lord's work must do it in vineyards corrupted by Original Sin; and since the overriding necessity is for the cause to succeed they must have no compunctions about resorting to the means that the enemies of the Lord feel free to use. Dulles represented the tradition associated with the name of Calvin, who had known how to combine the teachings of Jesus with a certain kind of practicality that went beyond them.

Foreign Service. In a remarkable interview that appeared in the *Sunday Register* of Des Moines, Iowa, on March 15, 1953, McLeod told what, now that he had 'all of the 40,000 State Department employees under his jurisdiction,' he conceived his duty to be. It was 'to clean out the State Department, and also to smooth the way for Republican-directed congressional committees to make a record against former Secretary of State Dean Acheson's administration.' This police-agent, with no experience in foreign affairs, professed himself concerned in his new post to change the whole character and conduct of American diplomacy, which had up to then shown too much regard, in his opinion, for what was fair to foreign countries and too little for what was good for the United States. He even proclaimed the need to change the way that American diplomats dressed, talked, and thought.

For approximately a year McLeod had a free hand with the American career service. It was during this year that blackmail, intimidation, and other pressures of a similar character were used to their fullest. The highly trained professional corps was decimated, demeaned, and demoralized; the whole apparatus through which the foreign relations of the United States had to be conducted was, in large measure, wrecked. Since even the American newspapers, at this time, were intimidated by McCarthyism, which was invading all the spheres of private life and private enterprise, there was almost no reporting of what was happening inside the State Department, although the correspondents in Washington were well aware of it; and there was virtually no public protest, since whoever protested was likely to find his career ended by public charges of pro-Communism.[3]

It was not until March 1954 that a series of television appearances by Senator McCarthy, in which he did not show to advantage, began to discredit him and his movement in the eyes of the American people. As this happened, the Administration and the American press began to show a courage in opposing McCarthyism that it had, until then, held in abeyance. As early as January 17, 1954, the *New York Times* had published a letter from five of the most respected elder statesmen of the Foreign Service,[4] speaking from

[3] It should be noted as a remarkable fact that, during the entire campaign to prove the personnel of the State Department and the Foreign Service disloyal, not a single case of disloyalty was found in a population of government servants totaling some 40,000.

[4] Ambassadors Norman Armour, Robert Bliss, Joseph Grew, William Phillips, and Howland Shaw.

retirement, who asked 'whether we are not laying the foundations of a Foreign Service competent to serve a totalitarian government rather than the Government of the United States as we have heretofore known it.' This letter, coming from such eminent and moderate figures, shocked many persons who had not known what was going on. By March 1, the tide had turned sufficiently so that it was possible quietly to relieve McLeod of much of his authority, although keeping him in his post. However, vast damage had already been done.

Secretary Dulles suffered personal distress at what was being done to the organization that came under his nominal jurisdiction, and on which he depended. He could hardly allow himself to interfere, however, since he had concluded that the overriding necessity was for him to retain public confidence by appearing to be as ruthless as anyone in his attitude toward all who had had suspicion cast upon them. (The President, himself, simply looked the other way during this year in which important parts of the Executive Branch were abandoned to McCarthy's depredations, maintaining that it would be undignified for him to get into personal conflict with him.)

Among McCarthy's targets were two distinguished career diplomats who had specialized in Chinese affairs. He insisted that Messrs. John Carter Vincent and John Paton Davies be dismissed as Communists or pro-Communists. Both men, highly respected throughout the Foreign Service, had been completely cleared of these charges, and completely vindicated with respect to their loyalty, in repeated hearings before impartial boards set up for the purpose; and both had, under McCarthy's pressure, been subjected to renewed trials after each acquittal. When Dulles became Secretary of State he solved the problem of satisfying McCarthy's demand for the elimination of Vincent by obtaining Vincent's resignation (under heavy pressure and in return for another vindication of his loyalty and security) on the grounds that, in the new Secretary's words, as a Foreign Service Officer his 'reporting of the facts, evaluation of the facts, and policy advice during the period under review show a failure to meet the standard which is demanded of a Foreign Service Officer of his experience and responsibility at this critical time.' The following year, after Mr. Davies's loyalty had already been completely vindicated nine times in nine successive trials, the Secretary dismissed him for 'lack of judgment, discretion, and reliability.' The new Ad-

ministration felt itself compelled to cut out the horses that had
been pulling the carriage in order to feed the wolves that bayed
on its trail. Granted that this was an ugly spectacle, no historian
can say that the Administration would not have been overcome
and destroyed by the wolves in the absence of such appeasement.
Judgments of what constitutes political necessity are not easily
made by those who stand outside of politics, which at its best is
still not a dainty profession.

The wrecking of the American Foreign Service was a disaster
that the United States would survive. One is reminded of the comment that Thucydides made on the disaster to Athens of the loss,
in the foolish Sicilian expedition, of its army and fleet. Athens
survived, he said, because 'so superfluously abundant were the
resources from which the genius of Pericles had foreseen an easy
triumph in the war over the unaided forces of the Peloponnesians.'
It had been true throughout the twentieth century that the United
States could afford great errors, and could go far toward tearing
itself to pieces, so superfluously abundant were the resources
available to it for holding its own in the world. Nevertheless, for
years to come, the American Foreign Service would have learned
the lesson that survival and advancement in the career required
the kind of judgment, discretion, and reliability that were manifested by reporting from abroad what conformed to the official
views of those at home, by analyzing foreign situations in such a
way as to come to conclusions that supported those views, and by
giving only such advice as accorded with them. Most of those who
could not meet this requirement left the Government service,
although some very honorable men stuck it out and remained un-
compromised. By 1954, briefings on Cold War situations that were
given the Secretary of State by the organization under his command were no longer to be relied on, and he would have done
better to depend on the more informed reporting in the press—
even though the press, too, had been in great measure corrupted
by the fears associated with McCarthyism.

To any historian who was present, as this writer was, no experience could have conveyed a more vivid appreciation of the problem posed for any doctrinaire and totalitarian regime, like that
of Moscow, in keeping itself truly informed. Without genuine
freedom, the rulers of men, like those they rule, have no choice
but to live in a world of myth.

CHAPTER XXVII

The new Administration and the problems of military policy

EVER since the great depression at the beginning of the 1930's there had been a basic difference between dominant opinion in the Republican and Democratic Parties, respectively, over what the nation could afford in the way of public expenditures. The thinking of the Democrats had been associated with academic economists, notably John Maynard Keynes, who minimized the importance of savings, who were not alarmed by a large and continuing public debt, who emphasized the point that nations cannot go bankrupt by borrowing from themselves, and who believed that any modern government has an overriding obligation to spend as heavily as need be for the maintenance of full employment and the stability of the national economy. Republican thinking, on the other hand, had been associated with business-men who were disposed to equate the soundness of a nation's economy with balanced budgets at a level of taxation low enough to give full play to the profit motive as an indispensable incentive of free productive enterprise. These business-men had been alarmed at the vast expenditures, the high taxes, the unbalanced budgets, and the mounting public debt under twenty years of Democratic rule. They felt that continuing on this course was bound to lead to some kind of economic disaster, and that it was, in any case, destructive of the free-enterprise system.

The Republicans, more than the Democrats, thought in terms of a norm represented by the period (remembered from childhood) before the successive emergencies of World War I, the great depression, and World War II. These emergencies had perhaps required an abandonment of what they regarded as sound fiscal practices, just as an emergency in the career of an individual may require him temporarily to live beyond his income by borrowing or drawing on his savings. Such lapses, however, must not be continued as a normal practice, and the dominant elements in the Republican Party were alarmed at the failure, so many years after World War II, to return to what President Harding, after World War I, had called 'normalcy.'

The national budget, which had fallen to $32,289 million in

Fiscal Year 1946–1947 (leaving a surplus of $754 million), had again risen, under the Truman Administration, to $73,982 million in 1952–1953 (leaving a deficit of over $900 million). For 1953–1954 the Truman Administration, before leaving office, had drawn up a budget of $78,587 million, and anticipated a deficit of $9,992 million. This sharp rise in expenditures and deficits represented, simply, the cost of containing Communism, of waging the Cold War. (Some three-quarters of President Truman's proposed budget for 1953–1954 was for expenditures on what were called 'national security programs,' about 60.% going directly to the armed services.)

The dilemma that confronted the new Republican Administration was clear. The only way it could move toward a balanced budget and, at the same time, lower taxes was by a substantial reduction in military and related expenditures. (This was the more true because the preponderance of the other expenditures represented fixed charges for interest on the national debt and for veterans' programs.) It had, however, promised that it would adopt a much more aggressive and dynamic Cold War policy, by which it would put Russia on the defensive. How, its opponents asked, could it risk doing this at the same time that it was reducing the military strength of the United States?

The answer, at least in principle, was to be found in the abandonment of a conception of containment that, by implication, imposed unlimited expense on the United States. In his *Foreign Affairs* article Kennan had written: 'Soviet pressure against the free institutions of the Western world is something that can be contained by the adroit and vigilant application of counter-force at a series of constantly shifting geographical and political points. . . .' Taken literally, this meant that the United States had to have 'counter-force' available for immediate application at any point along the frontiers of the Russian empire, from Kamchatka to the mouth of the Elbe, at which Moscow, having the unchallenged initiative, chose to apply pressure.[1] Russia had the interior position and could strike without notice in any direction she wished, while the United States had to be prepared to counter her

---

[1] Kennan had referred to pressure against 'the free institutions of the Western world,' but the Truman Doctrine had virtually eliminated this qualification, which, in any case, had not been clearly made in the article, and after 1949 Americans had assumed that Communism must be contained no less in Asia than in 'the Western world.'

at whatever point, around an outer line of many thousands of miles, she might choose to strike. Such preparation, if actually made, would be immense in its requirements for all sorts of fighting forces and their transport. Taken literally, it would have implied a budget many times larger than any that even the Democratic Administration had proposed. Although no one in the Government ever had taken it literally, there can be no doubt that this conception was genuinely vulnerable to the kind of attack the Republicans had made on it in the campaign of 1952. The weakness they alleged was a genuine weakness.

At this point we may note that one main issue, cropping up always in new guises, dominates the Western debate on political–military strategy at every stage of the Cold War. The issue, put crudely, is whether the West should depend entirely on the strategic nuclear power of the United States, its ability to destroy the Russian (or Chinese) society by nuclear explosives delivered across thousands of miles, or whether it should furnish itself with other kinds of military force as well, in order to have alternatives, where military action is called for, to such a drastic move as that of initiating all-out nuclear war. If the West, in the face of aggression, found itself without any choices between the two extremes of all-out nuclear war, on the one hand, and the abandonment of containment (in effect, surrender), on the other, prudence would presumably constrain it to adopt the latter choice wherever the aggression was not, in itself, of such importance as to warrant recourse to universal destruction. On the other hand, it was argued, if the West provided itself with alternatives to strategic nuclear retaliation, then the potential aggressor would be less likely to be deterred from any sufficiently limited aggression because he would know that the West had prepared itself to respond to such an aggression with other means than those afforded by its strategic nuclear force, that it therefore did not intend to use that force. He would, according to either of these opposed arguments, be able to realize his supposed objective of world conquest by the simple strategy of undertaking a succession of aggressions, each one of which was so limited that it would not, in itself, justify the unlimited destruction involved in a strategic nuclear response. The free world, in the witty phrase of the time, would be nibbled to death.

In sum—according to one view, the aggressor might commit limited aggressions if the United States had, as its only means of responding, a strategic nuclear armament that it would presumably be unwilling to use to meet any small aggression; according to the other view, the aggressor might feel encouraged to commit limited aggressions if, by providing itself with limited means to deal with such aggressions, the United States showed that it did not intend to respond to them with its strategic nuclear armament.

What is clear is that the provision of alternatives to the strategic nuclear response was far more expensive than dependence on it alone. Therefore, those who attached a high enough value to budgetary economy were bound to end up in favor of an approach, at least, to exclusive dependence upon it.

In the new Republican Administration, which was so largely dominated by business-men, a drastic limitation in Government spending took priority over the demands of military defense. At least initially, the Administration took the position that national security depended, in the first instance, on a sound economy, which in turn depended on fiscal policies that limited expenditures to a level substantially lower than those that the Democratic Administrations had accepted. The purpose of the Communists, it was maintained, was to induce the United States to bankrupt itself by its military expenditures, whereupon they would be free to take over the world. The conclusion was that one had to decide in advance how large a defense-budget the country could afford, and then design its defense accordingly. The Democrats, on the other hand, insisted that one had first to decide what the requirements of defense were, and then meet those requirements at whatever cost. There was, here, a clear issue in which the prevailing opinion in the Republican Party differed from the prevailing opinion in the Democratic Party.

After the new Administration took office a complete review of American strategy was undertaken by the National Security Council. The product of this review was one of those documents that reconcile conflicting views by ambiguity. Anyone who read it would find that its language lent itself to a variety of interpretations.[2]

[2] The contents of this document have been discussed in books on American strategy by writers who have never seen it, since it has remained a secret document. Their sources have been private reports of its general tenor by Government officials, or Secretary Dulles's address of January 12, 1954, which was based on what was, at least, his own interpretation of it. When one writer purports to reveal the contents of a secret document like this, other writers after him take him, and each other, as their authority, a process by which all doubt quickly disappears. What everyone says becomes what everyone knows, and what everyone knows is true.

Throughout 1953 there had been constant speculation, fed by hints from members of the Administration, that a new and better strategy, a 'new look' in defense policy, was being prepared. There was no doubt that such a new strategy, if only for reasons of economy, would involve a more complete dependence on strategic nuclear power, thereby decreasing the requirements for American ground and naval forces.[3] The anticipated 'new look' aroused anxiety in Europe, where it was feared that the United States would drastically reduce its ground forces, if it did not withdraw them altogether.

Finally, on January 12, 1954, in an address delivered at the Council on Foreign Relations in New York, Secretary Dulles ostensibly presented, what had been awaited so long, the new policy of the Administration. He began by observing that American policy hitherto had represented nothing more than a succession of responses to emergencies created by Russian initiative, and he implied that long-range planning had been neglected.

The Soviet Communists [he said] are planning for what they call 'an entire historical era,' and we should do the same. They seek ... gradually to divide and weaken the free nations by overextending them in efforts which, as Lenin put it, are 'beyond their strength, so that they come to practical bankruptcy.' Then, said Lenin, 'our victory is assured.' Then, said Stalin, will be 'the moment for the decisive blow.'[4]

He referred to the need to avoid 'military expenditures so vast that they lead to "practical bankruptcy,"' and added: 'This can be done by placing more reliance on deterrent power and less dependence on local defensive power.'

Referring to the previous inadequacy of policy and planning, he said that the new Administration had had to take 'some basic policy decisions.' 'This,' he added, 'has been done. The basic

[3] The chief instrument of American strategic nuclear power was the Strategic Air Command (SAC), with its intercontinental bombers based in the United States and its overseas air bases. The Navy had at least a secondary role in the delivery of nuclear weapons (from aircraft carriers). The Army, however, had no strategic nuclear role at all.

[4] In an article written immediately after this address (see pp. 282–3 below), Dulles put this differently. '. . . the Soviet rulers,' he wrote, 'seek gradually to divide and weaken the free nations and to *make their policies appear as bankrupt* [my italics] by overextending them in efforts which, as Lenin put it, are "beyond their strength." Then, said Lenin, "our victory is assured." Then, said Stalin, will be the "moment for the decisive blow."' What Lenin actually said, or what Stalin actually said, if anything, is not known to me.

decision was to depend primarily upon a great capacity to retaliate, instantly, by means and at places of our choosing.'

This last was the key sentence of an address that immediately aroused a storm of alarm and indignation throughout the Atlantic world. It was taken to mean that the United States was prepared to turn every local conflict into a worldwide nuclear war in which its allies, if not it as well, would be destroyed. The use of the word 'instantly' was interpreted as meaning that the United States would not take the time to consult its allies before acting to transform a local conflict into Armageddon. Within hours of delivering the address the Secretary of State was a severely embarrassed man. President Eisenhower felt compelled to deny, at his press-conference the next day, that any new 'basic decision' on defense policy had been taken at all; and on March 17 he would deny that the so-called 'new look' defense policy (a phrase which he said he deplored) was either new or revolutionary. Dulles, as was clear to anyone who knew the National Security Council document on which his address was based, had interpreted it to suit his own mind.

Ordinarily, when an important statement of policy is made on behalf of the Government of the United States, its text is prepared and checked in every phrase and nuance with the assistance of a corps of advisors. A fault of the Truman Administration, as we have seen, was to carry this procedure of corporate drafting too far, to the point where such statements lost the integrity and authority that depend on a single hand holding the pen. Dulles, up to January 12, 1954, had gone to the other extreme. Uncomfortable as he always was with the bureaucratic organization he had inherited, he had not known how to use it effectively. The 'massive retaliation' speech, as it came to be known, was written entirely by him, and apparently with only one exception even the members of his immediate professional staff in the State Department did not know about it until it was delivered and published.[5]

To this day, the 'massive retaliation' speech is a poignant document purely as an expression of Dulles's personal character. There was always in him something of the little boy who, in his day-dreams, is the master-strategist, outmaneuvering and foiling

[5] The exception was an able lawyer, brought into the Department from the outside and still new to foreign affairs, to whom the Secretary showed the text in advance, but who did not feel himself in a position to deal with it critically.

his dastardly opponents at every turn by his boldness and craft. All his life he had cultivated a legend of himself based on this youthful day-dream, and now for the first time, at sixty-five years of age, he was in a position to realize it before the eyes of the whole world. More than once it happened that he was unable to resist the temptation to strike public attitudes in fufillment of this dream, attitudes that, by their sheer exaggeration, provoked immediate public reactions highly embarrassing to him. One such occasion was when he briefed a reporter who wanted material for an article about him for *Life* magazine. He told the reporter, in the informal privacy of their meeting, and the reporter duly reported it in the issue of January 11, 1956, that 'the ability to get to the verge without getting into the war is the necessary art,' whereupon he proceeded to illustrate the practice of this art by showing how the United States, since he had assumed his position as master mind in the conduct of its foreign relations, had done precisely this with brilliant effect on three separate occasions. Published as an interview, the public impression that the Secretary of State's boasting gave was of an immaturity and recklessness in the United States, under the Eisenhower–Dulles Administration, that aroused widespread alarm throughout the alliance, just as the 'massive retaliation' speech had two years earlier.[6]

One may suppose that, as was the habit of his mind, Dulles was not thinking of the impact of his speech abroad when he wrote it. To some extent he was still fighting the electoral campaign of 1952 by contrasting, for the benefit of the American public, the weakness and confusion of the previous Administration with the strength, the long-range vision, the daring, and the command of events that distinguished its successor. He was cultivating the legend, he was realizing the dream on the world's great stage. At the same time, he was showing how the Republican Party was honoring its electoral promise to strengthen the position of the United States in the world while reducing expenditures, how it was foiling international Communism both in its designs for aggression and in its plot to reduce the United States to 'practical bankruptcy.'

The speech aroused such immediate and incisive criticism (much of it misrepresenting what he had actually said), and had such an effect on confidence abroad in the maturity and sense of international responsibility represented by the American leader-

---

[6] Important parts of this interview are given in Bell, p. 24, fn. 4. The contents should be read, not as history, but for their revelation of a romantic imagination.

ship, that remedial action had to be undertaken at once. For this purpose a shaken Secretary of State turned, the next day, to his professional staff to assist him in preparing a statement, which ultimately appeared as an article under his name in the April 1954 issue of *Foreign Affairs* ('Policy for Security and Peace'). In this article he expounded the strategy of the United States in terms that reduced the more extreme implications of what he had seemed to be saying in his 'massive retaliation' speech.

The President's denial that there was a revolutionary new defense policy, immediately after the speech announcing it, and the *Foreign Affairs* article in which the Secretary corrected himself, have since been largely forgotten by the chroniclers of these events, who generally maintain that the United States under the Eisenhower–Dulles Administration had a policy of 'massive retaliation,' which was abandoned in favor of an opposite policy (that of 'graduated response') under the following Administration of President Kennedy. In fact, the United States cannot be said to have ever had a policy of 'massive retaliation,' any more than it ever had a policy of 'liberation' as opposed to the policy of 'containment.'

Perhaps one could best put it that the United States, at all times from 1945 on, considered that it was of the utmost importance for the Atlantic alliance, and for itself, to have military means that provided an alternative to the strategic nuclear arm for meeting the wide variety of possible aggressions. To the extent that considerations of economy or lack of will resulted in failure to create such means (under whatever administration), it had, perforce, to depend on the deterrent effect of the threat of 'massive retaliation,' for what it might be worth. This dependence, at any given time, was therefore purely a matter of degree. It would, however, become less credible to the potential aggressor, and therefore less effective in deterring him, as he himself developed a nuclear arm that would tend to deter the United States from using its own; and this development was already advanced when Dulles made his speech. If 'massive retaliation' might have been a workable policy before the middle of the 1950's, it was less likely to be so from then on. We come closest to reality, however, if we regard 'massive retaliation' as a phrase rather than a policy.

*   *   *

Korean truce negotiations, which had been going on since July 10, 1951, were finally concluded by the signing of an armistice on July 27, 1953.[7] By the end of the year it was possible to announce a decision to begin withdrawing American troops by returning to the United States two of the eight American divisions that were in Korea. The *de facto* end of the Korean War, then, made possible a substantial reduction in the Army, as well as reductions in the Navy and Air Force, and a consequent reduction of the national budget. In fact, the Army was reduced only slowly, from a total personnel of 1·5 million in 1953 to just under a million in 1957, and to about 850,000 after 1958. However, when Secretary of Defense Wilson, at the end of 1954, announced plans for reducing it to a million men by the middle of 1956, the reason he gave was not that any new policy of 'massive retaliation' made it possible but, rather, that the threat of global war had decreased.

Under the two Eisenhower Administrations, from 1953 to 1961, the national budget rose, on the whole, establishing new records for peacetime, and was more or less heavily unbalanced except in fiscal years 1956–1957 and 1959–1960, in each of which a surplus of between 1,000 and 2,000 million dollars was registered.

These facts are to be noted because they suggest that, in spite of such phrases as 'liberation,' 'massive retaliation,' and 'return to fiscal orthodoxy,' the policy of the Republican Administration was essentially a continuation and development of the policy it had inherited from the Democratic Administration, just as the policy of the Democratic Administration that was to take office in 1961 would, in spite of certain nominal disguises, be essentially a continuation and development of the policy that its Republican predecessor had followed. The men who make the decisions of government, whatever party they belong to, do not make them as they would in some ideal world of their minds. They make them as circumstances require. So it was that even the Bolsheviks, after they had caputed power in Russia, found themselves constrained to continue the policies of the czars.

[7] Secretary Dulles told the reporter for *Life* magazine, in 1956, that he had personally brought the Communists to conclude this armistice by making it clear that, unless they did, the United States would bomb Manchuria from the air and would use atomic weapons. However, the War had become deadlocked long ago, and it was no longer profitable for either side to continue it. Without seeing the language that Dulles used to make this threat (in talk with Prime Minister Nehru of India, he told the reporter), one cannot weigh this claim. There is no evidence that any contingent decision had been taken in Washington to bomb Manchuria or to use the atomic bomb, and every reason to believe that, in fact, such a decision could not have been taken.

CHAPTER XXVIII

The extension of 'containment' to Asia and the beginning of American involvement in Indo-China

WHAT was it that the United States, in 1947, had undertaken to contain?

Kennan, in his *Foreign Affairs* article, had said it was Russia. The Truman Doctrine, which had not been carefully formulated, had gone to an extreme of generalization and vagueness, saying that 'it must be the policy of the United States to support free peoples who are resisting attempted subjugation by armed minorities or by outside pressures.'

In 1947, it was chiefly the containment of Russia in Europe that the authors of the containment policy had in mind. They were thinking of containment along a line from the Baltic to the Persian Gulf. They did not exclude the Far East and South-East Asia, but this was not where the greatest or the most immediate danger lay and, presumably, this area occupied only the margin of their vision.

To Kennan, the Stalinist state was the enemy. To less sophisticated persons, the enemy was a generalized evil called Communism, and it was the containment of whatever bore this label that they had in mind. Communism was a synonym for the forces of Satan that opposed God's kingdom, and to a large proportion of the American people the term came to signify anything that was socially unorthodox, radical, left-wing, or merely liberal. Communism, thus conceived, was to be contained, and it was to be fought wherever it might manifest itself, whether in Russia, in South-East Asia, in Washington, or in American intellectual communities.

So the containment policy, which in its earliest origins had relatively narrow limits, tended from the beginning to lose those limits, thereby involving the United States in ever larger obligations for policing the world.

By 1948, as we have seen, the containment of Stalinist Russia from the Baltic to Iran had been realized—at least for the time being. In 1949, however, Mao Tse-tung's peasant insurrection, which he called Communist, had won the Chinese civil war. Internal social pressures imposed on the Government of the United States the interpretation that this represented the conquest and enslavement of the 600 million Chinese people by Moscow, which had thereby extended its empire to the South China Sea. Then, in 1950, Moscow's Korean puppet had invaded South Korea. So Asia, along with Europe, became a primary theater of the Cold War, and the containment of China was added to the containment of Russia in the belief that it was, in fact, the containment of Russia.

Because of its long exclusion from power and responsibility, the Republican Party had, after 1948, come increasingly under the influence of its less moderate and less sophisticated elements. Consequently, its emphasis was, in subtle ways, more on the ideological aspects of the Cold War and less on its limiting geographical elements. This was represented by the new Administration's constantly reiterated identification of it as a worldwide crusade in which the forces of morality opposed the forces of immorality. So it was that, long after the internal threat of Communism in the United States had diminished to the point where it was no longer serious, the country turned inward upon itself and began to tear at its own vitals in the passion to eliminate from its body that wide range of unorthodox belief or behavior to which the name 'communistic' was applied.

The emphasis on Asia, which circumstances had made necessary, was also congenial to the less sophisticated elements in the Republican Party. What remained of the old isolationism took the form of a general anti-Europeanism, and found an expression in the slogan, 'Asia First.'

It should be recalled that the basic tradition of American foreign policy, which had been made obsolete by circumstances at the end of the nineteenth century—the tradition identified with the warnings against involvement overseas in Washington's Farewell Address—was based on the conception of a complete separation between the views and interests of the American New World, on the one hand, and something called 'the Old World,' on the other. 'The Old World,' however, had been the European Old World only. It was from the wicked power-politics of European potentates that the political morality of the idealistic New World had to be protected.

Those who upheld this traditional policy had tended, when communications opened up across the Pacific, to favor an actively interventionist American policy in Asia, which like the American continents had to be protected against the wicked scheming of the European empires. The 'Open Door' policy, so casually proclaimed by John Hay in 1900, and so enthusiastically embraced by the American people, had almost immediately developed into a policy of protecting the Chinese nation against the invasions and impositions of the imperialistic Europeans. From 1898 on, it had been the most anti-European and isolationist elements in the United States who had been most outspokenly in favor of showing the American flag far and wide in Asia.

After 1947, when isolationism was finally discredited, the old isolationists no longer appeared as such. They could be recognized still, however, partly by their advocacy of primary attention for the needs of Latin America (an implicit criticism of the Marshall Plan), and partly by their advocacy of a dynamic interventionist policy in Asia. The dominant conservative element in the Republican Party, with its nostalgia for what Herbert Hoover called 'the olden days' (and which it remembered as the golden days), was happier with American involvement in Asia than with American involvement in Europe.

It was the more natural, then, that Dulles, in the 1952 campaign, should have accused the Democratic Administration of neglecting Asia, and that, when he came into office, he should have given a higher priority to containment in Asia than it had had before. Here circumstances and the inclination of the Republican Party coincided. It would have been surprising if Secretary Dulles had dealt as roughly with, say, the Nationalist regime on Formosa as he did with France when he threatened that the United States would withdraw its support from France, and from Europe generally, if France did not ratify the E.D.C. treaty.

*   *   *

In his first State of the Union Message, delivered thirteen days after he took office, President Eisenhower said that his Administration had 'begun the definition of a new, positive foreign policy' that would be governed by certain fixed ideas. The first of these (that 'our foreign policy must be clear, consistent, and confident') may be dismissed as hortatory. The second was that 'the freedom we cherish and defend in Europe and in the Americas is no different from the freedom that is imperiled in Asia.' What was implicit here was that the American policy of resisting Russian expansion, which had been justified by the need to re-establish the international stability that depends on a balance of power, represented the discharge of a moral obligation to maintain freedom everywhere in the world, without discriminating in favor of Europe.

Here, in this second 'fixed idea,' was the fault of the original Truman Doctrine, which had also, by implication, imposed an unlimited commitment on the United States. It repeated, as well, the fallacy that had caused embarrassment to the Truman Administration even in the composition of the Address in which it had proclaimed the Truman Doctrine; for, on the false grounds of defending peoples who enjoyed freedom against the ambitions of dictatorships, the United States would find itself defending dictatorships from Korea to South America.

President Eisenhower then announced that he was 'issuing instructions that the Seventh Fleet no longer be employed to shield Communist China.' It will be recalled that, in the Blair House meeting of June 26, 1950, one of the spur-of-the-moment decisions had been to interpose the Seventh Fleet between Formosa and the mainland, the purpose being to impose a deterrent threat on the flank of Communist China. Since the United States had had no legal basis for overtly taking sides in the Chinese civil war, and since this would have been an imprudent as well as an improper thing to do, it had announced that the Seventh Fleet was to prevent attacks by either side against the other. This, however, was hardly more than a formal gesture. It was like claiming that, in interposing oneself between a cat and the mouse it is chasing, one is being strictly impartial, since one is preventing either from attacking the other. Similarly, it was a mere gesture, directed at the domestic audience, for President Eisenhower now to unleash the mouse, thereby removing the protection that the United States had hitherto accorded the cat.

It is characteristic of all parties that have been long out of power, whether in the United States or elsewhere, that when they finally achieve it the first thing they do is indulge in a series of dramatic gestures in fulfillment of the dreams on which they had lived and the promises they had made during their years in the wilderness. What came to be ironically known as 'the unleashing of Chiang Kai-shek' was symbolic, merely, of the promised policy of 'liberation' and of the decision that Asian problems were no longer to be ranked below those of Europe. It belonged to the initial play-acting stage of the new Administration.

The Truman Administration had felt immediate alarm at what the aggression in Korea might portend for Europe, fearing that it might be preliminary to a similar aggression there, and it had responded by the creation of NATO armed forces. What worried the new Eisenhower Administration, now, about the truce in Korea, was that it might release Chinese forces for aggression in Indo-China.

*   *   *

Indo-China (comprising Laos, Cambodia, and Viet Nam) had been a French colonial possession until World War II, when it was conquered by the Japanese. Thereupon, a Vietnamese nationalist, Ho Chi Minh, had organized in China a League for the Independence of Viet Nam—better known by its abbreviated Vietnamese title, Viet Minh. The Viet Minh had collaborated with the Western allies in underground resistance to the Japanese rulers. Its objective, however, had been the independence of Viet Nam rather than the restoration of French rule. Consequently, when the War was over and the French undertook to return to Indo-China, they were not welcomed by the Viet Minh and, in fact, soon fell into warfare with it.[8] This was the kind of warfare in which regular troops on the French side were fighting an invisible enemy, the Viet Minh forces that struck from ambush only to disappear immediately into the jungles from which they had momentarily emerged, or to make themselves indistinguishable from the peaceable local populations. It was not the kind of war that the French could ever win without a larger degree of support from the native population than, as we now know, they would be able to elicit either by the strength of the forces they could put into the field or by any attractiveness they might associate with their presence.

[8] The situation was not without its complexities. The French had obligations that, together with the desire to wipe out the consequences of their humiliating defeat in the War, provided arguments against not returning to Indo-China at all. The Laotians and Cambodians both wished the re-establishment of French power in Indo-China to protect them against the encroaching Thais on one side, the encroaching Vietnamese on the other. At the same time that negotiations were under way between France and the Viet Minh there was treachery on both sides. The fighting began with a surprise uprising and massacre of the French in Hanoi by the Viet Minh on December 19, 1946. The situation was essentially tragic, and the more one understands it the more one hesitates to reserve one's sympathy for one side only.

In 1948-1949 the French set up a Vietnamese Government that, opposing its own claim to that of the Viet Minh, thereby gave the war in Viet Nam the character of a civil war, with Vietnamese under the leadership of Ho Chi Minh fighting Vietnamese who, under the Government of the restored Emperor Bao Dai, were associated with the French.

The Indo-Chinese conflict was, in its origin and essence, independent of the Cold War. It was simply part of the general movement throughout south Asia, from the Persian Gulf to the Philippines, for escape from the erstwhile rule of the white man and the establishment of national independence. As such it represented the direction of history and the principle, now universally accepted, of self-determination. In a word, it represented legitimacy. The British, recognizing this, had granted independence to the Indian subcontinent in 1947 and to Burma in 1948. The Dutch had tried to re-establish themselves in the Netherlands East Indies at the end of the War, but they were to accept defeat, at last, as gracefully as they could manage it. The United States, to which the Philippines had been a burden and an embarrassment from the beginning, joyfully recognized Philippine independence in 1946. To the extent that these Western nations were able to disengage themselves from their former Asian empires they would find themselves better off for it—and this would apply, as well, to the French when, almost a decade after the War, they were finally driven from Indo-China.

Nominal and geographical circumstances, however, were at last to draw the Vietnamese struggle into the Cold War, of which it would become a part.

The chief nominal circumstance was that Ho Chi Minh, the leader of the only valid, authentic, and proved movement for Vietnamese independence, was a Communist. Any investigation of what such a label means in real terms, when applied to someone in Ho's position (even though he was a trained and dedicated Communist), immediately takes one into realms of fantasy. The scriptures on which Communism was based had foreseen the revolutionary overthrow of a feudal aristocracy by a bourgeoisie that had grown up under its rule (the French Revolution was the example of this), to be followed at some subsequent date by a second and final revolution in which the bourgeoisie was overthrown by an industrial proletariat that had, under its rule, grown up to constitute the immense majority of the population. This had no relevance at all to Viet Nam, a tropical land of pre-industrial people engaged largely in rice-farming. Certainly Ho Chi Minh was not thinking of making the Communist revolution, in any orthodox sense, among the Vietnamese.

It is true that Mao Tse-tung in China was establishing a precedent for attaching the Communist label to an entirely different kind of movement, having little to do with proletarian revolution, a peasant movement against land-owners that aimed to abolish private property and at least limit private economic enterprise—and this had its relevance to the situation in Viet Nam. One is bound to ask, however, why the Western nations should have felt that the form of social organization in either China or Viet Nam was a matter of vital concern to them. In fact, for what it was worth, Ho Chi Minh pointed out that his regime respected private property, favored private enterprise, and welcomed foreign investment.

It had been true of Mao Tse-tung, and it was still more true of Ho Chi Minh, that the movement which each headed represented nationalism (which orthodox Communism had always been against). Each was essentially a movement of national independence, and as such had, as we have seen, a legitimacy that the West accepted in principle and, for the most part, in practice as well.

Ho's Communist label strongly implied, it is true, that he served the international conspiracy directed from Moscow. In point of fact, however, there is no indication that his movement (which was not that of a Communist Party or in itself Communist) had any support or encouragement from Moscow, at least up through 1948. This accords with Stalin's repeatedly manifested opposition to the acquisition of power by nominal Communists beyond the area that he could be sure of controling. If he had been against a nominally Communist victory in Yugoslavia, in Greece, and in China, it is plausible that he was even more against such a victory in a land so remote as Indo-China.

Ho himself insisted that he was seeking independence for Viet Nam inside the French Union—the association of states representing the French tradition that Paris tried to create after 1945. He denied that his regime was a satellite of Moscow, and as late as March 1949 he denied that it had any relations with Mao Tse-tung. He was not advancing a Communist program.

The geographical circumstance that, in addition to the nominal circumstance, involved the Vietnamese conflict so completely in the Cold War at last was the existence of a common boundary between the part of Viet Nam dominated by the Viet Minh and a China that, in 1949, acquired the Communist label and was thereafter thought of, in the West, as part of the Russian empire. We may plausibly surmise, however, that the Viet Minh was not eager to rescue its country from the Japanese and the French only to have it fall captive to the Chinese, whether they called themselves Nationalists or Communists. A long history of domination and exploitation by China had made Vietnamese nationalism basically anti-Chinese.

We can come closest to grasping the implications of the nominal situation if we grasp the fact that, just as the term Communism connoted simply a generalized and undefined principle of evil to most Americans, so it connoted a notion of virtue and progress to many Asians who identified it with national independence and the equality of all men. (One is tempted, time and again, to declare that the problems of international relations are fundamentally semantic.)

American public opinion, and Washington too, had originally been sympathetic to the Viet Minh, which had cooperated with the Western allies against the Japanese and which represented a legitimacy that all Americans associated with their own struggle for independence against the British. The events of 1949 and 1950, however, were bound to change all that. When Mao's movement triumphed in the name of Communism, presumably adding China to the Russian empire, then the fact that the leader of the Viet Minh was denominated a Communist became decisive. In the simple view that prevailed, resistance to the Viet Minh then represented the containment of Russia. So, in the name of containment, the United States gradually found itself opposing the movement for Vietnamese independence and, in effect, supporting the hopeless French effort to re-establish an obsolete imperial position in Indo-China. The British, increasingly uneasy about Malaya, similarly accorded a half-grudging support to the French. At the same time, Ho Chi Minh naturally found himself looking for support to Mao Tse-tung's China, and becoming more dependent on it. So the Vietnamese struggle was forced into the mold of the Cold War, whose divisions were impressed upon it by nominal circumstances and geography.[9]

[9] If the American Revolution had occurred after the French Revolution, rather than before, would men like Edmund Burke still have supported it as they did, or would they have felt that it had to be resisted in the name of containing Jacobinism?

On January 18, 1950, Peking recognized Ho Chi Minh's regime as the Government of Viet Nam. Moscow did the same on January 30. A week later, the United States and Britain recognized Bao Dai's regime as the Government of Viet Nam. So the original policy of containing Russia, unconsciously transmuted into the policy of containing Communism, led the United States and Britain to oppose the independence of a tropical Asian country three thousand miles away from Russia.

It may be noted here in passing that, by opposing the Chinese peasant revolution and the Vietnamese independence movement, on the assumption that they represented Moscow, the Western powers forced the Russian, Chinese, and Viet Minh regimes into closer relations and greater interdependence than was natural to them. This represents something akin to the operation of a self-fulfilling prophecy. By the summer of 1950 the Communist Chinese were supplying arms, training, and ideological indoctrination for the Viet Minh, but not men. (One surmises that Ho Chi Minh did not, in any circumstances short of desperation, want Chinese armies in Viet Nam.)

On May 8, 1950, in Paris, Secretary Acheson said:

The United States Government, convinced that neither national independence nor democratic evolution can exist in any area dominated by Soviet imperialism, considers the situation to be such as to warrant its according economic aid and military equipment to the Associated States of Indo-China [i.e., Laos, Cambodia, and Viet Nam] and to France in order to assist them in restoring stability and permitting these States to pursue their peaceful and democratic development.

Secretary Acheson, like all Americans, was the captive of his time and place in sharing the excessively simple view, which the social pressures of the day no longer allowed to be questioned, that Communism throughout the world represented a single movement under the command of Moscow, which used it in the service of its own purpose.

President Truman, in his statement of June 27 (in which he interpreted the Korean aggression as showing that 'Communism has passed beyond the use of subversion to conquer independent nations and will now use armed invasion and war'), announced not only the intervention of the Seventh Fleet between Formosa and the mainland, but also that he had 'directed acceleration in the furnishing of military assistance to the forces of France and the associated States in Indo-China, and the dispatch of a military mission to provide close working relations with those forces.' From this time on, the depth of the American commitment increased steadily as American assistance rose to cover some two-thirds of the entire French expenses in Indo-China.

At the same time, the French at home became increasingly aware of fighting a hopeless war in which they had already lost the objective for which they had begun it. The Governments of the three Associated States, taking advantage of the French embarrassment, had bit-by-bit forced France to grant them complete independence, so that the original objective of re-establishing a French position in Indo-China had already been surrendered. The French forces that were needed in Europe to fill out France's contribution to NATO and, especially, to balance the strength of a restored Germany, about to raise forces of its own, were being drained off to the other side of the world to serve the general purpose of containing Communism, a purpose that had not existed when the fighting had begun and that was not a primarily French purpose. The core of the French Army, consisting of its professional and non-commissioned officers, was being swallowed up in the quicksands of Indo-China, leaving France progressively weaker at home, and thereby impairing the position as a great power that it had undertaken to re-establish by sending its troops to Indo-China in the first place.

While the French had gradually lost what enthusiasm they had ever had for the war in Indo-China, their Vietnamese allies had been without any from the start. How could they be enthusiastic in helping the foreigner to fight their own compatriots on their own soil? Among the Vietnamese, high morale was to be found only on the side of the Viet Minh. For the French and their Vietnamese allies the war no longer had any justification except the vague and dubious one that it was being fought to contain Communism, or to contain China. And there was no prospect that it could be won. Under the circumstances, the French were disposed to disengage themselves by any means they could.

Agreement was consequently reached—initially among the United States, France, Britain, and Russia—that a conference to discuss the restoration of peace in Indo-China should be convened in Geneva on April 26, 1954. As the date for the conference approached, however, the French military position began to deteriorate disastrously, with all this implied for its bargaining power when it arrived at the conference table. Plans for the conference went forward nevertheless. It met. And on the day before it took up the problem of an Indo-Chinese settlement French arms in Indo-China suffered their worst disaster since the fall of France in 1940.

CHAPTER XXIX

The United States takes France's place in Indo-China

At the end of 1953 the French had established a major strategic stronghold at Dien Bien Phu, in northern Indo-China,
into which they ultimately put some 15,000 of their best troops,
the élite forces on which they depended most. The Viet Minh proceeded, then, to surround and besiege Dien Bien Phu.

In the second half of March 1954, with the Geneva Conference
on Indo-China only a month away, Washington, which had taken
an optimistic view of French prospects, was suddenly confronted
with the certainty that, unless some radically new element was
introduced into the situation, the French garrison at Dien Bien
Phu was doomed—and with it, very likely, the French position
in Indo-China. This was an alarming prospect to Washington,
which regarded the Viet Minh as an instrument of Moscow. In its
view, if all Viet Nam fell to the spreading Communist empire,
Laos and Cambodia were bound to follow; and after them, like
as not, Thailand, Burma, Malaya, India; perhaps Indonesia, the
Philippines, Japan. In a press conference on April 7 President
Eisenhower was to compare the situation to a line of dominos
standing on end: if the first fell, the others behind it would fall in
succession, until the whole line had been brought down. The fall
of Indo-China, he said, would endanger the American defense
system from the Philippines to Japan.

This was one of the three occasions when Dulles, according to
what he told the *Life* correspondent some two years later,[1] practiced the art of going to the verge of war without getting into it.
He set himself to give the Communist leaders the impression that
the United States would intervene with military force if the trap
was closed on Dien Bien Phu. 'The imposition on Southeast Asia
of the political system of Russia and its Chinese Communist ally,'
he said in an address on March 29, 'by whatever means, would be
a grave threat to the whole free community. The United States
feels that that possibility should not be positively accepted, but
should be met by united action.' In the next days he claimed that

[1] See p. 282 above.
296

there were Chinese engaged with the Viet Minh in the siege of Dien Bien Phu,[2] and warned that their assistance was approaching a point at which retaliation by the United States might be called for. At the same time, two American aircraft carriers, bearing nuclear weapons, sped toward Indo-China.

By various devices, the Secretary of State gave the impression that Britain, and France as well, were with the United States in its supposed determination to take violent action, if necessary, for the rescue of Dien Bien Phu. This aroused such alarm in the House of Commons, as among the British people, that on April 27, the day after the Geneva Conference opened, Prime Minister Churchill felt compelled to assure it that the British Government had committed itself to no such thing.

Those who knew Dulles best would be the least likely to doubt that he had, from the beginning, counted on this denial by the British. It enabled him to give the impression that the failure to carry out the threat of American intervention at Dien Bien Phu was due entirely to British timidity and betrayal. Although a clear majority in Congress and among the American people, with the Korean War to sober them, were certainly opposed to such intervention, Dulles was now able not only to preserve but to enhance his image as the strong man of anti-Communism—deserted in a crucial hour by those who should have been marching at his side.[3]

On May 7, the day before the Geneva Conference took up the question of a settlement in Indo-China, Dien Bien Phu fell. There was no prospect, now, of a triumphant negotiation from the American point of view. Therefore Dulles had returned to Washington from Geneva before the negotiation on Indo-China began, leaving his unhappy deputy, Under Secretary Bedell Smith, to sit with the foreign ministers of the other powers and to face what had to be faced. In the final stages of the Conference Smith took the position that since the United States was not a belligerent in Indo-China it had no primary role in negotiating agreements and would not seek to impose its views.

[2] There is some doubt that this was, in fact, so. See Bell, p. 29, fn. 3.

[3] Readers who are not familiar with the way politics have been played at all times and all places may be more shocked by my interpretation of Dulles's actions than they would otherwise be. The men who worked intimately with him (of whom I was not one) knew that he was a master of such Machiavellian intrigue as I attribute to him here. Even his insistence on publicly identifying himself with religion and morality was something that Machiavelli would have understood and applauded.

The cease-fire agreement finally reached, on July 20, provided for the temporary partition of Viet Nam—the military-demarcation line not to be in any way interpreted as constituting a political or territorial boundary—pending internationally supervised elections to be held throughout the country in July 1956.

Looking back, one has to ask who it was who had agreed to this.

The agreement was concluded between the Franco-Vietnamese military command and the command of the Viet Minh Army. This is to say that, in a formal sense, Bao Dai's Vietnamese regime had not been a party to it. This regime confined itself to endorsing the agreement in an eight-nation 'declaration' that it signed along with France, Great Britain, Russia, Communist China, Laos, Cambodia, and the Viet Minh regime. (The United States, playing the role of mere spectator, refrained from signing this declaration.) Bao Dai's regime and its successors, as transpired in time, did not consider themselves bound by the provision for free nation-wide elections—elections which the Viet Minh would presumably have won—since it had merely endorsed an agreement entered into by its military command, without becoming a party to it. Therefore the projected elections of 1956 would not be held. Viet Nam would continue for an indefinite future to be divided, like Korea, between two states, a northern and a southern, that would confront each other as rival claimants to the government of the whole country. In this one instance, it was the Western side in the Cold War that would oppose those free elections that it demanded in other contested areas.

Considering the military weakness of the Franco-Vietnamese side, the final agreement (especially if the provision for elections was not to be realized) represented as good an outcome, from the standpoint of the Western powers, as they could have hoped for. There is reason to believe that Russia and China put pressure on the Viet Minh to accept it. Who can say that this pressure was not induced, at least in part, by fear that the United States would enter the fighting in Indo-China, thereby expanding it, perhaps, into a general war? Who can say, then, that a great power's deliberate affectation of international irresponsibility, however dangerous such a resort may be, and however damaging to its credit in the long run, does not have its uses?

A year after the partitioning of Viet Nam at Geneva, the political structure of South Viet Nam, which had never become established, was close to collapse. At this point the United States, providing necessary financial support, assumed the directing role. The South Vietnamese Government thereupon became, in effect, its puppet. By force of circumstances, by the very dynamics of the Cold War, Washington now found itself responsible for a regime that was its satellite in the same sense that certain East European regimes were satellites of Moscow. With the rapid decline of France's influence in Indo-China, the United States became progressively more involved. Inheriting France's role, it also inherited, as an outside power trying to impose its will on the native population, the stigma of imperialism. This was, in a sense, unjust, because it had no imperialistic ambition, no desire for overseas territory or the government of alien peoples, no wish for imperial responsibilities. The position it came to occupy in Indo-China was not what it had wanted or foreseen when, five years earlier, it had acted on the belief that the French efforts in Indo-China represented the containment of Russia.

*   *   *

In 1950 the United States had embarked on a policy of active containment in Asia as in Europe, in the Pacific as in the Atlantic. Pursuing this policy, it thought of itself as containing Russia, it thought of itself as containing China, or it thought of itself as containing something called Communism that was threatening to engulf the world.

It also thought of itself as supporting 'free peoples who are resisting attempted subjugation by armed minorities or by outside pressures.' In this, however, it took inadequate account of fundamental differences between Europe and other parts of the world. Freedom in Europe meant self-determination and freedom of speech for the individual. It meant freedom from the impositions of dictatorial government, or of any élite like the Communist Party, as much as it meant national independence. This was the sense in which the Europeans west of the Iron Curtain were free peoples, and these were the terms in which they had welcomed with relief and gratitude the intervention by which the United States, in 1947 and 1948, undertook to cooperate in saving their freedom and restoring their strength. They, themselves, enthusiastically constructed a foundation for American intervention, so as to make it possible, in the O.E.E.C. and the Brussels Treaty organization.

Such a situation, however, did not exist in Asia. It is true that in Korea an attempted international kidnapping had provided an urgent need for rescue by the United States, so that here the legitimacy and the welcome of its intervention had been clear. In Japan, the position of the United States was the product of legitimate conquest in war; and, as in Germany, the American presence had come to be welcomed for the protection it afforded the new and democratic regime of freedom that the nation had adopted. In the rest of Asia, however, the situation was different. The peoples and governments of south Asia, especially, did not consider that the containment of Russia had anything to do with them. Nor did they take the American view of Communism as a conspiracy for their enslavement. To them, Communism had, in fact, connotations of freedom from the imperialist yoke that they had been struggling to cast off. Therefore it was easy for them to regard their former Western masters, now the opponents of Communism, as the real enemies of freedom.

These Asian peoples and governments were not so intent on the fundamental freedoms of the individual, which were associated with Western democratic tradition and experience, as they were on freedom from the overbearing presence of the Western white man, freedom from the humiliation associated with his status as the overlord.[4] It was in this sense that, to them, the egalitarian ideals of Communism meant freedom. Dominant opinion throughout south Asia wanted to keep the white man's Cold War, which was over remote issues conceived to be irrelevant to Asia, at a distance. It was not disposed to welcome the political and military presence of the United States, especially not on the grounds that the United States was supporting free peoples who were resisting attempted subjugation by international Communism. This conception, that the Asians were free peoples resisting attempted subjugation by

[4] Generally I avoid using the common terminology that assumes the division of all mankind into two groups, the white and the colored races, if only because it is scientifically false. If we accept the anthropologist's tripartite division of mankind into 'white' Caucasians, 'yellow' Mongoloids, and 'black' Negroids, then the dominant peoples of India and Pakistan, like those of the Middle East and North Africa, belong to the 'white' Caucasian race. Human societies, however, are governed by mythical conceptions, among which none has been more assiduously propagated, by the North Atlantic peoples themselves, than the conception of the two groups, which not only lumps Hindus and Pakistanis with Chinese and Negroes, but sometimes goes so far as to lump the Arabs and, on occasion, even the Latin Americans with them, under the rubric of 'the colored races.' What I am describing here, however, is an Asian view, which is shared in Europe and America, not the true view.

international Communism, was simply an American myth associated with the Cold War.

It is true that the dominant opinion I have described was modified or overborne by local circumstances in important parts of Asia. Thailand, which had survived the era of Western imperialism without ever completely losing its independence (chiefly because it had been a buffer between the rival French and British empires), and which had a tradition of friendly relations with a disinterested United States (which had opposed both French and British imperialism), welcomed American support of its independence against the possible pretensions of its Asian neighbors. Pakistan, a country in the borderlands of the Middle East, was moved by its bitter rivalry with India to welcome any support it could get—and so it made little difference to it that the avowed motive of American support was alien to its preoccupations. The Philippines, to the eternal credit of American colonial policy, continued in its newly acquired independence to look on the United States as a big brother. Australia and New Zealand, almost beyond the rim of Asia, were simply Atlantic nations transplanted to the Pacific, and it would certainly not occur to any continental Asian that they represented Asia. The welcome that the United States had from these half dozen scattered nations, mostly for ulterior reasons, was the exception rather than the rule. In China, India, Ceylon, Burma, Indo-China, and Indonesia it was not welcome—and these nations represented the overwhelming preponderance of the Asian population.

The Eisenhower Administration took inadequate account of the real circumstances and the real issues in Asia when it proclaimed, as one of the fixed ideas on which it would base a new foreign policy, that 'the freedom we cherish and defend in Europe and the Americas is no different from the freedom that is imperiled in Asia.' This represented a mythical conception, illustrative of the human limitation described by Santayana in the statement that I have put at the front of this book as its epigraph. Because it represented a mythical conception native to the United States, it was better suited to appeal to an unworldly domestic audience than to provide the basis for a sophisticated foreign policy.

Europe had offered solid ground on which the United States could make a stand. By contrast, Asia was a swamp. In Europe the United States had responded to a call of distress from its own kind. In Asia its self-appointed role as the rescuer of free peoples from Communism was not accepted or understood. In the eyes of the Asians, the intruders in Asia were not the Russians whom they had never seen but the English, the French, the Dutch, and now increasingly the Americans. It is, in fact, hard to imagine what most Vietnamese made of Dulles's claim to be protecting their country against the imposition of Russia's political system. (Russia's political system, in any case, could not possibly have been imposed on their country.)

What a contrast we have here, in this lack of common understanding, with the understanding between the Americans and the West Europeans in 1947–1948!

*   *   *

By the beginning of the 1950's an equilibrium of sorts was developing on the European scene; but revolutionary events were rocking the Far East. The Truman Administration, having lost such freedom of choice as it had previously had, was compelled to address itself in haste and confusion to these Far Eastern developments, for which it had not been prepared. Under the pressure of an excited public opinion, it improvised action without making a policy.

The new Republican Administration found it both congenial and timely to react against the primacy that the Atlantic area had occupied in American thinking under the Truman Administration, as under the Roosevelt Administration before it.[5] It therefore set itself to rectify what it regarded as an unwarranted neglect of Asia and the Pacific.

Dulles was not a man of creative imagination and originality, nor was he sensitive to the psychological subtleties of human relations—even though we make allowance for the fact that he was not as crude in his private thinking as in his public utterances. From the point of view adopted by the new Administration, 'the freedom that is imperilled in Asia' called for a South-East Asia Treaty Organization as 'the freedom we cherish and defend in Europe' had called for a North Atlantic Treaty Organization. His predecessor having fathered NATO, Dulles now undertook to father a SEATO.

[5] The entire history of American foreign policy, certainly after 1829, could be written in terms of a tension between those who looked eastward toward Europe and those who, spurning Europe, looked westward away from it.

In his address of March 29, 1954, Dulles had said that the Communist threat to Indo-China and South-East Asia should be met by 'united action.' A few days later he conferred with representatives of Britain, France, Australia, New Zealand, Thailand, and the Philippines on the organization of a united front for the defense of South-East Asia and the western Pacific against Communist aggression.

In the weeks of negotiation that followed, the differences between the situation in Asia and the situation in Europe imposed themselves irresistibly on the general consciousness. For one thing, it became only too clear that the bulk of South Asia was actively hostile to the formation, under Western auspices, of a united front against Communism. This, in its view, was a Western project to bring the Cold War into its part of the world. As early as April 24, Prime Minister Nehru of India expressed 'concern and foreboding' at 'an invitation to Western countries, to ANZUS Powers [Australia and New Zealand], and to some Asian States to join in united and collective action in South-East Asia.' 'This,' Nehru continued, 'had been preceded by statements which came near to assuming a kind of Monroe Doctrine over the countries of South-East Asia.'

The opposition of its greatest partner in the Commonwealth was bound to make the British reluctant to go along with the United States in this project, as they nevertheless felt bound to do. The participation of France, on the basis of its claim to a vanishing remnant of colonial influence in Asia, did not commend the project. The Australians and New Zealanders, who already had a defense treaty with the United States, were not Asians. Since the Indo-Chinese, to the extent that they did not exclude themselves, were to be excluded by the terms of the Geneva agreement, there would remain only the Pakistanis, the Thais, and the Filipinos (with whom the United States already had a defense treaty) as the Asian representatives of the united front when it was formed by the conclusion, on September 8, of the South-East Asia Collective Defense Treaty. Among the territories of the adherents of this Treaty (the members of SEATO, as their association continued to be called, although the initials no longer fitted), there was only one frontier in common, that between Thailand and British Malaya on the Isthmus of Kra. Since the military forces of Pakistan were tied down by the confrontation with India over Kashmir, the only substantial military forces available to SEATO were those of the United States, which had no territory in Asia. Seeing the weakness of the whole arrangement, Washington now recoiled from any commitment to military action in case of such aggression as would invoke the provisions of the Treaty, nor was it willing to share control over its forces by pooling them with others under any rule that depended on joint decision by SEATO. Finally, Formosa and Hong Kong were excluded from the area in which the SEATO powers obliged themselves to cooperate for the frustration of aggression.

In effect, the burden of containing China's presumed expansionist tendencies in South-East Asia had come to rest, and would continue to rest, largely on the shoulders of the United States. In Malaya the British would successfully bear their part; and in 1962, when Chinese forces invaded the northern marches of India, it would fall to the Indian Army to offer such military resistance as they would encounter. For the rest, however, from Korea to the Middle East it would be the threat of American intervention that would provide the only effective military restraint.

The anomaly, here, is so evident as to invite comment and speculation. The presumed threat of Chinese expansion southward was, properly, a far more immediate concern of the South-East Asians than of Americans, whose security could be only indirectly and remotely menaced by it. Americans had reason to be concerned at the prospect of any Chinese advances in South-East Asia, but not to be more concerned than the South-East Asians themselves.

The United States, one judges, was too easily alarmed and too quick to react with extreme measures, or the threat of extreme measures, to what was, for it, only a remote threat. In the eyes of the Asians, as of others, it put itself in the wrong by its impulsive decision forcibly to prevent Mao Tse-tung's regime from extending its rule to Formosa, which Washington had itself recognized as belonging to China, and by its insistence on considering the ousted regime of Chiang Kai-shek, which was without credit among the Asians, as the Government of China. Then it put itself in the wrong by supporting the French forces against the Vietnamese forces that were fighting for the independence of their country. In China and in Indo-China alike, it put itself in the untenable position, for a Western power, of defending China against Chinese, Viet Nam against Vietnamese, Asia against Asians.

Not many Asians were likely to be persuaded by the American claim to be holding off the Russian empire, or the Russian political system, whether from Formosa, from Indo-China, or from South-East Asia generally. Its association, for these purposes, with the unhappy British and the unhappy French, inevitably tended to discredit its cause. For the South Asians had no experience of Russian imperialism to make them fear it, they saw no Russian masters standing over them; but they did have a vivid experience of French, British, and Dutch masters, masters from the North Atlantic world to which the Americans belonged. The Russians were not visible intruders, and the Chinese had not actually intruded into any territory not their own (although a tenuous question might be raised whether remote and inaccessible Tibet, which they had occupied, was properly Chinese territory); but the intrusiveness of the Americans and their European kinsmen was conspicuous. No wonder that the Asians associated the danger of imperialism with their presence, the danger of aggression with their aggressiveness (however well intentioned we know that aggressiveness to have been)!

One speculates that if the United States, less easily alarmed and more patient, had stood aloof, the South Asians would have found increasing reason for alarm at the growing threat of Chinese power under a fanatical and doctrinaire leadership. This, it is plausible to believe, would have been the predominant concern of Ho Chi Minh as ruler of Viet Nam. In the typical pattern of political reaction to an expansionist threat, repeated time and again over the centuries, the Indo-Chinese, the Indonesians, the Thais, the Malayans, the Burmese, and the others would have been impelled to move toward one another in a common resistance. The point might well have been reached at an early stage where the assistance of the United States would have been eagerly sought. Then the United States could, if it had seen fit, have contributed its strength, not as an unwelcome intruder but in response to an appeal for rescue.

There was time to be patient and unalarmed. Every advance that the Chinese made into territory not their own, every undertaking to hold down rebellious aliens in the jungles of south Asia, would have discredited them and taxed their strength. The thought of the Chinese undertaking to occupy and rule the Indian subcontinent, if they were ever so foolish as to attempt it, would at worst be occasion for qualified alarm. The United States leaped into the quicksands of Asia simply to forestall its antagonists from entering upon them.

But this is to reckon without the energy and the basic attitudes of our American nation, which always prefers dynamic action to the patient inaction that foreign relations so often demand; which believes in seizing the initiative even in situations that give the advantage to those who, by waiting, retain their freedom of choice; and which consequently goes awooing prematurely and unsuccessfully when, if only it had waited, it might have found itself in the stronger position of being wooed.

In 1947 Washington had behaved with extraordinary delicacy and restraint in making its own return to Europe await a European initiative to have it return. That delicacy and that restraint were abandoned after 1950, when the American people, in unnecessary alarm, began to lose the steadiness that great responsibility requires. So they acted, as we must believe, unwisely, and brought the good name of the United States into a spreading disrepute that could only weaken its influence and its cause.

CHAPTER XXX

The death of Stalin, the succession, and the attitude of the United States toward these events

FOR many years Stalin had occupied the position of a god in Russia. His dedication to the ideals of Marxism–Leninism, his vision, his military genius, his infallibility—these had been a constant theme of self-congratulation by the society over which he presided. This reverence had extended beyond the borders of Russia. Communists and Communist sympathizers all over the world shared it. In wide circles, Marx, Lenin, Stalin, and Abraham Lincoln were equated as liberators of mankind.

No one seriously doubted that, in the small circle of those who served under Stalin in the Kremlin, the reverence and the personal loyalty were complete. These men—Molotov, Malenkov, Beria, Khrushchev, Bulganin, Kaganovich, Mikoyan, and the rest—had repeatedly expressed, in their public utterances, the wonder and the gratitude that he inspired in them. They were, however, the younger contemporaries and the successors of the old Bolsheviks who, having made the Bolshevik Revolution with Lenin, had been killed off by Stalin in the purges of the late 1930's.[1] Each had come through the most extreme personal dangers only by a vigilant mistrustfulness of everyone, by conspiratorial skill, and by sheer nerve. In the winter of 1952–1953 these men may have apprehended preparations for another purge by which the eternally suspicious Stalin would replace them with still a new generation of officials whose loyalty he could feel sure of. His promotions and appointments at the 19th Congress of the Communist Party in October could be read as suggesting their coming replacement.[2] After the Congress there had been the

[1] Molotov was an exception, the only old Bolshevik surviving in Stalin's entourage.

[2] In his address to the 20th Congress of the Party in February 1956 Khrushchev said: 'It is not excluded that had Stalin remained at the helm for several more months, Comrades Molotov and Mikoyan would probably not have delivered any speeches at this Congress. Stalin evidently had plans to finish off the old members of the Politburo . . . this proposal, after the 19th Congress, concerning the selection of 25 persons to the Central Committee's Presidium was aimed at the removal of the old Politburo members and the bringing in of less experienced persons who would extol him in all sorts of ways.'

dramatic announcement, which could have been interpreted as preparing the ground for a purge, of an alleged plot by fifteen doctors to kill some of the top personages in the Soviet Government and Army. The implication was of delinquency by important elements in the Government, which should not have allowed such a plot to develop.

Stalin was seventy-three years old at this time. When men who have exercised great power for many years begin to age conspicuously while continuing to hold the reins of power, they become an increasing problem for those who serve under their rule. One can therefore imagine that Stalin's death, early in 1953, would have been timely for a variety of reasons.

The announcement of Stalin's death, which came on March 6, had been carefully prepared. In the days that followed, the stage-management of events was smooth and skillful. At the funeral, orations were pronounced by Malenkov, Beria, and Molotov. 'Joseph Vissarionovich Stalin,' said Malenkov, 'our teacher and leader, the greatest genius of mankind, has come to the end of his journey.' The other two spoke in like terms, which had long been customary.[3] It could be noted even at the time, however, without awaiting later events, that a note of genuine personal sorrow was to be detected only in Molotov's oration.

An American who had been a close observer of the Government in Moscow, and who attended the funeral, gave his private and informal comment on the occasion in Washington some days later. What had impressed him was that the men who had been close to Stalin, whose faces had always been severely expressionless when he had seen them before, seemed as if they had suddenly been released from bondage. For the first time in his experience they smiled, they chattered, they were animated. Resorting to hyperbole, he told us that the pall-bearers, hitherto always so impassive, did everything but kick the corpse. This was the first hint some of us had that the reverence for Stalin, among those who had been his high priests, might have been outward only.

Immediately after Stalin's death the promotions and appointments made by him at the 19th Party Congress were undone;

---

[3] The occasion of Stalin's death moved Dulles to use such terms about his own chief. At a press-conference on March 9 he said: 'The Eisenhower era begins as the Stalin era ends. . . . As he [Stalin] dies, General Eisenhower, the man who liberated Western Europe, has become President of our great Republic, with a prestige unmatched in history.' This is probably the only occasion on which President Eisenhower found himself mentioned as the successor to Stalin.

and less than a month later it was announced that the charge against the doctors had been a fabrication: there had been no doctor's plot at all!

However much they may have been relieved by the passing of the old tyrant, the men responsible for the government of Russia in the following days must have been keyed up by anxiety. For a quarter of a century the society over which they now found themselves presiding had been disciplined by the awe attached to the name of one man, who had been regarded by the masses as more than human. It was his name that had made the people of Russia bow their heads and bear their ills. What would happen now that this unique element of authority had suddenly been removed? No one could know whether, after all these years of suppression, the people had grown to accept the regime to which they had been submitted by force and terror. When the lid was removed would the pot boil over?

Russia, moreover, was surrounded by powerful enemies. Would they take advantage of a moment of confusion in the Russian society and its leadership to strike?

These anxieties are clearly apparent between the lines of the funeral orations.

In addition, there must have been tense anxieties in the breast of each individual over the succession. In Russia's Byzantine tradition, exemplified by the struggle for power after Lenin's death, the man who won the contest for supremacy encompassed the death of all who had been or might be his rivals. Only the winner survived. Inevitably, then, immediately upon Stalin's death a deadly game was implicit in the relations among Malenkov, Beria, Khrushchev, Molotov, Kaganovich, the Army leaders, and others.

Every indication, however, is that there had been some agreement among these men on the rules of the game, probably in advance of Stalin's death and in preparation for it—in any case, before its announcement.[4] An element of solidarity would have existed among them for the time being—if not as a matter of sharing a common secret then because of the mortal danger to

---

[4] The announcement on March 6 said that Stalin had died on the 5th, but in the atmosphere of conspiracy and stage-management that prevailed it is possible that Stalin's death had occurred earlier, that the announcement had been put off until arrangements for the immediate succession had been largely completed, and that the putative date of the death had been set to conform to the announcement.

the state that the death of Stalin must, in their view, occasion. It is reasonably clear, for example, that they had agreed on the principle of collective leadership, and on a corresponding rejection of what, in that period after Stalin's death, they were to denounce repeatedly as the 'cult of personality.'[5] They had also agreed on a complete reorganization of the top commands of the Government and of the Party, including the posts to be occupied by each, so that they were able to announce it at the same time that they announced Stalin's death. It was a remarkable performance.

One may surmise, as well, that one person among them, by the fear and hatred his power inspired, caused the others to form a common front against him. Even well before Stalin's death Lavrenti Beria had been increasing the sinister power over the whole society that his control of the secret police gave him. If, as there is reason to believe, the invention of the doctor's plot had been designed chiefly to discredit him, then Stalin himself had been planning his destruction. Stalin would hardly have been unconcerned by the steady growth of the secret police under Beria until they had come, at last, to number 1.5 million men. In addition, Beria had under his command a militia of 300,000 men, and through his control of the forced-labor camps it is estimated that nearly one-fifth of the entire labor-force in the Soviet Union was under his rule. One may well believe that none of the other members of the group that constituted the collective leadership, at the time of Stalin's death, was nearly so powerful as he. He had, in effect, his own praetorian guard. The fear that he might use his power to make himself absolute dictator, in succession to Stalin, may have drawn the others together in the kind of comradeship that only a great common danger makes possible. A struggle for power appears to have gone on through the spring between Beria and the others, including those who commanded the Party, the basic machinery of the state, and the Army. Apparently Beria, by putting his own men in key positions, tried to gain personal

---

[5] For example, in its issue of July 10 *Pravda* would observe: 'The strength of our leadership lies in its collective nature, its solid and monolithic unity. Collective leadership is the highest principle of leadership in our Party. This principle accords entirely with Marx's thesis that the cult of personality is harmful and impermissible.' I do not recall that anyone in the West, at the time, attached prime importance to the implicit indictment of Stalin that this represented. It may be that our preconceptions, before Khrushchev's dramatic denunciation of Stalin in February 1956, did not allow us to do so.

control of the Party and state machinery, and especially to make himself supreme in his native state of Georgia. A trap was set for him, however, and was apparently sprung on June 27, when tanks and soldiers were seen moving through the streets of Moscow. Two weeks later the world was informed of his arrest as 'an enemy of the Communist Party and the Soviet people,' charged with a whole calendar of criminal actions, including what *Pravda* referred to as 'his foul machinations for the purpose of seizing power.'

According to the official announcement, the death sentence was executed on Beria and six of his associates in December, after he had, in a secret trial before the Supreme Court of the Soviet Union, been found guilty of high treason.

From this point on the struggle among the members of the collective leadership took a more civilized form and, proceeding slowly, was not finally resolved until 1957, when Nikita Khrushchev, who had emerged as acting *primus inter pares* in 1955, expelled his rivals from their commanding positions in the Party and the Government on the grounds that they constituted an 'anti-party group.'

Khrushchev was a shrewd, tough, humorous but pugnacious figure with a peasant background and no formal education. He had climbed up through the ranks of the Party apparatus by his opportunism, his quickness, his energy, his daring, and a capacity for cajoling people. Making himself a somewhat crude comic figure wherever he went, impulsive, voluble, and jovial, with a folksy quality and a homespun wit, he had all the basic attributes of an American grass-roots politician rather than of a traditional Russian ruler. It was obvious that he liked people, that he respected them as Stalin had not, and that he was neither cruel nor vindictive by his own native instincts. (He had taken his part in carrying out the great purges of the late 1930's, but this would have represented a requirement of survival in the dangerous career that he was realizing under Stalin.) Add to this that he was a rapid improvisor of great daring rather than a man of deep and patient calculation. He would, one supposes, have made a first-class buccaneer on the Spanish Main. He had only a crude and superficial knowledge of Marxian dialectics, and like all practical operators of his type he must have had little respect for abstract theoretical considerations. This left him free to be the more flexible in his opportunism. As a virtuoso in political improvisation he knew how to advance boldly, and how to retreat when one would have thought he had burned his bridges behind him.

We must also credit Khrushchev with genuine impulses in the direction of liberalism. Even while he served as a tool of Stalin he had been revolted by Stalin's mistreatment of people, by the torture and death meted out to men for whom he may well have had great respect. This was expressed with a sort of personal passion that could not have been altogether affected in the speech denouncing Stalin before the 20th Party Congress.

One can imagine that Khrushchev's rise to pre-eminence after Stalin's death was in large part attributable to the fact that his rivals in the collective leadership could feel a confidence in him that they could not feel in one another. So far from having the qualities of a dictator like Stalin, he preferred to consult his colleagues and to act on the basis of a consensus among them. He was not a misanthrope who, achieving power, would be disposed to use it against them with the ruthless cruelty of a Stalin. And he had a self-deprecating quality which made it clear that he did not fancy himself in the role of dictator. Those who were moved by a revulsion against what Stalin had represented would naturally be drawn to Khrushchev.

Once Khrushchev had achieved his pre-eminence the dynamics of the situation impelled him to remove his rivals among the members of the former collective leadership; but he dealt with them humanely by the standards of the Russian society, and he never undertook anything like the self-deification that Stalin had practiced.

*   *   *

In his airgram of February 22, 1946, from Moscow, George Kennan had written: 'It has yet to be demonstrated that [the Soviet system] can survive supreme test of successive transfer of power from one individual or group to another. Lenin's death was first such transfer, and its effects wracked Soviet state for 15 years after. Stalin's death or retirement will be second.' In the seven years that followed, a constant topic of speculation and discussion, inside and outside of Government, had been: After Stalin, what? Only the inhibition against 'wishful thinking' held in check the hope, widespread throughout the West, that the Soviet state, unable to resolve the problem of the suecession, would fall into confusion and helplessness upon Stalin's removal from the scene.

Surely this might have happened. In the absence of effective constitutional provisions establishing the procedures of succession—
provisions that cannot exist in connection with illegitimate
personal rule—the door was open to anarchy. Beria, overthrown
in Moscow, might have found refuge in Georgia, which he had
been converting into a personal stronghold; and civil war might
have ensued. Or he might have seized power in Moscow and
found that he could maintain it only by the practice of such
terrorism as would itself have spelled chaos. Or the Army might
have moved against the Party, or against the secret police, with
incalculable consequences.

Even from the standpoint of the Soviet regime's enemies it is
doubtful that anarchy over the vast realm of Russia was desirable.
Anarchy tends to propagate itself. The breakdown of authority in
the Soviet Union would have been followed, immediately, by a
breakdown of authority throughout the eastern half of Europe.
There might have been violent clashes between rival leaders
with their respective followers. There would surely have been
interventions across state frontiers, probably amounting to invasions. Perhaps the Poles would have undertaken to reconquer
the territory they had lost to Russia in 1944 and 1945. Perhaps
the Chinese would have moved to occupy Siberia and Outer Mongolia. Perhaps the Germans would have crossed the Oder-Neisse
line. Perhaps the Greeks and Yugoslavs would have clashed over
Bulgarian Macedonia. Under such circumstances of spreading
anarchy the West would have been drawn irresistibly into East
Europe to provide rescue, to forestall rivals, to re-establish order.
Who knows what clashes this, in turn, might have led to? Anarchy
in Russia would have been like a fire spreading in a dry forest.

If one takes account of political possibilities one is bound to
conclude, I think, that what actually happened in Russia, upon
the removal of Stalin, was about the best that could have been
expected. Control was kept by relatively responsible men who, as
it later transpired, were animated by a genuine revulsion against
what Stalin had represented.

As the months lengthened into years, moreover, it became
apparent that in the era of Stalin's rule Russia had undergone an
evolution by which such rule itself had been rendered increasingly
obsolete. The Russian society had been outgrowing its traditional
barbarism. With industrialization—which had been advancing
rapidly under the czars and had continued under their successors

—a relatively sophisticated class of industrial managers and technicians had been rising to predominance. These men, whose role was indispensable, could not function under the conditions that, for a thousand years, had kept the Russian people in a state of servitude approaching that of domestic animals. They were not, like their forebears, illiterate peasants. Their role and their willingness to perform it required widespread freedom of debate and decision. And their training made them as apt to question political authority as to accept it. Russian scientists and scholars, upon whom the society depended more and more, had the same requirements and predilections in even greater degree. All this meant that the days when Russia could be ruled by an Ivan the Terrible or a Stalin were at their end.

The collective leaders appear to have appreciated this. They were, it seems, determined that a Caligula should not succeed to a Caligula. The principle of moderation had enough credit among them, and they had enough respect for orderly procedures, so that they were unwilling to settle their rivalries by assassination or mete out death to the losers as Stalin had done. The death of Beria, since it was the product of a secret trial on essentially political charges, must be accounted an exception; but what is notable is the fact that it was so. When Khrushchev, in successive maneuvers, defeated Malenkov, Molotov, Kaganovich, Bulganin, and Zhukov, he simply sent them into a comfortable retirement. And when he himself was overthrown in 1964 the like consideration was shown to him. This represented a hopeful improvement on the Byzantine tradition that Stalin had embodied. I doubt that many observers at the beginning of 1953 foresaw it.

The years that followed Stalin's death also showed that important aspects of his foreign policy were without honor in the minds of his successors. He had dangerously overextended the empire of which they found themselves the heirs. He had then united the West against it, provoking the restoration of West Europe under the leadership of the United States. He had alienated Yugoslavia, thereby producing the first great break in the Communist front. He had blundered in Korea, with incalculable consequences that included the rearmament of the nations banded together in the Atlantic alliance. In a world of nuclear weapons his conduct of foreign relations had raised international tensions to a point of extreme danger for the Soviet state. The new leadership, although it could not expect to disengage from the Cold

War and so bring it to an end in the immediate future, this being beyond the bounds of political possibility, showed itself anxious to relax international tensions and to retrench the over-extended empire where it could be retrenched without too much danger.

The fundamental change that all this represented was not only unappreciated in the United States, where the movement of opinion had been away from moderation, but was almost wilfully disregarded. As had been the case when the Japanese had been trying, a decade earlier, to find a way out of World War II, no one in Washington dared to accept the apparent new attitudes of the demonic enemy at face value. McCarthyism, beginning at the end of 1949, had only now achieved the heights of its supremacy, and anyone who suggested that Stalin's death had diminished the menace of the Communist conspiracy was likely to find himself suspect. He would, in any case, be silenced by the outspokenness of the opinion against him. Everyone agreed that no one must allow himself to be misled by the smiles of the new Communist leadership. Everyone felt impelled to make it clear how little he, in any case, was in danger of being taken in by them.

Just below the surface of consciousness in Washington there were powerful reasons for such a reaction to the outward appearances of a new moderation in Moscow. By 1953 the entire foreign policy of the United States, so painfully developed after 1946, was based on the Cold War. It made sense only in terms of the premises on which the Cold War was being fought. Specifically, the policy was based on the belief that Moscow was determined, by fraud or violence, to establish its ideology, its political system, and its domination over the entire world. The men in Washington, as a group, were the authors of that policy. They had created it, they had developed it, they had struggled to gain its acceptance by the American people. It was their baby. They were bound to react with alarm, now, to any suggestion that the premises of their policy might no longer be valid—just because there were smiles in Moscow where before there had been frowns.

More specifically, the United States was, at this time, making every effort to persuade its European allies that the Soviet menace was such as to require greatly increased contributions by them to the military forces being assembled under NATO; and that the danger was of such magnitude as to make the organization of a European Defense Community imperative. This was precisely the period when the United States was putting pressure on

France to ratify the E.D.C. Treaty. All this effort would be defeated, now, if the Europeans should be so gullible as to believe
that, just because the Russians were smiling, the danger had
passed. The tendency, therefore, was to become still more shrill in
pointing out the danger and in rallying the troops.

Finally, any great struggle like the Cold War creates vested
interests beyond those that represent intellectual commitment
alone. In the United States the top staffs of the three military
services have to give a major portion of their time, year in year
out, to preparing their requests for appropriations and to fighting
their case for those requests through the various committees and
subcommittees of both houses of Congress. They find themselves
asking the Congressmen for the largest possible budgets on the
basis of the magnitude of the foreign danger they have to meet.
It is not their business to underestimate that danger. On the contrary, they are moved to present, as the basis for their requirements, the most extreme estimates of the antagonist's intentions
and capabilities. If, now, Moscow's smiles should be taken
seriously, the military chiefs would see their budgets reduced by
the forces in Congress that favored economy and that now saw an
opportunity to practice it. (There is no question here of the
honesty of the military leaders: like human beings in other situations of the sort, they genuinely believe in what conforms to
the interests with which they identify themselves, interests that
in this case are directly identified, in turn, with the national
interest.)

Finally, there is the vast industrial complex, constituting a substantial part of the nation's economy, that depends on Government contracts. Those who produce war materials have a vested
interest no less marked than that of the military in the menace to
the national security, and are no less sincere in their defense of it.
They, too, identifying their professional interests with the national
interest, were bound to view with alarm any tendency to minimize
the Soviet menace in response to smiles from Moscow.

For several years after Stalin's death, then, the orthodox saying
in Washington, when the matter came under discussion, was that
the new regime in Russia was even more dangerous than the old
because, by its smiles, it threatened to betray the West into 'letting
down its guard.'

Inside the State Department the intelligence specialists on
Soviet affairs, who regularly briefed the Secretary of State and his

entourage, continued for at least a year and a half after Stalin's death to report that the succession represented no significant change in the objectives, the policies, or the basic attitudes of Moscow. Everything was essentially as it had been under Stalin. Continuity was unbroken.

Roberta Wohlstetter, referring to the conclusions that the intelligence experts draw from the factual data that they gather and collate, has observed that, 'without a very large and complete body of assumptions and estimates, the data collected would not speak to us at all.'[6] This is fundamental. No meaning can be elicited from unordered accumulations of factual data until they have been arranged in accordance with a conceptual framework that, in the realm of politics, represents for the most part such assumptions as it occurs to no one to question. It is common experience that we interpret the behavior of one whom we regard as a friend quite differently from the interpretation we would put on identical behavior in one whom we regarded as an enemy, simply because we make different assumptions about him. Presumably the Soviet intelligence experts interpret the data that they gather according to the tenets of Marxism–Leninism.

The tacit assumption that the intelligence experts in Washington made, when they set themselves to interpret the vast arrays of data before them, was that of a conspiratorial movement for the overthrow of capitalist society, founded by Marx and Engels a century earlier, which had been pursuing its fixed purpose with unalterable determination through successive generations to the present. The movement was one of men who were dedicated and disciplined, so that when one of them fell the others would immediately close ranks and carry on. Marx, Lenin, Stalin, Mao Tse-tung, Ho Chi Minh, Khrushchev—all were the servants of the one continuing movement. If there were from time to time variations in their conduct of the movement these represented tactical maneuvers only. Khrushchev's call for an international *détente*, for 'peaceful coexistence' of the 'socialist and capitalist camps,' was such a maneuver, designed to seduce our allies and to throw us off our guard. In the light of these basic assumptions, the figures on steel-production, the latest data on the development of the Russian aircraft industry, a reorganization of Red Army units, a statement in a Russian technical journal—all fitted

---

[6] Wohlstetter, Roberta, p. 706.

together to show that the succession to Stalin had brought no real change.

This conclusion began to be increasingly difficult to maintain, however, after the middle of 1955, when the new regime in Moscow had withdrawn the Red Army from East Austria, abandoning the occupation that it had been maintaining there as in East Germany; when it had publicly apologized to Tito for the errors of its predecessor, and had publicly agreed with him that each socialist state had the right to follow its own path to socialism without interference from outside; when it had evacuated Port Arthur and had returned to Finland the naval base of Porkkala; when it had taken the initiative to recognize the German Federal Republic and establish normal relations with it; when it had moved to normalize its relations with Japan; and when it had made notable concessions to the Western powers on the issue of disarmament. It became impossible to maintain after the text of Khrushchev's denunciation of Stalin and Stalinism at the 20th Party Congress in February 1956 became known.

The more generous and liberal line that Moscow pursued in foreign affairs after Stalin's death (and which had been foreshadowed at the 19th Party Congress before his death) could be discounted as representing simply a decision to pause in its career of world conquest, and to reduce, pending the completion of its own nuclear armament, the danger to itself inherent in the excessively high tensions that had been allowed to develop under Stalin. It was proper, as a matter of prudence, that one should so discount these changes. After all, Germany was still divided, Berlin was still besieged, East Europe was still under the tyranny of Moscow. Nevertheless, the changes, whatever motives they represented, were real changes, and they were not insignificant from the practical point of view. In international relations, what one does now is more important than what one may intend to do at some time in the future. Decisions made with respect to some time in the future are not operative. It is not until the future time comes that the operative decision will be made, and it will not necessarily conform to what had been projected earlier. Without prematurely abandoning its defenses, the West could properly recognize the change and explore its possibilities. This, in fact, is what it would begin to do in the summer of 1955.

CHAPTER XXXI

*The attempted reversal of Stalin's policy, leading to the
Polish and Hungarian crises of 1956*

CONFLICTS have their own dynamics, which tend to make
them self-perpetuating. In societies where feuding between
families occurs a feud may outlive the issue over which it began
and be continued by new generations that have forgotten what it
was about. Perhaps the mutual fear and hatred engendered by the
danger that each side represents to the other is enough to keep
it going.

Once the two sides had come to grips in the Cold War disengagement by either would be possible, at best, only gradually
over the years, or by the intervention of extraordinary new circumstances. Each side was in the position of the man who has a
bear by the tail. Even though the new leadership in Russia decided
that Stalin had overextended the area under Moscow's rule by
occupying the eastern half of Europe, the sudden liberation of
eastern Europe would have released hitherto suppressed forces,
inside Russia as well as outside, by which that leadership would
itself have been overthrown. Even though Washington decided
that it had been unwise to get involved in Japan, Korea, Formosa,
and Indo-China, an abrupt abandonment of these areas would have
been politically and strategically disastrous. International relations
would have gone out of control. Chaos would have ensued.

As we have seen in earlier chapters, the actions a state takes
to meet possible dangers may strengthen those dangers—may even
bring them into being where they had not existed before, thereby
justifying the actions *ex post facto*. The maintenance of a dam is
vital to hold back a body of water that had not existed before it
was built.

The international balance of power is always a dynamic
balance, a balance of forces that push actively against one
another. Every push that is set up provokes a counter-push. To
the degree that stability is achieved, it is not the static stability of
a pyramid but the dynamic stability of a Gothic cathedral, in

which the vaults, arches, and flying buttresses, thrusting against each other, thereby hold each other up in a single equilibrated structure. Abruptly remove one vault or one buttress, with its thrust, and the balance is destroyed, the whole structure collapses. It may be a delicate matter to build a Gothic cathedral; once built, however, to take it down is even more delicate.

The only safe way of ending the Cold War, when the circumstances that had brought it into being had lost their validity, would be by a gradual, reciprocal, and even reduction of the thrusts on both sides over a period that would certainly cover years. If the United States took active measures to liberate East Europe the Russians would automatically respond by tightening their hold. If, however, the behavior of the United States at last persuaded the Russians that its objectives were limited, that its policy was moderate, and that it accepted as inviolable the genuine security interests of the Soviet state, then they would be more likely to seek escape from their overextended position by a gradual disengagement—unless the American behavior appeared to represent, not the moderation of the strong but a weakness that tempted the Russians to expand their influence. Reciprocally, if Russian behavior at last persuaded the United States that the Russian objectives were limited, and that Moscow was not threatening West Europe, it would be more disposed to be limited in its own objectives and moderate in its own policy; and it would gradually be inclined to retire from West Europe, North Africa, and the Middle East. The legend of the contest between the Wind and the Sun, in which the objective was to make the man take off his overcoat, is not always inapplicable to international affairs.[1]

*   *   *

In his airgram of February 22, 1946, Kennan had written: 'Soviet internal system will now be subjected, by virtue of recent territorial expansions, to a series of additional strains which once proved severe tax on Tsardom.' The cruder view that came to prevail in Washington was that the Russian state had been immensely strengthened by the acquisition of all the populations and natural resources of East Europe—and, after 1949, of China

---

[1] In an address of November 11, 1956, Tito said that the development of independence among the satellites was being hindered by Western propaganda in favor of their liberation, which aroused Moscow's fears that, if it granted them a status similar to Yugoslavia's, 'reactionary forces' would gain control of them.

too. One may plausibly believe, however, that if Stalin's successors had spoken frankly they would have confirmed what Kennan had written.

In the second century after Christ Rome thought of itself as having suzerainty over the entire world—even though there were realms of outer darkness to which its rule did not reach in practice. (Brazil has suzerainty over large areas of Amazonian forest, inhabited by wild Indians, to which its rule does not reach in practice.) Rome's title to worldwide predominance was based on the assumption that it represented the only true civilization. In practice, however, its limited strength could extend just so far. Ancient China, similarly, had regarded itself as the suzerain of the whole earth, but this had not represented any practical danger for Europe and America, lying so far beyond its reach.

When Hadrian became Emperor of Rome in 117 it did not occur to him to abandon the claim to world domination in principle, but it was evident to him that in practice the Empire he had inherited from Trajan was dangerously overextended. He therefore set about retracting its frontiers in northern Britain and in Mesopotamia. This was the easier for him to do because no other power equal to Rome threatened its existence from beyond those frontiers.

It is evident that Stalin's successors were impressed by the overextension of the empire they had inherited as Trajan's successor had been impressed by the overextension of the empire he had inherited. They, too, set about the task of retraction, made the more difficult for them by the danger that the antagonized countries from which they withdrew would join with their powerful enemies. Their dilemma was not without precedent in history. 'What you hold,' Pericles is reported to have told the Athenians, 'is, to speak frankly, a despotism; perhaps it was wrong to take it, but to let it go is unsafe.'[2]

The difficulties and dangers of Moscow's overextension were dramatized for the new leaders by certain developments in East Europe during the months after Stalin's death. Early in June 1953 there were insurrectionary uprisings against Russian domination and the Communist regime in Czechoslovakia. In East Germany on June 24 the puppet Prime Minister, Grotewohl, made a speech in which he admitted that the flight of 'hundreds of

[2] Thucydides, Book II, Chapter 63.

thousands' of farmers to the West had caused serious food shortages. During that same month there was a spontaneous general uprising of the people in East Berlin, demanding liberation from the Russians and an end to Communist rule. This insurrection spread to cities all over East Germany. The local police forces were unable to cope with it, so that the Russians were compelled to use their own tanks and troops to put it down if East Germany was not to break away and join the West.

The new Russian leaders were confronted by the fact that the same explosive situation existed throughout their East European empire, where they were trying to hold a lid on a volcano. One can imagine the alarm among them at the possibility of Western intervention to support uprisings of the captive peoples, and at the prospect of what would happen throughout East Europe if war with the West should break out. They might have tried to deal with this danger by multiplying their means of suppression, by intensifying the reign of terror. But a reign of terror merely increases disaffection and thereby aggravates the long-term problem. The alternative was to appease the disaffected peoples by providing improved conditions of living, and by cautiously relaxing the suppressive measures to which they were being subjected. If the lid was kept tightly clamped on the volcano the pressure under it would simply increase; but if it could be lifted by small degrees over a long period then the pressure might be gradually relieved until someday, perhaps, it would be safe to take the lid off altogether. This delicate and dangerous alternative, in which the West had every reason to wish them well, was the one the new Russian leaders adopted.

Beginning in the summer of 1953, and continuing through 1955, there was a general relaxation of economic impositions on the captive populations throughout East Europe. Then, in February 1956, came Khrushchev's notable address to the 20th Party Congress. In it he not only denounced Stalin and Stalinism, he denounced the rule of the secret police, and he called for greater individual liberty, as well as for a general liberalization of government to give greater scope to debate and to the intellectual and artistic life in general.

This address was eloquent testimony to the desire of the new leadership to break with the past. If there was any hope of doing this, it was only by such a bold, clean stroke of outspoken repudiation—whatever the cost. And the cost was immense, for it discredited the Soviet Union as leader of the world Communist movement by discrediting its conduct of that leadership for a generation past. It told the Communists the world over, who had been taught to accept Moscow's direction as infallible, that for some thirty years Moscow had misled them. It told them what sheep they (and the new Russian leaders themselves, as Stalin's former henchmen) had been. After this, how could anyone again give unquestioning obedience to Moscow's orders? How could anyone again accept its leadership?[3]

In an earlier address at the 20th Congress Khrushchev had said that the main feature of the present era was 'the emergence of socialism from the bounds of a single country and its transformation into a world system.' The days of 'socialism in one country' were over, for now there were many socialist countries. This was said as a boast, but in fact it constituted the prime dilemma of Moscow and the world Communist movement in the 1950's. No longer could Moscow hope to dictate to the other Communist parties and regimes. On April 17, 1956, the Cominform was dissolved by its members because, as they announced, it had 'exhausted its function.'

Palmiro Togliatti, the powerful leader of the Italian Communist Party, summed up the situation. 'The Soviet model,' he said, 'cannot and must not any longer be obligatory. . . . The whole system becomes polycentric, and even in the Communist movement itself we cannot speak of a single guide but rather of a progress which is achieved by following paths that are often different.' In other words, the one church must now split into many churches. 'Polycentrism' was a euphemism for the fragmentation of the Communist movement.[4] Tito, who five years earlier had been the first great leader of a Communist movement to declare

---

[3] The address was secret. 'We cannot,' Khrushchev said, 'let this matter get out of the Party, especially not to the press. It is for this reason that we are considering it here at a closed Congress session . . . we should not give ammunition to the enemy; we should not wash our dirty linen before their eyes.' But it was too sensational to be kept secret long. The present generally accepted version of the address was issued by the State Department on June 4, 1956. It should be read from beginning to end, for its contents are nothing less than Shakespearian. Together with comments on it by Communist organs and spokesmen in other countries, it is available in *The Anti-Stalin Campaign and International Communism*, edited by the Russian Institute of Columbia University.

[4] The word is a contradiction in itself. How can anything have more than one center? 'Polycentrism' is a euphemism for no center at all. Togliatti's statement may be found in Russian Institute, pp. 138–9.

his independence of Moscow, and who had stood against it alone —Tito now had his triumph. Already the top leadership in Moscow had traveled to Belgrade, like the Holy Roman Emperor traveling to Canossa, and had publicly humbled itself before him, apologizing for the efforts Moscow had made under Stalin to compel his subservience.

Titoism, from now on, would become the rule in the Communist movement. The single ideological and political empire would never recover its credit. Everything was changed. The West no longer faced one mighty empire that seemed to be advancing inexorably toward world domination. Instead it now faced an empire that, in expanding, had fallen apart.

It would, however, be many years yet before the West would bring itself to recognize this, before it would begin to appreciate the implications of this triumph for Titoism. During that period it would continue to wage the Cold War along the old lines, as if nothing had happened, as if the time was still 1950.

*   *   *

The explicit discrediting of Stalinism was an implicit call for reform throughout the Communist world. To the extent that what was still said and done in that world represented Stalin's illegitimate prescriptions it could no longer be justified. The names of men whom he had condemned to disgrace or oblivion had to be restored to good fame. His self-serving falsifications of history had to be corrected. The elements of personal dictatorship associated with the 'cult of personality' had to be eliminated as well as condemned.

This posed a dilemma for the Russian leadership, which would lose control if it undertook too rapid or drastic a liberalization of a society that was far from ready for true liberalism. The dilemma was still greater when it came to the relaxation of tyrannical controls over the satellites. In surrendering to Tito, as the Russian leaders had already done at Belgrade, they had accepted the Titoist principle of equality among the socialist countries, each of which was, like Yugoslavia, to enjoy the sovereign freedom to go its own road. In principle, Moscow had renounced the Stalinist claim to the subordination and obedience of Communist regimes in other countries. In practice, however, it dared not let them go their own road because their own road might lead them into the enemy camp, with disastrous consequences for Russian security.

Considering the foreseeable consequences, then, the attempt to undo Stalinism, and especially the denunciation of Stalinism at the 20th Congress, was an extraordinary demonstration of good intentions on the part of men who supposedly represented the ultimate in cynicism. It confronted them immediately with the basic problem of all casuistry: that of how to apply ideal principles in the real world without thereby encompassing one's own destruction. In the final test, as it transpired, the Red Army would have to be used to insure that the satellite countries should not go too far along the road that Tito had taken, the road that Moscow had now officially approved.

The open rebellion against Stalinism in Moscow quickly spread to the satellites, where the old Stalinist leaders found themselves on the defensive against nationalistic and liberal forces, within the Communist ranks, that had been released by Moscow's new line. There was a general ferment in which the popular forces threatened to rise up and sweep away the despotic regimes that had been imposed upon them.

As soon as this threat became manifest, the chief concern of Moscow, and of its collaborators in the satellite regimes, was that it should not be realized. Reorganizations of the governmental and party leaderships, in accordance with the new line, could not be avoided, but they had to be prevented from going very far. After Stalinism had been publicly kicked out the front door, Moscow and its collaborators undertook to have it quietly brought in again through a rear window. For example, the Stalinist First Secretary of the Hungarian Communist Party, Matyas Rakosi, forced to resign, was replaced by his close associate, virtually his *alter ego*, Erno Gerö.

Everywhere the situation was delicate, but only in two countries, Poland and Hungary, did developments go so far as to require the intervention of the Red Army.

In Poland the anti-Stalinist reaction at last brought to power the man who had long ago established his identity as a Polish Tito. Wladyslaw Gomulka had, some years earlier, been deposed as First Secretary of the Polish Party, expelled from the Party, and imprisoned for 'nationalist deviation.' In April he was released and rehabilitated, although it was made explicit that this did not imply an endorsement of his views. In August, after an uprising of workers in Poznan had suggested the advisability of appeasing the people, he was readmitted to Party membership. The popularity of the Titoist views associated with him, his own astuteness, and his consequent political strength, were such that he now rose to predominance like a cork released below water. His emergence on top had the dramatic suddenness of a *coup d'état*, arousing an alarm in Moscow that appears to have bordered on panic. The Titoist defection of Poland, which his emergence might have betokened, would have been far more serious than that of Yugoslavia, partly because Poland was the greatest of the satellites, but chiefly because Moscow's communications with East Germany crossed its territory. If Poland broke away, East Germany would break away with it, and then what could stop East Germany from joining in a reunited Germany against Russia? No regime in Moscow could have taken a risk so alarming for the sake of an abstract principle like the right of nations to equality and independence.

The palace revolution by which Moscow's puppet regime would be replaced by Gomulka's Titoist regime was to occur at a meeting of the Central Committee of the Polish United Workers' (i.e., Communist) Party due to convene on October 19. As that date approached, it appears that tank formations of the Red Army began to move on Warsaw. Then, without warning, on the morning of the 19th the top leadership of the Soviet Union (Khrushchev, Kaganovich, Mikoyan, and Molotov) arrived in Warsaw. The meeting between the Russians and the Poles (including Gomulka) that then took place, while Russian troops were moving on Warsaw, was tense and dramatic, with shouting on both sides. Apparently the Russians had flown to Warsaw under the impression that Poland was about to defect completely to the Western camp. The attempt they made to intimidate the Polish leaders had little success. It may be, however, that the Polish leaders, for their part, were able to reassure them that, while declaring Poland's independence of Russia, they were not intending to break with it and join its enemies. Less than twenty-four hours after their dramatic descent upon Warsaw, the Russians had turned back to Moscow, and on the 20th the Central Committee was able to proceed with the business that had been so abruptly postponed.

Gomulka, as he was about to be elected First Secretary of the Polish Party, made a speech denouncing the preceding regime, affirming the right of Poland to follow models other than the Soviet Union, and asserting not only the 'equal rights' of all

Communist countries and parties, but also the 'full independence and sovereignty, and the rights of each nation to sovereign self-government.' To this he prudently added that 'Polish–Soviet relations based on the principles of equality and independence will give the Polish people such deep feelings of friendship towards the Soviet Union that any attempt to sow distrust of the Soviet Union will find no fertile soil among the Polish people.'

In the next few days Moscow accepted the Polish *fait accompli*, presumably on the basis of the limits within which the new independence would be kept, and the Red Army forces turned back to their bases.

This episode is a sort of parable that dramatizes the constant conflict between what men want and what circumstances require. Stalin's successors, with the best will in the world, could not abruptly release the countries that he had made captive. Nevertheless, Poland had, in a convulsive movement, regained a small measure of independence and sovereign dignity. Through the long hours of October 19, the Polish leaders had talked back to the rulers in Moscow as their equals, and this represented a new situation throughout East Europe that augured well.

In Chapter VII I drew a contrast between Finnish realism, with its sense of limits, and the Quixotic romanticism that had caused the Poles to disregard the limits of possibility. It should not pass unobserved now that, in the October crisis, the Poles (the public no less than the leaders) manifested such behavior as I had earlier identified with the Finns. We must conclude that they had been tempered by the disasters into which their romanticism had led them; and their new realism was the more effective because in Gomulka they had at last found what Stalin had told Churchill they needed, a Polish Paasikivi. Gomulka, by identifying himself with the Polish desire for independence of Moscow, had acquired an authority that he had then used to keep that independence from going beyond such limits as Moscow could accept. So Poland achieved for itself something approaching the qualified independence of Finland, and if that independence remained less than what the Finns enjoyed this was necessarily so, given the strategic importance that the Polish land had for Moscow.[5]

[5] A principal difference between the status of Finland and that of Poland is that the former was not compelled to embrace something called Communism. The difference was greater in appearance, however, than in reality. After the events of October, other political parties beside the Communist were allowed to exist in Poland and were

Essentially the same crisis as had been kept under control in Poland, developing at the same time in Hungary, at last went out of control. The political elements in Hungary that represented what Gomulka represented in Poland, the Titoist alternative to Stalinism, were never able to establish their authority. In the absence of such an alternative authority, the Hungarian liberation movement could not be kept within limits that Moscow could accept. Moscow had been able to accept the nominal independence and equality of Poland on condition that Poland remained faithful to its alliance with Russia.[6] It was ready to accept the nominal independence and equality of Hungary on the like condition. But the Hungarian leader who was in the position equivalent to Gomulka's, Imre Nagy, could not get the increasingly rebellious nation, which had nominally come under his authority, to subscribe to that condition. Driven by popular demand, he found himself constrained to announce, on November 1, the severance of Hungary's alliance with Russia and its claim to be regarded, from that moment, as a neutral state like Switzerland. Only by so doing could he remain in touch with the country, uniting it behind him. By so doing, however, he provoked the fatal intervention of the Red Army to put down the rebellion by brute force.

The choice that confronted Moscow, at the critical moment, was either to reassert the Stalinist dominion over Hungary by force or to see the Hungarian people overthrow Communism and make good their independence—in which case all the East Europeans would surely have undertaken to follow the successful example. The only alternative to forcible suppression, in other words, was the catastrophic withdrawal of the Iron Curtain to the Russian frontier, behind which Russia would, in effect, find itself besieged as for centuries past. In that case, history would probably record

---

given at least subordinate representation in the Polish Government. Agricultural collectivization was halted and other provisions identified with Communism were also abandoned. An alliance was made between the Government and the Roman Catholic Church, which thereafter played, quite openly, a dominant role in the Polish society. Any visitor to Poland could tell right away that it was a Catholic country, but he might be in that country a long time without finding signs of Communism.

[6] In formal terms, the alliance was the Warsaw Pact, which had been concluded between Moscow and the Communist regimes of East Europe in 1955. Because its importance was more formal than substantial, it does not merit the attention in such a history as this that it would properly have in a history concerned with institutional and diplomatic arrangements for their own sake.

that the revolt against Stalinism in Moscow had led, as by a train of fire, to the collapse of the Russian empire and of the world Communist movement. As Moscow must have seen it, a reunited Germany, allied with the Atlantic nations under the leadership of the United States, would then have threatened the very survival of the Russian state.

The Russian leaders had inherited from Stalin an explosive and unwelcome situation that they had set out to reform. They had thereby released forces that were almost beyond their control, and so were driven, at last, to desperate measures for their own salvation. The lid had been lifted a little way in Poland, after which it had been successfully held in place. Lifted a little way in Hungary, it blew off completely—whereupon it was reimposed by the Red Army, which clamped it on tighter than before. The new regime in Moscow, trying to undo a tyranny, ended by imposing a still greater tyranny. Destalinization, going too fast too far, led to restalinization—at least for the time being. The defeat of men's good intentions as a consequence of the very effort they make to carry them out is the essence of tragedy.

On November 1 the Government of Imre Nagy, having already announced its decision to hold free elections (which could result only in the overthrow of Hungarian Communism), declared Hungary's neutrality. At dawn on November 4 the Red Army attacked Budapest. For ten days the people of Budapest and of other cities, under the leadership of Communist workers' organizations, fought a hopeless battle with bare hands against Russian tanks and artillery. The Russians, having captured and broken to their will one of Nagy's principal associates, Janos Kadar, placed him at the head of a Hungarian puppet regime that owned the hostility of all elements in the Hungarian nation, Communist and anti-Communist alike. There was a month of anarchy. The barrier of the Austro-Hungarian frontier broke down. Across it streamed thousands and tens of thousands of refugees.[7]

In the end, as was inevitable, the foreign tanks triumphed over the bare fists of the native population. Quiet settled upon the land once more under a reign of police suppression. Shops opened again; the trams of Budapest returned to their rounds; little children went back to their schools to receive from intimidated teachers what passed for the heritage of human culture. Normal

[7] Before the flight was ended and the border resealed, over 195,000 Hungarians had escaped, some 2% of the entire population.

life was resumed. The slow process of secular evolution by which the Hungarians would gradually increase their independence continued after the setback as before. For a time, however, the name of Russia would be 'a dismal universal hiss' throughout the world.

In Moscow, those who were philosophically inclined must have found food for thought.

CHAPTER XXXII

The four-way division of the Cold War, manifested at the Geneva Conferences of 1955; the visit of Bulganin and Khrushchev to South Asia; the extension of the Cold War to the Middle East; and the muddle that culminated in the Suez crisis

To those who took the view that the Cold War was a contest between the good and the wicked for the mastery of the earth there could be no common ground between the two sides and the contest could end only with the total victory of one over the other. The objective of each side, in that case, must be to win it. On the other hand, if the purpose of the Cold War was simply to achieve a new international stability then both sides shared a common objective, which ought ultimately to provide a basis for agreement between them. They ought ultimately to be able to agree on terms, other than victory and defeat, by which each alike could expect to survive in reasonable security.

This difference in basic conception was fruitful of misunderstanding in Washington during the 1950's. Military men, especially, tended to feel that the Government should have a strategy for total victory in the Cold War, involving a calendar of projected offensives leading to it. Such a calendar, in the extreme form, would have a designated D-day on which the Western coalition would assume the strategic offensive against the enemy, and it would be completed by a V-day when the enemy power was finally broken. There would be a surrender scene and terms imposed by the victor. Others, recalling such historic struggles as the contest between Christendom and Islam, looked forward, rather, to a gradual resolution of the Cold War by the establishment, perhaps imperceptibly over a long period, of a stable equilibrium between the two sides, or by progressive shifts in the constellation of forces involving the gradual decentralization of power on both sides until there no longer were two sides. While the former were moved to intensify the Cold War (on Admiral Lord

Fisher's principle that 'moderation in war is imbecility'), the latter were moved to reduce its intensity toward the day when it should be no more, when men should ask one another what had ever become of it. In a convenient if slightly invidious verbal coinage, the former would come to be identified as 'hards,' the latter as 'softs,' and the public would read in the press of disputes between the two as particular issues of policy in the Cold War arose.

It was evident that the division between hards and softs existed no less in Moscow, where it tended to be equated with the distinction between those who still inclined toward Stalinism and those who had revolted from it.

These labels provide a convenient shorthand, although their application to individual persons, or in the context of particular issues, is at the risk of too crude a simplification. By his fundamental character as a mediator and a harmonizer of men President Eisenhower was clearly a soft. Secretary Dulles, on the other hand, as a man of Calvinistic disposition and an advocate, was clearly a hard. In Moscow, the relatively liberal Khrushchev was a soft, while Stalin's former confidant, Molotov, who continued as Foreign Minister until the summer of 1956, was a hard.

In a curious way, as the 1950's progressed the softs on the one side tended to become the tacit allies of the softs on the other, the hards on the one side of the hards on the other. This was because any indication of a soft policy on one side was bound to strengthen the position of the softs on the other, while hard behavior on one side strengthened the hards on the other by justifying them in their militancy.

This was exemplified in connection with the two abortive peace conferences, as we may call them, held at Geneva in 1955.

By the spring of 1955 great pressure had developed from many quarters for the convening of a 'summit' conference, a conference of heads of government, to resolve the issue of the Cold War. The successor regime in Moscow had been pressing for such a conference in accordance with its ostensible efforts to relax international tensions and establish an international regime of what it called peaceful coexistence. This met with a ready response in Western public opinion, where there was a strong disposition to believe that if, instead of their representatives, the heads of government themselves sat around the table to talk out their differences, mutual understanding and an abatement of hostility would ensue. Consequently, in May arrangements were concluded to hold at Geneva in July a conference of the American, British, French, and Russian heads of government. Since such a conference, of four days' duration only, could not possibly settle the wide range of issues that presented themselves for resolution, it was intended simply as an opportunity for the heads of government to agree on the course to be followed in more detailed negotiations that would be opened by a longer conference of the four foreign ministers to follow.

To the softs on either side, whose objective was a settlement rather than victory, these two conferences presented a hopeful prospect. For those whose objective was victory they wore a different aspect. Mr. Eisenhower might well look hopefully toward the forthcoming conferences; but Mr. Dulles would not, since he could have no expectation that the diabolical Russian empire, which had been constantly growing in its strength, would surrender at them. (Similarly, we may suppose that Messrs. Bulganin and Khrushchev[1] might be hopeful of the *détente* at which they were aiming, while Mr. Molotov would be more impressed with the unlikeliness of a Western surrender.)

There was reason for some hope of progress toward a general settlement on the basis of peaceful coexistence, if that was the objective. Russia had just agreed to withdraw from Austria, restoring the whole country to independence; it had approached the Government of the Federal German Republic (which had just joined NATO) in a move to establish normal relations with it; and it had suddenly made very large concessions to the West in the general disarmament negotiations that had for long been at a standstill. These moves, if not proof of good faith, were tokens of it that could be disregarded neither by those who wished for a settlement nor by those who, seeing no alternative to total victory, did not.

Dulles, whose course was quite different in this from Eisenhower's, appeared from the beginning to be trying to prevent any successful conferences from being held by publicly establishing that the objective of such conferences would, in effect, be Russian surrender. Immediately after the agreement to hold them he told the press that the question of Russia's East European satellites might be raised at them, and that the Russian concessions in

[1] Bulganin, as Premier, was the head of the Russian Government, although Khrushchev, as First Secretary of the Communist Party, was presumably more powerful and important.

Austria and in Yugoslavia pointed toward similar Russian re-
treats in the rest of East Europe. This line, which provoked a sharp
reaction from Moscow, was bound to strengthen the hand of
those in Moscow who maintained that, since the West was seeking
nothing less than total victory, to make any concessions to it at
all would be dangerous.

The four days of the Geneva 'summit' conference, at which
Dulles and Molotov remained in the background, brought no
substantial agreement, but they were not therefore without value.
The fact that the principal spokesmen of East and West dealt
quietly, courteously, respectfully, and humanely with each other,
instead of shouting abuse at each other like primitive warriors
about to enter battle, was of the utmost importance. This marked
an end to the unlimited violence of language that the Russians
had adopted in the fall of 1947, and that had inevitably provoked
some response in kind by the West, intensifying the whole conflict.

When the four Foreign Ministers met in October it was clear
that their positions on the main issues did not allow of an agreed
settlement. After the Russian concessions on disarmament, the
United States, for what may well be considered sound reasons,
had hardened its attitude, rejecting, now, disarmament proposals
that it had itself previously espoused. On the question of Germany,
which was the central issue between Russia and the West, it adhered to the position, clearly unacceptable to Moscow, that Germany must be reunified on the basis of terms that would allow it to
belong to the Western camp after reunification as before. Under
the circumstances one may well conclude that in 1955 it was still
too early to expect a solution of the central geographical and
strategical issues that, as the legacy of World War II, had engendered the Cold War. The best that could be hoped for (and
this was of prime importance) was the development of a tacit
understanding that the continuing struggle between East and
West would be conducted within limits of civility and moderation designed to prevent it from getting out of hand and ending in
universal desolation.

An interesting by-play at the Foreign Ministers' Conference
illustrates the implicit alliance between the hards (as between the
softs) across the battle-lines of the Cold War. After the first nine
days of negotiation, during which Molotov, reflecting the new
official attitude in Moscow, had appeared to be genuinely seeking
an agreed settlement, the Conference adjourned for three days.

Molotov took advantage of this break to return to Moscow, perhaps to seek instructions more to his liking. At the same time Dulles flew to Belgrade, where he indulged in the most provocative behavior possible. In a broadcast over the Belgrade radio, and in a statement made to the press after a meeting with Tito, he called for the liberation of Russia's East European satellites. Coming from the American Secretary of State, in Belgrade, and in the middle of the Geneva 'peace' conference, nothing could have been better calculated to support the arguments of the hards in Moscow. At the end of the three days, when he left Moscow Airport for his return to Geneva, Molotov announced happily that he was returning with 'new baggage.' From that moment he was once more the old Molotov of Stalinist days who responded negatively and with abuse to every Western proposal. When the Conference ended in total failure some ten days later, the hards on both sides could take satisfaction in the fact that the slight mollification of the Cold War produced by the meeting between the heads of government had now been undone by the foreign ministers. There is a sense in which we may say that, at the Geneva Conferences of 1955, Dulles and Molotov defeated Eisenhower and Khrushchev.

The fact that from 1955 on the historian has to think in terms of this complex four-way relationship across the battlelines of the Cold War speaks for itself. Let no one believe, however, that as early as 1955 a substantial settlement of the intractable issues involved in the Cold War would have been possible if it had not been for the hards on either side.

*   *   *

By the summer of 1955 the two sides in the Cold War appeared to have arrived at a tacit understanding that their conflict was to be kept within such limits as would obviate any extreme risk of a great nuclear war. This, essentially, was what Moscow meant by the 'peaceful coexistence' it had been calling for ever since Stalin's death. This appeared to be the significance of the Geneva 'summit' meeting.

However, while the two sides may have been in tacit agreement not to go to war over their differences, there was no question of discontinuing the conflict. It was to be carried on, still, by all means short of war; which is to say that it was to be carried on by political and economic competition. The Western allies would still pursue the objective of containment. Moscow would still strive to break out of its encirclement.

Along the original Cold War front from the Baltic to the Mediterranean, and in northeast Asia as well, there was deadlock. Throughout south Asia, however, from the eastern end of the Mediterranean through the East Indies, no stability had been achieved. Egypt, the Arab states, Pakistan, India, Burma, Indo-China, Indonesia, the Philippines—all these had just achieved their independence from their erstwhile Western masters. In varying degrees, all were inadequately prepared for self-government and responsible participation in international affairs. Like fledglings in their first flights, they fluttered high and low, almost out of control, uttering strident notes of alarm or outrage at the manifold disasters that seemed to impend. Just as Americans in the early 1950's had created the bogy of alien forces in their midst that were to blame for their failures and their insecurity, so the newly independent nations now cried out against the Western 'imperialists' from whom they had just gained their independence, denouncing the 'colonialism' of countries that had just abandoned its practice. At the same time, however, they depended on trade with those countries and, especially, on massive assistance from them if they were to survive at all. The Western governments, for their part, fearful of utter chaos across half the world, and with at least the vestiges of particular interests to protect where they had once invested so heavily, tried still to feed the clamorous fledglings that pecked at them in fury. It was an awkward relationship, lending itself to exploitation by Moscow.

We should recall that in Leninist doctrine, and to a large extent in traditional Western thinking as well, the Western powers lived by the imperialistic exploitation of their Asian and African empires. Only by mulcting the suffering masses of Asia and Africa, as by mulcting the proletarian masses at home, had the capitalist rulers of the West been able so far to keep themselves in power. If, now, they should be finally ousted from what had been their overseas empires, their power would collapse at home as well as abroad. Then the revolution foreseen by Marx and Lenin would come all over the world, and with it the catastrophic end of capitalism.

An irresistibly beckoning opportunity now appeared to offer itself to the men in Moscow. It was in south Asia that the Western lines, elsewhere unyielding, could be outflanked. The Russians had only to say to the south Asians: your Western enemies are our enemies too; we, too, are outraged by their imperialism; and we are the ones who can enable you, by training and material assistance, to dispense with their humiliating presence in your midst. Turn to us and be saved.

In November 1955 Prime Minister Bulganin and First Secretary Khrushchev embarked for India, Burma, and Afghanistan. Arrived in south Asia, they threw themselves into their salesman's role with the enthusiasm of inexperience. In their public addresses and statements they bewailed the sufferings of their Asian hosts under the yoke of the Western imperialists. Mr. Khrushchev commiserated with the Burmese because the English 'call you savages and barbarians.' The English had 'sat on the necks' of the Burmese, he said, and 'robbed them of the last piece of bread.' Marshal Bulganin, in the capital of Kashmir, undertook the role of spokesman for the Kashmiris, assuring his auditors, some of whom must have been astonished to hear it, that the Kashmiri people were loyally devoted to the Republic of India rather than to the Pakistani ally of the American war-mongers. Both men repeatedly made clear how the Soviet peoples, too, had suffered at the hands of the Anglo-Saxon militarists. In Bombay Mr. Khrushchev revealed that the Western powers had 'started the Second World War' by sending 'the troops of Hitlerite Germany against our country.' Like the Asians, the Russians, feeling the same reverence for the memory of Mahatma Gandhi, were outraged at the West's addiction to aggressive war and militarism. NATO, Marshal Bulganin explained to a joint session of the Indian Houses of Parliament, was an aggressive organization. (In Bangalore, however, Mr. Khrushchev departed momentarily from his role as a follower of the Mahatma to announce with undisguised pride the explosion by the Soviet Union of a hydrogen bomb 'of unprecedented power,' equivalent to 'millions of tons of conventional explosives.')

Prime Minister Nehru of India finally felt the need to point out in public, and in the presence of his guests, that India maintained friendly relations with England and the other Western powers— even while, like the Soviet Union, it deplored their taste for nuclear weapons and military blocs.

Messrs. Bulganin and Khrushchev also undertook, in terms that were generally vague, to give their hosts technical assistance in industrialization and agricultural development; and they entered into trade-agreements with them.

The Asian journey of the two Russian leaders revealed that, if there was a certain amount of crudeness on one side in the Cold War, generally identified with Mr. Dulles, there was crudeness on the other as well. In India and Burma, at least, the local leaders were constantly embarrassed and sometimes seriously disturbed by the behavior of their guests. *The Statesman* of Calcutta, representing a consensus in the Indian press, pointed out that Prime Minister Nehru, on his official visit to Russia earlier in the year, had conducted himself with a decorum, a dignity, and a propriety that the Russian visitors had not shown in India. Signs of barbarism in their guests caused misgivings among the intellectually subtle and refined heirs to the world's oldest civilizations.

* * *

As NATO had been the organization for the containment of the Communist empire from the Baltic to the Mediterranean, so SEATO had been created to serve the same purpose from the Philippines to Pakistan. We have already seen that it was hardly more than a nominal barrier to Communist expansion; but as a solemn legal instrument it was not without importance in the eyes of the lawyers who, especially in the West, play a dominant and distinguished role in shaping the conceptions and the conduct of international politics. To complete the system of containing alliances by closing the gap between SEATO and NATO, an alliance for the containment of Russia in the Middle East was devised in 1955. The Baghdad Pact (later the Central Treaty Organization or CENTO) comprised Pakistan, which was the westernmost Asian member of SEATO, and Turkey, the easternmost member of NATO. In between, it had Iran, Britain, and Iraq (which, however, withdrew after it underwent an anti-Western revolution in 1958), while the United States maintained a close but informal association with it.

The shifting sands of the Arab world, however, offered no reliable foundation on which to erect political and military defenses. The Western powers and Russia, alike, would find that, where they were able to make alliances with the Arab-speaking states, they could not count on those alliances. A local political convulsion might at any moment undo all.

The ablest and by much the most powerful leader in the Arab world was the Egyptian dictator, Gamal Abdel Nasser (who also found that his attempt to build solidarity among the Arabs was like writing in the desert sands what the first gust of wind would obliterate). Nehru had made a high moral virtue of not taking sides in the Cold War—however much his anti-Western animus and the influence of his environment impeded his efforts to achieve in practice the impartiality to which he adhered in principle. Nasser tried to follow essentially the same policy, but simply as a matter of *Realpolitik.* He did not fail to recognize how advantageous it was to be the object of competitive wooing by both sides, each ready with gifts. His experience was that he could generally draw offers of largesse from Washington and Whitehall by letting it seem that he was attracted toward Moscow; and he had reason to think that he could draw largesse from Moscow by intimating that, under certain circumstances, he might be prepared to break with the Western 'imperialists.'

The game he played had, however, its delicate and dangerous features. For one thing, his position as the principal Arab leader required him to commit himself to the only objective on which all the Arabs could unite, that of destroying the state of Israel in their midst. The powerful political support that Israel had in the United States, and the deep American commitment to its survival, made it virtually impossible for the United States to supply Nasser's Egypt with any significant quantity of arms that would, inevitably, be pointed at Israel. For these arms he turned, then, to the Communist camp. In September 1955 he was able to announce the conclusion of an agreement for the large-scale purchase of a variety of military equipment from Czechoslovakia.

The United States and Britain had long been considering whether to assist Egypt in a vast project for economic development based on the construction of a high dam at Aswan on the Upper Nile. The project did not seem promising to them and they were reluctant to become involved in it. But now Russia had embarked on an aggressive campaign to replace them in the Middle East as in South Asia, and the Egyptians were intimating that they could obtain the assistance needed to build the dam from Moscow if the West should refuse it. On December 17, then, the United States and Britain announced their decision to offer Egypt financial support for the first stage in the construction of the dam. On July 17, 1956, a variety of complications having been worked out, Egypt accepted the offer. Three days later, it was brusquely withdrawn.

The reasons for this sudden about-face will not be fully known until the relevant documents are published. It may be that Nasser had gone too far in his insulting denunciations of the Western powers and his ostentatious cultivation of Moscow. The presumed fact that future Egyptian cotton crops, needed to finance Egypt's economic development, had been mortgaged to pay for the Czechoslovakian arms was certainly a factor. Pro-Israel sentiment in the American Congress, plus the opposition of the American cotton states to assistance for a development that would improve the competitive position of Egyptian cotton, must have played their part. It is possible that the brusqueness of the withdrawal, and its timing, represented a deliberate attempt to bring about Nasser's fall by striking a blow at his prestige.

To save himself, Nasser had to react quickly and effectively. Within a week, therefore, he astonished the world by seizing and nationalizing the Suez Canal, the vital, internationally-owned waterway that traversed Egyptian territory. With the revenue from the Canal, he announced, 'we shall not look to Britain and the United States for their $70 million grant. . . . Egypt will build the Aswan Dam without pressure from any nation.'

The consternation of the Atlantic powers, caught by surprise as they were, was complete. Not only did the so-called 'life-line' of Britain's remaining empire in Asia pass through the Suez Canal, the petroleum from the Persian Gulf that kept the wheels turning in West Europe all came by way of the Canal. Nasser had closed his hand upon an essential artery supplying the economic life of West Europe. No one believed that Egypt, by itself, even with the best intentions, would be able to operate the Canal and keep traffic moving through it—and the best intentions could not be taken for granted. The West felt it had to do something.

There is no need to go into the ensuing history of blundering and bad faith that marked the exchanges between Washington and Whitehall. The British, preparing to take a strong line, thought they had the commitment of the United States, through Dulles, to join them in taking it. Proceeding on that basis, they found themselves, as they thought, betrayed and deserted by the United States. Dulles, having ostensibly taken one position at meetings in London to decide on common action, took a contrary position after his return to the United States, where a presidential election campaign made the contrary position opportune. In desperation then, the British Government under Sir Anthony Eden decided to reassert the former independence of British imperial policy by a bold stroke of which Washington should not be informed in advance. The British and French Governments now worked together in conspiratorial intimacy to prepare and execute this stroke. The Israeli Government, it is clear, also had a part in their plot.

On October 29 a long course of quarreling and skirmishing between Israel and its Arab neighbors culminated in the launching by Israel of an armed invasion of Egypt. The next day Israel and Egypt received an Anglo-French ultimatum demanding that, within twelve hours, both withdraw their forces to a distance of ten miles from the Canal (only the Egyptians had forces within ten miles of the Canal), and that Egypt accept an Anglo-French occupation of key points along the Canal. When the Egyptians refused to comply with the latter demand, Anglo-French forces attacked and invaded Egypt.

Taken quickly, the Anglo-French military action might have presented the rest of the world with a *fait accompli* before there was time to react. It was, however, delayed, and during the delay such overwhelming pressure was brought from all quarters to bear on Britain, especially, that the British Government found itself faced with the alternative of abandoning the entire enterprise or taking the consequences in the form of a financial disaster, a domestic political convulsion, the break-up of the Commonwealth, and what looked as if it might be a permanent rupture with the United States. Under the circumstances, it had no choice but to abandon the enterprise.

Moscow, which was at the time in the midst of the Hungarian crisis, was slow to react. On November 5, however, Prime Minister Bulganin sent a letter to Eden and another to the French Prime Minister, Mollet. In the letter to Eden he wrote: 'In what position would Britain have found herself if she had been attacked by more powerful States possessing every kind of modern destructive weapon? There are countries which need not have sent a navy or air force to the coasts of Britain but could have used other means, such as rocket techniques.' In the letter to Mollet he asked: 'What would be the position of France if she were attacked by other States having at their disposal modern and terrible means of destruction? . . . The Soviet Government is fully determined to apply force in order to crush the aggressors and restore peace in the East.'

Here was the first open threat by Moscow to use rocket-borne nuclear weapons against the countries of the West unless they conformed to its demands. At this date the threat was limited in its effectiveness by the general confidence that Russia did not yet have a nuclear armament capable of deterring an American nuclear response to a Russian attack on West Europe. What was ominous about the threat was simply the demonstration that, when Moscow did come to have such an armament, it would feel no compunction about threatening to use it on the free countries of Europe unless they submitted to its will. The day when it would, in principle, be in a position to do this effectively was rapidly approaching. Anxiety began to grip people, especially in Britain, where they felt themselves totally vulnerable to such an attack as the Russians were prepared to threaten.

CHAPTER XXXIII

Russian triumphs in the arms race, leading to a more dynamic diplomacy in 1958

Ever since 1945 dominant opinion in the West had held that the time was limited in which a settlement of the conflict with Russia would have to be achieved if general disaster was to be averted. Once Russia had a nuclear capability of its own, to neutralize that of the West, the West would never again be in as strong a bargaining position. In the most alarmist view, which had much plausibility, once Russia had achieved such a capability the defenses of the West would no longer be tenable. The United States could no longer be counted on to respond to a Russian invasion of West Europe by a nuclear attack on Russia when its own cities were hostages to Russia. So the Russian empire would expand over the Atlantic world, and over Asia, as the Roman empire had expanded at the beginning of the Christian era. When, in 1949, Russia produced its first atomic explosion years earlier than had been expected, the West, more than ever, felt itself living with a time-bomb.

No one outside Moscow could know precisely when Russia would have achieved a nuclear capability sufficient to match and deter that of the United States. There were signs that this point was approaching in 1955, and it appears to have been reached in 1958. During the three or four intervening years the world outside Russia awaited it with the most profound anxiety and pessimism.

In 1953, less than six months after Stalin's death, Russia had exploded its first hydrogen bomb. By the summer of 1955 it had in operation a heavy bomber roughly equivalent to the American B-52, which had a range of some 6,000 miles. This meant that American cities were at last within range of Russian hydrogen bombs, although it is evident that Russia had not as yet acquired a sufficient force to undertake the widespread devastation of the United States. That would have required a great many long-range bombers carrying a great many bombs, since it was to be expected that a large proportion of the bombers would be shot down before reaching their targets. Although Moscow presumably had, now, the capacity to destroy the cities of West Europe, the American ability to retaliate on Russian cities would continue to be an effective deterrent as long as that ability could still be exercised with a high degree of impunity. When that time was over, however, a Russian diplomacy based on the threat of nuclear attack might logically be expected to produce the surrender of one free country after another. Would the NATO alliance be able to hold together, for example, in the face of an ultimatum from Moscow that made the nuclear destruction of any of its European members the alternative to compliance with some limited demand, such as the withdrawal of Western garrisons from Berlin? Would not the West find itself surrendering piecemeal under the repeated application of such a threat? Russian diplomacy was well known for what was called 'the salami tactic,' the tactic of not attempting to achieve its objective at one stroke but of taking it, rather, slice by slice.

It is no wonder that, with this sword of Damocles suspended over their heads, the members of the Western alliance, especially its European members, had been anxious, in 1955, to achieve a relaxation of the Cold War tensions, if possible a settlement.

*   *   *

Hòw are we to judge Russian attitudes and intentions during this period that represented the twilight of the Western nuclear monopoly?

We must recall that, in the determination of what states actually do in their foreign relations, the pressing demands of the present tend to override the theoretical appeals of more-or-less distant futures, with their imagined opportunities or dangers.

Stalin's death in 1953 had introduced a period in which Moscow was less able and less inclined than it had been to conduct a militant foreign policy. The removal of the authority that the Russian people had associated with Stalin's name caused his collective successors to concentrate anxiously on the domestic scene. Their collective leadership was, in itself, unstable. In the absence of a firm constitutional framework for such leadership, those who shared it were bound to find themselves in a competition that would end only when one of them emerged victorious. So the First Triumvirate in Rome had eventuated in the dictatorship of

Julius Caesar, the Second in the dictatorship of Augustus. The period of collective leadership that followed Stalin's death was, essentially, an interregnum. It was to continue until 1957, when the single leader would emerge at last in the person of Khrushchev. During this interregnum the inner politics of the Kremlin were bound to preoccupy the competing leaders to such a degree that a militant foreign policy would have been difficult.

It was in June 1957, at a meeting of the Central Committee of the Party, that the contest between the rivals came to a head. In the outcome, Molotov, Malenkov, and Kaganovich were removed from their posts as Deputy Premiers and expelled both from the Presidium and the Central Committee of the Party.[1] After this, although he never became a complete dictator like Stalin, Khrushchev's primacy was clearly established, to be formalized, at last, in March 1958, when he took Bulganin's place as Prime Minister, thereby making himself the official head of the Government as well as of the Party.[2]

By the middle of 1958, then, Moscow was once more in a position to conduct a dynamic foreign policy. The very fact that Khrushchev did not wield an absolute personal power as Stalin had would, indeed, prove a spur to such dynamism. As all Latin American history shows, the leader whose position is not solidly established is always tempted to strengthen it by aggressiveness and resounding successes in the foreign field. Unlike Stalin, Khrushchev appears to have held his position at the summit of the Soviet society as much by political cajolery as by intimidation. He did not, for instance, seek to make examples of his defeated rivals by taking their lives, by casting them into dungeons, or by sending them to hard labor in Siberia. He depended, if not on the positive support of the top leadership in which he was *primus inter pares*, then on its collective unwillingness to undertake his downfall. This meant that he had to make a record of success rather

---

[1] The main charge against them was that they had set up an 'anti-party group.' Molotov was also accused of obstructing the foreign policy of peaceful coexistence. This latter charge was repeated by Khrushchev in a speech of July 6, in which he said that Molotov, preferring the policy of 'tightening the screw,' had been 'obstructing the measures for easing international tension and promoting world peace.' In Russian history since 1917, however, it has happened that a rising leader, having overcome his opponent by accusing him of error in the policies he advocated, has then felt free to adopt those same policies as his own.

[2] In November 1958 Khrushchev publicly identified Bulganin as having been a member of the 'anti-party group,' along with Molotov, Malenkov, and Kaganovich.

than of failure, for in the latter case the top leadership would at last find it imperative to replace him.

The emergence of a single leader at last, in 1958, coincided ominously with Russia's acquisition of a full nuclear capability to match that of the United States. The imminence of this acquisition had been dramatically revealed to the West on October 4, 1957, when Moscow was able to announce the launching of the first man-made earth satellite ('sputnik' in Russian) by means of a carrier rocket. A rocket capable of putting such a satellite into orbit would also be capable of delivering a nuclear warhead with considerable accuracy to any target in the United States.

A month later Russia put a second and much larger satellite into orbit around the earth, this one carrying a dog as passenger.

Not since the Communist attack on South Korea had the American people suffered such a frightening surprise. What the two *sputniks* demonstrated was that, in a vital aspect of the arms race, Russia had unexpectedly got ahead of the United States. It had been able, ahead of the United States, to produce rockets with a thrust amply sufficient for intercontinental ballistic missiles (I.C.B.M's.), and to direct them with astonishing accuracy.[3] This was alarming in itself, proclaiming the day when Russia would have on its own soil any number of I.C.B.M's., aimed at targets in the United States, while the latter would still be depending chiefly on its vulnerable and obsolescent B-52 bombers plus medium or intermediate-range ballistic missiles (M.R.B.M's. or I.R.B.M's.) deployed in ships or on the soil of allies who might, as the danger to themselves increased, be disposed to withdraw their cooperation.[4] What was equally alarming to the American public was the demonstration that Russia had developed the advanced scientific and technological capability that the achievement revealed. President Eisenhower, in a broadcast of November

[3] The accuracy required to put a package into a predetermined orbit around the earth was of the order that would be required to land a package of thermonuclear explosive on a city several thousand miles distant. The comment had been made by American experts that the problem of intercontinental delivery by missiles was less that of giving a missile sufficient thrust than that of hitting the right continent. As was not the case with the long-range bombers that had hitherto been the only means of intercontinental delivery, the defender could have no effective way of interfering with the passage of an I.C.B.M. to prevent it from reaching its target.

[4] The first successful firing of an American I.C.B.M., the Atlas, would carry it several hundred miles on December 17, 1957. On January 31, 1958, the United States would have its own first successful launching of an earth satellite—but the weight of 'Explorer I' would be less than 3% that of 'Sputnik II.'

13, admitted that 'the Soviet Union now has in the combined category of scientists and engineers a greater number than the United States, and is producing graduates in these fields at a much faster rate.' To many persons, in their secret hearts, it began to look as if the Soviet Union was the country of the future.

The unpleasant surprise produced by the Russian *sputniks* inaugurated a long period of alarm in the West. That Russia would ultimately achieve a rough nuclear parity with the United States had long been accepted, but no one had expected that it would suddenly achieve a 'break-through,' gain an advance on the United States that might assure its victory in the Cold War either by a diplomacy that compelled retreat in response to its nuclear superiority, or by the actual use of that superiority to destroy the power of a United States that had allowed itself to fall into helplessness.

What now confronted the West was the prospect of what everyone called 'the missile gap.' Russia, the experts agreed, was already so far ahead of the United States in the development of I.C.B.M's. that it was now too late to avoid a period in which it would enjoy a decisive superiority. During this period, which would begin about 1961, Moscow would be irresistibly tempted to destroy the power of the United States by a surprise attack that disarmed it at one stroke.[5]

The American nuclear armament was, and for the best part of a decade would continue to be, vulnerable to surprise attack. An important part of it consisted of long-range bombers at known airfields in the United States. Russia's I.C.B.M's., when they were ready, could presumably destroy a major portion of them on the ground. Another important part of the deterrent consisted of equally vulnerable medium-range bombers on airfields from Britain to Turkey, and in the Far East. Another part, just now being developed, consisted of Thor and Jupiter I.R.B.M's., also at known bases about the periphery of Eurasia.

[5] The situation moved President Eisenhower to appoint the so-called 'Gaither Committee' to report on the military balance between the United States and Russia. In its report (the general contents of which became known in spite of official secrecy) it foresaw that Russia would be able to launch a successful disarming and city-destroying attack on the United States by late 1959, using a hundred I.C.B.M.'s with thermonuclear warheads. This prediction, together with the associated prediction of the 'missile gap,' was based on the assumption that the Russians would realize the missile production of which they were thought capable. In 1961, after years of living with the nightmare, it transpired that they had not realized it, that the prediction of the 'missile gap' had in fact been a false alarm.

Some missiles were on aircraft carriers and submarines that could be tracked. In the years to come, Atlas and Titan I.C.B.M's. would be deployed in the United States, but they would be as vulnerable as the long-range bombers to a disarming surprise attack. Their fuel was liquid oxygen, which could be loaded into them only immediately before their dispatch, at the cost of a delay that would give the Russians time to destroy them. Not until the middle 1960's, when solid-fueled missiles became operational—land-based Minuteman I.C.B.M's. and Polaris I.R.B.M's. to be fired from submerged submarines—not until then would the United States have an essentially invulnerable deterrent.[6] Not until then would the 'missile gap' be closed—but by then there might no longer be a United States of America.

Even when the United States did have a full complement of operational Thor, Jupiter, Atlas, and Titan missiles, one might be sure that the closed nature of the Russian society, by contrast with the open societies of the West, would give Moscow a decisive advantage. For Russian intelligence, operating in open societies, would almost surely be able to locate every bomber and missile base, while Western intelligence could be less sure of locating the bomber and missile bases in the vast territory occupied by Russia.[7] Moreover, an all-out surprise attack on Russia would be constitutionally difficult, if not impossible, for the United States to undertake, and secrecy in preparing such an attack would hardly be feasible. The Soviet Union, for its part, would have no like difficulties.

In any case, with 1958 we enter the period of what an American strategic expert aptly called 'the delicate balance of terror.'[8] During this period each side would hold in its hands an armament with which it could, one supposed, destroy the other in one cataclysmic stroke. The supreme advantage, under the circumstances, would lie with the side that struck first, for only by so

[6] The Minuteman and Polaris missiles would be in a constant state of readiness. Upon word that enemy missiles were approaching, the former could be dispatched before the enemy missiles arrived. The latter, moving at speeds up to twenty knots along the bottom of the Arctic Ocean, the North Sea, and the Atlantic, in atomic-powered submarines that could remain submerged for weeks, would presumably be impossible targets.

[7] Apparently the chief device for this purpose was a swift reconaissance airplane, the U-2, which could silently cross the breadth of Russia at 65,000 feet altitude, taking photographs.

[8] See article by Albert Wohlstetter.

doing could it hope to destroy, in major part, the other side's capacity for retaliation. Consequently, if tensions between the two should begin to rise sharply neither would feel that it could afford to take the risk, by itself waiting to strike, that the other would get in the first blow, which would be final. Here, however, the constitutional obstacles would weigh heavily against the United States.

The situation appeared to be even worse than this, however, for Russia, according to the accepted theory of the 'missile gap,' would through a period of years have a decisive advantage over the West in its means of delivering the great thermonuclear explosives.

Under such circumstances, could the United States still be expected to fight for Berlin or West Europe? In another crisis, with tensions mounting, with the Russians under increasing compulsion to launch a pre-emptive strike in good time, would the United States still insist on their containment? Could the nations of West Europe and the Mediterranean continue to rely on its protection?

The position of America's European allies was awkward. Simply because American bombers and American missiles were based on their soil, they were bound to be targets in any surprise attack by Russia. What would be left of England after, say, a three hours' bombardment by thermonuclear weapons? What would be left of Turkey after a Russian attack? What would be left of West Germany? Of France? Of Italy? All these countries were, now, exceedingly vulnerable to a Russian diplomacy that threatened nuclear destruction.

It is clear that Khrushchev and his associates were no less aware than their antagonists in the West of the new possibilities that the acquisition of a full nuclear capability were opening to their diplomacy. They now seemed like men who, after many years in the Valley of the Shadow of Death, had at last reached the far side. For a dozen years they had lived in mortal fear that the United States would use its nuclear armament to strike down the Soviet state before it could develop a like armament of its own. It could hardly have seemed likely to men of their experience and ideological outlook that the 'capitalist imperialists' would not use their nuclear monopoly, while they still had it, in a preventive attack that would destroy the centers of Russian authority. The only hope had been that popular sentiment for peace, together with the threat that the Red Army posed for West Europe, would deter them. It must have seemed a precarious hope. On it, however, they had come through. Now, for the first time in its existence, the Soviet Union had a weapon that virtually insured it against deliberate attack. The 'capitalist imperialists' had waited too long.

The note of relief and exultation is unmistakable in Khrushchev's utterances about this time. Safe at last! he seems to be saying. At last Soviet Russia can march forward, the promise of world Communism can be realized.

Under Stalin Moscow had publicly given the impression that it did not regard nuclear weapons as having the decisive importance that the West attached to them. This, presumably, was slyness on its part, designed to limit the prestige that the United States derived from its nuclear monopoly and, perhaps, to cover up its own all-out program to break it. Following his death, however, when it was necessary to defend a foreign policy of caution and conciliation, Moscow had, after some internal bickerings between the hards and the softs, come to espouse the view that, in the nuclear age, the resort to general war was no longer a realistic option. Lenin had predicted that, in the death throes of capitalism, one or more great and devastating wars must inevitably occur; but it seemed only too evident in the 1950's that the Communist society of Russia was no more likely than the capitalist societies of the West to survive even one such war. Khrushchev had therefore amended Lenin's prophecy by making 'inevitability' a matter of degree. 'War,' he had told the 20th Party Congress in 1956, 'is not fatalistically inevitable.' [9] He all but said in so many words, on this and later occasions, that if, by not giving extreme provocation to the United States, it could be dissuaded from launching a preventive war until Russia had developed its own deterrent, then the worldwide triumph of Communism would come without war because the capitalist world would have let the time for a preventive war go by. The socialist camp would have become too strong to be fought. Now, at last, the day had come in which Moscow, safe behind its nuclear shield, could conduct a dynamic diplomacy before which the Western alliance would have to give way. The forebodings of the West were matched by a sort of exultation in Moscow.

At the end of the last chapter we saw how, in the Suez crisis of

[9] In a later statement he was to find that even a 'fatal' inevitability could get over being so. 'A new world war,' he wrote, 'is no longer a fatal inevitability.'

1956, Moscow had, albeit in a gingerly fashion, threatened England and France with nuclear attack. It had waited to do so until the situation had developed to the point at which the two countries were going to have to retreat anyway, and then it had done so only in terms that limited both risk and commitment on its part. The time was still early for an outspoken and convincing diplomacy of nuclear threat.

The launching of the first *sputnik*, on October 4, 1957, apparently encouraged Moscow to resort, five days later, to a somewhat more explicit threat.

Early in the year the constant conspiracies and changing combinations of Arab politics had brought Syria into an increasingly hostile attitude toward Turkey and the West. There was fear in the West that Syria, with its strategic control of a major pipeline from the Iraqui oilfields, was about to become a Russian satellite. Suddenly, in September, Moscow charged that Turkey, acting as catspaw for the United States, was preparing to invade Syria for the purpose of overthrowing its pro-Russian government. Then, five days after the *sputnik* launching, Khrushchev gave an interview to James Reston of *The New York Times* in which he claimed that Turkey, at the behest of the United States, was massing troops on the Syrian border in preparation for an American-sponsored invasion. 'If war breaks out,' he said, 'we are near Turkey and you [the United States] are not. When the guns begin to fire the rockets can begin flying, and then it will be too late to think about it.'

In a letter of October 12 to the British Labor Party, then in the opposition, Khrushchev wrote:

One cannot ignore the fact that Britain is a member of the North Atlantic bloc, and a military gamble by Turkey and the United States against Syria would in effect predetermine Britain's participation in it. Any extension of the conflict around Syria may plunge Britain into a new devastating war, with all its terrible consequences for the population of the British Isles.

The population of the British Isles was already becoming only too aware of what the consequences of Britain's continuing association with the United States might be, now that an increasingly aggressive Moscow had the means of neutralizing the American deterrent, on which Britain depended for its protection, and turning Britain itself into a radioactive desert at one stroke.

The British Isles, with or without American bases, would be a target because the British had developed a nuclear armament of their own, with bombers for the delivery of atomic and thermonuclear bombs. The actual deployment and use of this armament had been integrated with the deployment and use of the American armament, but as long as it existed England was an essential target, and utterly vulnerable.

Under the circumstances it is not surprising or altogether discreditable that a public movement to remove Britain from the firing-line got under way. The most conspicuous of the organizations formed for the purpose was the Campaign for Nuclear Disarmament (C.N.D.) with which some of the most distinguished scientists, artists, religious leaders, and intellectuals in England associated themselves. The objective was to have England rid itself, unilaterally, of its nuclear armament, and contract out of its alliance with the United States. If, by abandoning the general defense, of which its own was a part, it should ultimately fall captive to Moscow and be added to its satellite empire, that was still preferable to annihilation. 'Better Red than Dead' became the slogan.[10]

During the following four or five years (the period of 'the delicate balance of terror') there would be like stirrings in most of the countries so dangerously allied with the United States, and in the United States itself. The fact that powerful and conspicuous minorities in the West were advocating surrender, in response to Moscow's nuclear diplomacy, could only encourage Moscow to intensify it in the hope of thereby breaking up the Western alliance and its defenses.

In November 1958 Khrushchev announced that the time had now come for the occupying powers to withdraw from Berlin, handing the city over to Moscow's East German satellite, the German Democratic Republic (G.D.R.). If, at the end of six months (i.e., by May 27, 1959), the West had not reached an agreement with Moscow on this, Moscow would act without the West. It would turn over to the G.D.R. control of the West's access routes to Berlin, and if the West then attempted to use

[10] The slogan was surely right in terms of its premise, which was surely wrong. The people who adopted it had persuaded themselves that 'Red' and 'Dead' were the only alternatives. A broader view was taken by the governments of the Western alliance (including the British) whose objective might have been summed up by: 'Neither Red nor Dead.'

them without the G.D.R.'s consent Moscow would support the G.D.R. Force would be met by force. A series of such threats was brought to a climax on Christmas day, when Foreign Minister Gromyko said before the Supreme Soviet in Moscow that 'any provocation in West Berlin,' or any attempt at 'aggressive actions against the German Democratic Republic,' could start 'a big war, in the crucible of which millions upon millions of people would perish and which would bring devastation incomparably more serious than the last world war. The flames of war would inevitably reach the American continent. . . .'

The United States, Great Britain, and France had been handed an ultimatum, giving them six months to decide whether they would withdraw from Berlin or fight Russia.

CHAPTER XXXIV

The resumption of Moscow's attempt to capture West Berlin

THE moment that had for so many years been dreaded in anticipation had come at last. Having provided itself with a nuclear armament of its own to neutralize that of the West, Russia could presumably move forward with impunity, now, at points like Berlin where the West had little if any local strength.

It is not hard to see why Moscow was impatient to eliminate the Western presence in Berlin. Khrushchev described it as a bone in Russia's throat. More than just an annoyance, it represented an acute and constant danger, threatening Moscow's control over East Germany and thus over its whole satellite empire.

Since the first establishment of the occupation regimes, the population of East Germany had been escaping to West Germany in such numbers as to raise the question of how much longer the East German society could continue to function. From 1949, when records began to be kept, to the end of 1958, 2,188,000 East Germans had escaped into West Germany—out of a total population, in 1949, of some 17·5 million. The flight of doctors, dentists, pharmacists, and teachers was threatening breakdowns in the essential services that depended on them. The flight of farmers was threatening a crisis in food-production. The whole economy of East Germany was being undermined.

In 1958 the East German authorities succeeded in virtually sealing off the long frontier between the two Germanys by establishing a forbidden zone along it, bounded by barbed wire, surveyed from watch-towers, and patroled by police dogs. Still, however, the escape-route through Berlin remained open. Any East Germans who succeeded in traveling to East Berlin, on one pretext or another, could then take the S-Bahn (the underground and elevated railway) to West Berlin and freedom. The East German plain-clothes police were constantly removing passengers from the trains going to East Berlin or from the S-Bahn, and many of those removed were put to forced labor; but still the wholesale escapes continued, with all they implied for the destabilization of the satellite empire.

354

To Khrushchev and his associates it must have seemed that now, at last, they had the means to put an end to this uncontrolable situation with which they had had to live for a decade. At the same time, and by the same means, they could break out of the military encirclement that the West called 'containment.' For now that the United States could presumably no longer protect its European allies by the deterrent threat that its nuclear monopoly had hitherto enabled it to pose, those allies would find the risk of continuing to hold their places in the forces of encirclement too great. Whether in Berlin or the eastern Mediterranean, the members of NATO could be expected to break ranks before a Russian diplomacy that offered the threat of what had now become an irresistible force.

The garrisons of the three Western powers in Berlin totaled only some 11,000 men. They were more than a hundred miles inside what had to be regarded as enemy territory, surrounded by hostile forces estimated at 550,000 men. Access to Berlin on the ground was through narrow gateways held by the Russians, who checked all traffic in either direction and, by frequent delaying and harrassing tactics, demonstrated how easily they could close them. The only access by air was along three 'air corridors,' and the Western aircraft that plied them were buzzed by Russian fighter planes in order to display their helplessness. Developments in electronics, available to the Russians, would prevent any repetition of the 'air-lift' that had kept the city supplied during the Berlin Blockade of 1948–1949. President Eisenhower was merely acknowledging the obvious when, in a press conference on March 11, 1959, he said: 'We are certainly not going to fight a ground war in Europe. What good would it do to send a few more thousands or indeed a few divisions of troops to Europe? With something like . . . 175 Soviet divisions in that neighborhood [i.e., the neighborhood of Berlin and East Germany] why in the world would we dream of fighting a ground war?'[1] If the West

---

[1] NATO had only 21 divisions. A reporter asked the President whether, if the United States would not fight a ground war, it would fight a nuclear war. He replied that he did not know 'how you could free anything with nuclear weapons.' This, implying that the United States would not fight a nuclear war either, provoked a further question to which he replied: 'I didn't say that nuclear war is a complete impossibility.' The President could not say that the United States would not fight for West Berlin without thereby encouraging the Russians to proceed with its seizure, but he could not say that yes, it would fight for Berlin, without thereby alarming the European allies and public opinion everywhere.

was going to fight a real war for Berlin the only kind it could fight would be a general nuclear war in which the big cities on both sides of the Atlantic would be targets.

During the months of the Berlin crisis that began with the Russian ultimatum of November 27, 1958, each side took the position that if a war started over Berlin it would be the other side that started it. On December 11, in an official statement, Moscow asserted that 'any attempt to force a way into Berlin,' after it had handed over the controls to the East German regime, would be regarded as 'an attack on the German Democratic Government.' Such an attack would lead to a 'military conflict,' the extension of which into a general war involving 'the most modern means of annihilation, including nuclear and rocket weapons,' it would be 'hardly possible' to avoid. On February 18 President Eisenhower stated that if any attempt was made to prevent the Western powers from carrying out their responsibilities to the people of West Berlin 'it will be somebody else using force,' not the Western powers.

To maintain the independence of West Berlin the three Western allies would have to keep open the overland communications with it. After May 27, if it carried out its threat, Moscow would hand over the control of those communications to the East German regime, which the allies did not recognize and with which they had no agreement, as they did with Moscow, for access to Berlin. Then if the East Germans closed the gates, simply lowering the barriers across the access roads at the frontier, what would the allies do? Would they claim that it was the Communists who had initiated the use of force by lowering the barriers? Would they put a tank at the head of a column of troops and break through a barrier? If they did so, Moscow said, it would consider the action an armed attack on the Soviet Union, and it would reply in kind. Then the Western allies would either have to accept defeat or face a nuclear war that might be expected to entail their own destruction without saving Berlin.

The logic of the military situation appeared to call for the Western abandonment of Berlin. Politically, however, such an abandonment was all but unthinkable. It would constitute a betrayal, not to be disguised, of 2·2 million people in West Berlin alone who had, for a decade now, put their entire trust in the protection of which the Western allies had given them guarantees. Relying on this protection in 1948–1949, and ever since, they had given their leaders solid support in defying the Communists by whom they were surrounded and virtually besieged.

Moreover, because of the dramatic events of 1948–1949, when the Berlin Blockade had been broken by the Western airlift, Berlin had become the principal symbol of the Western determination not to give way before Moscow. This meant that, if the West should now abandon the city, its action would not only be regarded as an historic betrayal; it would be taken by all those peoples who had put their trust in Western protection as a demonstration that they could no longer count on it. The West Germans, the Scandinavians, the South Koreans, the Japanese, and peoples everywhere would feel that they had better make the best terms they could with Moscow. The allies who were about to take the risk of allowing the United States to set up nuclear missile bases on their territory (the I.R.B.M's. that might compensate for the Soviet priority in the development of I.C.B.M's.) might well, under a threat of annihilation by Russia, change their minds. It might be expected, then, that all the defenses of the West would begin to crumble, so that, having retreated from Berlin, the United States and such allies as remained to it would find no other point at which they could make the stand they had failed to make at Berlin. Or, avoiding the risk of war at Berlin, they would have to take a greater risk of war later on. The Munich betrayal of 1938 was in everyone's mind.

In the immediate test the three Western governments held their ground. On the last day of 1958, in their formal replies to the Russian notes of November 27, they affirmed their determination to stand fast in Berlin, saying that they would not accept the transfer to the East German regime of Moscow's responsibility for Berlin and the access routes.

The formal positions of Russia and the West, respectively, had now been established. Adhered to, they would lead to a military collision on or shortly after May 27, 1959. Each side continued, in the first months of the new year, as the final date drew nearer, to make statements declaring that it would not retreat from its position. Moscow continued to repeat its warnings of war. Joint contingency planning by Washington, London, Paris, and Bonn went forward apace. On February 9 Dulles was able to report publicly that general agreement had been reached on the steps to be taken if the access of the Western powers to Berlin should be blocked. Moscow, and the rest of the world with it, were left to guess what those steps would be.

No historian today can know how much reality there was behind the impressive façade of unity, among the Western governments, in their refusal to retreat from Berlin. Presumably Moscow, at this time, could not know either. That the populations on whose support the governments depended were not indifferent to the danger of nuclear war over Berlin, and that they might not support their governments all the way to the brink of such a war, was clear. It was not only that the peoples of the West had to contemplate the destruction of all their hopes, of everything they cherished, of their civilization, their families, their homes, and themselves, in a sudden exchange of blows that might, it seemed, leave the northern hemisphere a radioactive desert. They were being asked to accept the risk of this for the sake of one local community belonging to the nation that, in the course of bitter and still recent experience, they had learned to regard as the enemy of mankind itself. To many who not only remembered Hitler vividly, but who still identified the whole German nation with what he had represented, it seemed intolerable that they should be expected to take such terrible risks for the inhabitants of Hitler's capital, the traditional center of Prussia and Prussianism. In 1939, when Britain and France went to war, there were many in their midst who asked: Why die for Danzig? Inevitably, now, there were many to ask: Why die for Berlin? In this, rather than in the declarations of the governments, lay Moscow's hopes that its nuclear diplomacy would succeed.[2]

*   *   *

The confrontation over Berlin in the winter of 1958–1959 was essentially like the confrontation over Serbia in 1914. If it were to

[2] A personal note may help make vivid, although it cannot truly recall, the fear that now gripped the populations of the West if not of the entire world. One who, living in Geneva, is on record as having consistently supported a firm stand at Berlin, recalls how, nevertheless, he lay awake night after night, thinking of his wife, thinking of his children one by one, thinking of what might be the end for them after so much of love, of promise, and of hope as had become associated with them in his mind over the years. Still he recalls the physical sensation in the abdomen, preventing sleep, that the imagination of the possible horror in store for them produced in him. Multiply this man, now, by millions, spread over half the earth, think of the sum of their fear, with its physical manifestations, and it seems a wonder that the very air which wrapped our planet was not visibly altered by it. Yet men everywhere stood firm, and the danger passed.

follow the same logical development it would eventuate in a general war. In 1914 the governments had been willing to risk such a war because they expected to survive it and even to profit by it. The governments involved in the Berlin confrontation, however, could feel no assurance that such a war would not result in the loss of all they had at stake, perhaps with irreparable damage to mankind. Consequently, we must suppose that neither side was willing to engage in such a war or even, perhaps, to take a considerable risk of it.[3] All the two sides were doing was to see which would be the first to turn back as, together, they approached the brink of war. Moscow had assumed that the logic of power, made eloquent by an overtly menacing diplomacy on its part, would move the West to retreat. Now, however, the formal attitude of defiance that the West had adopted must have begun to introduce an element of increasing uncertainty.

In circumstances like this, where neither side can risk the ultimate showdown, the defender of the *status quo* has an advantage over the challenger. For it is the challenger, not the defender, who is proposing to take the action that will produce the showdown. Add to this that a possible need to retreat had always been native to the Russian outlook, representing as it did a thousand years of national experience, while it was almost unthinkable for the Western democracies, especially the United States.

Having by its ultimatum begun the movement toward the brink, Moscow, as the scheduled date of arrival approached, began to cast about for ways of postponing it. While it was clearly not prepared to give up its objective of prizing the Western powers out of Berlin, we cannot doubt its determination to achieve that objective by the threat of war only, not by its realization, and this required at least a modification of the ultimatum to allow more time for achieving it.

On March 2, then, Moscow proposed a meeting of heads of government, a 'summit' meeting at which a settlement of the Berlin issue would be negotiated. The West, however, could hardly regard the issue as negotiable. Its position in Berlin was like that of a mountaineer holding on to the face of a cliff by his fingers and toes only: there is no point of attachment at which he can relax his hold without losing it altogether. The position in Berlin was already so precarious that there was nothing the West could

---

[3] Until the relevant documents are published we cannot know how far the Western governments were willing to go.

concede in negotiation. If, by a compromise, the Western allies abandoned only a few of the rights to which they held, the Berliners would see that they could no longer count on their protectors, who would presumably retreat at each successive test. Already the more pessimistic among them were moving with their families to West Germany; the population was beginning to decline; doubts about West Berlin's future were threatening the economic and cultural life of the besieged community. This growing exodus might easily become a mass movement, and the decline in vitality might reach the proportions of a disaster—until, at last, those who remained in the dying city would feel themselves obliged to make whatever terms they could with a triumphant East German regime acting as the catspaw of a triumphant Moscow.

Moscow now accompanied its proposal for a summit meeting with an obligato of saber-rattling. This put the Western governments under pressure from their own populations by making it appear that the choice was between such a meeting and an intolerable risk of nuclear annihilation. The proposal, moreover, seemed altogether reasonable to an important part of Western opinion, especially in Britain and the United States, which shared a traditional belief that all disputes could be settled amicably if only the top men on either side, as distinct from professional diplomats, would sit down together, get to know each other, and talk matters out. The American Government, however, was conscious of the fact that a formal summit conference would inevitably be held on the world's great stage, with every syllable and gesture of the principals reported around the globe. The principals would necessarily find that they were playing to the galleries rather than talking to each other. While the Western negotiators would be under the embarrassment of constantly having to negotiate among themselves a common position (which was likely to represent the views of the least resolute among them), and would be constantly having to glance back over their shoulders to see whether public opinion at home was still with them, Khrushchev would be under no like limitations. He would be able to set a new trap for his Western opponents every hour. By offering guarantees of the continued freedom of the West Berliners, albeit on terms that made them worthless, and guarantees of their communications across a sovereign German Democratic Republic, he could easily make it appear to the world audience that the Western governments were stubbornly advancing toward the holocaust of all civilization, not for the freedom of Berlin, which could not be saved, but simply on grounds of abstruse legal quibbles and a pedantic aversion to recognizing the German Democratic Republic.

Eisenhower might have resisted Moscow's demands for a summit conference, which were to be so generally supported in the West, on the understandable grounds that he refused to negotiate under the pressure of an ultimatum. Now, however, Khrushchev began to play the role of the reasonable and conciliatory statesman. On March 5, three days after proposing the summit conference, he said in an address at Leipzig that there was no question of an 'ultimatum' over Berlin, or of regarding May 27 as an irrevocable 'deadline' for the transfer of Soviet control to the German Democratic Republic. If negotiations were begun 'in a reasonable way,' that date could be moved to June, to July, or 'even later.' On the 9th he told an audience in East Berlin: 'If need be, we are ready to have the United States, Britain, France, and the Soviet Union, or neutral countries, maintain in West Berlin a minimum of troops to assure the observance of the free-city status, without the right, however, to interfere in the city's internal life.' Two days later, the leaders of the German Democratic Republic joined him in a statement that it was prepared to guarantee free access to West Berlin from both east and west, and to respect its status as a demilitarized free city.

Finally, on March 19, after Moscow had maintained for four months that the Western powers had no rights entitling them to remain in Berlin, Khrushchev told a press-conference: 'I believe that the United States, Britain, and France do have lawful rights for their stay in Berlin. These rights ensue from the fact of German surrender as a result of our joint struggle against Nazi Germany.' This was precisely the argument that the Western powers had made from the first, and that Moscow had been rejecting categorically. Here was a poignant demonstration of a traditional Russian strategy, learned during the long centuries when the Russians had been dealing so deviously with the Mongols, the strategy of what might be called opportunistic retreat while awaiting some new occasion for opportunistic advance.

The sword of Damocles, however, was not removed. At any time—if not in May then in June, if not in June then in July, if not in 1959 then in 1960—Moscow might abruptly turn over to its East German puppet responsibility for Berlin and for the access of the Western powers to it. Therefore the suspense would continue. The war of nerves would go on, perhaps for years to come, with such varying degrees of intensity, from month to month, as Moscow might find opportune. Under this manipulated pressure, Moscow would continue to call for a summit conference.

*   *   *

At the same time that Moscow moved to absorb West Berlin it also moved to detach the more vulnerable members of NATO from their alliance with the United States. It pointed out to them that, in case of war, their association with the United States would entail their complete destruction by nuclear weapons. Italy, Greece, and Turkey were directly and explicitly warned that they were exposing themselves to nuclear annihilation. Norway and Denmark were admonished that, for their own good, they should contract out of the Western alliance and assume for themselves the same status as Finland.[4]

This diplomacy, like the move to oust the West from Berlin, was not immediately successful. However much it stimulated such unofficial and pacifistic movements as the Campaign for Nuclear Disarmament in Britain, however great its effect on large sectors of public opinion in the threatened countries, the governments themselves held fast to the NATO alliance, not shrinking from the obligations and the dangers that it entailed. Britain, which had from the beginning provided bases for American nuclear bombers, now provided bases, as well, for American Thor missiles and for American submarines armed with Polaris missiles. Italy and Turkey, in the early months of 1959, during the period of high tension over Berlin, entered into agreements with the United States for the basing, on their territory, of Jupiter missiles.

---

[4] In April 1959, ten days after the Italian Senate had approved the relevant agreement, a note from Moscow was delivered to the Italian Government. 'In the event of a conflict,' it said, 'precisely these bases will be the target which, by way of retaliation, will have to be destroyed with the help of all types of modern weapons. It is superfluous to say that ... not only people living in the vicinity of the rocket bases, but the population of the whole country, would be subjected to a grave danger.' A few weeks later Greece was similarly warned. Both the Italian and Greek Governments, however, responded defiantly. The former went ahead with the establishment of an American missile base, the latter proceeded to stockpile American nuclear warheads (*The Times*, London, December 2, 1965). The invitation to the Norwegians and Danes to follow the Finnish example was contained in Khrushchev's address at Riga of June 11, 1959.

Moscow's aggressive diplomacy, and the refusal of the West to retreat before it, represented the kind of situation that in past ages had commonly been resolved by the test of armed conflict. In this case, the Government with the initiative saw that, in the nuclear age, this test was no longer acceptable even as a last resort. It could threaten, but the instinct of self-preservation, itself, told it that it must not force matters to the point of carrying out the threat. While not prepared to abandon the new diplomacy after a trial of only a few months, after what was only an initial failure, we now see how, on repeated occasions over the next few years, Moscow advances toward the brink of finality, while the world holds its breath, only to stop short of it on each occasion.

After 1956 it had appeared to those who were the most sophisticated in the time-tested principles of power-politics that the altered balance of power consequent on Russia's acquisition of a nuclear armament would have to be registered, now, in victories for Russian diplomacy from Berlin to Turkey. The West would have to give way at points which its relative strength no longer allowed it to hold. The logic that led to this conclusion was accepted by the best minds in the West as well as by Moscow. Nevertheless, it was a logic that would have to be revised, at last, in the light of experience.

CHAPTER XXXV

*Khrushchev's visit to the United States to make peace;
its failure; and the collapse of the summit conference of
May 1960*

Moscow's diplomatic offensive had failed in its first stage,
during which it had raised tensions between East and West
to a pitch unequaled since the winter of 1950–1951. Consequently,
its diplomacy was now aimed at bringing the Western heads of
government to a conference at which, by the arts of demagogy,
they might be subjected to the pressure of a public opinion that
would, in the ostensible interests of peace and reasonableness,
compel their retreat from Berlin. Toward this end, Khrushchev
had withdrawn his ultimatum by the device of declaring that the
deadline for the conclusion of a treaty with East Germany was
moveable. He presented himself to the world, now, as a man of
good-will who wished only for a peaceful settlement of the Cold
War, such as, he felt sure, could be readily achieved if only President Eisenhower would adopt the same reasonable attitude and
sit down with him at the conference-table.

We should resist the temptation to believe that this new public
attitude represented a diabolical dissimulation. Khrushchev, having tested Western determination over the period from November
to March, may well have concluded that a *détente* was desirable—
may even have concluded, for reasons that will come out in the
next chapter, that a general settlement of the Cold War must
now be sought. He was, one supposes, simultaneously pursuing
two goals that were not incompatible to his mind: a resolution of
the Berlin problem, without which there could be no stability,
and a general settlement with the West. His alternate hostility and
conciliation, each genuine in its way, had been virtually the hallmark of Russia's relations with its neighbors ever since the centuries of Mongol domination.

President Eisenhower, hanging back from the proposed conference, said he would agree to it only if there were reason to believe that it would be fruitful. This meant, *inter alia*, that the issue

between the two sides should be explored in preliminary fashion at a level below the summit. Khrushchev, accepting this condition in a spirit of indulgence, agreed to a Western proposal of a Foreign Ministers' Conference in Geneva, which was held from May 11 to August 5, 1959.

All that this meeting demonstrated was that, as had been suspected, the respective positions of the two sides were not truly negotiable. Perhaps all the meeting accomplished was to provide a face-saving occasion for postponing the realization, as scheduled, of Moscow's threat to deliver West Berlin and its western approaches to East Germany.

The Foreign Ministers' Conference could hardly be said to have fulfilled Eisenhower's condition that, before he went to a summit conference, there should be evidence that such a conference would be fruitful. Therefore, another preliminary move was now in order. On August 3, 1959, two days before the end of the Foreign Ministers' Conference, Moscow and Washington simultaneously announced that Eisenhower and Khrushchev had agreed to exchange amicable visits, that each had accepted the invitation of the other to enjoy the hospitality of his country. This would provide two successive occasions for them to talk informally about their common problems. Khrushchev made it clear, in press conferences, that there would be no rude threats to mar these get-togethers. Good manners and friendship would be the order of the day.

Suddenly, with this announcement, the terrible tension seemed to be relieved. 'When we look back upon the story of the last few months,' said Prime Minister Macmillan of Britain, 'we realize how great an advance there has been. Last November we were talking in terms of threats and ultimata. Now we are talking in terms of personal visits and discussions.'

Mr. and Mrs. Khrushchev, with their son and two daughters, and with a train of Soviet dignitaries, arrived in Washington on September 15. At the airport he said he had come 'with an open heart,' that 'we and all peoples should live in peace and friendship who inhabit our common mother Earth.' The Khrushchevs sat down to dinner with the Eisenhowers in the White House that evening. Speaking before the National Press Club the next day, Khrushchev said that he had come to America to end the Cold War. Two days later he created a sensation, in an address to the United Nations in New York, by proposing 'universal and complete disarmament,' to be achieved within four years—an end to all armed forces, war ministries, general staffs, and nuclear weapons. The next day the Khrushchevs, having flown across the continent, had lunch in Hollywood with Marilyn Monroe, Frank Sinatra, Bob Hope, and other stars of the American screen. After touring California like an American politician running for office, Khrushchev returned to Washington, stopping for visits in Corn Rapids, Iowa, and Pittsburgh, Pennsylvania.

Back in the East, he spent three days with Eisenhower at Camp David in the Maryland woods. Much of the time the two men walked together in the woodlands or sat about informally, alone except for their interpreters. This was followed by a visit with the Eisenhower grandchildren, aged three to ten, at the Eisenhower farm in Gettysburg. Press and public had the impression that these two benign men, both of them grandfathers, had become partners for peace.

The next day Khrushchev, about to depart on the return flight to Russia, spoke his farewell to the American people over television. 'Good evening, American friends . . .,' he began, 'we like your beautiful cities and wonderful roads, but most of all your amiable and kind-hearted people.' He went on virtually to declare the Cold War at an end, although recognizing realistically that there were residues of feeling, at least among the Americans, that could not be expected to disappear immediately. 'You will realize,' he said, 'that it is not so easy to overcome all that has accumulated over the many years of the Cold War. Consider how many speeches were made that did not promote the improvement of relations but, on the contrary, aggravated them.' He cited the Bible and identified the 'socialist system' with Christianity. He ended in English: 'Good-bye, good luck, friends!'

The original plan had been for President Eisenhower to pay his return visit promptly, but it was put off until the following spring, as Mr. Khrushchev explained before his departure, by a grandchildren's agreement. At Gettysburg the President's grandchildren had told the kind Mr. Khrushchev that they would like to come with their grandfather when he went to visit the Khrushchevs in Russia. Mr. Khrushchev had concluded (and he knew his own grandchildren would agree) that the spring, with its mild weather and its blossoms, would be a better time for them to come.

All this is not a dream. The record of the visit is there. More-over, those who remember what had come before, and what was to come after, should not jump to the conclusion that Khrushchev was not, himself, genuinely moved by the good-will that he expressed so warmly. Especially in the heart of a Russian, hate can pass over into love in an instant. Both emotions have a relationship to fear that makes them akin. What a man fears, he may either try to kill with hate or to mollify with love.[1] In any case, during part of Khrushchev's visit to America the intractable international issues, which would confront the statesmen so soon again, got lost in the great and ennobling generalizations.

*   *   *

Khrushchev's visit to Eisenhower had ended the Cold War in principle. All that remained was to end it in practice. The long projected summit meeting would now be held, presumably, for the realization of this happy objective. In the state of relief and euphoria that had been produced, it seemed possible that the meeting would be one of friends and partners.

At this point, however, reality began to reassert itself. To the hards in the Communist world, to those who were ideologically passionate, Khrushchev's fraternization with the 'capitalist imperialist' enemy must have appeared as if the Archangel Michael had gone off on a drinking-party with Beelzebub. He did not have enough personal authority to assure unquestioned acceptance by the whole movement over which he presided of such abrupt shifts in policy as Stalin had undertaken when, in 1939, he had entered into a pact with Hitler. From this point on it becomes increasingly apparent that Khrushchev, as dictator only by consent of the governing oligarchy in Moscow, is in some sense on probation. Unless he can justify his course by successes that will silence his detractors, he is going to have to revert to a more prudent and conservative course, or he is going to find himself replaced.

Much more was involved, however, than the internal politics of the Kremlin only. As we shall see in the next chapter, under the surface of international Communist unity, a great and historic rift was now developing. Peking was in a state of growing rebellion against Khrushchev's leadership in Moscow. Two days after he had said good-bye to Eisenhower in Washington Khrushchev had landed in Peking to attend the tenth-anniversary celebrations

---

[1] Surely the Mongols had experienced this time and again in the days of their dominion over the Russians. It is often easier to love one's enemy, whom one fears, than to love one's neighbor, whom one doesn't.

of the Chinese People's Republic and, presumably, to see to it that the policy of the Chinese Communist regime conformed to the line set by him—a line that the outraged men of Peking regarded as pro-American. There he discovered to what a degree his courtship of the Americans had been viewed with alarm and indignation as a betrayal of the sacred cause. To the Chinese leaders, struggling with desperate internal problems, and feeling themselves in frightful danger from the United States, it must have seemed that the bond of kinship between white European peoples was showing itself stronger than the bond of ideology, that the two nuclear powers might even be moving to associate themselves in a common enterprise to dominate and police the rest of mankind, which was without nuclear weapons to resist them. Already Moscow had opposed the Chinese desire to have nuclear weapons of their own, and had set itself against militant action by Peking to 'liberate' the island of Formosa, since such action would provoke a clash with the United States.

The growing rebellion of Peking, which Khrushchev's conduct had been stimulating, would have provided the basis for the most serious charge that his opponents in Moscow could bring against him. It was not, however, the only possible charge. His record, by now, was one of mounting failures and near failures. In the domestic sphere he had sponsored an immense and costly program to overcome Russia's deficiencies in food-production, and it had failed utterly. His incautious liberalism had failed to bring Tito's Yugoslavia back to the paths of obedience, and it had almost resulted in the complete defection of Poland and Hungary. He had made bold forays in south Asia and the Middle East with nothing to show for them. Now he had made a spectacular play, at great risk, to get the West out of Berlin, and in that, too, he had failed up to now. Finally, he had lowered Russia's prestige in the world by undignified behavior on repeated occasions.

It is clear, then, that by the fall of 1959 Khrushchev needed a success. Perhaps he hoped for such a success at the summit meeting toward which everything was at last moving. Now, however, there were increasing indications that with the passage of time Moscow's diplomatic momentum over Berlin had been lost, that the West, having by its firmness brought about a tactical retreat on Khrushchev's part, was now increasingly set to yield nothing at the forthcoming summit meeting.

*   *   *

Moscow's increasing difficulties with its Chinese ally were matched, now, by difficulties that Washington was beginning to experience with its French ally. France had been sorely humiliated, first by the Nazi occupation and then by a necessary dependence on its American rescuer. In the years after 1947, when the West Europeans were still helpless, Americans had got into the habit of directing them in a manner that was often officious, as if they were, like children, inferior in judgment and experience. The French suffered from a sense of being under barbarian tutelage. Once the occasion for enduring such tutelage had begun to pass, it was a foregone conclusion that they would rebel against it. This rebellious disposition was personified in the strong man who had now risen to power in France.

General de Gaulle, a man formidable in character and intellect, had long made a distinction between the French people, for whom he had no respect, and something called France, which he identified with himself.[2] Even while the land and people of France were held captive during the War, he had insisted that France would not allow itself to occupy second place in the councils of the nations; and he had quarreled with Roosevelt and Churchill because they would not concede to him *qua* France (although he had no mandate) a voice equal to their own in the direction of the War. For the rest, he represented the essential world-outlook indentified with late nineteenth-century nationalism. He was a latter-day Bismarck, who like Bismarck was exclusively concerned to achieve the greatness of the national community for which he acted. The generation of statesmen before Bismarck's, the post-Napoleonic generation, had still been concerned with the happiness and tranquility of Europe, but Bismarck had been concerned only that Germany be great—with consequences, after his time, that Germany and the rest of Europe would suffer alike.

For more than a dozen years after the War France had lain in political confusion, leaderless, politically paralyzed, almost incapable of governing itself. By late 1958 differences of opinion about how to deal with a rebellious Algeria had brought the unhappy nation to the verge of a civil war that threatened to match,

---

[2] It is customary to say of any great man that he is a complex personality. What was striking about de Gaulle was the uncomplicated and unambiguous nature of his basic beliefs and attitudes. His *Mémoires de Guerre* already testified to his mistrust of the French people, and his devotion to the France that was represented by himself. See also such statements as his address to the French nation of November 4, 1965.

in its magnitude, the Spanish Civil War of the 1930's. This was the moment when de Gaulle took command. On January 8, 1959, he became President of France with powers not inferior, in any practical sense, to those of Louis XIV. In the months to come he had to concentrate on extricating France from Algeria and other overseas commitments, and to restoring order at home. Once he had accomplished this (which would not be before the middle of 1962), he would be ready to address himself to the rectification of a situation in which France found itself part of an alliance in which it did not occupy first place. Where opportunities for such rectification came earlier, however, he was ready to exploit them.

One such opportunity came now. He had not been happy to follow the leadership of Eisenhower, who was distinctly his inferior in intellect and education, and he had not relished France's position as an excluded party while Eisenhower and Khrushchev discussed between them the future of the world in which France was included. There is a parallel, here, between the positions of Paris and Peking.

Khrushchev and Eisenhower together had now set the stage for a summit conference that, if it was to be centered on the Western presence in Berlin, could hardly be profitable to the West, which was already in so weak a position in Berlin that it had virtually nothing it could concede without disaster. Events were taking their course, however, carrying the West along with them, and it was understood that the summit conference would be held not later than mid-December. President Eisenhower and Prime Minister Macmillan, it was understood, had agreed to this.

On October 21, however, the French Government caused surprise by making public its view that a summit conference should not be held unless there was proof, presumably to be given by Moscow, that a genuine abandonment of Cold War pressures could be expected, not just in Berlin, but in South-East Asia, in the Middle East, in Africa, and in the United Nations as well. Once such proof had been furnished, then the conference might meet, but not to discuss some local or topical issue. It should meet to discuss nothing less than 'the problems that divide the world.' In France's view, such a conference should not be held before the spring of 1960 at the earliest.

Eisenhower, whose leadership was thus challenged, moved to resolve the Western position by an immediate meeting of the American, British, and French heads of government, announcing his willingness to go to Europe for the purpose. De Gaulle, however, saw no need to hurry. Paris announced that France would not be ready for such a meeting before mid-December. So France made its will felt by leaving the others with no choice but to accept a postponement of the summit conference.

The British Government, faced with popular alarm in Britain at the danger of war, had from the beginning been pushing for a summit negotiation on Berlin. The Governments of Adenauer and de Gaulle, however, took the position that the rights of the West in Berlin were not negotiable and therefore should not be the subject of any negotiation. Eisenhower, confronted with this difference among the allies, appears to have played the role in which he had always been happiest, that of the detached and impartial mediator. His mediation was so far successful that the three Western heads of government were, at last, able to get together on an invitation to Khrushchev to a summit conference in Paris, the agenda to be nothing more specific than 'the main problems affecting the attainment of peace and stability in the world.' Khrushchev accepted, and the date of May 16, 1960, was set.

*   *   *

An unforeseen incident now upset all plans. Since the summer of 1956 the United States had been sending reconnaissance planes especially designed for the purpose to fly over Russia at such a height (over twelve miles) that they might escape detection, gathering data on military installations. Moscow had known about these flights all along, but their altitude and speed had been such that it had not been able to interfere with them.

The mission of the U-2's, as these planes were called, was of vital importance to the defense of the West. Russian intelligence, operating in the open Western societies, presumably had no difficulty in locating air and missile bases, and would have no difficulty in detecting such extraordinary activities as would herald hostile military action by the United States. In the closed Russian society, however, the United States could obtain the same kind of information only by resorting to U-2 reconnaissance. It may well be that, in the period of 'the delicate balance of terror,' the information elicited by both sides, through their respective devices of espionage, contributed to stability and security for both alike. If the United States had been entirely ignorant of what was going on inside Russia, knowing only that the Russians had the means to launch a devastating surprise-attack on it, it would have been more susceptible to alarm and more disposed to desperate measures during any period of crisis in the relations between the two countries. One function of espionage was reassurance.

On the other hand, given the Soviet obsession with the danger that foreign agents might penetrate Soviet society, and given the fact that unidentified planes over Russia might carry nuclear bombs, Moscow could hardly view the U-2 flights with serenity.

On May 5, eleven days before the summit conference was to convene, Khrushchev announced that an American plane had been shot down over Russian territory. It later transpired that the plane was a U-2, that it was crossing the heart of Russia from Pakistan to Norway, and that it was shot down some 1,250 miles inside the Russian frontiers.[3]

In his original announcement of the U-2 incident on May 5, Khrushchev expressed himself with restraint and gave the matter remarkably little importance. He also deliberately laid a trap for Washington, as he later admitted, by withholding the information that the plane's espionage equipment had been recovered and its pilot captured unhurt. Washington, in accordance with established practice in such matters, proceeded to issue a false account of what the plane was and what it had been doing, saying that it had been gathering weather-information along the Turkish frontier. Thereupon Khrushchev sprang his trap by revealing the true facts and the evidence. His purpose, clearly, was to lower the standing of the United States in the eyes of the world on the eve of the summit conference.

I mentioned in Chapter XXXII that a tacit alliance had developed, across the battle-lines of the Cold War, between the softs in Moscow and Washington, as between the hards, and that both Eisenhower and Khrushchev, by contrast with Dulles and Molotov, represented the softs, the advocates of relaxed tensions. In an address to the Supreme Soviet on May 7, Khrushchev professed himself 'quite willing to grant that the President knew nothing about the plane having been sent into the Soviet Union.' If this was a hint to Eisenhower he did not take it, nor did he follow the

---

[3] There are grounds for speculating that Washington, recalling how in 1941 the Japanese Government had resorted to negotiations to cover the surprise attack on Pearl Harbor, ordered this particular flight at this particular time to determine whether the Russians were making preparations for a like surprise in connection with the summit meeting. See the report of June 26, 1960, on the investigation of the U-2 incident by the Senate Foreign Relations Committee.

accepted practice whereby governments, if only in formal terms, refrain from acknowledging their acts of espionage. His army training had taught him that a good commander always accepts responsibility for the actions of his command, and he was also sensitive to the charge, which had been made repeatedly, that he was not in effective command of the Government over which he presided. So he admitted the true facts, and he assumed personal responsibility for them. By taking this position, he betrayed his tacit alliance with Khrushchev, who would now find it politically impossible to minimize the incident.

Worse than that, however, in a press conference of May 11, with the summit meeting only five days off, the President justified the U-2 flights in terms that could leave little doubt of an intention to continue them. Khrushchev hardly had any choice, after that, but to react in outspoken and menacing terms.

As soon as the four had seated themselves about a table in the Élysée Palace, on the morning of May 16, Khrushchev demanded, as a precondition of going ahead with the Conference, that the Government of the United States 'condemn the inadmissable provocative actions of the U.S. Air Force with regard to the Soviet Union,' that it commit itself to the discontinuance of such actions, and that it undertake to 'punish those directly guilty of such actions.' He proposed that otherwise the Conference be postponed for six to eight months. He also proposed that Eisenhower's return visit to Russia, scheduled for the following month, be postponed.

The President, in reply, would go no further than to say that the U-2 flights had been suspended after the recent incident and were not to be resumed.

So the summit Conference ended without ever having begun. Efforts to overcome the impasse would continue for another day or two, but in vain.

The morning of the 17th, Khrushchev gave an impromptu press conference in a Paris street. Then, accompanied by Russian Defense Minister Marshal Malinovsky, he drove to the village of Pleurs-sur-Marne as a tourist on holiday. There, in a farmyard, surrounded by newspapermen, farm laborers, chickens, and pigs, he repeated his demands on the President. The next day, at a formal press conference in Paris, he said that if the President sent any more planes over the Soviet Union, not only would they be shot down, but the foreign bases from which they had taken off, and 'those who have set up these bases and actually dispose of them,' would suffer 'shattering blows.'

Those who observed Khrushchev during these days, with the watchful Marshal Malinovsky always by his side, could hardly doubt that he was under pressure from the hards in Moscow to strike bellicose attitudes before 'the capitalist imperialist aggressors.' Again, now, he said that his Government was planning 'to conclude a peace treaty with the German Democratic Republic . . . thereby to deprive the Western powers of the right to have occupation troops in West Berlin. When we consider it necessary, we shall take up our pens—the drafts have already been prepared —sit down, sign the treaty, and announce it.'

The day before the abortive summit meeting, when the four heads of government had arrived in Paris, and when it had become clear what the nature of the next day's confrontation was likely to be, the American Secretary of Defense, with the President's concurrence, had instituted a 'communication alert' of American military forces all over the world. This, he later explained, had been 'a sound precautionary measure.' [4]

With tensions once more at the danger-point, then, on the morning of May 19 Khrushchev flew to East Berlin. There he met with the East German leaders while the world braced itself for the announcement that might mean war.

Again, however, he turned back from the brink. While he said, in a speech of May 20, that the perpetuation of the occupation regime in West Berlin would not be permitted, he also said that Moscow would do nothing to worsen the international situation. 'Therefore . . . the existing situation will apparently have to be preserved until the heads-of-government meeting which, it is hoped, will take place in six to eight months' time.'

The world, having held its breath for four days, breathed again.

But the dignity of statesmanship recovered only slowly and incompletely. Back in Russia, Khrushchev publicly declared that, when Eisenhower's term as President ended, he would offer him the job of manager of a kindergarten. As for the Vice President of the United States, he said that he would remind him of 'the

---

[4] One may speculate that the failure of the U-2 flight had deprived Washington of intelligence that might have made it less apprehensive of a Russian surprise attack. This was the period of 'the delicate balance of terror,' when victory seemed likely to go to the side that struck the first blow. In Washington the military, especially, remembered Pearl Harbor.

message sent by the Zaporozhian Cossacks to the Sultan of Turkey: "What kind of knight are you if, without your trousers, you can't kill a hedgehog with the part of your body on which you sit."' It had been many centuries since the relations between states had been conducted with such informality.

The Zaporozhian Cossacks, however, had not had missiles tipped with thermonuclear warheads to aim at the Sultan of Turkey. Speaking from the same platform as that from which Khrushchev made his picturesque remarks about the President and the Vice President of the United States, Marshal Malinovsky reminded his listeners that Russia had the means to strike 'both at the satellites and at the leader' of the Western alliance—'no matter what seas and oceans they may hide behind.'

CHAPTER XXXVI

The break between Moscow and Peking; Moscow's abortive intervention in the Congo

THE formal alliance of Russia and China, concluded in the winter of 1949–1950, was an artificial arrangement between Greeks and Persians, not a natural association of Greeks with Greeks. Their two cultures were distinct, without any common heritage of experience, language, or thought. The obeisance that both Governments made before the altars of a common ideology could only add, in the long run, to the difficulties of their relationship, since each was bound to regard differences at the level of casuistry as signs of heresy in the other.

As we saw in Chapter XIX, the agrarian movement headed by Mao Tse-tung had been born of a rebellion against Moscow's authority and leadership. Not until 1949, when its victory in the Chinese civil war was being completed, did Moscow, accepting the accomplished fact, move to bring the new Government into the same subordinate relationship to itself as the governments of the other Communist regimes, the Yugoslav excepted.

If the circumstances of 1950 had been less unfortunate, and if they had combined with a more-than-human insight on the part of Americans generally, the artificial relationship between Moscow and Peking would hardly have maintained even the semblance of solidarity as long as it did. But the American people and their Government, taking the semblance for the reality, pursued in the blindness of anger a policy that would have confirmed their misconception, *ex post facto*, if anything could have. By applying the policy of containment to both realms alike, as if they had become one, the United States encircled them and pressed them together. Under its pressure the semblance of solidarity was maintained for almost a decade—especially as the new China desperately needed massive support for its economic and military development that, in the circumstances, it could look for only in Moscow.

From the beginning, however, the partnership must have been as uneasy as it was unnatural. The 4,500 miles of boundary between Russia and China, from the Himalayas to the Sea of Japan, was not a natural frontier in terms either of physical features or ethnography. All it represented was the line where a European empire, expanding steadily into Asia since the seventeenth century, came up against a declining Asian empire. As such it was, essentially, a line of imperial confrontation, the kind of line that bends back and forth with changes in the balance of the opposing powers. On the Chinese side, moreover, was a land-hungry population of some 600 million, while on the Russian was an abundance of empty land. After 1949, even more than before, the problem of containing China must have been a nagging worry for those who ruled in Moscow. In fact, it was now for the first time that China appeared as a potential menace to the Russian empire. Hitherto, a weak China had always been on the defensive against an expanding Russia. But the China of Mao Tse-tung was an awakening giant. It was industrializing, it was modernizing, and it was undertaking to set up a nuclear military establishment of its own on Russia's southern borders—just as the United States had set one up on its western borders.

China's nominal communization in 1949 gave it claims on Moscow for economic and military assistance that Moscow would not feel itself in a position to satisfy, and that it would be reluctant to satisfy in important respects for strategic reasons. The implications of Moscow's refusal to help the new China become a nuclear power were not lost on the new Chinese rulers, who took a bitter view of it.

Even under the pressure of American containment, then, a powerful China was not to remain in meek subordination and obedience to alien rulers in faraway Moscow. It would, in fact, come to contest Moscow's leadership of the Communist movement, at first in Asia and then throughout the world. By visiting Afghanistan, India, and Burma in 1955, Khrushchev and Bulganin were staking a claim in Asia of which Mao was expected to take notice. It is clear that he did take notice, regarding the claim as an impertinence and a challenge.

We must remember that, at least as early as 1946, Mao had set himself up as a supreme ideological leader in his own right, independent of Moscow, not under the tutelage of Stalin or anyone else.[1] In Peking's view the Chinese Revolution, rather than the

---

[1] See Crankshaw, pp. 20–21; and Fitzgerald, p. 168.

Russian, was the proper model for the countries of South Asia (indeed, for the countries of Africa and South America as well) to follow. Moscow, however, full of scorn at Peking's program of short-cuts to Communism, could not agree.

At the 20th Congress of the Russian Communist Party in 1956 Khrushchev, in addition to posthumously expelling Stalin from the Communist movement, rescinded Lenin's dicta on the inevitability of war and on the indispensability of violent revolution for the achievement of Communism in capitalist countries. At a time when China felt itself in desperate embattlement, he proclaimed that 'peaceful coexistence' between the capitalist and socialist camps was possible, that the latter could overcome the former by political and economic competition without physical combat, and that in certain countries Communism might be achieved without violent revolution, perhaps through parliamentary means. At the same time, his Russia was offering to bourgeois capitalist states like India (with which China was having a border dispute) assistance for development, and even implements of war, that China needed urgently for itself. It was seeking a *détente* with the North Atlantic powers at summit conferences, and it was manifesting, sometimes outspokenly, its unwillingness to support China in any dangerously militant pursuit of its claims in the Straits of Formosa. In 1959, after three days of apparent camaraderie with Eisenhower at Camp David, Khrushchev had flown to Peking to insist that it not press these claims against the United States. In the winter of 1959–1960, when the Sino-Indian border dispute exploded in a clash of arms between the two countries, Moscow adopted an attitude of neutrality that implied opposition to any Chinese success.

Under these circumstances it would have been strange if the men in Peking had not begun to reason that the men in Moscow were, after all, white Europeans with a special affinity for the European civilization of the North Atlantic; that fear of war had led them to abandon their Marxist–Leninist militancy; and that their Russia was, in fact, on the way to becoming a defender of the *status quo*, like the United States, more interested in peace than in revolution. This interpretation could not have made more tolerable the arrogant disposition of Moscow to keep the Chinese in guiding strings as if they were children, telling them what they might not do, pouring scorn on their efforts to transform their society quickly by the attempted establishment of peasant communes.

The new regime in Peking was pursuing the traditional interests of China under the rubric of Marxism–Leninism, while the regime in Moscow was pursuing the traditional Russian interest under the same rubric. The traditional interests of the two empires clashed.

The Sino-Soviet quarrel, as it became steadily more intense, was disguised, even for the Communist leaders in other countries, as merely a debate between fraternal parties over ideological formulas. At the Third Congress of the Rumanian Communist Party, however, in the summer of 1960, it broke through these restraints. The fraternal delegates were shocked by a sudden exchange of recriminations between Khrushchev and the representative of Peking. This exchange was followed by Moscow's abrupt recall from China of all the Russian technicians who had been sent to help in its industrialization. The technicians, on their departure, took with them the blueprints of the factories in course of construction, so as to make it virtually impossible for the Chinese to continue the construction on their own. Apparently Moscow had decided to show Peking that it had the will, as well as the power, to enforce obedience. Its action was not essentially different from its chastisement of Belgrade in 1948; and, like the Yugoslavs in 1948, the Chinese responded by defiance.

The rift was now irreparable, like the Great Schism between Western and Eastern Christendom in 1054. A spokesman for the Chinese Communist Party formally declared that it alone was the correct interpreter of Leninism. The succession to Marx and Lenin, in other words, had now passed from Moscow.[2] So Khrushchev's Russia, already so completely preoccupied with the Cold War on its western front, found itself engaged in a new cold war of increasing intensity on its eastern front.

The Sino-Soviet quarrel, although hidden from the world for months and even years, had become acute in 1958. This, be it recalled, was at the very time when Moscow had experienced the sudden access of self-confidence incident to its simultaneous resolution of the internal struggle for Stalin's succession and its achievement of full nuclear power. Undoubtedly its new self-confidence under Khrushchev caused it to overestimate its ability to deal with the Chinese difficulty, just as it caused it to overestimate its ability to break the ranks of the West.

[2] Crankshaw, pp. 112–13. There is reason to believe that, by this time, border clashes between Chinese and Russian forces had occurred. See Zagoria, p. 344 and p. 446, fn. 4.

The new access of strength had encouraged Khrushchev to embark on an aggressive anti-Western diplomacy. On the other hand, Peking's growing defiance foreboded a weakening of Russia's position that had the opposite implications for policy. If Russia was going to have to meet a major challenge in Asia it would feel the need of a settlement in Europe so as not to find itself embattled on two fronts at once.

To maintain Moscow's prestige and leadership throughout the revolutionary world, especially in the face of the Chinese challenge, Khrushchev would have to provide the spectacle of an increasingly powerful and militant Russia overbearing the declining strength of the West and compelling its retreat. Otherwise the revolutionaries of Asia, Africa, and Latin America, responding to the mutinous appeal of the Chinese, would be inclined to turn away from Moscow's leadership. The West, however, was standing firmer than had been expected, and to carry militancy beyond a certain point would be to take a risk of nuclear war as unacceptable to the European satellite regimes that followed Moscow's leadership as to Moscow itself. And it would intensify the Cold War in the West precisely at a time when Russia was having to give increasing attention to a challenge in the East.

If, however, the West continued to prove so strong and stubborn that it could not be moved, without unacceptable risk, from the positions that it occupied, then it would be better to work for an accommodation with it that would enable Moscow to turn its attention, in good time, to the danger from an increasingly strong and militant Chinese empire.

In sum, Khrushchev had to have either a triumph over the West or a *détente* with it. There was danger, however, in the inconsistency of pursuing both virtually at once, for in the end he might incur the penalties of both courses without the rewards of either. From November 1958 to March 1959 he had pursued the objective of a triumph, and had failed when the West stood fast at Berlin. From March 1959 to May 1960 he had pursued the objective of a *détente*, and had failed when the U-2 incident had discredited the attempt. From this point on he would again pursue the objective of a triumph, and he would pursue it in an increasingly reckless manner as, with the passage of time and the accumulation of failures, he felt his own weakening position in the Kremlin at stake. It is hardly too much to say that at times in the next two years he presented the spectacle of a fish thrashing about in shallow water. It was spectacular but, considering the power of destruction he represented, frightening.

* * *

From the beginning of the Cold War the West, with its world-wide responsibilities and its consequent vulnerabilities, had been the defender of an established if evolving order. Soviet Russia, its vulnerability confined to the areas in its immediate vicinity, had used all the devices of propaganda and subversion to embarrass the West by supporting the spread of chaos beyond those areas.

Shortly after the explosion at the Paris encounter of May 16, 1960, the proliferation of chaos in Africa appeared to provide Khrushchev with an opportunity, in an area far beyond Russia's existing influence, to score such a success as would suggest the triumphal march of Communism in the world.

At the close of World War II the prewar empires of the European powers in Asia and Africa were clearly obsolete. Like slavery a century earlier, their existence violated the principles of freedom and equality that had come to be generally accepted the world over, principles that were now applied to nations as they had formerly been to individuals. These empires had, moreover, become political, economic, and military burdens to the powers that owned them. They were also, however, symbols of national prestige for the populations of those powers, and this made it difficult for the governments to adapt to the times by withdrawing from them.

There was, in many cases, a more fundamental obstacle to withdrawal. Just as those who were emancipated from slavery in the United States in the middle of the previous century, and those who were emancipated from serfdom in Russia at the same time, were often not prepared for the problems that go with freedom and the responsibilities that belong to citizenship in a political democracy, so many of the colonial dependencies of the European powers were not ready for self-government in the years immediately after the War. The abrupt and total withdrawal of the established administrations would mean chaos, bloodshed, and terrible human suffering—conditions such as would inevitably require foreign intervention. It would also mean the catastrophic loss of economic properties that the citizens of the governing powers had in them, and this could not fail to complicate the task of withdrawal. What complicated the task most was the problem of assuring the safety of the Europeans who, having struck roots in these territories, remained in them, often constituting an appreciable part of the population.

Finally, as the Cold War developed, the governing powers were inhibited by the fear that, upon their own withdrawal, they would be replaced by the expanding Russian empire.

In spite of all these difficulties, by the middle 1950's the British, the French, and the Dutch had disengaged themselves from almost all their dependencies in Asia, and the United States had realized the desire it had cherished for almost half a century to cut loose from the Philippines. In all these dependencies an élite class, more-or-less capable of carrying on government by itself, had grown up under the respective occupying regimes, and there was generally a long history of civilization.

The case was different in Africa south of the Sahara. Here, over large areas, virtually the entire native population consisted of savages still at the cultural level of the stone age, organized in warlike and mutually antagonistic tribes. Even the most complete ideologist, if he knew the level of their development, would have been without compunctions in arguing that they were hardly ready as yet to form self-governing states that could protect the interests of their peoples, administer an equable justice, and discharge the responsibilities of membership in the worldwide community of nations. At the end of the War there was general agreement that a long course of cultural development was necessary before they would be able to maintain and justify their own independence.

The European occupying powers, however, found their position increasingly embarrassing as the 1950's passed. In the eyes of most of the world it represented a self-serving and wickedly conspiratorial imperialism, involving the obnoxious heritage of racial discrimination. The subject populations, themselves, became increasingly rebellious, and there was a mounting demand for complete and immediate liberation. Moscow, and the whole world Communist movement, promoted this and took every advantage of it to discredit the West and to earn golden opinions for itself throughout the world that was in rebellion against the West. The Western governments began to find themselves under heavy pressure, as well, from liberal opinion in their own populations.

Under the circumstances, the concept that independence must be preceded by a long course of preparation was no longer workable.

Britain withdrew from the Gold Coast, now known as Ghana, in 1957; France withdrew from Guinea in 1958; and in 1960 sixteen colonial territories in Africa, with some 85 million inhabitants, were set free. All the rest of Negro Africa—outside the Union of South Africa, Southern Rhodesia, and the Portuguese colonies— was set free in the following two or three years.

Some of these territories, having been better prepared for self-government than others, managed to establish an order of their own to replace the order that had been imposed on them. This was not the case with the Belgian Congo, a territory of forest and savannah almost as big as India, inhabited by a variety of primitive negroid peoples including pygmies.

This savage region, unknown before 1875, had thereafter been explored and exploited by an association of Belgians under the personal patronage of King Leopold II. Civilizing the savages was a prime objective of the association, but remained largely nominal. Instead, the natives were enslaved, in effect, by white traders interested in the profits to be had from ivory, at first, and later from mineral resources as well. This early exploitation, with its nominal good intentions and its abominable cruelties, is vividly described by Joseph Conrad, who knew it at first hand, in what is one of the masterpieces of English literature, *Heart of Darkness*. Until the late 1950's it had hardly occurred to anyone that this savage wilderness might some day be an independent nation-state, and the Belgians had done nothing to prepare the scattered peoples who inhabited it for such an eventuality.

Then, suddenly, at the end of the 1950's, voices were raised in the halls of the United Nations and all over the world, demanding that the Congolese nation, which was presumed to exist as such, be liberated and allowed to govern itself. The primitive peoples of the area had, undoubtedly, suffered terribly under a Belgian rule that had not been well organized for the discharge of humane responsibility, and the Belgians at home did not have a good conscience about it. When leaders among the Congolese began to demand independence and to create mounting disturbances, the Belgian Government, rather than resist them by force, abruptly decided to get out of the unpleasantness once and for all. On January 27, 1960, it undertook to grant complete independence by June 30—even though no kind of constitutional or administrative structure had been created to replace the colonial administration.

In the few months before June 30 a constitution was devised and a Government of sorts was produced for the new Republic of the Congo, proclaimed on that date. There was a President, a Parliament of two Chambers, and a Cabinet—exactly as in Belgium, except that the chief of state was a president rather than a king. The only persons available to man this sophisticated structure, however, were at best partially educated individuals whose forebears had only recently emerged from the savage life of the forests; and most of the scattered populations in whose name and under whose mandate they were to govern were, as yet, without any relevant political experience.

The Congo became independent at midnight on June 30. On July 1 tribal fighting began in Leopoldville, the capital. On July 5 the Congolese Army mutinied and anarchy spread over the land. European men, women, and children who had remained in the Congo, now the helpless objects of atrocities by soldiers run wild, fled pell-mell which way they could. Troops were rushed from Belgium and went into action against the mutineers on July 10. The next day, the richest and most developed province of the new Republic, the Katanga, seceded. At the request of the new Congolese Government for help in saving itself from 'Belgian aggression,' the Security Council of the United Nations authorized the dispatch of a United Nations military force, the first contingents of which arrived in the Congo on July 15 to help the Congolese Government re-establish order and to make the Belgian military presence unnecessary.

The Congo had, by then, been independent two weeks. All over the world the Belgian 'imperialists' were being denounced for conspiring to keep the wealth of the Katanga for themselves, and for intervening by force in the internal affairs of the new Republic.

In Moscow on July 13 Foreign Minister Gromyko accused Belgium, Britain, the United States, France, West Germany, and NATO of armed aggression against the Congo for the purpose of liquidating its independence. Two days later Mr. Khrushchev announced the receipt of a letter from the Congolese Government in which it is said that it might be 'compelled' to ask for the Soviet Union's intervention, unless the Western camp discontinued the aggression against the sovereignty of the Congo Republic. In the reply, which he published forthwith, he said that 'the Congolese Government may rest assured that the Soviet Government will render the Congo Republic all the assistance which may be necessary for the triumph of your cause.'

The next day the American representative at the Security Council, referring to reports that Russia 'might intervene in the Congo directly with troops,' said that with other members of the United Nations the United States would do 'whatever may be necessary to prevent the intrusion of any military forces not requested by the United Nations.'

The record of history is consistent in showing that the most fertile cause of general war is the collapse of political authority in any area surrounded by rival great powers. The disintegration and collapse of authority over the area of the ancient Turkish Empire had led to a series of wars that began with the Crimean War in 1853 and culminated in World War I. The crumbling of authority in China had led to a series of wars that began with the Opium War in 1840 and culminated in the Pacific war of 1941 to 1945. The Cold War, itself, was the product of the collapse of authority in Germany and the states surrounding it. Now, overnight, between June 30 and July 1, the same situation had occurred over an immense area in the heart of Africa. There was a vacuum of authority into which the two sides in the Cold War were likely to be drawn.

In the weeks that followed, the official Government of the Congo was in the hands of Prime Minister Patrice Lumumba, a former clerk in the tax and postal administrations who, suddenly finding himself the focus of a worldwide political struggle beyond his understanding, responded with quasi-hysterical passion in a succession of moves that were consistent only in their mutual inconsistency. One day he announced an 'immediate appeal' for Russian troops that would be deferred pending developments. A week later he was asking for the immediate dispatch to the Congo of 'thousands of United States and other troops.'

By the middle of July such order as was being kept in the Congo was being kept by Belgian forces under the authority of the Government in Brussels, and United Nations forces under the authority of the Security Council. The Security Council, which was feeling the severest pressure from virtually all opinion outside the North Atlantic area, was demanding the withdrawal of the Belgian troops, while the Secretary General of the United Nations, Dag Hammarskjöld, was desperately gathering and dispatching a variety of national troop-contingents made available by United

Nations members to replace the Belgians and make their presence unnecessary.

The United Nations forces, which would amount to almost 20,000 men before the year was out, were required to keep order in a vast ungoverned land rent by civil strife, but without interfering in its internal affairs. It was an impossible assignment. The only alternative to their presence, however, seemed to be an invasion of the Congo by armed forces of other African states, possibly by armed forces from both sides in the Cold War; which in turn might set off a third world war in which the northern hemisphere would be subjected to nuclear devastation.

The Congolese Government, itself, quickly fell apart, with President Kasavubu and Prime Minister Lumumba each announcing the deposition of the other. In these circumstances Moscow espoused the cause of Lumumba, sending him airplanes and lorries for troop transport. Hundreds of its agents swarmed into the country in the guise of diplomats, technicians, and instructors. At the same time, Moscow suggested in repeated statements, many of an inflammatory nature, its readiness to send Russian forces or 'volunteers' to support Lumumba's Government against NATO and other forces of 'imperialism.'

Inevitably, a dispute developed between the Russians and Hammarskjöld, Hammarskjöld having suggested, in a statement on August 8, that an objective of the United Nations in the Congo was to 'permit the Congolese people to choose freely its political orientation in the world of today, independent of any foreign elements the presence and role of which would mean that through the Congo we might introduce in the continent conflicts extraneous to the African world.' (To this he added, in terms that under the circumstances were not exaggerated, that the immediate achievement of such a solution 'is a question of peace or war—and when saying peace or war I do not limit my perspective to the Congo.')

Lumumba demanded that the United Nations forces be put at the disposal of the Congolese Government that he headed, to be used by him for ejecting the Belgians and for recapturing the seceded province of Katanga. Instead, and without reference to him, Hammarskjöld negotiated the withdrawal of the Belgian combat forces directly with the Belgian Government and the leader of secessionist Katanga, and declined to use the United Nations forces in actual combat against the forces of Katanga.

Again, however, Khrushchev had embarked on a gamble that he would lose. Lumumba, to whose cause he had committed himself, fell from power, and on September 16 the entire staff of the Russian Embassy was expelled by the Congolese Army leader, Mobutu, who had taken the reins of power into his own hands. The Russian presence, which had been building up in the Congo for two months, in the form of men and machines, was abruptly and completely ejected. In the course of the years that followed, an order of sorts was re-established in a neutral Congo to which the Katanga was finally reunited, chiefly by political pressure and negotiation.

The expulsion of the Russians was humiliating for Moscow, and especially for Khrushchev, who could ill afford such a spectacular failure. In what must have been an increasingly reckless frame of mind, he now proceeded to new gambles.

CHAPTER XXXVII

Khrushchev's attempt to reshape the United Nations;
the advent of the Kennedy Administration;
Moscow's third attempt to prize the Western powers
out of Berlin

I N an unanticipated crisis, when the established forces of order
no longer function, a private citizen on the scene may have
to assume an authority with which he has not been formally
vested. This was the position that Hammarskjöld had found himself in when the Congo had suddenly fallen into anarchy. His
mandate from the Security Council had been to furnish the
Government of the Congo 'with all the military assistance which
may be necessary until . . . the national security forces are, in the
opinion of the Government, in a position to deal fully with their
tasks.' But the Government of the Congo was itself manifesting the
Congolese anarchy and unable to function responsibly. With the
support of the Security Council, then, Hammarskjöld did not allow the United Nations Force to come under the Government's
command or to be used in factional combat. It remained under
his direction, with the consequence that he found himself exercising, in detail, a personal authority that was sometimes difficult to
distinguish from governmental authority. The principal objective
toward which he exercised this authority was the exclusion of such
outside forces as were eager to fish in the troubled waters. So it
was that, by a role improvised to meet an unforeseen emergency,
the Secretary General of the United Nations contributed to Moscow's frustration.

From Khrushchev's point of view this was an abandonment by
the Secretary General of the abstinence from international partisanship required of him. What it showed, as he saw it, was that the
Secretariat under Hammarskjöld was in the service of the West.
Khrushchev now undertook, therefore, to remove Hammarskjöld and to destroy the dominating position that the West undoubtedly had been enjoying so far in the United Nations.

He set the stage for this move by a successful undertaking to convert the Fifteenth Session of the General Assembly into a summit conference of sorts. On the argument that disarmament negotiations, which had failed in other forums, should be carried on by heads of government at a regular session of the General Assembly, he succeeded in making the Fifteenth Session an Assembly of Notables. At that Assembly, before an audience including kings, presidents, and prime ministers, the ex-miner from the Ukraine was to play the spectacular personal role that he so evidently relished.

In his initial speech to the General Assembly on September 23, 1960, he demanded Hammarskjöld's resignation, accusing him of illegally intervening in the Congo's internal affairs and of 'siding with the colonialists.' [1] He then proposed that the office of Secretary General be abolished, its function to be entrusted to an executive committee of three persons who should represent, respectively, the countries of the West, the Communist countries, and the countries that were uncommitted in the Cold War. Since the committee would be empowered to take decisions only on the basis of unanimity, any of its members would be able to prevent it from acting against the interests of any one of the three groups, as Hammarskjöld was accused of having done in the Congo. He also suggested that the headquarters of the United Nations be moved out of the United States, saying that it would be welcome in the Soviet Union.

By casting all the issues he raised during his three weeks at the General Assembly in terms of the fight against 'colonialism,' Khrushchev was clearly counting on the support of the African and Asian members, who with the Communist members would have constituted a majority. In this, however, he misjudged the situation. On the whole, the African and Asian members were attached to the international organization that, as it was constituted, provided them with a means of influence in world affairs that they could not have enjoyed otherwise; and they had reason to be grateful to Hammarskjöld for acting to prevent the threatened confrontation in the Congo between Russia and the United States that would have made Africa a principal arena of the Cold

[1] His personal attacks on Hammarskjöld continued in crescendo to the point where, in a letter of the following February to the heads of government in sixty-six countries, he said that Hammarskjöld had 'sullied himself by foul murder,' a charge quite unrelated to any reality.

War. On the two occasions Hammarskjöld had to reply to Khrushchev's attacks by defending his office and his conduct in it he was roundly applauded by almost all present. The second time, he received the longest ovation ever accorded any speaker in the history of the General Assembly, while Khrushchev pounded his desk with his fists in sign of disapproval. It was evident that Khrushchev's proposals for organizational reform had no chance of being carried. He had again taken an initiative that would result in discredit for Moscow and humiliation to himself.

In subsequent meetings of the General Assembly Khrushchev repeatedly engaged in behavior that was impulsive and dramatic to the point of being disorderly. His language, in the violence of its terms, was so unsuited to parliamentary procedure that on occasion he had to be called to order by the Chairman, who in one instance directed that his remarks be expunged from the record as improper in such an assembly. Once, when the Philippine delegate was speaking unfavorably of Moscow's policy, Khrushchev took off his shoe, brandished it at the speaker, and then banged his desk with it while shouting that the speaker was a 'lackey of American imperialism.' The turmoil that followed was so great that the Chairman, who broke his gavel in the attempt to re-establish order, was constrained to adjourn the meeting to the following day.

*   *   *

This may be the best point for a digression on the personal element in the conduct of the Russian state during the years in which Khrushchev was at the head of its Government.

One always felt about the rotund old man, with his rude peasant manner, his bald head, and the impish twinkle in his eyes, that in the combination of wit and good humor with which he tended to redeem his outbreaks of petulance he had the qualities that make the Falstaff of *Henry IV* such an endearing figure. Speaking his farewell to the General Assembly, the day after his disruptive attack on the Philippine delegate, the old man said: 'I beg you not to be offended if I have said anything in a way I should not have done. I hurt the Philippine representative a little, and he hurt me. I am a young parliamentarian; he is an old hand. Let us learn from each other.'

One also had the impression, as with Falstaff, that old Nikita Khrushchev regarded humanity at large with a sort of affectionate gusto, that he enjoyed his association with it, and that he wished it well. His indignation at Stalin's inhumanity, and his desire for good-will among men, were undoubtedly genuine. He was not an ideologist by disposition, although in the untutored state of his mind he accepted the ideological myths of his time with a simple credulity.

The fact remains, however, that he represented a capricious personal conduct of the affairs of a power that had the life of mankind under its hand. Without the element of legitimacy in the control and direction of political power—legitimacy both constitutional and essential—the affairs of the Russian state were being conducted with less than full responsibility.

Although the czars had represented a greater formal legitimacy than their successors, on one occasion after another they had represented as little essential legitimacy; for no personal rule that does not limit itself by boundaries of custom and the accepted ethics of the day, if not by explicit constitutional provision, can be essentially legitimate. The classic example is that provided by some of the more sensational among the successors to Augustus Caesar, who had himself played in ancient Rome the role that Lenin played in Russia. The world had suffered from mad emperors of Rome, and in the absence of institutional safeguards there was no assurance that it would not suffer from mad rulers of Russia. Czars Ivan IV and Paul had provided precedents to match those of Caligula and Nero. The capricious rule of Stalin and the capricious rule of Khrushchev, each in its way, suggested this danger, which was the more alarming in a world where the Roman short sword had been replaced by the long-range missile bearing a nuclear warhead.

On the other hand, the sobering effect of this weapon was the distinguishing feature of international politics in the second half of the twentieth century. There was reason to hope that the consequently strengthened forces of sobriety, in Russia as in any other country that might find itself in a position of similar responsibility, would in the future prevent madness from holding the seats of supreme power as it had held them, on occasion, in the past. We cannot, as I have already suggested in Chapter XXX, altogether exclude the possibility of some parallel between the end of Stalin and the end of Paul.

*   *   *

By the fall of 1960 Moscow had failed, as yet, to make headway at Berlin. It had moved impulsively to establish a sphere of influence in Africa, and had failed there. It had tried to bend the United Nations to its will, and had again failed. In the West the *status quo* remained unyielding in spite of Russia's acquisition of a nuclear arsenal, while in the East the Chinese challenge was developing apace.

As the 1960's began one was increasingly inclined to ask what the Cold War was about. The West was encircling the Russian empire, to contain it, because fifteen years before it had been expanding so dangerously. The Russian empire was pushing against the encircling forces, trying to break them, and this appeared to confirm the premises of containment. The operative motive on both sides, however, was merely the search for a security that, if it was to be attained by either, would have to be a common security based on common agreement.[2]

The fact that only the United States and Russia possessed independent nuclear panoplies created unacknowledged bonds of common interest between them. Each needed an understanding with the other (even though it was only a tacit understanding between enemies) whereby both could feel some assurance that, in a crisis, there would be no sudden exchange of nuclear blows between them—provoked, perhaps, by some misapprehension. Together they had a common interest in the establishment of international arrangements to prevent other countries from acquiring, one after another, nuclear arsenals of their own; for as that happened the problem of preventing nuclear war might become insuperable. Finally, it would now become increasingly evident that the United States and Russia had a common interest in containing China.

On the other hand, the problems of the division of Europe, including the problem of Berlin, were not susceptible, and would not be for as long as anyone could foresee, of any diplomatically arranged and categorical solution. Moscow would be inviting disaster to itself if it withdrew within its traditional frontiers, allowing the rest of East Europe to come under the control of anti-Russian forces; or if it allowed East Germany to join a profoundly hostile West Germany. The West, as we have seen, could not

---

[2] This did not mean that each side did not have to keep the other within the limits of this motive by its own defensive strength. If (to take the extreme case) either side surrendered, the dynamics of the situation would immediately remove the limitation by which the motive of the other was defined.

withdraw from Berlin without disaster; although Moscow, and Khrushchev personally, were now deeply committed to compelling its withdrawal.

If the basic geographical issues between Russia and the West were not susceptible of a categorical diplomatic resolution, then the question that arose was whether the unresolved issues could be lived with. Time had already invested the situation, imperceptibly, with a certain stability. What had seemed so dangerously abnormal in the later 1940's had come to seem less so; what had seemed intolerable as a persisting phenomenon had proved, for fifteen years now, not to be so.

The real grounds for hope arose out of the fact that this irresolvable situation had been evolving, almost of itself, in the direction of what, in terms of history and culture, represented normality. As early as 1949 Yugoslavia had once more become an independent state, self-ruled. Poland had regained a measure of independence and had come to be essentially self-ruled; and its nominal Communism had come to mean little or nothing. By 1960 Albania, so recently a satellite, was in defiance of Moscow. Rumania, too, was to assert a greater independence as the 1960's passed. The Iron Curtain would tend to become constantly more shadowy as contacts between East and West Europe—through economic and cultural exchanges, through tourist travel—developed. Some day one might ask what had ever happened to it. So, by gradual, natural processes, normality might some day be restored.

The division of Germany presented a less encouraging prospect, since the concept of one German nation had become so firmly established in normative thinking that virtually no one could adjust his mind to the conception of two separate German states continuing to exist indefinitely alongside each other. Even here, however, time might be expected to make tractable the intractable. The two states were growing apart as new generations, with distinct educational formation and experience, respectively replaced the old generations in each. By this process they would, in time, no longer quite be one people. While the West Germans continued to demand reunification, there was reason to believe that the demand was acquiring, in some degree, the character of cant. Privately, it was widely recognized that most of the principal political and economic interests in West Germany would view reunification with alarm if it should appear to be abruptly imminent.

What one might expect was that, in time, the East German state would, like the other East European satellites or ex-satellites of Moscow, gradually loosen its bonds. As it achieved independence, then, it might gradually develop a multiplicity of ties with West Germany, perhaps to the point where some kind of federation between the two came into being. By that time, however, both states might be associated, somehow, in a larger community of Europe.

As one surveyed the western scene in 1960, then, the only problem that the Cold War antagonists might find it impossible to live with indefinitely was the problem of Berlin. The draining away of essential elements in the East German population, through the escape-hatch that the Western allies continued to hold open at Berlin after the border had been effectively sealed elsewhere, constantly threatened the breakdown of the East German society and state. As we shall see, however, Moscow would in 1961 resort to a device designed to overcome this danger, and thereby to make it possible for it to live indefinitely with the problem of Berlin.

At the beginning of the 1960's there were signs in the West that people were beginning to weary of the Cold War, and to ask what sense it made. In the late 1940's everyone had been alarmed at the thought of the Red Army, which had already marched so far, continuing on to the English Channel; but this was no longer a plausible fear. The hysterical anti-Communism that had gripped the American people and their Government at the beginning of the 1950's had largely spent itself by the beginning of the 1960's. A disposition to move in the direction of a reasonable peace on the basis of live-and-let-live was beginning to have faint manifestations in the United States, while in Britain there had long been a popular tendency to blame the American ally for the continuation of the Cold War. If this tendency was not more overtly marked at the beginning of the 1960's it was because of the wild behavior with which the head of the Russian Government was repeatedly alarming the world.

This was the evolving situation at the beginning of 1961, when the Eisenhower Administration was replaced by the fresh Administration of President Kennedy.

*   *   *

'On the Presidential coat of arms,' the new President told the nation, 'the American eagle holds in his right talon the olive branch, while in his left is held a bundle of arrows. We intend to give equal attention to both.' By the 1960's the dominant disposition of the American people and of the Western governments was to be equally ready either for possibilities of ending the Cold War or, in the absence of such possibilities, for holding their own in it—to be at once conciliatory and armed, to talk softly but carry a big stick.

It is evident, however, that Khrushchev's whole policy, and consequently his survival as ruler of Russia, now depended on his driving the Western allies out of Berlin. One can well imagine the mounting doubts among his associates in the Kremlin about his leadership, countered by his insistence that his policy needed more time to achieve the success he was sure it would bring; and one can imagine a reluctant decision to let him have the time. By now he must have felt like a man who goes about his business with a gun at his back.

Khrushchev's hope appears to have been that he would succeed with the new Administration of President Kennedy where he had failed with the Eisenhower Administration, which had proved un-expectedly stiff. On these grounds he had bought time, holding the campaign against Berlin in abeyance until the new Admini-stration should establish itself in office. The new Administration, less blatantly anti-Communist than its predecessor, and disposed to look for possibilities of accommodation by compromise, might find itself freer to retreat at Berlin. It might also prove more re-sponsive to the clamor of idealistic intellectuals throughout the West, who tended to regard a firm stand at Berlin as the demon-stration of a criminal willingness to let the world be destroyed by nuclear war.

Once the Kennedy Administration was installed, however, Khrushchev could not delay for much longer the resumption of the drive on Berlin. Both the external situation, in which East Ger-many was being drained of its population through the Berlin escape-route, and the position in which he found himself at home required it. First, however, the possibilities of an amicable settle-ment with the new Administration had to be tested. Friendly words for President Kennedy, and friendly gestures toward the United States, flowed from Moscow and were reciprocated by ex-pressions of peaceful intent from Washington. The two rival leaders of the world, neither yet sure what to expect of the other, then agreed to meet each other face-to-face in private.

The meeting took place in Vienna on June 3 and 4. It must have been revealing for both men, but especially for Kennedy.

Khrushchev, who presented the Russian position in writing (perhaps because his colleagues in Moscow had to be assured of what he presented), appears to have left no doubt that he was determined to end the *status quo* in Berlin, if not by agreement with the West then in defiance of the West. The President appears to have been taken aback by the expression of that determination, and to have left Vienna with the sombre conviction that in the next few months the world was to face a danger of imminent disaster.

In confirmation of this, on June 15 Khrushchev delivered an address in Moscow at which, as in November 1958, he again issued an ultimatum to the West. Russia, he said, was prepared to go ahead on its own to conclude with East Germany the peace treaty by which any rights of access to Berlin that the West might have would be terminated. Then, if the West violated the frontiers of East Germany it would 'receive a due rebuff.' The conclusion of such a treaty, he said, could not be 'postponed any longer,' but 'must be attained this year.' Again, as in 1958, the time-bomb was set a-ticking for all the world to hear.

On July 8 Khrushchev announced that, because of Western intransigence, Russia was abandoning a hitherto projected reduction in its armed forces and was increasing its defense expenditures by over a third. On July 25 Kennedy called for a substantial build-up of NATO forces and an increase in the American Army. 'We do not want to fight,' he said, 'but we have fought before. . . . We cannot and will not permit the Communists to drive us out of Berlin, either gradually or by force.' Khrushchev responded in a speech of August 7 by accusing the United States of 'carrying out mobilization measures, threatening to unleash a war.' He said it might be necessary to increase the numerical strength of the Red Army on the western frontiers and call up the reserves. Continued stubbornness by the West, he implied, might turn Berlin into another Sarajevo, and he spoke of what the Soviet Union could do to the United States and its allies in a third world war.

The international tension, reaching the proportions of a full crisis, now prompted increasing numbers of East Germans to flee through the last door still open to them, fearing that at any moment it would be shut forever. During the first six months of 1961 over 103,000 had made their escape. Then, suddenly, the door was indeed slammed shut, although not in a way that anyone had expected.

Under the terms of the relevant agreements, Berlin had been

administered as one city, with free circulation throughout. Many who lived in the Soviet sector had their places of work in the Western sectors; members of the same family might be living some on one side and some on the other of the imaginary line that separated the area of Soviet administration from the areas of American or British or French administration. At 2.30 a.m. on August 13, however, the East Germans sealed off West Berlin, except for a few official crossing-points where individuals could pass in and out under official inspection, and during the night of August 17–18 they began, on a crash basis, the construction of a concrete wall, topped with barbed wire, to cut the city in two.[3]

The Western allies would have been within their legal rights if they had forcibly interfered with the construction of this wall, and it seems improbable (in tranquil retrospect) that such interference would have led to war. The risk hardly seemed sound at the time, however, and in any case a sober intergovernmental decision to take it could not have been reached in the middle of one night. Weeks and months later, the failure to interfere would be a cause of bitterness in the hearts of those who knew the human suffering and the sense of outrage that the Berlin Wall had produced. A still later judgment, however, can hardly overlook the evidence that the Wall, by stopping the disastrous drainage of the East German population, at last enabled Moscow to live with the situation created for it by the presence of the Western allies in Berlin.

The immediate effect, nevertheless, was not to lessen but to heighten the crisis. Each side had suffered a blow to its international prestige, the West by allowing the Wall to be built, the Communists by providing such visible evidence of the captivity in which their populations were held.[4] For the moment, then, each side was impelled to strike heroic attitudes. Vice President Lyndon Johnson flew from Washington to Berlin, to be followed by General Lucius Clay, the symbol of the resistance to the 1948

[3] The East German puppet dictator, Ulbricht, justified the building of this wall in a broadcast of the 18th on the grounds that those whom he referred to as 'our dear brothers and sisters, the West German people' had allowed their Government to 'fall into the hands of Fascists, Nazis, militarists, revanchists, warmongers, slave traders, and head-hunters.'

[4] The Communists claimed that the purpose of the Wall was to prevent criminal aggressive forces from penetrating into East Germany, but anyone could see for himself (as I did) that the policemen who patrolled it on the Communist side, tommy-guns at the ready, had their backs to it.

blockade, and a reinforcement of 1,500 American soldiers. Moscow accused the West of misusing the air-corridors to Berlin by flying in West German 'revanchists, extremists, saboteurs, and spies.' Emergency military preparations were made on both sides.

Crisis was now being piled on crisis. Again people all over the world stopped sleeping. Again the Western governments had to resist the pressure of articulate intellectuals who were morally outraged by the apparent willingness of the politicians to risk a third world war rather than make peace with Moscow on its terms. Round-about Trafalgar Square in London marched little groups of men and women in single file, the flame of righteousness in their eyes, bearing placards that demanded unilateral nuclear disarmament now.

Since the beginning of November 1958, the United States, Britain, and Russia, by tacit agreement, had discontinued the nuclear test explosions that had been poisoning the atmosphere of the whole northern hemisphere and thereby endangering the future of mankind. Now, on August 21, Moscow announced that, because the United States and its allies were threatening to unleash a war 'as a counter-measure to the conclusion of a peace treaty with the German Democratic Republic,' its obligation to 'cool the hotheads in the capitals of certain NATO powers' required it to resume nuclear testing. Beginning the following day, the Russians successively produced some fifty nuclear explosions, culminating in one of over 50 megatons on October 30, that were designed to intimidate a Western world which, however frightened it might be, was still standing firm.[5]

The continuing firmness of the West, making it constantly more unlikely that Berlin could be won without war before the end of the year, together with the fact that the Berlin Wall reduced Moscow's need for haste, now induced Khrushchev to remove, once again, the deadline from his threat. In an address of October 17 to the 22nd Congress of the Communist Party of the Soviet

[5] A megaton is the equivalent of a million tons of T.N.T. The October 30 explosion, estimated at 57 megatons, was by far the largest ever produced, and with the others caused a sharp rise in the permanent level of radioactivity all around the northern hemisphere, as well as increasing the iodine-131, the strontium-89, the strontium-90, and the caesium-137 in the food and milk supplies of all the countries affected. An explosive in the 50-megaton range was many times more powerful than what would be needed for the complete destruction of any city in the world, so that it would be hard to find any use for it that would justify it even in purely military terms. The detonation of so much explosive power, as Khrushchev privately said, was designed to shock the West into a more yielding attitude.

Union he said that 'if the Western powers show a readiness to solve the German problem the question of time-limits will not be so important. We shall not then insist on having the treaty signed before December 31.' But all the other elements of pressure on the West were maintained, if only in abeyance, and this time there was no campaign to relax tensions such as had followed the withdrawal, in March 1959, of the first ultimatum on Berlin.

We may hardly doubt that, with the passage of the years and the constant deferment of diplomatic victory, Khrushchev was losing his freedom of action. For one thing, he was increasingly constrained by the quarrel with China, which finally came out into the open at the 22nd Congress and was henceforth conducted in public. We cannot dismiss the possibility that two incidental purposes of the great explosion on October 30, while the Congress was still in session, were to impress the Chinese, as well as the West, and to reinforce Moscow's diminishing prestige inside the Communist world.

Through most of 1962, then, the crisis in East–West relations remained unresolved while the crisis in Russo-Chinese relations continued to mount. Khrushchev's power inside Moscow, Moscow's influence throughout the Communist world, and the consequent capacity to meet the Chinese challenge—all now depended on the achievement of that victory in Berlin to which Khrushchev's regime had by this time committed itself almost beyond possibility of retreat. It was in 1962 that Khrushchev's most reckless gamble would come, and it would prove final.

CHAPTER XXXVIII

*Khrushchev's gamble in Cuba, its failure, and the ending
of a chapter in the history of mankind*

REFERRING to Frederick the Great's campaign against
Silesia, Macaulay wrote: 'In order that he might rob a
neighbor whom he had promised to defend, black men fought on
the coast of Coromandel and red men scalped each other by the
Great Lakes of North America.' In Khrushchev's campaign
against Berlin, the final battle would be waged about an island in
the Caribbean.

Cuba, having been liberated from Spain by American arms in
1898, had ever since given a lamentable demonstration of its inability to achieve responsible self-government. Throughout Latin
America from the beginning, disorder and dictatorship had characterized the efforts at self-government, but the scale and continuity of corruption in Cuba had been unsurpassed.

For the United States, the quality of government in Cuba had
constantly posed the standard dilemma of its relations with Latin
America: either it accepted whatever government was in being as
the government with which it had to transact the business of
Cuban–American relations, no matter how disreputable that
government might be, or it violated the principle of non-interven-
tion by deciding for itself what kind of government Cuba should
have. In the latter case, if Washington used its influence to bring
about the downfall of a Cuban government to which it objected,
it was likely to find that the successor government was no better.
Whether it intervened or did not intervene in the domestic affairs
of Cuba, the United States was bound to suffer the condemnation
of all those who, not bearing the responsibility, were free to disregard the dilemma.

The chronic situation was particularly uncomfortable for the
United States because of Cuba's strategic location, ninety miles
from its own coast and in an area of vital importance to its military
security. If disorder in the Congo, by tempting Moscow to establish a position there, had worried the United States, a like situation

in Cuba was bound to be regarded as not tolerable at all. The necessity of excluding from Cuba the military presence of even a potential antagonist from overseas had never been questioned by the American people or Government. Before the nuclear age one assumed that the United States would go to war rather than allow a power like Russia to achieve a lodgement in Cuba.

From 1952 to 1958 Cuba was under the normally corrupt and arbitrary dictatorship of General Fulgencio Batista. The domestic opposition to that dictatorship, which had to operate clandestinely and by the violent devices of insurgency, found its most effective leader in a young man of ebullient personality, Fidel Castro. Castro was moved more by antagonism to the Batista regime than by an ideological doctrine. When asked what kind of political society he intended for Cuba, if he should succeed in unseating Batista, he had resorted to the standard formulations of the Jeffersonian tradition: he was for constitutional democracy based on free and impartial elections; he was for the rights of the individual as opposed to the tyranny of the state; he was for 'free enterprise and invested capital.'[1]

Revolutionary opposition, for most persons who engage in it, is a generalized protest against established society. As such it tends to become a way of life rather than a means to any proximate end. Time and again, therefore, revolutionary leaders have found themselves quite unprepared for the exercise of power when an unexpected collapse of the established system has left it in their hands. This is essentially what had happened to Lenin in 1917. In 1958 it happened to Castro. The Batista regime suddenly collapsed of its own weakness, and Castro found himself at the seat of power without a considered program of any sort. In the event, he improvised measures from day to day, until in a short time he had gone a long way toward wrecking the Cuban society and its economy. To cover the confusion of the wreckage, then, he resorted to impassioned rhetoric, haranguing the Cuban people over television for hours on end, keeping them in a state of emotional excitement that made them willing parties to the sacrifice of their own freedom and welfare, while his lieutenants struggled with the intractable problems of government for which they were so unprepared. Inevitably, the institution of the freedom in which he had once believed proved beyond Castro's capacity. He was

[1] See Draper, Chapter I.

driven by circumstances to establish, rather, a tyranny more complete than Batista's, just as the Bolsheviks in Russia had been driven to establish a tyranny more complete than that of the czars.

Every revolutionary regime, to gain the acquiescence of the people in the sacrifices it imposes on them, has to madden them with the specter of a monstrous external enemy. Now Castro, driven by this necessity, embarked on a campaign of verbal violence against the United States, which he depicted as getting ready to invade the Cuban fatherland and enslave the Cuban people. The devices of the *agent provocateur* were used to provoke responses from Washington that would tend to bear out the accusations of its hostility and its monstrous intentions. American properties were seized, American diplomats were arrested. Washington held itself in check, but it was in the position of a man who is being stoned in the street by an urchin: it could hardly help but act to defend its interests and its dignity. At last, when Castro ordered all members of the American Embassy in Havana above the number of eleven to be out of the country within forty-eight hours, Washington broke diplomatic and consular relations.

Castro and his associates, being crisis-driven from the moment they seized power, had taken one desperate measure after another with little regard for any consequences beyond the immediate. The Cuban economy, as they found it, was entirely dependent on the United States, which in effect subsidized the sugar crop by accepting it at prices above those prevailing in the open market. Political compulsion, however, proved stronger than economic reason. So, by provoking the United States to such actions as the reduction of the Cuban sugar quota, the Castro regime cracked the foundations of the Cuban economy. The only way it could save itself, then, was to turn to Moscow for rescue. Khrushchev was irresistibly tempted. He saw himself being offered in Cuba the kind of triumph that was eluding him in the Congo. He began, then, in various ways to assume for the Russian Government the considerable burden of supporting the Cuban economy. He even went so far, in a speech of July 9, 1960, as nominally to put Cuba under Russia's military protection, saying: 'Figuratively speaking, in case of necessity Soviet artillery can support the Cuban people with its rocket fire if aggressive forces in the Pentagon [the American Defense Department] dare to start an intervention against Cuba. . . . We . . . shall make use of everything to support Cuba. . . .'

As Castro became increasingly dependent on Russia and the other Communist states he was moved by the association to identify himself as a member of the family, thereby establishing his claim to their support and protection. Before 1961 was out he had by this process gone so far as to denominate his Cuba a Communist state and a member of the Communist bloc. He had reached out for a corner of the Iron Curtain to place between himself and the United States.

This was an extraordinary situation that, in the long run, could hardly fail to be as embarrassing for Moscow as for Washington. If Stalin had been opposed to the establishment of Communist regimes in Yugoslavia and Greece because they would be beyond the area of Moscow's control, one can imagine how much more reluctant he would have been to involve himself in bonds of ideological brotherhood with an unpredictable regime on the other side of the world from him but within the very ramparts of his great opponent's defense system. Stalin, denouncing Yugoslav support of the Greek Communists, had said to the Yugoslav Vice President: 'What, do you think that Great Britain and the United States—the United States, the most powerful state in the world—will permit you to break their line of communication in the Mediterranean? Nonsense. And we have no navy.'[2] Now the situation was essentially the same, except that the sea was the Caribbean.

The measure of Khrushchev's recklessness is shown by the fact that he involved the prestige of Russia in a growing commitment to protect a country far beyond its reach, and to protect it against an enemy at whose feet it lay.

The fact that Moscow was putting itself in such danger did not, however, mean that the situation was without very great danger for the United States as well. In the world's eyes the United States appeared as a brutish Goliath under the attack of a gallant David, and all over Latin America the traditional resentment against 'the Colossus of the North' was taking the form of support for Castro, whose agents were actively stirring up disorders. The chief danger for the United States was that its self-control under such provocation might fail, that at some point it might make a premature or impulsive response by which it would bring endless trouble upon itself. If it should be provoked into taking direct

[2] See p. 86 above.

military action to unseat Castro it would arouse an impassioned opposition throughout Latin America, and it might well end up in the position of having to hold the Cuban people down by force, not daring to let them go. What the authoritarian Russian Government had been able to do in Hungary only with the greatest difficulty would, however, prove impossible in Cuba for the liberal government of the United States. The end would surely be political disaster of some sort.

The dilemma arose out of the fact that, as we have seen, the establishment in Cuba of a base for Russian power, if that should appear to be under way, could not be regarded as other than intolerable by the American people. It was hardly conceivable that any administration in Washington could, in such a contingency, hold back from taking whatever measures might be required to prevent it. Here valid strategical considerations would be powerfully reinforced by the fundamental tradition of the United States identified with the Monroe Doctrine. Over the long run, then, it was a dangerous situation for Washington and Moscow alike. In the case of Washington, the risks of acting and the risks of not acting might prove equally great.

*   *   *

As Russian technicians, advisers, and agents entered Cuba in their thousands to assist in economic planning, in industrial development, and in military training as well, it became increasingly difficult for Washington to remain in the attitude of a disinterested spectator. More and more voices were being raised in Congress, in the top ranks of the military services, and elsewhere, to express a mounting alarm and to demand action. Inside the Government it seemed only prudent to make preparations in good time for the not unlikely contingency that, in the near future, there would no longer be an acceptable alternative to forcible action.

By the end of 1960 Cuban refugees were arriving in Florida at the rate of 1,000 per week. The number of refugees in the United States and other countries about the Caribbean would soon be over 100,000. Here were the makings of a Cuban army in exile that might, if it should come to seem advisable, invade Cuba, join hands with the increasing number of rebels in the island's interior, and march to overthrow Castro. Cuba might be invaded, then, by Cubans only, rather than by a foreign army. The project would work if popular dissatisfaction with Castro's regime had reached a point at which an invasion, however inadequate in itself, should start a general uprising.

During the winter of 1960–1961, through President Eisenhower's last and President Kennedy's first days in office, preparations were made for the contingency. Cuban refugees were secretly armed, organized, and trained by the United States—in Florida, in Guatemala, and in Nicaragua. So a movement to overthrow Castro by means of an invasion got under way simply as a matter of readiness in case an invasion should seem advisable. It gained momentum as it increased in scale, until the possible invasion became a vested interest for the enthusiasts in the American bureaucracy who were giving so much to its preparation. President Kennedy, when he came to office, found everything going forward, even though there had been no decision actually to undertake an invasion. Matters were apparently coming to the point where the decision that would be called for would be whether to stop an undertaking already in motion rather than whether to embark on it. Politically, this was a much harder decision for the inexperienced President to take, and it was not made easier by the excessively optimistic reports, from Cuban refugees and from advisers who had become psychologically committed to the enterprise, that the Cuban people were ready to rise up in support of an invading force. So the President agreed to the projected invasion, which took place at the Bay of Pigs on April 17, 1961. But the Cuban people did not rise up, and Castro's forces were able to round up the invaders in short order.

This was a major political disaster for Washington, which could not dissemble the fact that it had been behind the adventure. Goliath had struck at David and missed. All over the world the United States was denounced for a brutal and bullying imperialism. Khrushchev, joining in the denunciation, hinted at possible Russian military intervention to protect Cuba from its would-be ravisher.

This incident, in simultaneously humiliating the United States and enhancing Castro's prestige, was bound to make the United States more reluctant in the future to try military intervention again; and this, in turn, would encourage Khrushchev to take even greater risks.

*   *   *

After the erection of the Berlin Wall, in August 1961, Khrush-chev had once more allowed the intensity of the Berlin crisis to diminish. But nothing was settled, and the position remained that, at a moment of its own choosing, Moscow would enter into a treaty with its East German puppet whereby the latter would claim sovereign jurisdiction over all Berlin and over the routes by which the Western allies had been having access to it. Therefore, the lull that continued month after month in 1962 seemed ominous. There was a general apprehension that a final confrontation over Berlin was being prepared, and the growing expectation was that it would take place in November. In fact, on September 11 Moscow announced that it was willing to keep the issue of Berlin in abeyance only until the Congressional elections in the United States, scheduled for November 6. Again one could detect the ticking of the time-bomb.

Throughout the West, now, the question in men's minds was what surprise Moscow was preparing to spring in November. It was clear that the diplomatic device of the ultimatum, by itself, had been too discredited by successive failures for further use, and it was doubtful that Khrushchev could afford a third defeat at Berlin. Presumably, then, Moscow was developing some new tactic for bringing pressure on the United States and its allies, some tactic that might be expected, this time, to prove irresis-tible. The Western nations braced themselves and waited in dire suspense. That suspense would be relieved, at last, in the second half of October.

The increasing presence in Cuba of Russian military personnel and Russian military equipment had been causing mounting alarm in Washington and among the American people. Conse-quently, Washington had been keeping an eye on military developments in Cuba by means of its U-2 photographic-recon-naissance planes. On October 14 one such plane took photographs that, developed in Washington the next day, showed that Russian medium-range missiles, capable of delivering nuclear warheads up to a distance of 1,200 nautical miles (almost 1,400 statute miles), had been emplaced in western Cuba. Further photo-graphs in the next two days showed sites under construction for the launching of intermediate-range missiles, capable of deliver-ing nuclear warheads to a distance of some 2,000 nautical miles—that is, to any point in the United States short of California and the Northwest. At the same time, it transpired, Russian bombers capable of carrying nuclear bombs were being uncrated and assembled in Cuba.

This, evidently, was the surprise that Moscow was getting ready to spring after November 6, when it planned to renew its campaign against Berlin. It would then be in a position to reveal that, with its new bases in Cuba, it could destroy most of the major cities of the United States in a matter of minutes if Washington still refused to retreat from Berlin.

A week of secret staff preparation in Washington culminated, on October 22, in a television broadcast by the President. After revealing what had been going on in Cuba he said:

> This secret, swift, and extraordinary build-up of Communist missiles in an area well known to have a special and historical relationship to the United States . . . is a deliberately provocative and unjustified change in the *status quo* which cannot be accepted by this country. . . . Our unswerving objective, therefore, must be to prevent the use of these missiles against this or any other country, and to secure their withdrawal or elimination from the Western Hemisphere.

Toward this end, he said, he had ordered a blockade of Cuba to prevent the delivery of any further offensive military equipment.[3] If the offensive military preparations now under way in Cuba should be continued, he said, further action would be justified, and he had therefore directed the armed forces of the United States to prepare for any eventualities. Any nuclear missile launched from Cuba against any nation in the Western Hemisphere would be regarded as an attack by Russia on the United States, requiring a full retaliatory response on Russia. He then said: 'I call upon Chairman Khrushchev to halt and eliminate this clandestine, reckless, and provocative threat . . . and to join in an historic effort to end the perilous arms race and transform the history of man.'

Alert to the possibility of a move against Berlin while Washington was preoccupied with Cuba, the President added: 'Any hostile move anywhere in the world against the safety and freedom of peoples to whom we are committed—including in particular the brave people of West Berlin—will be met by whatever action is needed'.

The United States Navy was ordered to stop and search any

---

[3] Since a blockade in time of peace is forbidden by international law he called it a 'quarantine.'

ship believed to be carrying the forbidden weapons to Cuba, and
to use force against it if necessary. On the day these orders went
into effect, October 24, twenty-five Russian ships were traversing
the sea on courses to Cuba, while work on the missile bases in
Cuba was continuing at full speed. That night, twelve of the
twenty-five Russian ships (presumably those carrying the forbidden cargo) turned around; but the construction of the missile
bases continued. The following evening, amid widespread reports
that Washington was ready to take military action to insure the
removal of the offensive weapons from Cuba, a letter from
Khrushchev to Kennedy indicated that Moscow was willing to
comply with Washington's demands.[4] Then, on the 28th, Moscow
announced that Khrushchev had ordered all work on the missile-
sites to be stopped, the missiles to be returned to Russia.

With the end of the relatively short and sharp Cuban missile
crisis, the long Berlin crisis was at an end too. Now whatever plans
Moscow may have had for action against Berlin after November 6
would not be carried out.[5]

*   *   *

October 1962, like July 1947, was a turning-point in relations
between Russia and the West. The contending sides in the Cold
War had been like two men fighting in the vicinity of an abyss
who come so close to its brink that, all at once, they see it opening
at their feet. In sudden alarm, then, they leave off fighting to
concentrate on their common safety. After that, the shared experience of so great a danger proves to be an unexpected bond
between them. For the time being, at least, they are less concerned
with the ultimate issue of victory or defeat than with the achievement of some mutual understanding whereby their conflict will
be kept within tolerable limits of safety. Together, and by agreement between them, they move back from the brink.

The initiative in the Cold War had, from the beginning, been
with Moscow. Obsessed throughout its history with the fear of
foreign encirclement, it had throughout its history been pushing

[4] Everything shows that there had been no contingency planning in Moscow for
what had happened, that Moscow was improvising its reponses in a state of alarm and
confusion. Khrushchev's letter of October 26, bearing all the signs of haste and excitement in its composition, was immediately followed by another of the 27th that con-
tradicted it. The second letter was disregarded by Washington, which found it more
advantageous to act on the basis of the first.

[5] See Kaufmann, pp. 270-1.

against the encircling powers. At the end of World War II, with the total collapse of all power on its western borders, this push had resulted in the cataclysmic expansion of its empire. The United States, then, in sudden alarm had committed itself to the containment of that expansion. This, in turn, had provoked atavistic impulses of alarm in Moscow, which saw containment as encirclement by powers intending its destruction. So it had committed itself to breaking the ring of containment. Throughout the Cold War that had followed, Moscow had had the initiative simply because it had been in the position of trying to break a line that the West had been in the position of trying to hold.

What the years of the Cold War showed was that, in the radically altered circumstances of a world come under the domination of the new arsenals, the advantage that the *status quo* normally enjoys had been decisively enhanced. While its defenders had only to stand firm, any who challenged it were bound to find themselves inhibited by the fear of what might be detonated if they should move forcibly against it. The advance against the *status quo* in Korea had proved to be a mistake, and the danger it had entailed must have been sobering in its effect on those in Moscow who had given the signal for it. In Berlin, despite the advantage enjoyed by the challenger in the disparity between his military forces and the defending forces on the scene, he had repeatedly felt constrained to draw back from the final test when the greatness of the risk became evident. Sober and responsible men, while they may accept a large risk of limited disaster, cannot accept a much smaller risk of unlimited disaster. Even if the odds should be only one in twenty that a particular move would fail, they could not accept them if its failure would entail the final destruction of civilization.

As in Berlin and Korea, Moscow had successively moved against the *status quo* in the Middle East, in Africa, and even in the Caribbean—only to draw back each time when the magnitude of the danger had become apparent. The same consideration had prevented the United States and its allies from moving to liberate the East European peoples, even when the populations of East Germany and of Hungary had risen up, in the hope of help from the West, to break their bonds.

By the end of 1962 there could have been little doubt left in Moscow that the positions occupied by the West were too firmly held to be overcome without a risk of general destruction that it could not accept. Moreover, Russia's possession of a deterrent nuclear arsenal, by reducing the insecurity identified with American encirclement, had lessened the need to break through that encirclement.

On the Western side as well, the issues of the late 1940's had become attenuated or had disappeared altogether. West Europe had been restored to strength, and there was no longer any fear that the Red Army would march to the Channel. Equilibrium and stability had gradually returned to the North Atlantic world since the years when a total breakdown had appeared imminent. A geographical *status quo* that had seemed too abnormal for endurance had endured so long, at last, as to begin to seem normal. While withstanding all the deliberate and forceful attempts made against it, the *status quo* had also showed that it was subject to the gradual transformations of historical evolution. For some years now the Iron Curtain had been becoming less substantial, the division of Europe had been losing its sharpness. The East European nations that had fallen under the power of Moscow in the cataclysms of the 1940's were, step by step, regaining their independence. Ideological considerations were losing their force as the meaning of the tag 'Communism,' applied to countries like Poland and Yugoslavia, became increasingly doubtful. Across what was supposed to be the line of confrontation between two warring camps communications, travel, and trade were increasing. If the nations on either side of that line were still enemies, there was constantly increasing fraternization between them. As with the conflict between Christendom and Islam centuries earlier, the slow churning forces of secular change were transforming the conditions on which the Cold War had been based. The question arose, then, whether the old conceptions of the Cold War were still relevant to the changed times.

History does not lend itself to neat terminations like those of fiction. For many centuries Russia had been in conflict with the West, and no final end to that conflict could as yet be foreseen in the 1960's. The Cold War constituted one chapter in this long history, being a spasm in the conflict brought on by a collapse of the Western power structure. While the spasm lasted it had been characterized by the apparent imminence of military destruction on a scale never before possible. But the destruction had been averted and, with the lapse of time, stability had been restored. By the end of 1962 the spasm appeared to be over.

The shock of the Cuban crisis and a common concern with the growing menace of China now moved Russia and the West to abate their quarrel and to undertake the development of cooperative relations between them. Within a year Moscow and Washington had concluded a treaty in which they, together with others, limited the arms race by agreeing to conduct no further tests of nuclear devices in the atmosphere, in the sea, or in outer space. They had also set up a special telegraph circuit between them whereby, in case of another crisis that threatened sudden war, the President of the United States and the Russian Prime Minister would be able to communicate with each other instantly, so as to avert the danger by joint action.[6]

Hardly more than a year after the Cuban crisis, when President Kennedy was assassinated, Khrushchev sent his successor a warm message of grief and condolence. The President's death, he said, was 'a severe blow to all who cherish the cause of peace and Soviet–American cooperation.' There was public grief throughout Russia and East Europe. In Poland, the Government proclaimed a national day of mourning.

Less than a year after that, Khrushchev himself would at last be removed from office by his associates, who in defiance of a long tradition would attempt to set up in Russia a legitimate and sober government that, taking account of the responsibility imposed by nuclear power, would avoid the dangerous excesses of Stalin and Khrushchev alike.

[6] During the Cuban crisis Kennedy and Khrushchev had communicated with each other through diplomatic channels that required several hours for the transmission of each message. Intercontinental missiles, by contrast, could span the distance in a few minutes only. It was conceivable that, in another crisis, both nations would be destroyed unless the words traveled faster than the missiles. The special communication link between Moscow and Washington had, in any case, an important symbolic significance.

EPILOGUE

The embroilment of the United States in Asia as a consequence of the Cold War, and the prospects for the future

ALL nations cultivate myths that endow them with dignity and, when occasion arises, give nobility to the causes in which they fight. A simple view would have it that myths, being fictional, must therefore be false. In a more sophisticated view, myths belong to the conceptual world by which, alone, we are able to interpret the existential world that constitutes our raw environment. This conceptual world, even if fictional, provides interpretations of the existential world that we must assume to be true in some degree. Most of us would agree that Shakespeare's *Hamlet* is a piece of fiction that represents truth in a high degree. Einstein's special theory of relativity is also a piece of fiction that, we suppose, represents truth in a high degree.[1]

We men have to live, then, in two worlds at once, the conceptual and the existential, and our central problem is to maintain the correspondence between them. It is when these two worlds diverge excessively that we find ourselves in serious trouble.[2]

Under circumstances of conflict between individuals or societies, and to the degree that conflict becomes passionate, the respective conceptual formulations of the parties tend to diverge from the existential realities they ostensibly represent. Fear, hatred, and the need for self-justification find their expression in conceptual falsification, whether innocent or deliberate.

---

[1] 'Physical concepts are free creations of the human mind, and are not, however it may seem, uniquely determined by the external world. In our endeavor to understand reality we are somewhat like a man trying to understand the mechanism of a closed watch. He sees the face and the moving hands, even hears its ticking, but he has no way of opening the case. If he is ingenious he may form some picture of a mechanism which could be responsible for all the things he observes, but he may never be quite sure his picture is the only one which could explain his observations.' (Einstein and Infeld, p. 31.)

[2] I have developed this thesis in my *Men and Nations*, and have exemplified it in *The Society of Man*.

Whenever an international conflict breaks out, each side is impelled to construct what we might call an advocate's account of the existential circumstances by which to identify itself with righteousness and its opponent with evil. At its crudest this takes the form of deliberately fabricated propaganda. More commonly it takes forms that are, at least in a subjective sense, less corrupt. When a people is called on by its national leadership to sacrifice all comfort and happiness for the sake of victory, the leadership is driven to create a mythology (in which it generally believes itself) that will serve to justify such sacrifices in their eyes. So it creates, for example, the myth of a proletarian struggle against wicked capitalists that is destined to bring about, at last, a classless society in which universal justice and happiness will be established forevermore; or it creates the myth of a worldwide contest between 'peace-loving' and 'aggressor' nations; and so the divergence between the existential and the conceptual is widened, with potentially tragic results. The false myth that inspires a people to fight successfully may obviate the possibility of crowning its success by the conclusion of a peace. This tragedy, represented in the two World Wars and their consequences, was not to be spared mankind altogether in the conclusion of the Cold War.

*   *   *

At the outset of the Cold War, the specific objective of the Western allies, however it was generalized for rhetorical purposes, had been to contain Russia's westward expansion at the line it had already reached in Europe. The specific objective of the Russians had been to prevent the restoration, on the western side of this line, of a strength they regarded as menacing. In the event, Western strength was restored in spite of the Russian opposition, and so the Russian empire expanded no farther. This result, however, left the two sides still at grips with each other in a conflict with diminishing relevance to the particular issues over which it had begun. Like all great conflicts, it had become its own reason for being; it had taken on implications of life and death for each side. On each side voices rose to proclaim the necessity of finally eliminating the menace that the other represented. What this history exemplifies is the tendency in any great conflict for the issues to become generalized and unlimited. The conflict called the Cold War quickly expanded until it encircled the globe—as had been the case with both World Wars, each of which had at first been confined to Europe. Generalization, expansion, and intensification gave increased scope to the conceptual corruption that, as we have seen, is an element in every conflict.

From the beginning the West was governed by the myth of a single conspiracy for world conquest under the direction of a satanic band in the Kremlin to whom all who called themselves Communists, the world over, gave blind obedience. On the basis of this myth the United States, especially, identified the triumph of a native uprising on the mainland of Asia in 1949 as the extension of the Kremlin's empire to include China, whose 600 million people were, accordingly, thought to have fallen captive to the conspiracy. Under Washington's leadership, then, the line of containment was extended, from the Middle East across South Asia and north to Korea, in order to embrace what was regarded as the enlarged Russian empire. Along the 38th parallel in Korea, along the line of islands from Japan to the Philippines, in the Straits of Formosa, and along the 17th parallel in Viet Nam, the United States deployed its military strength. So it was that, even after it had become clear that China was, in fact, independent of Moscow, the United States found itself committed to the siege it had already mounted.

If there was misapprehension on the part of the United States that led to this new Asian conflict, there was more extreme misapprehension on the part of China. When Mao Tse-tung and his collaborators came to power in 1949 they were as ignorant of the international world, in its existential reality, as Lenin and his collaborators had been when they came to power in 1917. In both cases, an ideological myth that had almost no correspondence to that world, standing for it in their minds, had misled them. It had led Lenin to expect that the workers and peasants of the countries that were neighbors to Russia, if not the workers and peasants of the whole world, were ready to rally behind the revolutionary banner that he held aloft, to overthrow the bourgeois states of the day at his signal, and to establish the international dictatorship of the proletariat that the prophets, Marx and Engels, had foreseen. Over thirty years of disillusioning experience had, by the 1950's, taught first Lenin and then his successors that the existential reality did not correspond to the conceptual vision on which this expectation had been based.

In the winter of 1949–1950 Mao and his associates had been at the same stage of innocence as Lenin and his associates in the winter of 1917–1918. Their ideological preconception presented to them a world divided between the evil capitalist-imperialists and the victims of their exploitation, the peasants and workers who, at this stage in history, stood increasingly ready to fulfill the hundred-year-old prophecy of the *Communist Manifesto* by breaking the chains that bound them, destroying the slave states of the capitalist-imperialists, and establishing forever the ultimate society of mankind in which all men were free and equal.[3] The United States, in this entrancing vision, was the leader of the imperialist camp in the worldwide struggle that was now reaching its climax. Therefore, by *a priori* conception, the United States was the chief enemy of the new China, which represented the peasants and workers of the world in their historic movement of liberation.

The fact that over the years the United States had become so closely identified with the *ancien régime* of Generalissimo Chiang Kai-shek served to confirm this view. Washington's intention of disengaging itself from this regime, when it had clearly lost the Chinese civil war, had been frustrated by an access of ideological passion among the American people and the consequent prevalence over their minds of concepts that misrepresented the existential circumstances in China. The final and inescapable commitment of the United States to the losing side had occurred, then, at that nocturnal meeting in Blair House when the unpondered decision had been taken to intervene with military force in the Straits of Formosa.

Even before this decision had been taken, however, the new Chinese regime had embarked on a campaign of anti-American propaganda and of atrocities against American citizens who fell into its hands. It is evident that, in addition to the ideological motive, what this represented was the need that every revolutionary regime feels, upon its acquisition of power, to create the bogy of a monstrous external enemy as a basis for enforcing on its own population the discipline without which it could not survive. The Sino-American conflict had already attained a considerable

[3] Marx and Engels had had only industrial workers (the proletariat) in mind. Lenin had discounted the peasants as a revolutionary force. Mao, raised in a peasant country with few industrial workers, had in effect given them the role that Marx and Engels had reserved for the proletariat. (This had been his heresy in Moscow's eyes after 1927.) So the authority of the prophets was maintained for a prophecy that had been conveniently transmuted.

intensity, then, before the decision was made to intervene in the Straits of Formosa. That decision, however, made the conflict irresolvable, perhaps for a generation to come. Self-deception on both sides, in 1949–1950, must be held accountable for the extension of the Cold War to the Far East in a form in which it could not be brought to an end when the original conflict in Europe had at last reached the point of resolution.

At the same time that the United States committed itself to the defense of the defeated Chinese regime in its Formosan refuge it also began to commit itself, by a more gradual process, to the defense of the regime in Viet Nam that had been improvised largely by the French and that, although possessing questionable authority in the country, qualified for American support by its identification as anti-Communist. Just as the United States had committed itself to the containment of China in the belief that it was thereby containing the Russian empire, so it committed itself to the containment of the Vietnamese liberation movement under the impression that it was thereby containing the Chinese (or the Russo-Chinese) empire.

*   *   *

The original Cold War had been set off by the sudden expansion of Russia in Europe. Consequently, there could be little doubt in any impartial mind that, when the West rallied under American leadership to halt that expansion, it was acting in its own legitimate defense rather than in a spirit of aggression. But China, when the United States undertook its containment, had not expanded beyond its traditional boundaries.[4] To anyone familiar with the dynamics of revolution a theoretical danger of expansion did exist, and this justified vigilance on the part of its neighbors and of those powers that bore a responsibility for the maintenance of international order. Because it had not in fact expanded, however, and because the United States was in the position of denying the new Chinese Government's right to govern even in China proper, the United States was, in this case, the party that appeared to be playing the role of aggressor in Asia. In Viet Nam, as everyone could see, the foreign forces were not Chinese; they were those

[4] The occupation of Tibet in 1959 was the occupation of a land that had traditionally belonged to the Chinese empire. The occupation in 1962 of certain areas on the Himalayan frontier with India was the occupation of areas to which India had no clearer title than China.

of the United States and its allies, and the forces opposing them in the field were native Vietnamese. This represented an essentially false position into which the United States, acting on the misconceptions that conflict engenders, had got itself; for it was in fact without expansionist ambitions, in Asia or anywhere else. By the middle of the 1960's, however, its essential commitments in Asia had become inescapable—just as its ancient commitment to the defense of China, however unwise in its origins, had become inescapable by the 1930's.

The position that the United States was in with respect to China and Viet Nam was only superficially similar to the position it had been in with respect to Russia when it embarked, with Russia's European neighbors, on the original policy of containment. A better parallel was that of the period from 1918 to 1920 in Russia, when Britain and the United States had refused to recognize Lenin's revolutionary new regime and had deployed their military forces against it.[5]

By the middle of the 1960's both sides in the original Cold War were disposed to discontinue the contest and to seek the development of more rewarding relations between them. Although far from ready to swear friendship, the powers that had been led by Moscow and those that had been led by Washington were ready to make peace. Unless the international situation got altogether out of control, eventuating in some wide catastrophe, such a peace would gradually be achieved, although its achievement would be delayed by all the repercussions of the American involvement in Asia. The time would come, then, when the division of Europe that had characterized the period immediately after World War II would have faded away, when new combinations and new conflicts had established new divisions across the world. And, all the time, the inexorable pressure of technological development would be enforcing a constantly growing association of the European states, and more widely of the states opening on the Atlantic, just as the once independent and sovereign Swiss cantons had been forced into the increasing association that had at last taken the form of their confederation. In such an association the boundary between the two Germanies would lose its importance, and so the Berlin problem, without ever being solved, would disappear. All

---

[5] This involvement in Russia had been a by-product of Anglo-American belligerency in World War I, just as the American involvement with China and Viet Nam, now, was a by-product of America's struggle in the Cold War.

this, it might be expected, would come about imperceptibly, like the movement of the hour-hand on a watch.[6]

What one could not foresee the end of, as yet, was conflict. In the constant recombinations of international society there would be new and sometimes alarming confrontations of power. Formerly, conflicts between societies had always been subject to the dynamics of escalation, which led to their resolution, at last, by the test of military combat. Since 1945, however, the presence on the scene of weapons that could, presumably, destroy the greatest societies in one blow, had had a major inhibiting effect on this tendency. What was historically unique about the Cold War was the restraining influence of the new weapons, which had prevented a conflict on the grand scale from culminating in general war. In the new weapons, then, lay the hope of the world, no less than its peril, as it moved on into an unknown future.

[6] All prediction is based on the perception of some order that has extension in time. Every order, however, is subject to disruption by unpredictable accidents. I can predict of a child that it will, in a certain number of years, be a man, but my prediction assumes that it will not be killed by an automobile first. Our world may be in evolution toward a more complete order than exists at present, but accident still plays a major role in it.

Publications Cited

In writing the foregoing chapters I made constant use of the eleven volumes of the *Survey of International Affairs* (London, 1955–1965) produced by the Royal Institute of International Affairs since World War II, and the seventeen volumes of *The United States in World Affairs* (New York, 1948–1965) produced by the Council on Foreign Relations since the War. I resorted for documentation to the Royal Institute's series, *Documents on International Affairs* (London, 1951–1965), to the *Documentation Française* (Paris), and to the back files of *The New York Times* and *Le Monde* (Paris). What I relied on most heavily, however, was *Keesing's Contemporary Archives* (London). Without this treasure-house of information and documentation the task I had set myself would have required additional years of work.

The following list of the publications cited in these chapters gives some of my other sources of information:

ACHESON, Dean, *Sketches from Life*, New York, 1961.

ASPATURIAN, Vernon W., and KEEP J. (editors), *Contemporary History in the Soviet Mirror*, London, 1964.

BAILLIE, Hugh, *High Tension*, New York, 1959.

BELL, Coral, *Survey of International Affairs*, London, 1957.

CALVOCORESSI, Peter, *Survey of International Affairs: 1947–1948*, London, 1952.

—— *Survey of International Affairs: 1949–1950*, London, 1953.

CHAMBERLIN, William Henry, *The Russian Enigma*, New York, 1943.

CHURCHILL, Winston S., *The Grand Alliance*, Boston, 1950.

—— *The Hinge of Fate*, Boston, 1950.

—— *Triumph and Tragedy*, Boston, 1953.

CRANKSHAW, Edward, *The New Cold War: Moscow v. Peking*, London, 1963.

DEDIJER, Vladimir, *Tito Speaks*, New York, 1953.

DINERSTEIN, Herbert S., *War and the Soviet Union*, New York, 1959.

DJILAS, Milovan, *Conversations with Stalin*, New York, 1962.

DRAPER, Theodore, *Castroism: Theory and Practice*, New York, 1965.

DULLES, John Foster, 'Policy for Security and Peace,' *Foreign Affairs*, Vol. 43, July 1965.

EINSTEIN, Albert, and INFELD, Leopold, *The Evolution of Physics*, Cambridge, 1961.

FEIS, Herbert, *The China Tangle*, Princeton, 1953.
—— *Churchill, Roosevelt, Stalin*, Princeton, 1957.
—— *Japan Subdued*, Princeton, 1961.

FISCHER, Louis, *The Life of Lenin*, New York, 1964.

FITZGERALD, C. P., *Revolution in China*, New York, 1952.

FORSTER, E. M., *Abinger Harvest*, New York, 1936.

FRANKLIN, William M., 'Zonal Boundaries and Access to Berlin,' *World Politics*, Vol. XVI, October 1963.

GROOM, A. J. R., 'U.S.-Allied Relations and the Atomic Bomb in the Second World War,' *World Politics*, Vol. XV, October 1962.

HALLE, Louis J., *Choice for Survival*, New York, 1958.
—— *Dream and Reality*, New York, 1959 (published as *American Foreign Policy*, London, 1960).
—— *Men and Nations*, Princeton, 1962.
—— *The Society of Man*, London and New York, 1965.

HIGGINS, Trumbull, *Korea and the Fall of MacArthur*, New York, 1960.

HULL, Cordell, *The Memoirs of Cordell Hull*, New York, 1948.

JONES, Joseph M., *The Fifteen Weeks*, New York, 1955.

KANT, Immanuel, *Critique of Pure Reason*, (trans. by J. M. D. Meiklejohn), New York, 1934.

KAUFMANN, William W., *The McNamara Strategy*, New York, 1964.

KENNAN, George F., *Russia and the West under Lenin and Stalin*, Boston, 1961.

KEYNES, John Maynard, *The Economic Consequences of the Peace*, New York, 1920.

MARSHALL, George C., *The War Reports*, Philadelphia, 1947.

MOSELY, Philip E., 'The Occupation of Germany,' *Foreign Affairs*, Vol. 28, July 1950.

NOEL-BAKER, Philip, *The Arms Race*, New York, 1958.

OPPENHEIMER, J. Robert, *Science and the Common Understanding*, New York, 1954.

PARES, Bernard, *A History of Russia*, New York, 1950.

PICKERSGILL, J. W., *The Mackenzie King Record: 1939–1944*, Chicago, 1960.

REES, David, *Korea: The Limited War*, London, 1964.

ROVERE, Richard H., and SCHLESINGER, Arthur M., Jr., *The General and the President*, New York, 1951.

Russian Institute, Columbia University (editor), *The Anti-Stalin Campaign and International Communism*, New York, 1956.

SCHWARTZ, Benjamin L., *Chinese Communism and the Rise of Mao*, Cambridge (Mass.), 1951.

STEBBINS, Richard P., *The United States in World Affairs, 1949*, New York, 1950.

—— *The United States in World Affairs, 1950*, New York, 1951.

STIMSON, Henry L., and BUNDY, McGeorge, *On Active Service in Peace and War*, New York, 1948.

THUCYDIDES, *History of the Peloponnesian War* (trans. by R. W. Livingstone), New York, 1944.

TOCQUEVILLE, Alexis de, *De la Démocratie en Amérique*, Paris, 1961.

TOYNBEE, Arnold and Veronica (editors), *Survey of International Affairs: The Realignment of Europe*, London, 1955.

TROTSKY, L., *My Life*, New York, 1930.

TRUMAN, Harry S., *Year of Decisions*, New York, 1955.

WOHLSTETTER, Albert, 'The Delicate Balance of Terror,' *Foreign Affairs*, Vol. 37, January 1959.

WOHLSTETTER, Roberta, 'Cuba and Pearl Harbor,' *Foreign Affairs*, Vol. 43, July 1965.

The epigraph by George Santayana is from his *Character and Opinion in the United States*, the third paragraph of the chapter entitled, 'Materialism and Idealism in American Life.'

The passage by Herbert Butterfield quoted in the Preface is from *History and Human Relations*, London, 1951, pp. 16–17.

Index